Foodservice:
A Managerial Approach

Foodservice:
A Managerial Approach

BRUCE H. AXLER

A NIFI Textbook

William C. Brown Company, Publishers
in cooperation with the
National Institute for the Foodservice Industry

Developed in collaboration with the
National Sanitation Foundation

Published simultaneously in Canada.

Printed in the United States of America.

International Standard Book Number: 0–697–00079–6

Library of Congress Catalog Card Number: 78–70714

2-00079-03

*On behalf of the
people in our industry
who will benefit, the Institute
is pleased to thank*

MARRIOTT CORPORATION

*for the financial support
which has made possible the
development of this book and
related course materials.*

Contents

Foreword

The increasing complexity of the foodservice industry calls for new approaches to the management of foodservice operations. Formerly, the foodservice industry was limited to the elegant restaurants and opulent hotel dining rooms where the well-heeled took their meals. Only the few boarding schools and colleges of the time (with much smaller enrollments than today) offered what we now call "school foodservice." Few people traveled, and those few ate aboard the trains and steamships that they relied upon for transportation.

In the past fifty years, the foodservice industry has changed greatly, and its role in the American economy has expanded to the point where it is now one of the most important service industries in the country. Several advances in technology and several changes in American culture have proven to be opportunities for the foodservice industry to grow. The increase in air travel (and the decrease in fares) has caused a travel "boom"; not only do Americans visit other regions of their own country more often, but the United States has also become a favorite destination of Europeans and Japanese. The rise of the fast-food chains has changed Americans' ideas about restaurants; one of the results is that Americans are more likely to eat away from home than ever before. Finally, the continuing prosperity of the United States and the increased numbers of women who hold jobs have caused a large growth of disposable income (money left over after necessities are paid for), and people often spend this money eating away from home in foodservice operations.

The foodservice industry has risen to these challenges by adopting increasingly sophisticated management techniques. In doing so, the growing number of trained managers are better able to turn these challenges to their own advantage. A management technique stressed throughout this book is the systems approach to foodservice operations. The systems approach, which takes into account the great changes in the foodservice industry, is based on the simple idea that any complex organization—

whether a society, or a corporation, or the human body—is made up of parts that are related and that act on one another in certain ways. By studying these parts and the interactions of parts and systems, management is better able to adapt the foodservice operation to its surroundings and make improvements in the operation. In the highly competitive foodservice industry, a manager can no longer rely simply on the "best" equipment or the "best" chef for success. Instead, managers must constantly examine the workings and organization of their operations and make needed adjustments; the careful and farsighted manager will "fine-tune" his or her operation.

The reader will also note a heavy emphasis on marketing throughout the book. The marketing system (Chapters 4 and 5) includes market research and promotion as well as the menu-planning and service systems (Chapters 6 and 11, respectively). Although many people regularly eat away from home, no foodservice operation can be "all things to all people." Commercial operations, such as restaurants, must determine what specific kind of patron to attract and how to design their menus, atmospheres, and service styles accordingly. Noncommercial operations, such as college dining halls, also need to make use of marketing techniques in order to please their clientele. Good marketing techniques are needed if a foodservice operation wants to enter a market, gain a share of that market's dollars, and hold on to that share. Every manager of every part of a foodservice operation must be familiar with the operation's marketing program and must put that program into effect.

A management approach based on the systems concept can lead to flexibility in dealing with problems and changes—two constants in the fast-paced foodservice industry. By watching and monitoring the various parts of their foodservice operations while they work—rather than relying on the "received truths" of "classic cuisine," the "dinner hour," or the "proper order of courses"—managers can use their skills and judgment to make innovations and adaptations that will lead to the continued growth of their operations and to their personal success as well.

Bruce H. Axler

Foodservice:
A Managerial Approach

Chapter 1
Foodservice:
A Perspective

The American foodservice industry is comprised of more than 500,000 individual establishments and employs more than 5 million people. As this industry approaches and exceeds sales revenues of $100 billion, it is possible to glimpse a reflection of its past and a suggestion of its future in present-day operations. Today's foodservice corporations and institutions, offering many of the same products as the cookshops of Mesopotamia that sold fried fish and grilled meats to the city dwellers of 2300 B.C., will share essential qualities with future successful foodservice operations.

All effective foodservice organizations of any type, in any place, and at any time have had three qualities in common:

1. The ability to offer people the products they want.
2. The ability to prosper in prevailing economic and social conditions.
3. The ability to adapt either when people's wants change or when conditions change, or both.

Those great foodservice operations of the past which have now disappeared possessed the first two qualities and lacked the third. Today, several billion-dollar companies in the foodservice industry have demonstrated all three qualities. Those future foodservice operations that will last only a short time will most probably fail because they fall short in all three areas.

This book, then, attempts to explain the successful functioning of foodservice organizations. It discusses how foodservice organizations survive, grow, and prosper by catering to people's diverse wants under conditions of change. It provides a generic framework of judgment for managers in creating, operating, and perpetuating foodservice organizations. It presents concepts, principles, and strategies that, in implementation, promise that the lessons of the past and present will not be lost to foodservice managers of the future.

1

THE FOODSERVICE INDUSTRY

The success of the foodservice industry is related to the success of individual foodservice organizations. As previously mentioned, successful foodservice organizations are distinguished by three qualities: the ability to offer people the products they want, to prosper in prevailing economic conditions, and to change appropriately when change is warranted. Attaining these qualities becomes the general objective of both the individual foodservice organization and the foodservice industry as a whole. These objectives are the standards by which the industry and the individual foodservice organization can be measured.

For the foodservice industry, success in attaining these objectives can be measured by such year-to-year economic indicators as total sales or rate of growth. For the individual organization, success in accomplishing its general objectives is measured by such financial and nonfinancial indicators as sales volume or percent of return patrons. However, the most important indicator for the individual organization is its survival from year to year.

Foodservice organizations that comprise the foodservice industry achieve their general objectives by varying methods. One foodservice operation that offers certain products to one group of people under certain conditions may differ in the way it accomplishes its objectives from another operation offering different products to different people under different conditions.

It is possible to describe the foodservice industry on the basis of these different methods of achieving objectives. Foodservice operations may be grouped on the basis of the specific products they offer—the *product perspective;* on the basis of the specific groups of people they serve—the *people perspective;* and on the basis of the specific conditions under which they operate—the *operational condition perspective.*

Product Perspectives The most apparent product of the foodservice operation is some kind of food. Therefore, the foodservice industry is sometimes described and categorized by the food products foodservice operations offer. Trade publications, foodservice industry associations, or government agencies that use the product perspective method of describing the foodservice industry identify the number of operations offering such food products as chicken, hamburgers and franks, pizza, Mexican food, seafood, pancakes and waffles, steaks and roast beef, sandwiches, or ice cream. These data are compiled for a given year and/or describe a given area of the country.

But the food product itself is only part of the product of the foodservice operation. Further description of the foodservice industry from a product perspective leads to categorization by extent of menu, service style, atmosphere, and consumer orientation.

Extent of menu   Since few foodservice operations offer only a single product, a description is frequently extended to suggest the total number of products an operation offers. On this basis, foodservice operations are classified as limited menu (less than 15 items total), full menu (from 15 to 40 items total), and extensive (more than 40 items). A limited-menu hamburger restaurant would be a foodservice operation principally offering hamburgers with a small selection of other items.

Service style   Another element of product perspective is the type of service the consumer receives. Service styles usually are categorized first by whether the consumer can eat in the foodservice operation. Thus a limited-menu hamburger restaurant could be further described as take-out (consumer cannot eat on premises, usually called a *stand*); take-in (consumer eats in facility, usually called a *restaurant* or *shop*); or take-in/take-out (consumer may eat in or carry food out).

If the consumer can eat in the facility, foodservice operations are further categorized on the basis of seating style. Using this basis, the categories might include the following: no seating (surfaces used for stand-up consumption of food); counter (counters and stools); booth (fixed tables and benches); or table (freestanding tables and chairs).

Finally, operations where the consumer will eat at a table or a booth are further categorized by the amount of personal service received. This amount may range from little or no personal service to a great deal of personal service by many attentive service workers. These categories are as follows: no service (usually called a *cafeteria*); minimal service (usually called a *coffee shop*); moderately attentive service (usually called a *family restaurant*); very attentive service (usually called a *tablecloth restaurant*); and extremely attentive service (usually called a *luxury* or *continental* restaurant).

Atmosphere   A third element of the product perspective is the atmosphere a foodservice operation offers. The appearance of a restaurant, its decor, and other factors that affect patrons' image of the foodservice operation are collectively called its *atmosphere*. Though definitions of the term "atmosphere" are regrettably vague, some categories based on this concept include the following: contemporary (modern and informal); theme (decorated in some definite style such as English pub or Polynesian); luxury (the decor probably includes expensive wall hangings, carpets, and fine table appointments); family (bright and cheery, nonbreakable tableware); and traditional (homelike and functional).

Consumer orientation   A fourth element of product perspective is consumer orientation, or what food or nonfood features a patron seeks from a particular foodservice operation. The categories based on these features are vague and overlapping, but widely used. These categories of operations include the following: fast food (usually refers to operations that prepare food on an assembly-line basis so the consumer gets the food quickly); coffee shop (operations suitable for coffee breaks or light snacks); lunch room and dinner house (operations primarily serving lunch or dinner, but not open or not convenient for other meals); bar or tavern (operations serving alcoholic beverages as well as food); refreshment places (usually operations with limited menus and serving a clientele that does not expect a meal); club (operations where food service may be interrelated with other services offered; patronage is restricted); and drive-in (operations where consumers do not have to leave their cars to order and receive food).

People Perspectives

Operations within the foodservice industry can be divided into three major groups on the basis of the people they serve: customers, guests, or clients. These categories are based on the relationship between the foodservice operation and the people it serves.

Customers   Customers are the patrons of commercial foodservice restaurants—the foodservice operations in business to make a profit for their owners. Customers have almost complete freedom of choice. They elect to patronize or to avoid a foodservice operation. The principal motivation of customers is a desire to eat in a particular foodservice operation.

Guests   Guests are distinguished from customers because they choose to eat in a foodservice operation in connection with choosing some other purchase or activity. Their choice of a particular purchase or activity consequently limits their choice of a place to eat. People using a recreational park or staying in a resort hotel are guests.

Clients   Clients are people who are largely obliged to eat in a particular foodservice operation and who may depend on it for their entire sustenance. Clients may be paying clients such as boarders at a school or university, factory employees, or hospital patients. Or clients may be nonpaying, such as prison inmates or patients in a state institution.

Foodservice operations are not always limited to serving only one type of patron. For example, a hotel foodservice operation may cater to guests as well as to outside customers. A university or military base foodservice operation may have some meal plan clients and some customers who have the option of patronizing the facility or eating elsewhere.

Beyond these three broad categories, the foodservice industry is sometimes described on the basis of the number and type of operations catering to patrons who are identifiable on some basis other than their relationship to foodservice establishments as customers, guests, or clients. For example, foodservice operations can be classified as appealing to people over fifty, people under thirty-five who went to college, families with young children, business travelers, unmarried persons over twenty-one, tourists, college students, or sports lovers. The usefulness of this method of describing the foodservice industry is more fully developed in Chapter 4 which deals with the marketing aspects of foodservice establishments.

Operational Condition Perspectives ③ The foodservice industry can be further described by categorizations based on social and economic conditions confronting foodservice operations. These social and economic factors represent the environment in which a foodservice establishment must operate. Descriptions based on these environmental factors reflect the operational condition perspective.

① *Categorization by business motive* Exhibit 1.1 shows a classification based on operational conditions; in this case, the profit-making or nonprofit-making nature of the foodservice establishment. In this classification, the foodservice industry is partitioned into three categories.

ⓐ*Commercial* feeding establishments are composed of eating and drinking places operated to make a profit. Note that institutional foodservice operations such as those in schools, factories, and hospitals are included in this commercial group when they are operated by profit-making contract feeders. Commercial foodservice establishments are most often open to the public.

ⓑ *Institutional* feeding establishments are comprised of business, educational, government, or institutional organizations which operate their own foodservice facilities. Usually these foodservice facilities are operated for the benefit of those who work at, travel on, live in, or are associated with, these institutions. Institutional feeding establishments most often do not have profit as a major goal and usually do not have service to the general public as a primary aim.

In Exhibit 1.1 *military* feeding establishments form a third, smaller category which consists of foodservice establishments serving the armed forces and other defense personnel. This third category could legitimately be considered a part of institutional feeding establishments.

Categorization by business association From the perspective of operational conditions, another category of foodservice operations includes those establishments functioning as subordinate facilities of entirely different kinds of businesses. When foodservice organizations are classified as hotel, motor hotel, drugstore, department store, variety store, or gasoline station foodservice operations, this identification is based on categorization by business association.

Categorization by business type The way in which a foodservice establishment is organized to do business may form a basis for categorization. Classifying or describing some foodservice operations in manufacturing plants, commercial and office buildings, and hospitals as food contractors (organizations which contract to operate foodservice facilities for other organizations) is categorization by business type. Other divisions in this category might be franchise operations (foodservice organizations in which each unit is owned individually but which has a menu, method of food preparation, purchasing system, and identification

EXHIBIT 1.1　The Foodservice Industry—Estimated Food and Drink Sales and Purchases, 1976

Number of Units	Type of Establishment	Estimated F&D Sales (000)	Percent of Total F&D Sales	Estimated F&D Purchases (000)	Percent of Total F&D Purchases
Group I — Commercial Feeding[1]					
112,180[2]	Restaurants, Lunchrooms	$26,541,072	33.88	$10,539,791	33.43
3,944	Social Caterers	1,037,451	1.33	421,464	1.34
8,222	Commercial Cafeterias	2,499,595	3.19	948,122	3.01
80,609	Limited Menu Restaurants (Refreshment Places)	14,903,154	19.03	5,360,366	17.00
5,550	Ice Cream, Frozen Custard Stands	551,025	0.70	187,348	0.59
44,112[3]	Bars and Taverns	6,308,491	8.05	385,953[4]	1.22
		$51,840,788[5]	66.18%	$17,843,044	56.59%
5,836[6]	**Food Contractors**				
	Manufacturing & Indus. Plants	1,450,683	1.85	676,018	2.14
	Commercial & Office Bldgs.	379,368	0.48	176,786	0.56
	Hospitals and Nursing Homes	565,293	0.72	226,117	0.72
	Colleges & Universities	755,783	0.97	267,540	0.85
	Primary and Secondary Schools	448,177	0.57	210,643	0.67
	In-transit Feeding (Airlines)	301,041	0.38	144,500[7]	0.46
	Recreation & Sports Center	603,967	0.77	223,468	0.71
13,438	Hotel Restaurants	2,463,415	3.15	826,175	2.62
2,498	Motor Hotel Restaurants	608,650	0.78	204,806	0.65
13,551	Motel Restaurants	1,367,656	1.75	496,994	1.57
9,323	Drug & Prop. Store Restaurants	489,114	0.62	185,863	0.59
1,269	Gen. Merchandise Store Restaurants	38,996	0.05	14,818	0.05
3,882	Department Store Restaurants	809,163	1.03	323,665	1.03
6,509	Variety Store Restaurants	542,180	0.69	211,449	0.67
3,299	Food Stores ex. Grocery	157,717	0.20	53,624	0.17
12,579	Grocery Store Restaurants	360,272	0.46	133,301	0.42
7,738	Gasoline Service Stations	173,731	0.22	64,280	0.20
3,384	Drive-in Movies	107,097	0.14	35,342	0.11
3,622	Misc. Retailers (Liquor, Cigar, etc.)[8]	127,372	0.16	46,491	0.15
2,750	Vending & Nonstore Retailers[9]	1,500,306	1.92	510,104	1.62
	Mobile Caterers	295,017	0.38	103,256	0.33
3,866	Bowling Lanes	329,840	0.42	135,234	0.43
	Recreation and Sports Centers	448,249	0.57	165,852	0.53
	Total Group I	$66,163,875	84.46%	$23,279,370	73.84%

[1] Data are given only for establishments with payroll.
[2] Figures are latest Census Area Reports or Merchandise Line detail counts or updates when reliable data become available.
[3] Unit count includes only those establishments serving food; however, sales figure is for all bars and taverns with payroll.
[4] Food only. Cost of alcoholic beverages totaled $1,914,312,000.
[5] Food and drink sales for nonpayroll establishments totaled $2,488,276,000 with eating places accounting for $1,666,027,000 and drinking places $822,249,000.
[6] Individual businesses, not locations. Contract feeders are included in eating place totals in all Bureau of the Census publications although their sales volume figures for contract feeders are significantly understated.
[7] Food purchases only.
[8] Includes SIC 59, except 591 and 596.
[9] Includes sales of hot food, sandwiches, pastries, coffee and other hot beverages.

From "The Foodservice Industry: Part I," NRA Washington Report, 27 March 1979. Reprinted by permission.

Number of Units	Type of Establishment	Estimated F&D Sales (000)	Percent of Total F&D Sales	Estimated F&D Purchases (000)	Percent of Total F&D Purchases
Group II — Institutional Feeding — Business, Educational, Government or Institutional Organizations Which Operate Their Own Foodservice					
	Employee Feeding				
4,000	Indus. & Comm. Organizations	$ 955,050	1.22	$ 467,065	1.48
548	Sea-going Ships (1,000+ Tons)	43,866	0.06	26,320	0.08
4,248	Inland Waterway Vessels	133,909	0.17	81,348	0.26
92,297	Public & Parochial Elementary & Secondary Schools (89,381) (National School Lunch Program)[10]	1,734,482	2.22	2,337,845	7.41
	Colleges & Universities[11]				
980	Public	1,133,325	1.45	646,947	2.05
1,407	Private	450,069	0.57	257,196	0.82
	Transportation				
61	Passenger/Cargo Liners	71,650	0.09	39,407	0.12
32	Airlines	284,744	0.36	141,838	0.45
2	Railroads	22,512	0.03	14,828	0.05
10,310	Clubs	737,929	0.94	355,298	1.13
4,120	Voluntary & Proprietary Hospitals	3,223,485	4.12	1,289,394	4.09
1,836	State & Local Short-term Hospitals[12]	481,640	0.61	346,789	1.10
746	Long-term General, TB Nervous & Mental Hospitals	733,707	0.94	293,482	0.93
380	Federal Hospitals[12]	215,354	0.27	190,229	0.60
26,672	Nursing Homes, Homes for Aged, Blind, Orphans, Mentally & Physically Handicapped[13]	1,638,299	2.09	1,052,214	3.34
3,165	Sporting & Recreational Camps	85,769	0.11	51,461	0.16
16,010	Community Centers	224,750	0.29	265,198	0.84
	Convents & Seminaries	***		109,123	0.35
	Penal Institutions				
620	Federal & State Prisons	***		156,976	0.50
3,921	Jails	***		126,612	0.40
	Total Group II	**$12,170,540**	**15.54%**	**$ 8,249,570**	**26.16%**
	Total Group I & II	**$78,334,415**	**100.00%**	**$31,528,940**	**100.00%**
	Food Furnished Food Service				
	Employees in Groups I and II			2,099,741	
	Total Groups I and II and FSE	**$78,334,415**		**$33,628,681**	
Group III — Military Feeding					
	Defense Personnel			799,527	
	Officers & NCO Clubs ("Open Mess")[14]	370,992		126,972	
	Food Service — Military Exchanges[14]	203,011		89,325	
	Total Group III	**$ 574,003**		**$ 1,015,824**	
	Grand Total	**$78,908,418**		**$34,644,505**	

[10] School lunch program commodities furnished in the calendar year 1976 under Sec. 6,32,416, are worth $473,224,487. In addition, 2,282,051,651 half pints of milk worth $147,786,139 were supplied to 83,555 outlets.
[11] Total number of colleges and universities which have foodservice whether contracted or not.
[12] Represents only sales or commercial equivalent to employees.
[13] Sales (commercial equivalent) calculated for Nursing Homes and Homes for Aged only. All others in this grouping make no charge for food served either in cash or in kind.
[14] Continental U.S. Only.
***These institutions make no charge for food served either in cash or in kind.

in common with the other units of the same organization), chain operations (foodservice organizations in which the overall operation is owned and managed centrally, with each unit manager responsible to the central organization), proprietorships (individually owned foodservice establishments), and so on.

Other categorizations that reflect operational conditions to some extent are *categorization by area of the country or by state; categorization by number of employees,* or *categorization by sales revenues.* The U.S. government publishes descriptions of the foodservice industry on the basis of area of the country, number of employees, and volume of sales. Major foodservice industry trade magazines attempt to rank leading foodservice operations on the basis of dollar sales.

On an informal basis, it is often the practice to classify foodservice operations—and hence describe the foodservice industry—on the basis of particular social and economic issues that cut across other categorizations. Such issue-oriented categories might include the following: operations with high labor costs; operations competing with major foodservice chains; operations affected by inflation; operations in central cities, and so on.

Limitations of These Perspectives

Though classification of the foodservice industry using product, people, and operational condition perspectives can make the role of the foodservice industry clearer, these classifications are somewhat deficient for the purposes of foodservice management.

On the one hand, if these perspectives are combined into an integrated classification, literally thousands of categories and subcategories must be considered. For example, a description of the foodservice industry from a product perspective alone would become exceedingly complex. If there are nine major product descriptors, three menu descriptors, three service-style descriptors, five atmosphere descriptors, and seven customer-orientation descriptors, each of these descriptors may be combined to produce approximately 50,000 different categories. Even eliminating half of these as being repetitious or mutually exclusive leaves 25,000 combinations. It would be necessary then to consider "limited-menu, contemporary, no-service, booth-seating, steak restaurants" and "full-menu, traditional, table service, seafood clubs" as well as 25,000 other categories in an attempt to classify a given restaurant or to describe its operation.

No one would dispute that a limited-menu, contemporary, no-service, booth-seating, steak restaurant exists, or that there are a number of them, or that they require a particular management approach. But it does not seem reasonable to suggest that a person who could manage a limited-menu, contemporary, no-service, booth-seating, *seafood* restaurant successfully, or even manage any restaurant successfully, could not manage that steak restaurant. From the standpoint of managerial skills, it does not seem reasonable to treat that steak restaurant as a separate case.

On the other hand, if the categories are too broadly drawn, for example, if one speaks of "institutions" meaning any foodservice operation serving the client, or speaks of "limited-menu restaurants" meaning any commercial operation with less than 15 menu items, it suggests that any operation which shares these characteristics is identical to any other in the same category. And this conclusion, also, is patently untrue.

The dilemma presented by these two extremes is a familiar one. It has in fact been resolved numerous times by identifying the essential elements that a great many otherwise different things have in common and analyzing them. A good illustration of this approach is offered by plane geometry. There are millions of flat surfaces in the world, from table tops to wheat fields. Faced with the impossibility of studying them all individually, mathematicians reduced them to their essential elements (points, lines, angles, planes) and, with obvious success, studied their relationships. They identified elements and combinations of elements generalizable to all plane surfaces of any kind, anywhere, however they are described.

Since foodservice organizations (like plane surfaces) are also complex, this more sophisticated approach of identifying essential elements and relationships and arriving at generalizations is used in this book. For this purpose, foodservice organizations, whether cookshops or mammoth corporations, are viewed from the standpoint of a *system*.

FOODSERVICE OPERATIONS AS SYSTEMS

The systems approach has been widely successful in analyzing complex organizations. The term "system" or "systems approach" has a technical connotation that may be awesome to a few; but in fact the concept of a system is a relatively simple one. In the broad sense of the word, a system is a set of parts united by some form of interaction for the attainment of a purpose, or objective. Examples of systems include the circulatory and digestive systems of the human body, transportation systems, communications systems, and the solar system.

The systems approach to organizations is based on common sense. It attempts to arrange the parts of an organization so that all the essential factors are taken into account and so that the processes, or functions, of the organization will produce outcomes that match stated objectives.

In a way similar to a telephone system or a digestive system, individual foodservice operations can be viewed as systems. Foodservice systems possess the following four characteristics:

1. They are composed of interrelated *parts*, or *elements*, that are common to all foodservice organizations.
2. They possess a recognizable *structure*, though some degree of structural difference among foodservice systems can be identified.

3. They have particular *objectives*.
4. They have internal *processes* for dealing with external elements such as materials, equipment, labor, and capital (called *inputs*), but also for dealing with social and economic conditions. These processes transform inputs, resources, to obtain *outputs*, or results, that satisfy objectives.

Interrelated Parts of Foodservice Systems

A foodservice system is composed of interacting parts, or elements. For example, in an electric-lamp system, the collection of parts is most commonly a bulb, wire, switch, stand, and shade. In a foodservice system, the interrelated parts consist of management, marketing, menu planning, work, purchasing, supply, production, service, business, and control.

These parts, or elements, of a foodservice system are complex—so complex that they themselves have the characteristics of systems. In fact, in this text they are called *systems*, although they might be more precisely called *subsystems* of the total foodservice system. Exhibit 1.2 presents these systems (or subsystems) and indicates something of their interrelationships. And the following chapters discuss each of these parts of the total foodservice system.

Clearly these parts are interrelated. Each element depends on the others in order to function properly and play its role in attaining the objectives of the whole system. Thus the contributions of each element must be coordinated since some of their activities overlap. For example, if a sports team is viewed as a system, and if its general objectives are to be achieved, then the activities of each team member—to block opponents, to gain an advantageous position, to score—must be integrated with the objectives of the other team members. It would be highly unsatisfactory if team members only blocked each other, or if they focused their individual efforts on personally scoring.

Structure of Foodservice Systems

The parts of a total foodservice system are arranged in a meaningful order. It is this structure that enables them to be recognized as a system. For example, if the bulb, wire, switch, and stand—the parts of the electric-lamp system are not united in a functioning, patterned whole, all we have is a lack of a lamp and, consequently, no system.

The structure, or framework, of a system also enables the system to be distinguished from other entities that also have the characteristics of a system. For example, it is possible to view the bulb, wire, switch, and stand as partial components of a Christmas tree, and not an electric lamp. It is the arrangement of parts that helps define a system.

As a further example, a sports team and an assembly line in a factory can be considered as systems, but they are obviously not foodservice systems. A commercial restaurant and a hospital foodservice operation, although quite different in some respects, do have a similar systems structure. This structural similarity of the hospital foodservice facility

EXHIBIT 1.2   Schema of Foodservice Systems

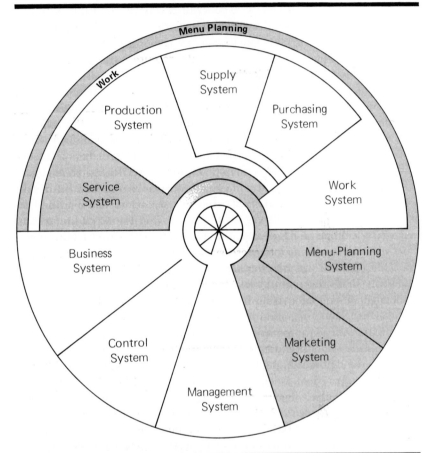

The ten subsystems (in this diagram and in later chapters, referred to as systems) interact to form the total foodservice system. Management-*the core system-joins with* marketing, business, *and* control *to form the steering mechanism of the foodservice organization.* Menu planning, work, purchasing, supply, production, *and* service *are the operating systems. The functions of the operating systems are programmed by* menu planning *and* work. *Marketing is closely allied with* menu planning *and* service, *and these three systems are shaded to indicate this connection. It is clear from this diagram that the integrated functioning of all the systems is essential to the success of the foodservice organization as a whole.*

and the restaurant allows the development of concepts and principles that are generalizable to them both—and to all foodservice systems.

In addition, a recognition of the structural similarities of foodservice systems allows the unessential differences to become apparent. These variations can be analyzed and related to the success of a particular operation in achieving its objectives. In the same way, the differences between two football teams can be examined, and though they are both similar systems, structured in similar ways, the success of the winning team can be analyzed by comparison with the losing team.

Specific Objectives of Foodservice Systems   The general objectives of foodservice systems—to offer people the products they want, to prosper in prevailing economic and social conditions, and to change appropriately when changes are warranted—have already been considered. These general objectives must be translated into specific objectives particular to each individual foodservice operation. For example, both a hospital foodservice operation and a commercial restaurant share the general objective of offering people the products they want. For the hospital foodservice operation, this general objective might be particularized as this specific objective: "to offer patients nutritious, appetizing, healthful meals." For the commercial restaurant, it might be particularized as a different specific objective: "to offer families with children traditional American cooking in a fun atmosphere." These two statements of specific objectives differ in their definitions of "people" and "product," but both are entirely consistent with the first general objective of foodservice systems.

Likewise the second general objective can be made specific for a hospital foodservice operation and for a commercial restaurant by defining the word "prosper" in ways appropriate to the different conditions that each operation faces. To prosper in prevailing social and economic conditions, the hospital foodservice operation must act consistently with the general program of therapy for patients and according to the priorities established by the hospital management for the allocation of its funds. In contrast, the major social and economic conditions confronting the commercial foodservice operation are related to the competitive pressure on it, and its need to make a profit. If the hospital foodservice operation does not act consistently with the general program of therapy or within budget limitations established by the hospital, it will be replaced by a new operation that does. If the commercial foodservice operation does not compete successfully and make a profit, it may become bankrupt or be closed or sold by its owner/investors.

For the hospital foodservice operation, then, the second general objective can be restated to suggest that a specific objective of a hospital foodservice facility is "to function as part of a general program of therapy in ways consistent with budget limitations." For the commercial foodservice operation, this second general objective might be restated to suggest that a specific objective of a commercial foodservice operation is "to achieve dollar sales sufficiently in excess of expenses to provide a profit that satisfies owner/investors."

Although the three general objectives of foodservice systems are universal, many different specific objectives consistent with each of them can be formulated by the management of a particular operation. Exhibit 1.3 suggests typical examples that may or may not be generalizable to operations of similar types.

Once a general objective has been particularized for an individual operation, it must be broken down further into a series of specific, explicit objectives. Each specific objective in this series applies to a particular subsystem within the total foodservice system, and suggests some partial means of attaining the foodservice system's general objective. A commercial restaurant's specific objective—"to achieve dollar sales sufficiently in excess of expenses to provide a profit that satisfies owner/investors"—could be stated as a series of specific objectives: "to gain a 75 percent market share (competitors together would have only 25 percent of patronage); to reach a sales volume of $1 million a year; to reduce food costs by 20 percent," and so on. It then becomes possible to identify these specific objectives with the particular elements, or subsystems, of the foodservice system. It becomes the function of the marketing element, or subsystem, to gain a 75 percent market share; it becomes the function of the food production subsystem to reduce food costs by 20 percent, and so on. In practice, it soon becomes apparent that certain types of specific objectives are legitimately the concerns of particular elements of the foodservice system, and these can then be identified as the objectives of marketing, of food production, of purchasing, and so on.

If a foodservice operation is not oriented toward achieving its general objectives by establishing such specific objectives, or if the general objectives are not used as clear guidelines for managers and people of each part in establishing the specific objectives of their own element, or if the specific objectives of parts of the operation are not really consistent with the general objectives of the operation as a whole, then the operation is in peril.

—Consider the vulnerability of a foodservice operation if its management does not recognize how prevailing economic and social conditions affect the operation and does not set its specific objectives accordingly—if, for example, the managers establish prices without any consideration of the operation's competition or the amount of money the operation's potential patrons have to spend.

—Consider the vulnerability of a foodservice operation if its production managers do not relate the specific objectives of their department to the general objectives of the organization as a whole—if, for example, the food production managers order the kitchen to produce the food they personally like.

—Consider the vulnerability of a foodservice operation if a specific objective works against a general objective—if, for example, an operation's managers establish the specific objective of reducing food costs and concentrate efforts to attain this goal on cutting food quality, thus causing the operation to fail to offer people the products they want and conse-

EXHIBIT 1.3 Some Specific Objectives of Particular Foodservice Operations

Type of Operation	Specific Objective	General Objective Category
Hospital or health care facility	To function as part of the therapeutic program	1
	To provide preventive nutrition education	2
	To encourage positive attitudes regarding the institution by enhancing the patient's stay	1, 2
	To comply with state and federal regulations	2, 3
	To speedily supply patients with meals	1
Employee foodservice facility	To provide refreshment and nutrition in order to increase worker effectiveness	1
	To boost morale	2
College and university	To encourage student involvement with the college or university	3
	To reduce food waste	2, 3
	To compete with commercial operations for food and/or entertainment dollars	2, 3
Military	To increase the civilianization of military foodservice operations by using more non-military personnel	2
	To encourage positive attitudes toward the military	2
	To provide individual options for socializing that are comparable to those in civilian life	1
	To minimize the effects of inflation by encouraging military personnel to accept meal allowances in money rather than in meal plans	2
Transportation (airline)	To provide foodservice options so travelers may purchase only the type and portion of food desired	1
	To entertain passengers	1, 2
	To reduce the cost of passenger meals and snacks	3
School	To reduce waste	2, 3
	To increase participation in the Type A lunch program	2
	To merchandise foods in such a manner that the school program is competitive with commercial operations	2, 3
Club	To attract new members	2
	To offer members personal service equal to that in a fine home	1
	To attract outside catering business	3
Hotel	To provide an adequate departmental profit	2
	To attract outside patronage	3
	To establish the hotel's competitive difference	2

quently jeopardizing the operation's prosperity in prevailing economic conditions.

In each of these examples, the specific objectives of the parts are somehow not in harmony with the general objectives of the whole operation, and, under such conditions, the foodservice operation cannot function smoothly and successfully.

Inputs, Outputs, and Processes of Foodservice Systems   The concept of inputs, outputs, and processes is essential to the systems approach. After management has structured the parts of the organization and directed them toward specific objectives, the operation, then, processes inputs into predetermined outputs. Inputs include all raw materials, labor, energy, equipment, financial data, marketing information, and so on; inputs are all the things used to produce the desired results. Processes are all the work done to achieve these results. Outputs are the results themselves, the marketable product of the foodservice operation; outputs should meet the standards and objectives of management and the standards and tastes of the market.

A very simple example of how inputs and processes are coordinated to produce the desired output can be found in the different workings of a drive-in hamburger operation and a Mexican chili parlor. Some inputs, such as ground beef, onions, tomatoes, spices, bread, and cooks' labor would be the same in both instances. But their equipment inputs would be different as well as their processes. The processes in the hamburger operation would include forming and seasoning the beef, grilling, assembling the inputs into a sandwich, and wrapping and bagging the sandwiches. The processes in the chili parlor would include browning and crumbling the beef, adding the correct amounts of spices, and ladling and serving the chili. Though using many of the same inputs, the different processes used by these two foodservice operations result in different outputs. The output of the hamburger operation would be ground beef formed into patties served with raw onions and tomatoes on a bun. In the chili parlor, the same inputs would result in an output of crumbled ground beef cooked with onions and tomatoes and served with bread on the side.

MANAGEMENT OF FOODSERVICE SYSTEMS

Discussing foodservice operations as systems does not change the foodservice industry, the foodservice operation, or foodservice activities such as preparing food and serving patrons. The systems approach to foodservice operations is a management tool, an aid to managing more effectively. Whether a foodservice operation—a total foodservice system —or individual subsystems such as production or purchasing are being considered, the systems approach is useful to management in different ways at three stages.

1. The systems approach provides a methodology for *creating or designing* a foodservice operation.
2. It aids its smooth *operation and management.*
3. It provides a means of *diagnosing functional difficulties and making improvements* in the operation.

Creation and Design   Approaching the foodservice operation as a system made up of parts or subsystems (which in turn are made up of parts) facilitates the work of the manager. A methodology for creating a particular foodservice operation or part of that operation (such as a purchasing department) is readily available. Consider the creation of a very simple foodservice operation, a doughnut bakery. In order to decide the best operational design, the bakery manager can apply the systems approach by considering all the characteristics of a foodservice system.

Specific objectives   What is the doughnut bakery supposed to do or accomplish?

Parts or subsystems   Of what parts, or subsystems, is it composed? What are the specific objectives of these parts? How do they work?

Interactions   How do the subsystems relate to each other and affect one another? How do these relationships affect the performance of the total system?

Structure   What general principles or concepts have demonstrated usefulness in creating the particular system? How does the structure affect the choice of processes and the interactions among the subsystems?

Inputs and outputs   What material and equipment inputs are necessary to produce the desired output? What external factors—favorable (opportunities) or unfavorable (limits)—will influence the performance of the system?

Processes   How will the operation accomplish the transformation of inputs into outputs? What steps will be involved in these processes?

Variations   What are the different ways of creating a system to achieve the same objectives? In a given situation, which variation is the most appropriate?

By using this methodology, the bakery manager can plan the operation in a thorough, logical, and orderly fashion. A manager can establish specific objectives for the doughnut bakery, i.e., to produce an acceptable doughnut that sells for 35 cents. The manager can set up the parts necessary to such a foodservice operation—marketing, purchasing, supply, and so on—and align them to create a structure that will make possible the attainment of the bakery's specific objective. Inputs, outputs, and processes would be determined by the manager. Inputs might include flour, yeast, water, sugar, the baker's labor, energy for running mixers and cooking vats, and all the equipment used, as well as both the initial investment in the bakery (capital), which limits purchase of materials, and the expectation of a favorable opportunity for marketing. The processes involved would include all the steps necessary to convert the raw materials into satisfactory outputs; the purchasing of raw materials and equipment, the actual measuring, mixing, and frying, and the means of serving the doughnut to the consumer. The desired product output would be saleable doughnuts.

When establishing the operation using a systems approach, the bakery manager must be aware of the possible variations of the system that could achieve the same objective. Of these variations, at a particular time, one might suit available inputs or changed objectives better than another. In such cases it would be good management strategy to use that systems variation.

If the specific objectives of the bakery, or of any other foodservice operation, are clear and attainable, if the inputs are available, if the processes for achieving the end result are known, then it should be possible to design or redesign a system to produce a satisfactory output. It should be clear that this is a better way to approach the creation or redesign of a foodservice operation than by simply copying someone else's operation or using some trial-and-error method that results in a succession of failed or flawed operations until the right design is found.

Operation and Management

Once the foodservice operation is organized as a system, it becomes easier to manage on a day-to-day basis. The systems approach provides an organized way of looking at an operation that facilitates the manager's understanding of how it works and of what it is capable. The bakery manager can accomplish more knowing how the system works and what to expect of it than not knowing.

The performance of a system is also predictable, at least more predictable than that of nonsystems. If a system performs well one time, with the same input and the same processes, the output should be the same the next time. Or, if the input is known—say, if the doughnut bakery uses a different flour for the first time but knows that it is flour of acceptable quality—and the processes are the same, then the output should be acceptable. Because managers use the systems approach to analyze their operations, changes can be made within these operations with some certainty of the effects of those changes.

Diagnosis and Improvement

The same questions that are asked in creating and redesigning a foodservice system can be asked in diagnosing possible deficiencies of an already created system. Results can be compared with objectives. To evaluate a system's overall performance, the system can be analyzed to determine if there are ways of making it work better, or if there is a need to alter it in some fashion to make it function better in changed circumstances. Because each part, or subsystem, of the foodservice system has its own specific objectives and responsibilities, the systems approach allows management to pinpoint where difficulties are occurring in order to make remedial adjustments. By knowing the interrelationships among subsystems, management can see how an adjustment in one subsystem will affect the other subsystems, and the system as a whole.

When it is determined what improvements a system needs, the systems approach eases implementation of these adjustments. A manager can use a good diagnosis to pinpoint exactly where the difficulty lies and what should be corrected. If the system does not produce a desirable output or produces undesirable outputs, then some factor of the system needs to be changed. For example, if the bakery produces burnt doughnuts, then the amount of time that the doughnuts cook should be reduced. If the system is too costly, that is, if it requires an unacceptable amount of input to produce the desired output, then it should be improved by changing processes or changing the parts of the system. For example, if the doughnut bakery is spending too much in labor costs making its own dough, the manager might decide to buy ready-made dough instead and concentrate production on cooking the doughnuts. Such a decision would affect the purchasing, supply, and production subsystems, which, in turn, would affect the business and work subsystems. The systems approach allows management to follow each reaction to the use of ready-made dough, or any other improvement to a system, throughout the system, thus facilitating the diagnosis of any new difficulties caused by this improvement. The systems approach gives management the key to understanding and evaluating its operations through all stages of development.

FOODSERVICE MANAGEMENT AS A PROFESSION

The profession of foodservice management consists of the creation, operation, and improvement of foodservice systems. Foodservice management positions are usually described in terms of the systems they concern. Hence the general manager is concerned with the total foodservice system, a food production manager with a production system, a business manager with a business system. That sometimes the purchasing manager is called the purchasing agent, or the general manager is called the company president, does not affect this fundamental relationship.

Because of the size, complexity, and diversity of the foodservice industry, there are enormous numbers of foodservice managers concerned with foodservice systems of every size and description. The National Institute for the Foodservice Industry reports that each year an additional 25,000 foodservice managers will be needed to sustain and expand current operations, and many other individuals will create their own new foodservice operations as owner/managers.

It is central to the systems approach to suggest that while the tasks of foodservice managers vary, they do not vary substantively. Different managers' tasks may vary in complexity, in the techniques management brings to them, and in the demands on management for knowledge and information, but none of these variations impedes the consideration of diverse foodservice operations as similar systems with similar ways of functioning. In essence, the tasks of the management of the small foodservice operation are very much like the tasks of the management of the giant corporation; the tasks of the management of the purchasing department of a foodservice operation are very like the tasks of the management of the production department.

This assertion has important implications for the individual foodservice manager or prospective manager. It promises that the lessons learned in managing any foodservice system can be applied to any other. It promises that through training in particular techniques or by using specific information a professional foodservice manager can meet the challenges of performing successfully in increasingly complex foodservice systems. It promises that the manager can also meet the challenge of effectively managing such diverse foodservice subsystems as production and purchasing and such diverse foodservice systems as a hospital foodservice facility and a commercial restaurant. In sum, it suggests that the understanding of the foodservice operation as a system can be the basis for a successful career in the foodservice industry, wherever an individual's efforts, education, and abilities may lead.

Chapter 2
The Management
System:
Part I

This book concerns the management of foodservice organizations. It is about nothing else. There are no recipes, no handy hints for cleaning stainless steel, no do's and don'ts for dining room personnel, and no buying guides for frozen foods. The management system spans the entire foodservice organization, relating the organization to its environment, setting its objectives, and planning and organizing its activities.

Foodservice management includes two areas: strategic management and personnel management. Through strategic management, the leaders of a foodservice organization formulate objectives and arrive at decisions in order to adapt their organization to changing conditions both within and outside the organization. The managers of an organization decide when and how something is to be done and even whether it is to be done at all. Strategic management causes the various systems to adapt, change, and interact.

Personnel management, on the other hand, is the effective use of people, their skills, and abilities. Since the foodservice industry is "people oriented"—an industry of people serving people—the employees of a foodservice operation are a major factor in its success or lack of success. Because of the importance of personnel management, it is treated separately in the following chapter.

Although every system in the foodservice operation has its "managers," management must be treated as a separate system. However integral management activities are to the operation's other systems and whatever variation in methods or emphasis occurs when particular management activities are performed, the responsibilities of a manager are distinct enough to merit separate treatment. Thus, this book limits the term "management system" to strategic management and personnel management in order to deal more appropriately with the managerial activities involved in initiating and implementing various courses of action. (Though closely allied to both strategic and personnel manage-

EXHIBIT 2.1   Interaction of the Management System with Other Systems

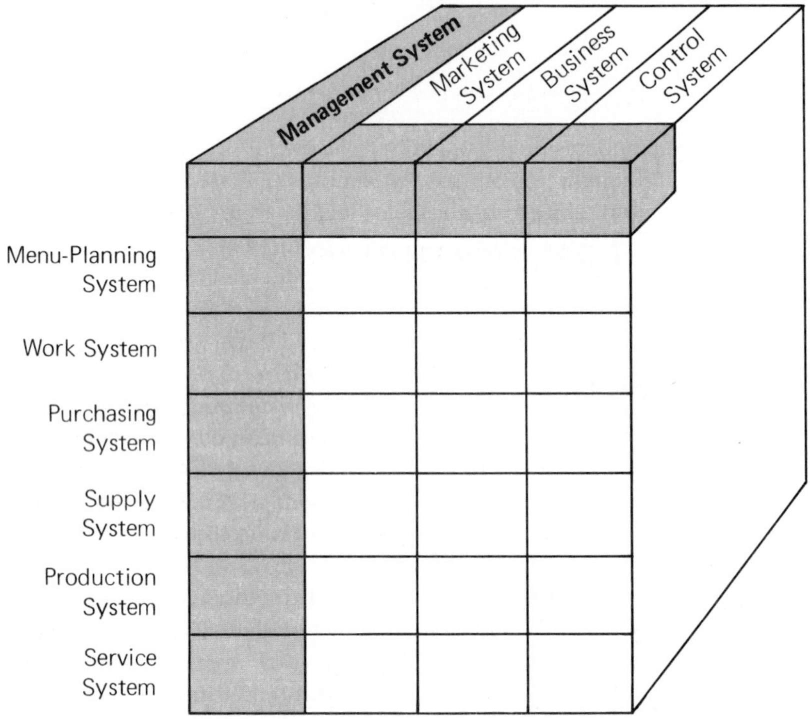

The management system interacts with every system of a foodservice operation. The activities of management are directed toward and flow through the other systems of the operation.

ment, the control system of a foodservice operation is treated as a separate system in Chapter 13.)

While it is valid to treat these universal management activities as a separate system for the purposes of presentation and study, this treatment should not lead to the conclusion that the management system functions in isolation. In fact, it interacts with, and depends upon input from, all other systems of the organization. For example, a particular managerial activity—planning—may start with data from the control system regarding flawed performance in the purchasing system. Managers draft plans to correct the problem and possibly develop guidelines for future action and adaptation. The effectiveness of that managerial activity is measured by the subsequent performance of the purchasing system for which the plan was formulated.

Exhibit 2.1 depicts the interaction of systems in a functioning foodservice operation. From this diagram it is evident that there is, for example, no marketing or food production activity that does not involve interaction with general management activities.

MANAGEMENT CONCEPTS

An analysis of the management system—those elements of a foodservice organization primarily dealing with strategic management and personnel management—yields a number of concepts central to the successful functioning of this system.

1. Managers set objectives.
2. Managers promote the successful integration of the tasks of a foodservice organization.
3. Managers are influenced by the external and internal environments of a foodservice organization.
4. Managers' activities are limited by available resources.
5. Managers' activities require the development of special skills.
6. Managers are people who have identifiable character traits.

Managers Set Objectives   Managers set objectives for their foodservice operations. The relationship between good management and established objectives is important to an understanding of the management system and to the actual management of a foodservice operation. Managers use standards for performance to gauge progress toward organizational objectives; every managerial activity must have an objective as a reference point. The objective can be short term (unloading a truck) or long term (improving profits). Without such reference points, it is difficult to measure the activities of the people in the organization. Without specific objectives, none of the information managers receive can be weighed or evaluated; and none of the situations that confront the manager can be assessed. An organization without objectives tends to stagnate, and managerial effectiveness diminishes. In the absence of well-defined goals, doing nothing makes more sense than performing meaningless tasks.

Objectives may be formulated by the manager who is directly responsible for their attainment or by other managers elsewhere in the organization. Higher-level managers, the executives, tend to establish long-term objectives—those affecting the organization's overall functioning and its growth and development. Higher-level managers set goals such as the percentage of profits they wish the operation to produce; they also decide, with input from the marketing system, which market segment the operation should be designed to attract. Managers of operational units (a purchasing department, a receiving platform, or a pantry section in a kitchen) more often formulate short-term objectives rather than long-term ones. These short-term objectives include such matters as how many loaves of bread a baker should produce daily and how many tables a waiter or waitress should be able to handle well each day.

Since all management activities are oriented toward some goal or objective, managers must involve the people with whom they work in activities that are meant to achieve some purpose: accomplishing a certain task—such as unloading a truck; attaining a particular standard—such as meeting a certain food budget; or bringing about some desirable change —such as improved profits. Ultimately, a management system is judged on the basis of its performance in reaching established objectives. Have the objectives actually been reached? If so, what resources have been expended in the effort and what are the incidental effects of the effort?

Managers Promote Interactions Between Systems

Because the foodservice operation is a system of integrated elements functioning together for some purpose, managers must recognize and promote the successful interaction of these elements. A manager of one system or part of a system cannot undertake actions without considering how these actions will affect other systems or their parts. A specific goal may be realized by independent action, but the overall objectives of the organization might well be compromised by such isolated action.

Because the problems caused by the interaction of different systems are foreseeable, successful organizations give their managers a set of guidelines, sometimes called *policies* or *procedures*, against which proposed activities must be measured. A policy is a statement of management's standards and objectives. Policies define acceptable performance. A procedure is an established method for performing some task; properly designed procedures guarantee an efficient flow of work. Properly drawn-up policies communicate management's objectives to every employee. In addition, if the guidelines are well drawn, they will protect the operation from activities in any one area that might be harmful to the total organization. They also limit the activities a given manager's department is authorized to undertake.

Managers Are Limited by the External and Internal Environments

While objectives and methods for achieving those objectives are being established, consideration must also be given to the limits that the internal environment of a foodservice operation and the external environment, that is, society, place on the attainment of certain objectives. Government—in the form of health department officials, tax agents, labor department officers, and police—is an instrument of social limits and society's values. The manager cannot violate any of the dozen or so codes affecting foodservice operations, nor do anything that society as a whole may disapprove of, even if it is within the bounds of the law.

The external environment influences foodservice operations to such an extent that managerial activities are undertaken only after consideration has been given to health codes, fire codes, safety regulations, the minimum wage law and other regulations, truth-in-menu requirements, local environmental standards, and many other regulations. Managerial activities are begun only after consideration has been given to public standards of decency and morality, and society's sentiments concerning such things as ecological preservation, architectural values, outdoor decorations and signs, drinking on Sunday, and the service of alcoholic beverages near schools and churches. All of these social values must be taken into account even if they are not governed by local statutes.

The attainment of objectives is also limited by the internal environment of a foodservice operation. The nature of the foodservice operation as a business often requires quick, but accurate, decision making, although a manager might prefer planning and careful assessment instead. A manager must learn about the workings and interactions of the various systems of a foodservice organization so that he or she is able to make on-the-spot decisions that further efficiency and the attainment of objectives. Foodservice operations are extremely fast-paced; changes are constantly occurring. Frequently, managerial activities must take place under less than favorable circumstances. Thus, much management activity is limited by the immediate situation. The choice of alternatives in a particular situation may be less desirable than the manager's ideal solution. However, one of them is likely to be more desirable than failure to respond to the situation at all.

Consider, for example, this situation: a major highway is closed by an accident, and busload after busload of tourists descends on the dining room of a small hotel located on a secondary road. Had anyone known of the highway's closing, more help would have been hired; several special function rooms would have been converted into auxiliary dining rooms; more food would have been purchased. The additional customers would have been served well.

Inasmuch as the upsurge of business was unexpected, the manager is faced with a number of less desirable alternatives: limit the menu; provide cafeteria service instead of table service; turn away busloads after the operation's capacity has been reached; and so on. Of course, the manager could simply do nothing at all—and allow the kitchen staff to collapse with fatigue, let waiting customers remain seated for hours at dirty tables, and allow service personnel to abandon the procedures for tallying and recording guest checks. Clearly, the manager's possibilities are limited by the immediate situation; however, a good manager is creative and turns any situation to advantage.

Managers' Resources Are Limited   Managers seldom have unlimited resources (people, equipment, or capital). Therefore, an ordering of objectives, especially of long-term objectives, is almost always necessary. For example, if an operation lacks capital, management must establish objectives that will ensure continuous, safe growth and avoid financial crises; if an operation can draw only from a small labor pool, the managers must seek to hire and retain help that is as skilled as possible from the limited number of applicants.

Management activities are undertaken only after careful assessment of the best possible use of currently available resources.

The quality of resources may also restrict managerial activity. For a specific operation, it may not be possible, regardless of financial resources, to obtain food products, space, skills, equipment, and information of optimum quality. The success of many managers lies in their ability to attain organizational objectives even though they are aware of a better, cheaper, or easier way that is beyond their reach.

Managers Display
Special Skills

Skills necessary to strategic management and personnel management will be surveyed in the remaining sections of this chapter and in the next. Some generalizations about effective managerial performance will also be offered. But even an entire book or several books devoted to management could not alone equip a person to function effectively as a manager. A thorough knowledge of managerial tools plus experience in management are needed for full effectiveness.

Strategic management and personnel management can profitably involve aspiring managers in the study of such diverse subjects as the behavioral sciences—sociology, psychology, and social psychology—and higher mathematics as it applies to budgeting and to techniques of planning and forecasting. Skills in these areas must be given as much attention as culinary knowledge, control procedures, merchandising, product specification, and service skills.

Obviously, it would be a gross exaggeration to suggest that detailed knowledge of these areas is actually necessary to the management of a small foodservice operation. However, the progress of a manager in an industry that is gradually developing into larger and larger economic units may ultimately depend on a grasp of such knowledge.

Managers Are
People with
Certain Traits

A manager is a person who makes a unique contribution. Within a particular operation, no one else has as much freedom to act, to make innovations, to learn and to teach, to prosper and to cause others to prosper. With this freedom, however, come numerous obligations: to superiors, to the organization, to the profession, to subordinates, and to the public.

How individual managers use their freedom of action and how they meet their obligations often determine the quality of their management and, therefore, the success of their operation. The effective manager creates that particular work environment in which each foodservice system functions best. The effective manager serves as a channel for information from society to the operation. On behalf of the operational unit and its members, the manager interacts effectively with both the organization and with its customers, guests, or clients. Within the operational unit, the manager encourages, directs, and teaches other individuals so that the organization can prosper.

There is a personal quality to management that is difficult to fit into a rigid pattern. Although management can validly be described as a system, as a profession, or as a series of activities involving specific skills, much of management remains an art. As practitioners of an art, successful managers seem to share a number of qualities. These qualities include flexibility, genuine leadership, the ability to initiate innovation, and an orientation toward processes and participation.

Flexibility   Successful managers exhibit an intellectual, emotional, and professional flexibility that allows them to respond to new situations and ideas. They regard new situations and ideas as opportunities, and they respond to people as unique and valuable individuals. A flexible manager is sensitive to changes in society's values and to changes in the tastes and attitudes of his or her market segment. Because of this flexibility, a manager seeks to adapt the operation to new situations and trends and to pursue new opportunities.

Leadership   Successful managers receive their authority by earning the respect and confidence of their superiors and subordinates. Successful managers do not rely on their position as "leader." They are recognized as being in charge because of their excellent decisions, forceful and forthright personalities, and clear perceptions of their operations' potentials and problems.

Innovation   Successful managers welcome opportunities to make innovations. They critically question prior assumptions. If such assumptions are no longer valid, successful managers discard them no matter how convenient they may have been.

Process orientation   The successful manager understands that the means by which an objective is reached and its cost to the organization, to its employees, and to society at large are as important as the objective itself. This statement may seem to imply that objectives are ignored. On the contrary, what is meant is that objectives must be defined in a broad context. The manager who does not have this larger perspective may see, for example, making the most profit as the immediate objective. On the other hand, the manager who has a process orientation understands that making the most profit at the moment may not result in the maximum profit in the long run, and he or she acts accordingly. As a simple example, a shortsighted manager might sell flood victims food and drink at the highest price the market will bear, whereas the process-oriented manager might donate whatever the operation had or simply maintain regular menu prices.

Participative orientation   The successful manager wants to involve the work group and other individuals in decision making that affects the unit. This involvement does not mean that every decision is shared, but rather that the manager endeavors to create circumstances in which the best decision is made, regardless of how it is made or by whom. For example, a manager may ask a chef to assess various brands and types of equipment before placing an order. Successful managers do not use their roles as leaders to make every decision singlehandedly.

STRATEGIC MANAGEMENT

In general, strategic management is the careful allocation and direction of the resources of a foodservice operation, be they money, equipment, or personnel. The manager directs the operation through careful decision making, thus adapting it to changes and ensuring optimum performance. In managing, the successful manager would seek to attain as many of the following specific objectives as possible.

1. *To develop plans and objectives*   The primary activity of management is to set objectives and then develop workable plans to accomplish those objectives. In Chapter 1, three general qualities of successful operations were mentioned: (1) the ability to offer people the products they want; (2) the ability to prosper in prevailing economic and social conditions; and (3) the ability to adapt either when people's wants change or when conditions change, or both. The responsibility of management is to develop a specific program for the attainment of these general goals. A plan is a program of action to accomplish goals.

For example, the management of a small chain may want to set an objective of opening 100 additional units within ten years. The managers begin to gather information to determine whether the objective is feasible and also to prepare a plan. The marketing system reports on consumer preferences and new products, and on the eating patterns and the competing chains in various parts of the country. Market research would establish which products are popular and which products may become increasingly popular in the near future. The business system would report on the availability of capital, the economic climate throughout the country, and the long-term effects of rapid growth. The control system would report on how to develop policies and procedures to ensure proper training of employees and high quality products in all units.

After receiving this information, management chooses among alternative courses of action and formulates plans. Management may decide to open 100 similar units in nearby states because it believes that the original product still has appeal, or it may decide to test-market a new product and then sell franchises. Management then must reevaluate its original objective and also ensure that each new unit maintains the same standards as the original restaurant. As the chain grows, management must reassess its objectives continuously; a pizza parlor chain with the same plans and objectives as a single independent pizzeria is doomed to failure. In fact, the objectives and plans of any operation must be reevaluated continuously to ward off stagnation and failure.

In addition, successful strategic management results in the formulation of guidelines that help the organization remain focused on its primary objectives. For example, a commercial operation generally has profit making as a primary objective. Unless strategic management is effective, this objective can become debased: high volume, not high profits, may become the objective. The operation may be kept open for several additional hours to increase volume. As volume is increased, profitability can decrease because the extra costs of keeping the operation open are not balanced by the extra business.

2. *To allow the operation to anticipate, rather than react to, situations and change*　As in other industries, managers in foodservice operations are sometimes thought to have performed well if they have weathered a crisis. They have reacted successfully to a rush of business, a shortage of a critical item, or to something similar that threatened the functioning of the operation. In contrast, genuine excellence lies in anticipating situations and planning to cope with them. A good manager recognizes that these situations could occur and gathers information and makes plans for dealing with them.

Reaction is always more expensive than anticipation. It can cost immediate dollars—for example, customers walk out because they have not been served, or efficiency is reduced as workers get the job done but with wasted time.

The systematic activities involved in strategic management make the manager address the strengths and weaknesses of the operation before they are critically tested. A staffing error—for example, too many salad workers and too few utility workers—can be revealed in the planning of the work schedule. Purchasing effectiveness, as another example, can be evaluated if the manager has information on the number of orders under five dollars that the operation executes. Small orders are as expensive to process as large ones. Hence, having too many small orders indicates a lack of efficiency.

This objective also includes gathering information to protect the operation against crises that can lead to complete business failure in commercial operations or to total functional inadequacy in noncommercial operations.

3. *To promote the maximum use of resources and increase the operation's opportunities*　Unless management is foresighted and monitors the use of resources (labor, equipment, facilities, information, and money), these resources tend to be allocated poorly: too much in some areas and too little in others. Too much money may be spent on new equipment, for example, and not enough on preventive maintenance programs. Strategic management provides the means for managers to oversee the allocation of resources.

In addition, by gathering information of various kinds, opportunities for increased profitability or increased service may be revealed. To realize these benefits, it is necessary to anticipate the opportunities before they occur. It should be apparent, for example, that the operation has a new market before the first new customer walks in the door.

Current Practices in Strategic Management   In commercial and noncommercial operations, in snack bars and school lunch programs, in every segment of the industry, one can find examples of excellent management and of poor management. Everywhere there are managers who do not know what is going on in their operations, managers who know what is going on and do not know what to do about it, managers who know what is going on and what to do about it but who do not take action, and managers who are in complete control of their operations.

A number of operational problems are symptomatic of deficiencies in management: lack of solid data on the operation's market; a loose menu program; uneven menu-pricing procedures; ignorance of fundamental costs of food and labor; loose accounting procedures; production planning by nonmanagerial workers; comparatively high costs of management per patient meal or per dollar sales, of products purchased, and of debt service; many leftovers and much waste; overstaffing; and no clear food and beverage cost-control procedures. While it is difficult to generalize, it is safe to say that foodservice operations owned by large conglomerates probably suffer least from such faulty management, and independent operations of all types suffer most.

However, one should not confuse effective management with the use of sophisticated management techniques. The manager of a foodservice operation can definitely plan successfully without using the complex techniques that the largest foodservice chains are able to use. The manager of a large operation who has sufficient technical support and automatic data processing equipment can use complex methods more easily, although a lack of sophisticated equipment and techniques should not cause managers to abandon a specific activity. The use of such equipment and techniques should not serve as a substitute for solid management and careful thinking and decision making. Even if the world's best computer is employed, bad methods, inaccurate data, and irrelevant instructions still would result in inappropriate information for decisions and plans.

ACTIVITIES OF STRATEGIC MANAGEMENT

Three activities are crucial to strategic management:

1. Operational analysis: gathering and organizing information.
2. Planning: interpreting information and setting standards for future performance.
3. Implementing: putting plans into effect.

These activities may involve a variety of processes. For example, planning involves processes such as forecasting, decision making, and budgeting. Decision making, in turn, can be accomplished by various sophisticated management techniques—or by the more familiar and sometimes more effective use of human judgment, logic, and experience.

Conducting an Operational Analysis

As a management activity, operational analysis is used to collect information relevant to the operation and to appraise resources and assess the current level of performance of the operation's activities. A manager should seek out information on the various external and internal factors which affect the performance of a foodservice operation, such as consumer preferences, business trends, financial climate, and internal organizational structure. Exhibit 2.2 lists various sources of this information. A consultant studying an operation might collect data in these areas; management also requires the same information to operate successfully. But management's operational analysis must be ongoing. A constant flow of up-to-date, accurate information is the only sound basis for managerial planning and decision making.

Some items listed in Exhibit 2.2 such as the reports and documents that contain information on business and finance have traditionally been the concern of executives only—of the very top managers of a company. It is the middle-level and operational managers who are concerned with information related to day-to-day activities. While the practicality of this allocation of information—to allow middle and operational managers to concentrate on operating performance—is understandable, the practice itself is questionable. Can anyone really make fundamental decisions about menu pricing or scheduling or purchasing without knowing the facts about the operation's financial health or about its market or its competition? If a manager is not deeply involved in this flow of information, the title of "manager" is of questionable significance.

A foodservice operation usually also undertakes a program of operational analysis for specific purposes and thus produces market studies, make-or-buy analyses, cost-benefit analyses, cash-flow projections, and similar information. Often, managers of operating units participate in these studies, especially when such studies concern actual operational performance. Outside consultants with particular specialties such as marketing, auditing, engineering, or personnel frequently supplement the internal resources of the organization in an operational analysis program.

Operational analysis techniques vary widely. Large corporations use the most sophisticated quantitative techniques—for example, statistical methods, dynamic and linear programming, and marginal utility analysis. Smaller operations that are concerned with operational analysis but which cannot afford the development of elaborate informational resources rely on the intelligent interpretation of logs, journals, inventory records, sales histories, menu analyses, and similar materials produced in

EXHIBIT 2.2 Types of Information Used in Operational Analysis

Information relevant to each of the following areas is necessary for some aspect of both executive-level management and the management of specific operational activities. Market information, for example, might be supplied by a series of studies: consumer preference studies, demographic studies, and so on. Without them, management decisions in the area of marketing and menu-program development are not validly made. Business information, for example, can be supplied by the various documents produced by accounting activities; without this information, decisions concerning financial management are difficult, if not impossible, to make.

If there is an inability to produce information that corresponds to most of the categories listed, management is deficient because of an ignorance of the fundamental functioning of the operation.

Market Information

Customer	*Competition (cont.)*	*Market (cont.)*
Preferences	Offerings	Trends in lifestyle
Characteristics	Customer reaction to	Unemployment
Response to operation regarding	competitors	
products	Competing social events (parades,	*Profitability*
prices	ball games, and so on)	By menu item
service		By meal segment
advertising	*Market*	By day of the week
	Characteristics	By time of day
Competition	Size	Cost centers
Characteristics	Location	Profit centers
Number	Demographics	Vulnerability to competition
Policies	Trends in education	Demand factors
Prices		

Business Information

Expenses	*Expenses (cont.)*	*Trends*
Cost of food sales	Cost of advertising and sales	Profit
Cost of beverage sales	Cost of utilities	Growth
Uniforms	Administrative expenses	Trends of expense items
Laundry and linen	Rent	Break-even points
China and glassware	Real estate and other taxes	
Kitchen utensils	Insurance	*Financial Status*
Kitchen fuel		Current assets
Cleaning supplies	*Financial Ratios*	Cash
Paper supplies	Current ratios	Accounts receivable
Guest supplies	Acid test ratio	Inventories
Bar expense	Receivable turnover ratio	Fixed assets
Menu and wine list	Inventory turnover ratio	Debt
Contract cleaning	Debt to net worth ratio	Cash flow
Exterminating	Gross profit margin ratio	Return on investment
Flowers and decorations		

Organizational Information

Strategy
Plans
Policies
Objectives

Procedures
Organization chart:
 by area
 by function
 by activity
 by persons
 by responsibilities

Procedures (cont.)
Control procedures
Accounting procedures
Communications procedures

Operational Information

Standards
Work standards
Productivity standards
Quality standards
Portion standards
Specifications
Standard recipes
Economic order quantity

Status
Operational data compared with standards
Percent of total sales of
 china breakage
 pilferage
 bad checks
Physical inventories
Percent storage used
Percent stock-outs
Purchasing effectiveness

Status (cont.)
Service facility use:
 dining room turnover
 covers per hour
 total space available
Value analysis
Cost analysis
Make-or-buy analysis
Lease-or-own analysis

Trends
Cost of raw materials
Cost of labor

Physical Resources
Age
Condition
Life expectancy

Physical Resources (cont.)
Current value
Depreciation
Cost of operating
Cost of maintenance

Personnel
Staffing table
Job classifications
Job specifications
Work rules
Labor contracts
Incentive programs
Appraisal procedures
Compensation scheme
Rates
Pensions
Fringe benefits cost

Environmental Information

Regulations
Trade practices
Wage standards
Health and safety
Food handling
Sanitation
Alcoholic beverages
Credit and collections
Facilities design
Construction
Fire
Pollution
Noise

Regulations (cont.)
Affirmative action
Antitrust
Price discrimination
Zoning

Agreements
Contracts
Labor-management
Franchise
License
Trademark and patent

Societal Values
Sentiments concerning:
 business operations
 alcohol
Competition
Public decency
Esthetics

Weather
Climate as it affects all other factors

the course of business. The information is interpreted by careful and experienced managers rather than through abstract "management science," often with excellent results.

Formulating Plans   Operational analysis leads naturally to the second large function of strategic management: formulation of plans. A plan is a detailed course of action for the foodservice operation. The plan is based on a careful interpretation of information produced by operational analysis.

Formulating a plan consists of three distinct processes: (1) forecasting; (2) decision making; and (3) planning.

FORECASTING   The goal of forecasting is to predict an event or situation that will occur at a certain time or within a certain time frame. However, a forecast is not a substitute for a plan. Because a forecast is an estimate of future activity, it cannot be used as an outline for action. Instead, forecasts are a principal source of information needed in planning. A foodservice operation makes use of numerous forecasts. For example, the purchasing department attempts to forecast price changes and product availability so that supply can be assured at the best possible price. The production department attempts to forecast product needs so that labor can be used effectively. The accounting department attempts to forecast cash flow so that money is available for day-to-day operations. Schedules, advertising campaigns, menus, and investments all rely on forecasts of one sort or another.

Forecasts are based on information about past performance of the operational area for which the forecast is being made. If the manager is forecasting the number of customers the operation can expect, then the number of customers that the operation served in a comparable period in the past is the basis of the forecast. If the information is accurate and complete, the forecast will be correct. If there is a great difference between forecast and fact, the information on which the forecast was made is inaccurate or incomplete.

In any forecast there is the added risk that past information is not completely relevant to the future. Circumstances may change, or a factor in the past that was relatively unimportant may suddenly be very important for the future. The noncommercial operation serving the continuing client—for example, a boarding school foodservice operation —may be assured that with a constant population of students and one menu choice, the forecast for food production for next week will prove to be accurate if it is based on the past week. However, the commercial operation, which has no commitment from its customers or guests and several menu choices, has an element of uncertainty in the forecast. This Thursday's patronage may or may not be just like last Thursday's.

Basic methods of forecasting attempt to minimize uncertainty. For example, instead of using only last week's records, the manager might analyze trends in patronage and menu selection over a period of time.

If the information on which the forecast is based is expanded sufficiently, short-term variations will tend to become less important. Forecasting methods also take into account recently occurring variables: managers forecasting for a commercial restaurant would consider changes in the operation's environment—a convention in town, the advertising campaign of a major competitor, the weather—and use this information accordingly.

As the complexity of the forecast and the number of variables or the length of time for which it is being made increase, the amount of information required also increases and the techniques used in interpreting it become more complex. A large foodservice company operating limited-menu restaurants might require several years of research to develop enough data to forecast the demand for a new menu item. It would require the most sophisticated forecasting techniques to make sure that the data were being interpreted correctly, that incidental variables were not obscuring the trends seemingly established by the information. One major foodservice company that has been researching acceptance of chicken for ten years and of ice cream for five years is still not sure enough of the results to rely on them in revising its menus.

DECISION MAKING   Decision making—the second step in formulating a plan—is choosing among alternative courses of action, each of which has advantages and disadvantages. Decision making is management's response to the information gathered.

The process of decision making is straightforward: define the objectives; gather information; determine the alternatives; weigh the alternatives; and make the best choice. The process can be complicated by difficulties at each step.

Defining the objective of a decision can be difficult. Frequently, the need to make a decision is not apparent. For example, a health care foodservice operation may simply drift, by a series of small, though correct, decisions, into buying most of its main courses as prepared frozen products. At no time does the manager make a choice between committing the kitchen to efficient production of its own main courses or committing it to efficient preparation or finishing of purchased pre-prepared products. Either alternative may be less expensive than the present course of action: inefficiently preparing purchased frozen products. A commercial restaurant that has enjoyed immediate success may not come to grips with decisions about its market, its market image, or its competitive position until sales decline. At that point, decisions may come too late.

Similar problems may occur at each step in the decision-making process. In gathering information to make a decision, the manager must decide what information is relevant. In developing alternatives, the manager must determine that all reasonable alternatives have been presented. In weighing the alternatives, he or she must decide whether the information on which the alternatives are based is accurate. In making the choice, the manager must determine whether external factors—such as personalities, traditions, or prejudices—have intruded into the decision process.

Managers must choose information that is appropriate and straightforward so that decisions are not obscured by unneeded or tangential information. Often, decision making that involves quantification—expressing information in numbers—helps eliminate the problems described above by showing the manager the factors involved in a particular decision. For example, the decision factors that relate to a health care foodservice operation's decision to make or buy main course items include the cost of labor, the cost of inventory, and the cost of processing, among others. Without first knowing that these are the areas in which information must be developed, a manager cannot make a good decision. Decisions in other areas involve other kinds of decision factors.

Once the factors appropriate to the decision are known, a specific technique for decision making can be selected. Most decisions are made by the logical method—simply assessing the information once it is organized around the decision factors. Complex decisions—those that involve long-range planning for the development of a foodservice chain, for instance—may involve many more factors and much more information.

PLANNING   Once forecasting and decision making have occurred, planning can take place. A plan is a formalized course of action. A budget is a type of plan that is expressed in numbers. Plans—whether expressed in words or in numbers—are the result of a decision or of a series of decisions. In other words, a course of action has been chosen from several alternatives. The plan specifies the details of the course of action, making it possible to implement it.

Many decisions in foodservice operations are best made ahead of time. A manager, for example, plans this week for next week's personnel schedule using decision factors such as the number of customers forecast, production requirements for that week, and employee vacations and productivity. Everyone could report to work next Monday morning, and the decision could be made then, but at the risk of coping with a crowd of grumbling workers.

Planning ahead is possible because decisions that must be made in the present can be based on decisions that have already been made satisfactorily—that Robin works in the pantry and Toby works in the bakery are the results of decisions that have already been made. These decisions could be made on the spot as needed; but, as Robin's and Toby's abilities are known and are unlikely to change in a week's time, prior decisions are justified. Plans as reflected in schedules, production orders, menu programs, purchasing policies, advertising budgets, and preventive maintenance programs are all based on prior operational decisions.

A plan to anticipate or remedy a specific situation may be defective because the plan did not result from the critical decisions—that is, it is inappropriate to the situation. The following example makes this point clear. A restaurant chain recognized that a great number of hamburgers were being cooked and then discarded because customers did not purchase them within the three-minute limit that the hamburgers were allowed to remain under the warming lamps. Chain headquarters developed a plan for reducing waste. After alternatives were considered, headquarters decided that the unit managers should record and report the number of hamburgers wasted and that they should be held accountable for any number above a certain amount related (as a percent) to the unit's volume of business. The plan worked in that fewer hamburgers were reported wasted. But the plan also failed because factors critical to the decision were ignored. To reduce waste, managers violated other rules. They did not remove all the hamburgers within three minutes; they sold hamburgers burnt on the grill to make up for those that were discarded after three minutes; or they did not use warming lamps all the time. To solve the problem, the decision process should have scheduled production of hamburgers to correspond more closely to the customer demand for hamburgers at a given time of day. It is also evident from this example that a plan must be evaluated before it is actually implemented. A plan must be evaluated to ensure that it conforms to the objectives and standards of the foodservice operation. An irrelevant or impractical plan is guaranteed to cause confusion and inefficiency among workers as well as managers.

Implementing Plans

Plans—whether schedules, production orders, or larger operational plans—must be implemented, that is, put into action. A manager facilitates the implementation of a plan in four basic ways:

1. Communicating: giving people the essential information about the plan and the situations in which it is applied.
2. Organizing: structuring people's behavior so that the plan can be implemented.
3. Interacting: directing the performance of operational systems in terms of the plan.
4. Problem solving: assessing and correcting variances and deviations from the plan.

COMMUNICATING

The objective of communicating is to relay information relevant to some course of action to the people who need it. Communicating is difficult or easy depending on the nature of the information, the abilities of the person communicating, and the ability and receptivity of the person to whom the communication is addressed.

Communication in the foodservice industry may involve any aspect of the operation's activities. Forecasts, instructions, orders, praise, news, procedures, health warnings, and dress codes can all serve to help individuals adapt their behavior to specific situations according to plan.

In the foodservice industry, all conceivable means of communication are used in order to give people the information they need to be effective in work situations. These means include conversations, conferences, meetings, classes, demonstrations, letters, memos, manuals, slide presentations, brochures, newspapers, television programs, radio shows, films, and teaching machines, among many others.

With regard to a specific communication directed to a specific group or individual, choosing the objective and the information to be conveyed is more important than choosing the medium of communication. Unless the objective—the desired change in behavior on the part of the recipients of the communication—is clearly identified, the communication tends to become confusing, trivial, boring, and ineffective regardless of the medium used. When choice of medium does arise, its selection will depend much more on the people to whom the communication is addressed than on the content of the communication.

As an example of a situation requiring communication, consider the safety hazards posed by the average foodservice kitchen. Numerous hazards can reduce an individual's productivity by causing injuries, delays, and loss of efficiency. Ultimately, the worker's reduced ability to function will compromise the production plan. Thus, the question is how best to inform the people in the kitchen of hazards so that they can adjust their behavior to the situation—i.e., work safely—and not compromise the plan.

In solving this problem, various communications media will be effective for different groups or individuals depending on their receptivity. If the kitchen is a large central commissary with sophisticated automated equipment operated by skilled and well-trained engineers, a formal lecture with some demonstrations and an operation manual may easily accomplish the objective. The group's literacy and high motivation make it easy for them to understand a formal conversation. On the other hand, if the kitchen is in a small foodservice operation staffed by people with varying educational backgrounds and differing competencies in spoken and written communication—and with varying willingness to understand—this type of communication will be largely unsuccessful. People may not understand the message—either from lack of ability or from lack of desire. Communication in the forms of printed signs, photographs, cartoons, films, and single sheets of do's and don'ts in several languages might provide the information necessary to accomplish the objective.

The manager must acquire skills in using basic communications techniques. Typically, he or she should know how to write a letter, produce an understandable schedule, conduct a business meeting, demonstrate a piece of equipment, and perform other similar duties. A manager should aim to improve the effectiveness of the communication by reducing the barriers people may set up between themselves and the information. For example, some people may simply ignore a communication. Soliciting their opinion or a confirmation of their understanding—"feedback," as it is called—makes them participate in the communication process and denies them the opportunity to ignore communications from management. Demonstrations and other visual techniques help overcome people's difficulties with abstract concepts. Describing desired changes in behavior as a personal benefit to the individual being asked to change reduces the "so-what" barrier.

ORGANIZING Organizing is another important activity in plan implementation. Through organizing, the elements of a plan and the workers' behavior required by the plan are formalized and carried out in day-to-day operations.

Once organization has been established, the plan and its objective, the people and their relationships to the plan, and the situation and workers' behavior in response to it can all be treated as a unit. In practice, these organizational units are called departments, groups, sections, teams, task forces, divisions, operating units, or a variety of other names that indicate a functional association exists between the elements of these units.

In the traditional restaurant, work stations have been organized to correspond to menu-item categories: soup, fish, sauce, vegetables, grill, pantry, bakery, and so on. The situation facing these kitchen departments will not vary radically from day to day. Therefore, after initial communication of information relevant to the operation's plans—such as portion-control information, recipes, and style of presentation—a certain standard behavior can be expected from the department. Little additional communication is necessary unless there has been a radical change of plan.

The performance of a department in restaurants organized in this fashion can be evaluated from day to day because the work situation does not change substantially. If 6 gallons of each of ten soups must be made every day by the same people, why should the quality of the soups vary? Few significant new decisions are needed; only new situations that arise need to be dealt with. In practice, instead of giving the department less attention, general management (the *chef de cuisine*) gives it a junior manager, a station head called a *chef de partie*. Some of the head chef's authority and responsibility are thus delegated to the station chef.

Many foodservice operations of all types are organized on this basis: a rigid hierarchy of departments headed by individuals who report to other managers who are a step higher in the organization. There may be operating departments—such as purchasing, marketing, and production —and within these departments there may be operating sections—such as the buying, receiving, and warehousing sections within the purchasing department.

Other foodservice operations which cannot be ensured of situations as unchanging as those that this rigid organizational arrangement implies must be organized differently. For example, more flexibility is needed by a social catering company that produces parties of widely different types; its organizational structure tends to be less rigid, to have more day-to-day communication, and frequently to have more intensive management. On the other hand, foodservice operations assured of situations that change even less than those of the traditional restaurant can permit an even greater degree of specialization in their organizational units. For example, the commissary of a large foodservice contractor serving continuing clients may have departments that make only a single item, like ham sandwiches, rolls, or tuna salad.

Organizing involves identifying the type of structure that is best suited to a particular operation. It entails evaluating similar existing organizational structures and determining how the organizing process can be made more efficient.

INTERACTING　A manager may also smooth the way for plan implementation through interaction. A manager interacts when he or she enhances the functioning of people and organizational units by manipulating elements in situations that face the operation. In essence, the manager interacts with these elements and modifies their relationship to the operation. Successful interaction results in a better implementation of the operation's plan. It reduces possible interference with the plan's implementation, or even makes the situation favorable to it.

Interference with implementation of a plan can come from a number of sources: government, the public, competitors. Government steps in, for example, if the operation fails to comply fully with the law. Thus, management interacts with government agencies by obtaining permits and licenses, and by complying with laws, codes, statutes, and other regulations in order to protect the operation.

To counteract interference by potential and actual customers, management relies on public and press relations efforts. By interacting successfully with the public and with the media that influence the public, management can induce a climate that encourages smooth functioning of the operation. For example, the management of a limited-menu restaurant chain that is expanding into a new city may spend considerable time and money in preparing the public to accept such a restaurant in a semiresidential or historic neighborhood. If the public relations effort is successful, contractors hired to construct the unit and the operations and marketing divisions will have little interference in implementing the plan to open the restaurant. If the public relations program is unsuccessful, pickets may delay construction; zoning boards may prevent it entirely; newspapers may refuse advertisements; suppliers may avoid it; and potential customers may boycott it.

Interference can also arise from competitors in the form of promotional activity, price changes, and advertising campaigns. Marketing strategies of various sorts may be seen as programs of interaction that attempt to neutralize potential interference from competitors.

A manager also interacts with, and influences, elements within the organization. Production plans may be facilitated by seeking cooperation with suppliers in modifying delivery schedules. Or the manager of one department may coordinate efforts with those of another department so that the operational plan may be more easily implemented. For instance, the banquet manager of a hotel may ask that the housekeeping department reschedule the cleaning of a function room so that there is more time available to prepare it for a convention group.

In summary, a foodservice manager has many opportunities to interact with individuals and groups to modify situations to favor the implementation of plans. These groups include government agencies; customers, guests, or clients; suppliers; subordinates; supervisors; consultants; neighboring businesses; the press; trade associations; and others.

PROBLEM SOLVING   However excellent the processes of operational analysis, planning, and implementing may be, the unforeseen still occurs. There must be a response that maintains the integrity of the operation's objectives. The process of problem solving—of adapting the plan to the situation—must provide that response.

In some respects, problem solving resembles decision making. Information about unforeseen events is gathered; alternatives are developed and weighed; and a course of action is chosen. But a critical difference exists between the two approaches. In problem solving, the response is not meant to be formalized, while the results of decision making *are* meant to be formalized.

This distinction is apparent in this simple example of problem solving. The griddle cook in a limited-menu restaurant is injured in a car accident and cannot report to work. After examining the information, developing the alternatives—among them, not serving grilled items—the manager decides that the operation is best served by the manager's working at the griddle station. This solution to the problem is only temporary. Immediately after that meal, the manager will, by decision making, formulate a more enduring plan for the operation.

Problems of this kind are common in foodservice operations: supplies are not delivered; equipment breaks down; workers are absent; the volume of business increases because of some event. Solutions to problems require a quick assessment of the seriousness and urgency of the situation and a quick response implementing the best workable solution. In problem solving, unlike decision making, the alternatives need not be exactly weighed on the basis of cost and effectiveness, inasmuch as the course of action used to solve the problem is unlikely to be repeated often enough to have much impact on profitability or the operation's effectiveness.

In most foodservice operations, managers actually involved in the situation usually solve the problem. Large organizations train managers to handle problem solving by providing them with simulated situations that require solutions to problems. Some organizations maintain teams of troubleshooters or crisis managers that have the ability and authority to mobilize the operation's resources to react immediately to the symptoms of a problem. Thereafter, the routine processes of management are used to eliminate the problem's underlying causes. For example, a large limited-menu restaurant chain will send a troubleshooter or crisis management team to the aid of a unit manager or franchisee at the earliest signs of difficulties. While these individuals are managing the crisis situation, any related problems of cost control, employee retraining, recipe standardization, production specifications, or market image are addressed, more slowly, by the appropriate departments of the chain's organization.

MAKING STRATEGIC MANAGEMENT EFFECTIVE

Delegation, decentralization of authority, and the entire process of organizing can increase managerial efficiency by allowing some people to specialize in more routine management tasks within individual operational units while general management takes care of challenges to the organization as a whole. In a large organization, for example, a worker may be principally concerned only with operational analysis or planning or forecasting.

There are, however, specific approaches to making strategic management more effective. They are as follows:

1. Application of the concept of managerial responsibility.
2. Assistance of persons with special skills.
3. Use of special techniques.
4. Use of forms and devices.

Managerial Responsibility   The effectiveness of strategic management can be improved by making individual managers responsible for the formulation of plans to attain goals. To this end, authority is given to individual managers, and each manager is made accountable for the results of the plans designed to attain the objectives chosen. The results are controlled, either by the individuals concerned or by other managers. Finally, the results are compared with the desired results or goals, so that the lessons learned from meeting goals, exceeding them, or failing to meet them can be applied.

At its broadest, this process is the practice of *management by objectives.* At its narrowest, it is often called *responsibility accounting.* In foodservice operations, managerial responsibility generally falls somewhere between these two extremes. The responsibility of most managers is limited; managers are held responsible for the results of certain plans, rather than for the attainment of general goals. The progress of their efforts is revealed by control devices specific to the activity and not by the general accounting system of the operation. Instead of being asked to set and attain a goal of 10 percent of overall profitability, for example, the manager is asked to establish more limited objectives. The goal might be a 2 percent reduction in the cost of service, a 3 percent increase in the volume of business, or the development of a more efficient method of ware handling.

Instead of measuring success or failure on the basis of the profit and loss statement at the end of the year, managers' performance is measured against the achievement of these limited objectives using routine control devices such as payroll, sales, and budget reports. From the information provided by these devices, the planning processes, the information used for planning, and the managerial efforts in facilitating the implementation of the plan can be evaluated. The individual manager alone, or a group of managers—including those more experienced and knowledgeable—will discover where the plan fell short of, or exceeded, expectations.

The process of control is basic to the concept of managerial responsibility. This subject is more fully discussed in Chapter 13; however, it can be stated here briefly that, for the effective use of managerial responsibility, controls must be designed to reflect the nature of the goals and the plans made for achieving these goals. And they must be tailored to the needs of the individual manager and the situation.

The concept of managerial risk is also frequently associated with managerial responsibility. Some foodservice organizations allow managers at all levels to set objectives and to make and implement plans. Therefore, by extension, these organizations accept the risk of error, partial failure, or total failure as part of the cost of developing managerial effectiveness. Other foodservice organizations do not wish to incur this risk and centralize the responsibility for strategic management in the executive levels of management. Some organizations assume only partial risks by restricting the authority and responsibility of individuals while allowing them some opportunities for risk taking.

A number of recently opened concept restaurants practice a high degree of managerial responsibility. Institutional foodservice operations, large chains of limited-menu restaurants, and foodservice contractors all are likely to adopt either centralized responsibility or the limited concept of responsibility accounting.

Assistance of Persons with Special Skills
To make strategic management more effective, a manager can seek the assistance of numerous individuals and groups. Sometimes this help is informal, and the people involved in assisting the manager have other operational responsibilities. Superior managers, managers on the same level, workers with special skills or experience, the leaders of informal work groups, suppliers, and union representatives can all be of assistance. They bring to the operation useful knowledge, competence in specific techniques, the benefits of experience, an objective view, or the ability to help facilitate the implementation of a plan.

In addition to these informal sources of assistance, many organizations provide formal assistance to a manager. Assistance may come from staff or support personnel within the organization or from consultants outside the organization.

Large organizations have staff or support departments in many areas: engineering, accounting, public relations, and others. The function of staff departments, in contrast to the work systems involved in production, is to assist the operating manager, not actually to manage the operation or an operating system.

Both large and small organizations call on outside consultants to assist operating managers at all levels in making strategic management effective. These consultants are usually associated with advertising agencies, marketing agencies, engineering firms, or accounting firms.

Use of Special Techniques
Numerous techniques in strategic management may have useful applications. These range from decision trees to the sophisticated Program Evaluation and Review Technique (PERT). A decision tree is the graphic representation of the various factors and contingencies involved in short-term planning. A manager using this technique would literally mark out all factors (and their relationships) on paper and then determine at which points decisions are required. PERT is a method for determining how long particular activities and procedures last; it is based on the shortest, average, and longest times an activity may take. For example, by determining how many hours plasterers, bricklayers, and other craftsmen need to complete a specified job, a restaurant could determine how long extensive remodeling would take. Management then could formulate a plan using the figures it has derived for man-hours and probably will be able to compute the cost of the project as well. While a detailed discussion of these techniques is not germane at this point, it is sufficient to point out that appropriately applied, they can make strategic management more effective.

In addition, the use of computers in the areas of operational analysis and information processing can also have the same result. Foodservice operations, ranging from independent restaurants to the dietary departments of hospitals, use such techniques for payroll analysis, inventory control and presentation, forecasting, facilities planning, labor utilization, work-methods analysis, and so on.

Use of Forms and Devices Strategic management is facilitated in most operations by the use of a number of forms and devices. Most of these materials are used in connection with specific operating systems; hence, they will be found throughout this book.

Chapter 3
The Management
System:
Part II
Certain concepts which are central to an understanding of the management system are developed in detail in the preceding chapter, "The Management System: Part I." There the activities of the management system are characterized as (1) being directed toward objectives; (2) promoting the successful integration of the tasks within the organization; (3) being influenced by the external and internal environments; (4) being limited by available resources; (5) requiring the development of special skills; and (6) being best performed by people who have certain character traits. The present chapter, "The Management System: Part II," is concerned with personnel management, which, like strategic management, is based on these concepts.

PERSONNEL MANAGEMENT

Theories of personnel management tend to extremes. One extreme treats people as "human economic resources" and uses principles similar to those used in the management of other resources such as equipment, information, and so on. The other extreme makes people the most important, indeed, the critical factor in the organization. According to this view, personnel management is an extension of sociology, psychology, and cultural anthropology.

A more constructive approach to personnel management is simply to recognize that people make many contributions to a foodservice operation: they are an economic factor in the functioning of the organization, and they bring to it the various social, psychological, political, and cultural facets of their personalities. Using this approach, a manager attempts to give people exactly the importance they merit according to the particular circumstances: sometimes they are very important and sometimes they are not.

47

Conceiving of personnel management in these terms avoids some very dangerous assumptions to which practitioners of other management approaches often fall prey. Neither control of "labor cost" nor effective "human relations" guarantees success to a foodservice organization or to any other enterprise. Rather, it is the management of people both as people and as they stand in relation to the other parts of the organization that brings success.

Specific Objectives of Personnel Management

A number of specific objectives of personnel management can be identified and are listed below. At a particular moment for a particular operation, some of these objectives may have higher priority than others.

1. *To integrate as fully as possible the people of an organization with its operating systems*   The objective of personnel management is to maximize workers' contributions to the organization. Attaining this objective requires the recognition of the needs of both the organization and the people it employs, and an assessment of the impact of that organization and its employees on each other.

2. *To attract individuals to satisfy current and future labor needs*   The departure of workers, ongoing expansion, and departmental reorganizations require the addition of new people to the organization. Plans for growth and expansion may call for additional people who can be integrated into the organization.

3. *To reduce the operation's labor costs*   A reduction in the labor cost can be achieved through increased productivity, better work design and better labor utilization, or through a decrease in some of the costs associated with labor, such as the costs of absenteeism, waste, breakage, pilferage, and patron dissatisfaction.

4. *To meet demands for new skills*   Changes in the operation, such as changes in consumer tastes, menu, equipment, work systems, or management, can require different skills or abilities. Employees must have or be taught the necessary skills.

5. *To design an operation sensitive to the rights of workers*   Legal, moral, and contractual imperatives call for a work environment that favors, or at least does not threaten, human health and safety. These imperatives also call for hiring and employment practices that recognize individual and civil rights.

Current Practices in Personnel Management

Although many foodservice operations successfully meet all these specific objectives, there is enough literature about the problems and challenges in personnel management to suggest that many operations do not meet or are unconcerned with these objectives. The following five observations on the present state of foodservice personnel management bear directly on the five objectives listed above:

1. The foodservice industry currently needs qualified workers and managers. Statistical evidence, pronouncements of industry leaders, the incidence of help wanted advertisements in newspapers, and the listings

of employment agencies specializing in foodservice managers support this contention.

2. Projections based on statistical models developed by the Bureau of Labor Statistics point to a considerable growth in the number of employees in the foodservice industry, as a result of general growth in population and income, to perhaps 6.5 million workers by 1985. Extrapolation from current trends reveals a growing need for management employees.

3. While the statistics are incomplete, those available indicate that the productivity of foodservice industry employees has not kept pace with the productivity of industrial workers and other service industry workers. Proposed changes in the minimum wage law and the use of the tip credit (that portion of the minimum wage assumed to be contributed by tips) in federal and some state income tax schedules can only compound this problem. The costs associated with labor—turnover, absenteeism, pilferage, consumer dissatisfaction—are still major concerns of foodservice management.

4. The increasing use of pre-prepared food products (those that include substantial purchased labor); the consolidation of foodservice enterprises into larger economic units, including a number of billion-dollar companies; and data from the Bureau of Labor Statistics, all suggest that the foodservice industry requires improved technology and new skills. Relatively fewer crafts (such as baking, sauce making, and butchering) and more managerial skills will be needed. In addition, there is an increasing demand for technical skills that involve machine operation and maintenance and for marketing skills aimed at patron accommodation in the sale, presentation, and service of food.

5. Vigorous application of federal legislation—the Occupational Safety and Health Act, the Equal Employment Opportunity Act, the Equal Pay Act, and Title VII of the Civil Rights Act—suggests that the health, safety, and civil and individual rights of workers will be of increasing concern in personnel management.

The challenge to the foodservice industry is clear. Personnel management in all its dimensions—from job design and recruitment to training and employee motivation—will demand increasing sophistication. For the individual operation, the challenge is to adapt successfully to changing circumstances, to reexamine the particular operation, and to remedy deficiencies in personnel management as these deficiencies occur.

ACTIVITIES OF PERSONNEL MANAGEMENT

Personnel management involves six different activities which collectively can achieve its stated objectives. These activities include:

1. Personnel planning: determining the operation's needs for personnel through analysis of the jobs performed by its present employees,

with due consideration of the operation's work structure and work environment.

2. Staffing: attracting, selecting, and inducting the people the operation needs.

3. Facilitating development: assisting people in developing the skills and competencies the operation needs.

4. Coordinating: integrating the operational activities of the foodservice organization and the abilities and personalities of the people it employs.

5. Motivating: sustaining and supporting workers in their efforts.

6. Evaluating: appraising the success of the individual in meeting the operation's needs and the effectiveness of the operation in meeting the individual's needs.

Each of these six activities will be discussed in turn in the following sections of this chapter, where they will be broken down into the more specific processes which comprise them. These processes may be directed by general management, a specialized personnel department, the operations managers of the organization's departments, or, frequently, all three.

Personnel Planning

Personnel planning is the process of defining and enumerating the skills and manpower that an operation requires. Gathering information is essential to the three activities of personnel planning: job analysis, job specification, and labor projection. Before these activities can take place, however, the work system for the foodservice operation should be established. It is impossible to formulate the personnel requirements of a foodservice operation without deciding how best to perform an operational task and how each task fits into the overall system.

For example, if a foodservice operation requires rolls, the alternative methods for producing them would have to be explored. Only then could it be stated definitely that a certain number of people with certain skills will be required to perform a set of defined tasks—that is, a job. One alternative might consist of nothing more than an oven, some small equipment, a table, and a person. Another might consist of an oven, a dough-kneading machine, a dough-rolling machine, automatic portioning equipment, and a person. Quite obviously, the skills required by these two jobs would differ. The matter of designing a work system is treated extensively in Chapter 7, "The Work System."

JOB ANALYSIS

After the work system is designed, individual jobs can be outlined. Though of course jobs often require equipment as well, a job analysis is concerned only with the human contribution to the job. Job analyses focus on the activities of individual workers.

A narrative method is most frequently used in preparing a job analysis. Either an operating manager or a person in the personnel department reports on the job after observation and/or interviewing. Sometimes a standard written job description, produced by the federal government or by various trade and professional groups, is used as a model. A few foodservice organizations use more sophisticated methods of task determination, like activity analysis and time and motion analysis, which are discussed in Chapter 7.

The ideal job analysis describes five areas: the assigned tasks; how these tasks are performed; how this job relates to other parts of the organization; the demands the job makes on the individual; and monetary and other compensation (like fringe benefits) available to the employee.

The usefulness of job analysis is dependent on whether the study is approached creatively or merely affirms the status quo. If workers are asked to describe their jobs, and the tasks (parts of the job) they identify are uncritically accepted as the tasks necessary to the job, the management process has been bypassed. When job vacancies are filled automatically without any job analysis taking place, old work habits are perpetuated, even if they are inefficient or harmful to the operation. For example, a general manager with a "take-charge" attitude may assume tasks belonging to other departments, such as purchasing or marketing. This centralization of management may be highly effective and desirable. However, the manager may have assumed responsibilities best left to other departments. A judgment has to be made on the basis of a critical evaluation of the job analysis. Properly used, job analyses can help regulate an organization so that it functions efficiently and smoothly.

JOB SPECIFICATION   Job analysis tells the actual activities that comprise a job. Job specification describes the abilities necessary to perform these job activities. In job analysis, the person doing the job has been implicitly described along with the job, while job specification focuses on the qualities which make this person fit for the job. The job analysis is translated into a job specification when the understanding of what tasks a job entails is turned into a sketch of a person possessing an inventory of specific skills and attributes befitting the job.

For very simple tasks, job specification is straightforward. Since most people could perform the tasks of the job, only rather broad qualifications must be specified: the ability to do manual labor, stand for three hours, and the like. When many tasks, or especially complex ones, are included in one job, the inventory of skills and attributes required by the job specification becomes more difficult to establish. In fact, many personnel managers avoid establishing a comprehensive job specification: the job specification tends to become a reworded job analysis. Instead of stating the qualities a person needs to perform the job, many job specifications simply vaguely call for a person who can do the job. The actual abilities that this person might need are not mentioned at all. A defective job specification—for example, based on a job analysis that designates the tasks of a job as cooking French entrées—would simply require a person who could prepare French entrées without mentioning the qualifications necessary to do so.

To avoid being empty exercises, job specifications should express qualifications in terms of education or experience. However, this approach assumes, questionably, that education or experience guarantees competence, and that only those persons with a certain amount of education or experience are competent. When education or experience criteria are applied rigidly, capable people may be excluded from consideration because of improper evaluation of their abilities or suitability for the position.

If these possible defects in the job specification process are recognized, job specification can be constructive. Job specifications can be used to establish rough guidelines for eliminating totally unqualified individuals and assist in matching qualified people to suitable jobs.

LABOR PROJECTION   It is necessary to determine not only which skills are required by the operation, but also how many people with particular skills are required. After analyzing the job of baking rolls, and determining the qualifications a person needs to bake rolls, an operation must determine how many bakers are needed. In practice, decisions concerning the number of employees required are made on a variety of bases. These bases include guesswork, experience, perpetuation of the current work system, directives from executive management, clauses in union contracts, and careful study of available information through operational analysis, forecasting, decision making, and planning. Many sophisticated planning techniques can be used: computer staff projections, statistical methods, model construction, and so on.

②Staffing   Foodservice managers involved in staffing their operations implement the results of personnel planning by finding the people to fill the jobs. Even in a small foodservice organization, some persons are regularly involved in staffing. Staffing involves three activities: recruitment, selection, and induction.

RECRUITMENT   The object of recruitment is to inform potential employees of the operation's personnel needs and to encourage such people to seek employment in the operation.

For many foodservice operations, government agencies have added another dimension to recruitment: affirmative action. Affirmative action programs are attempts to ensure fair procedures in staffing. In order to correct hiring and employment practices that have resulted in discrimination—against blacks, Hispanic-Americans, Orientals, American Indians, women, persons of a certain age, religion, or national origin, and the handicapped—the operation must, by law, actively recruit from among these groups. Employment goals reflecting the composition of the population from which the operation hires may have to be achieved.

The traditional methods of recruitment (such as newspaper advertising, visits to educational institutions, use of employment agencies, and radio and television advertisements) may have to be modified to ensure that particular groups of people are reached. For example, it would be unacceptable to recruit foodservice managers only in all-male colleges.

SELECTION   Selection, the second step in staffing, generally consists of application, interview, and screening phases.

Application   A job application usually entails rather formal clerical procedures. The candidate for employment may present credentials in the form of a resume (job history), curriculum vitae (brief biography), work samples, and recommendations or may simply fill out an application form eliciting some of this information. While job candidates are free to submit any materials they wish, the Equal Employment Opportunity Act, Title VII of the Civil Rights Act, the Equal Pay Act, and various state and local regulations, which may be stricter than federal law, prohibit the employer from requiring written or verbal information that may lead to discrimination.

Information concerning the personal life of the candidate may be solicited only when such information is a Bona Fide Occupational Qualification (BFOQ). Thus, a candidate cannot be asked for a picture, information regarding place of birth, membership in organizations, name before marriage, and so on. The hiring practices of an employer that requires information about military status, arrest or conviction, or prior bonding may also be questioned by agencies regulating this process.

Interview   The interview, either a structured or informal conversation with the candidate, is probably the most widely used selection tool in foodservice hiring. An interview is used to elicit information to the extent that the law allows, to allow the interviewer to evaluate the personality of the candidate, and to communicate to the candidate the important features of the job and the company. Within this limited scope, the interview can be useful. Too often, however, too much is expected of it.

Unless the interviewer has been carefully trained to assess job-related psychological characteristics during an interview, little about the potential on-the-job performance of the candidate will be learned. More often than not, the interviewer comes to the interview with a preconception of the ideal employee and intends to measure the candidate against this model. Clever candidates understand this situation and attempt to present themselves and their credentials so that the proverbial square peg will fit the round hole. For this reason, a series of interviews or a meeting with several interviewers tends to be more effective. In the latter instance, the interviewers can see how well the candidate relates and reacts to various individuals, stressful situations, tension, and pressure (abilities which may be job requirements).

Screening   The process of selection can proceed more formally by presenting the candidate with a standard test or situation, a method called *screening in/screening out*. Any formal test used must measure job-related abilities and attributes. If it does not, there is little sense in administering it. Such a test—either developed by the operation or purchased from outside the organization—should be validated by the Equal Employment Opportunity Commission (EEOC) as testing only job-related abilities. Otherwise, it may seem discriminatory, leaving the operation open to government or employee-candidate suits.

Work-sample or work-assessment testing is often appropriate. Asking a griddle cook candidate to prepare two fried eggs is neither unreasonable nor illegal. More complex methods for assessment—for example, two- or three-day group problem-solving sessions for potential managers —also can be useful if they are well structured. The objectives and the subject matter of the test must be well-defined, based on a reasonable and experimentally determined standard, and affirmed by the EEOC as nondiscriminatory.

INDUCTION   The final step in staffing is induction: introducing the newly hired employee to the organization and the job. Proper induction starts the employee working productively with the least amount of disruption of normal production and eases the inevitable personal stress that accompanies starting a new job. It also orients the employee to the organization's structure and gives the employee information relevant to compensation, privileges, and medical plans.

In practice, proper induction often does not happen: a new worker may be given too much information, too many rules, too many introductions, and too many names all at once. At the very least, the highly desirable objective of reducing personal stress is compromised. A potentially productive worker may quit because of unnecessary pressure at the time of induction.

A program of orientation, introduction, and acclimation planned by management to attain trouble-free induction is the best approach. In preparing the program, it is necessary to consider the particular worker or worker group and the particular operation. The matter should be approached as a communications problem. What are the operation's priorities for the transfer of information? What are the worker's priorities? After the priorities of each have been satisfied, perhaps through the use of a very simple information sheet and a conversation with a supervisor, then the secondary concerns of each can be taken up in turn.

Induction can be very important with regard to the worker's eventual contribution to the operation. In the absence of managerial attention to induction, worker loyalties may be won away by a labor organization or by an informal work group, and thus the new employee's reactions to the company may be prejudiced by the opinions of particular individuals.

<table>
<tr><td>③</td><td>*Facilitating the Development of Foodservice Personnel*</td><td></td></tr>
</table>

Facilitating the Development of Foodservice Personnel

The third major activity in personnel management is personnel development. In the past, foodservice operations were able to acquire skilled and competent people through staffing activities; there were enough qualified candidates to provide an almost continuous flow of new employees. However, several fairly recent phenomena have disrupted this pattern of staffing. First, the technological skills and knowledge needed by foodservice employees have changed radically. Moreover, the general expectations of many workers have changed from wanting a job to wanting a career.

The managers of a foodservice organization cope with these changes by facilitating the growth of personnel through *training* and *career development*. The operation must educate both the newly hired worker and the long-term employee in foodservice skills, procedures, and objectives. It has become increasingly necessary to provide an opportunity for each worker to develop sufficiently to advance in economic, social, and professional status in the operation and the community. If workers' needs are not met, the operation will suffer from a shortage of capable people for the maintenance or expansion of its activities and from costs due to high turnover, low productivity, absenteeism, theft, and indifference.

TRAINING   The training of foodservice personnel is the process by which workers' abilities are adapted to the needs of the operation. In order to determine if training is worthwhile, a particular training plan has to be weighed against its alternatives. For example, instead of training all personnel so that they have the skills required by an operation's work system, the work system can be reshaped so that the operation's needs correspond to the abilities of available workers, thus eliminating the need for extensive training. The limited-menu take-out/take-in restaurant that serves hamburgers, pizza, or fried chicken has, through a rigorous program of work-system design, succeeded in simplifying its food production process to such an extent that it has relatively little need for training. As long as a personnel pool of high school students and other part-time workers is available, this type of operation can function efficiently. Were this situation to change, perhaps because more interesting work became available to students, the operation might redesign its work system, replacing unskilled labor with an automated production/service

EXHIBIT 3.1   Guide for the Continuing Evaluation of Training Effectiveness

Short Range	*Long Range*
1. Does training increase the speed at which employees reach minimum performance standards? Is the speed at which trainees reach these standards predictable?	1. Are trained employees more likely than untrained employees to improve their performance over minimum standards?
2. Does training begin at the trainees' starting skill level?	2. Do trained employees maintain learned skills? Is "refresher" training needed periodically?
3. Does training encourage employee interest in the job?	3. Does training affect worker turnover or absenteeism?
4. Can training be integrated with on-going operations?	4. Do trained employees maintain job interest? Do they make suggestions to improve their jobs?
5. How much time and effort do supervisors (trainers) spend on training? Does training detract from their other job demands?	5. Does training improve a department's overall work performance?
	6. Is training cost-effective or would it be more viable to alter the work system so that training is not necessary?

Evaluating the effectiveness of training will enable the foodservice operation to modify future training to enhance the strengths and correct the weaknesses of the current training program.

machine. As a consequence, the operation's training needs would change as well: operating the new machine might require a highly skilled, specially trained technician.

Once training needs are established, the total commitment of the operation is needed if training is to be effective. A number of practices can be recommended:

1. Base training on the same criteria as the communications process discussed in Chapter 2: define goals and choose a medium that fits the needs of the individual or group being trained.

2. Provide thorough training of instructors, especially informal instructors such as supervisors and senior workers.

3. Establish incentives for the employees being trained: increased compensation, recognition, or promotion. The operation can only facilitate training and development by providing the opportunities; the individual worker still must want to benefit from them.

4. Make certain that training addresses the total individual. A long-range view of the training process should be taken, and subjects which will indirectly increase the employee's contribution should be considered: academic subjects, instruction in management techniques, subjects of personal concern, and so on.

5. Try to guarantee that the training process provides genuine opportunities for individual development. Sometimes training programs are used as conciliatory gestures to employees who are disenchanted with their rate of advancement. Exhibit 3.1 offers a guide for evaluating training effectiveness.

Training techniques in the foodservice industry vary greatly. For non-managerial workers, the principal method is an adaptation of the job instruction technique offered as Exhibit 3.2. Management workers are trained by individual instruction from a senior employee; by formal course work in the operation or at a business or professional school; by structured management games simulating decision-making and problem-solving situations; by observation of work activities (internship); or by a combination of these methods. Every conceivable instructional medium and method is employed, from talking puppets to sophisticated computer systems. Some of the large foodservice operations maintain special schools, often called "colleges," which provide the opportunity for academic instruction and simulated on-the-job training. There are also several widely used programs of correspondence instruction.

CAREER
DEVELOPMENT

Training paves the way for career development. Consideration of career development is vital to successful personnel management and to the foodservice operation itself, for a number of reasons:

• Job candidates with the skills and abilities needed by the foodservice operation may require the prospect of career growth in order to enter the operation's employ.
• As the operation grows larger, it may require an increasing number of supervisors and managers familiar with its systems and procedures.
• The growth of an organization can be attributed at least partially to the growth of the people who are a part of it.

The problem is not that career growth is impossible in the foodservice industry. Judging from the number of corporate executives of major foodservice companies who entered foodservice organizations as non-managerial workers, career growth is certainly possible. The problem is not that today's manager, or graduate of a school of management, will not rise beyond an entry level position. No other industry gives young managers as much responsibility and potential for personal advancement. It is not unusual to find a 21-year-old in charge of 30 people and

EXHIBIT 3.2 How to Instruct

Step I   Prepare the worker

      Put the worker at ease.

      Describe the job.

      Find out what the worker already knows about it.

      Place the worker in the proper work position.

Step II   Present the operation

      Clearly explain and patiently demonstrate one step at a time.

      Emphasize each key point.

      Repeat the operation with the worker telling you how it is done.

Step III   Try out performance

      Have worker do job; correct errors.

      Have worker explain key points of each step as the worker does the job again.

      Make sure the worker understands job procedure.

      Repeat the process until you are sure the worker knows procedure.

Step IV   Follow up

      Leave the worker alone to do the job, telling him where help can be found.

      Check frequently.

      Encourage questions.

      Taper off coaching.

Orderly, methodical instruction assures that the trainer does not leave out a step and reinforces each skill as it is learned, before progressing to the next step. Such instruction lessens the personal stress of the trainee.

a million dollars worth of equipment. The problem is that career growth is not offered as a prospect to those current employees who were hired as nonmanagerial workers.

Many companies do not offer a career ladder progression to someone hired as a utility worker or as a service worker. People with higher career expectations either seek employment in another foodservice operation or move into entirely different occupations. Many of the costs associated with personnel (costs of turnover, indifference, and so on) can be attributed to this problem. The failure of many foodservice operations to recruit minority workers, or even to recruit sufficiently productive workers, stems in part from the image created by this apparent lack of potential for individual growth.

Career development involves several steps:

1. The design of definite programs of career progression.
2. The establishment of identifiable standards for career progression.
3. A publicity effort to inform persons who might benefit from career development and who could, in turn, benefit the organization, that such a program exists.

Exhibit 3.3 offers a model career ladder for a traditional restaurant organization. Other types of foodservice operations can chart career progress on the basis of their own organizational structure. A social catering company, for example, probably would equate the size of a party managed with career progress.

 *Coordinating*   People must work effectively with other people and use the products, machines, and systems of their operation effectively if that operation is to achieve its objectives. Management's contribution to this integration of activities is coordination. This fourth major activity in the management of people ensures that this effective interaction takes place.

In successful coordination, the basic question is how much managerial attention each of the organization's elements requires. Traditional, relatively simple foodservice operations have given priority to the coordination of people's efforts with the other elements of the system. More sophisticated organizations, such as large foodservice contractors, have directed managerial attention to the correction of poor planning, lack of organization, inefficient work-system design, and inefficient use of equipment. In any operation, some attention to the coordination of people's efforts is necessary. How much depends on management's recognition of where its priorities lie.

Once management establishes how much attention must be given to coordinating people's efforts, it must decide upon the way that it will coordinate those efforts. In the foodservice industry, the techniques used to coordinate the efforts of people vary considerably in their applicability to a specific operation and in their basic assumptions. These techniques involve *leadership, direction,* and *supervision.*

LEADERSHIP   In coordinating the efforts of people, leadership basically consists of setting goals, with or without the participation of those for whom the goals are set, and either selling the goals to the workers or inspiring the workers to try to achieve them. *Selling* suggests that individuals can be motivated to see a personal economic benefit in integrating their efforts with those of other individuals and with the other elements of the system. *Inspiring* suggests that people can be made to identify their own objectives (monetary or otherwise) with those of the operation. Leadership is generally used to coordinate the efforts of managers and their

EXHIBIT 3.3   Model Career Ladder for a Traditional Restaurant

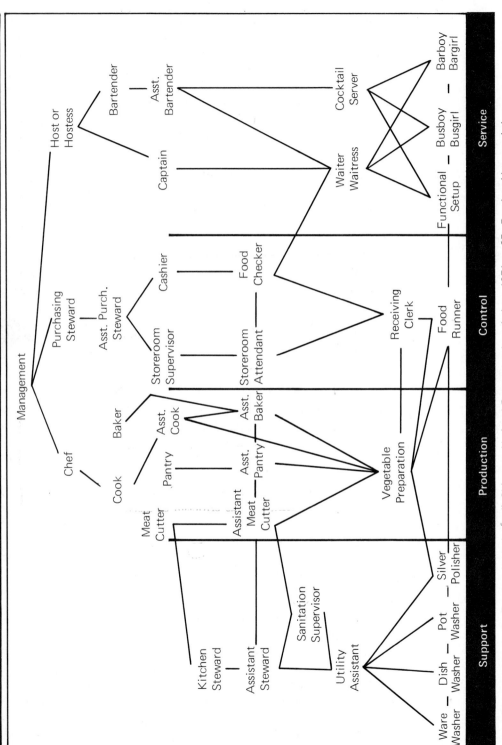

From "Career Ladders in the Foodservice Industry." Chicago: National Restaurant Association. 1971, p. 25. Reprinted by permission.

Functionally Integrated Career Progression Model for a Foodservice Facility

subordinates and the fairly well-educated persons (for example, college students on summer vacation) who may be doing nonmanagerial work. The basic assumption in leadership is that people, or more specifically the persons who are being led, are rational and will either try to maximize rewards or recognize and accept a mutuality of interest with the organization. Such a participative process as group decision making is the kind of coordination of people's efforts that results from the leadership of persons assumed to hold rational and well-thought-out opinions.

DIRECTION   As a technique of coordinating, direction consists of ensuring that people understand what is expected of them, whether or not they agree with the course of action, and then making them accountable for following that course of action. Although there are some similarities between direction and leadership, the differences are significant. Direction grants individuals far less autonomy than leading does. In direction, the primary motivation is the worker's fear of the unpleasantness associated with failure; in leadership, the primary motivation is the worker's anticipation of the pleasant results of success.

Direction is used with the same groups as leading is. The basic assumption in directing is that people, at least the people being directed, are rational and will try to minimize any unpleasant consequences of their actions.

SUPERVISION   Supervision, the third technique in coordinating people's efforts, largely consists of suggesting, requesting, or ordering people to do limited tasks; watching their performance; correcting their efforts; and constantly reinforcing the original suggestion, request, or order. Supervision grants people little autonomy to coordinate their own efforts. Either the promise of reward, such as praise or immediate monetary gain, or the threat of punishment, such as criticism or discharge, makes supervision effective.

Supervision is used primarily with nonmanagerial workers, hence, with most workers in foodservice operations. The basic assumption underlying this technique is that workers, or specifically the workers being supervised, are not goal-oriented or self-directing; that the only way to coordinate their efforts is by the promise of immediate reward or punishment and by constant reinforcement of the relationship between acceptable performance and reward, and unacceptable performance and punishment. The reward sought and punishment feared by people who are supervised are on a much more basic level than the success sought by people who are led and the unpleasantness avoided by people who are directed. It is assumed that supervised workers are simpler in their desires and easier to guide toward these potential satisfactions than workers who are led or directed.

The use of a particular technique of coordination, then, results from management's attitude toward its people. Attitudes can be the result of empirical evidence that a particular technique is necessary, or they can be the result of certain assumptions—which may or may not be true—about people and the way they work. The danger of such assumptions is that they will be applied to the wrong individual or group. The intensity and quality of managerial coordination must be related to the situation, the people involved, and the needs of the other elements of the organization.

Some companies attempt to train managers in the specific techniques of leadership, direction, and supervision. Others attempt to develop the manager's understanding of the nature of the human personality. They try to build sensitivity to the effects of managerial action and the organization on its people. Whether a company is teaching its managers "command and control" or enrolling them in "sensitivity training" sessions necessarily depends on its views of how best to motivate people.

(5) *Motivating*   Any approach to personnel management is based on either an accurate assessment of or definite assumptions about the worker or worker group's attitudes regarding work—the worker or worker group's motivation. Thus, motivating is the fifth activity in the management of people. The object of motivating is to cultivate behavior and attitudes that favor coordination and to remove obstacles to the development of such behavior and attitudes. Instead of accepting current behavior and attitudes as the permanent basis of the relationship between the worker and the organization, management attempts, by motivating the worker, to effect changes for the better.

Much controversy surrounds the question of how management can best improve workers' motivation. The debate concerns fundamentally differing views of human nature and individual needs. The three prevailing views lead to different methods of motivating. The view that people act rationally and that their needs are economic suggests that monetary rewards (or the fear of economic punishment) would motivate workers. The view that people are basically social beings whose needs for affiliation and association dominate their behavior suggests that company baseball teams, newsletters, recognition programs, and the like would motivate employees. The view that people want self-fulfillment suggests that group decision making and participation in the establishment of goals and objectives of the organization would motivate employees.

These views are irreconcilable when carried to extremes, since they suggest conflicting conceptions of the relationship between the organization and its employees. There are, however, a number of general guidelines to motivation that are acceptable from all three viewpoints.

These guidelines, as listed here, could form the basis for effective motivation in a foodservice operation:

1. Behavior and attitudes can be influenced and changed: styles of management and approaches to the coordination of people's efforts—no matter what conception of human nature and needs they correspond to —really respond to circumstances, to the momentarily perceived behavior and attitudes of workers. As behavior and attitudes change, so must management's responses.

2. People have diverse motivations: people differ; individuals are complex; people—whether in groups or individually—react differently to motivation at different times.

3. Motivation is influenced by factors outside the organization: background, education, and other personal factors, as well as current social climate and other environmental factors, limit the activity of motivating within the organization.

4. A person's motivation is influenced by the social setting of work: the interaction of the individual and the worker group must be considered when attempting to motivate either individuals or groups.

5. Management must be trained to motivate effectively: individual managers base their relationships with workers on their own views of human nature that may be partially untrue or simply inapplicable to the situation at hand. Such simplified views on motivation as everybody wants more money; people just want to be treated with respect; two-way communication always motivates effectively; happy people are more productive; all workers should be treated like children; or all workers want a part in decision making; are obviously not always appropriate. Special training in motivating techniques would make managers recognize and correct erroneous assumptions.

Particular approaches to motivation, such as wage incentives or good human relations, are frequently suggested as the single universal motivator. Bearing in mind the above guidelines, a more reasoned approach would be to consider motivating an ongoing activity, with emphasis on three important techniques: morale building, compensation, and protection.

Morale-building efforts provide motivators directed either at satisfying people's personal and social needs or at removing factors that they find personally or socially unpleasant. Compensation efforts are directed toward providing people with satisfactory direct and indirect monetary or economic rewards. Protection efforts are attempts to remove conditions that are physically unpleasant—the removal of which, in turn, will provide conditions conducive to motivation efforts.

The use of, and emphasis given to, each of these activities requires managerial flexibility. Most motivating activities are a combination of all three. However, the choice of method for motivating workers depends on a clear assessment of the specific situation and the individuals or groups involved. At least five different factors must be considered in determining effective motivation techniques including (1) the needs of persons involved; (2) the influence of the group on individuals; (3) the particular objective toward which people are being directed; (4) the cost of a particular motivational approach compared to its potential benefits; and (5) the environmental influences on people's behavior and attitudes that might affect their receptivity to specific motivation techniques.

MORALE BUILDING   As a method of motivating, morale building attempts to cause workers to identify their own objectives more closely with those of the organization, as is done if the coordinating technique of leadership is successful. Morale-building efforts should cause people to cooperate and approach their work with willingness and zeal. A low rate of employee turnover and absenteeism, high quality production with minimal waste, and a general spirit of cooperative effort are signs of successful morale building.

The list of morale-building techniques is diverse. Each technique can be appropriate or inappropriate to particular individuals in a particular situation. Morale-building techniques usually are based on giving workers personal attention, granting them recognition and dignity, or fostering their participation in work planning and management decisions. Exhibit 3.4 offers some examples of each of these approaches to morale building.

COMPENSATION   Monetary and economic benefits from work and the individual's future expectations about these benefits are significant influences on current behavior and attitudes. People take jobs or refuse them, stay with companies or leave, cooperate or withhold effort, all because of the level of satisfaction they derive from their pay or prospects.

Compensation can come in the form of cash wages paid, economic benefits offered, or the prospect of more pay and more benefits.

Cash wages paid   Direct wages paid to an individual and such monetary compensation as shift premiums, weekend and holiday premiums, reporting pay, recompense for travel time (portal-to-portal pay), washup time, bonuses, and, indirectly, the opportunity to earn gratuities are included in cash wages paid.

The actual compensation that a person receives can be determined in different ways. In craft, supervisory, and managerial jobs, negotiation between the employer and the individual is the most common method. Sometimes, compensation for a particular individual is determined objectively by a job analysis. The job is analyzed; each com-

EXHIBIT 3.4   Approaches to Morale Building Used in Foodservice

Approach	Applications
Personal attention	Employee counseling on personal matters
	Flexible work schedules
	First-name relationships with management
	Good induction and orientation procedures
	Positive management attitudes
	Treatment of employees as individuals
	Development of social aspects of job
	Small gifts
Recognition and dignity	Praise in public, criticism in private
	Dignified job titles
	Limited supervision
	Communication about rationale of work
	Requests for, and possible use of, suggestions and ideas
	Grievance procedures for airing complaints
	Protection of sensitivities
Participation	Worker-requested job rotation
	Role in setting objectives
	Consultation in decision making
	Job design

ponent is weighed on the basis of the difficulty, skills, or knowledge involved, and then these factors are translated into monetary terms. Often, nonmanagerial jobs in operations that have contracts with labor unions are rated through such job analyses.

In many foodservice operations, the remuneration for a particular category of work is pegged at the minimum wage. Persons employed in those jobs are traditionally paid the lowest wage federal or state law allows.

It should be obvious even from this brief overview that some of these methods of compensation have motivational value while others do not. The negotiated wage offers at least the prospect of reopening negotiations. On the other hand, compensation at the minimum wage, with little prospect of rising above it, has little motivational value except to those persons who have no alternative prospects for employment.

At times, all these methods of compensation have worked well for foodservice operations. In the past, there have been waves of immigrants eager to take any job and attracted by a wage that was greater than what they could expect in their homelands. Ironically, the minimum wage, although accelerating upward at an unprecedented rate, is now proving to be an inadequate inducement in recruiting people and an inadequate motivator in keeping them.

Economic benefits   Economic benefits, or fringe benefits, can contribute considerably to foodservice compensation plans. Economic benefits might include vacations, paid holidays, medical care, educational allowances, meals at cost or less, lodging, clothing allowances, pensions, and so on. In foodservice operations, such benefits as food and lodging traditionally have compensated for somewhat lower cash wages. For some individuals, these benefits are positive motivators since, by appearing to virtually eliminate personal expenses, they seem to offer an opportunity to accumulate capital.

Fewer and fewer foodservice operations currently can offer such benefits as lodging and free meals. The change to pre-prepared food items has eliminated the by-products ordinarily used for workers' meals, and with today's construction costs, few modern operations can afford to build staff housing.

Prospect of future cash compensation or benefits   The expectation of more pay or benefits, or both, is a powerful motivational device that is used widely. To motivate employees by such expectations, foodservice operations can offer any combination of the following.

1. Cash bonuses related to sales volume.
2. Stock-option plans whereby the worker can acquire shares in the company at a discount from the stock market price.
3. Wage incentives such as premium pay for exceeding quotas or standards.
4. Promotions to higher rank.
5. Additional fringe benefits such as special meal privileges or extra vacation time.
6. Bonus plans that relate the amount of the bonus for the worker group to a reduction in the cost of labor for a given time period.
7. Opportunities for premium pay or overtime pay.

The workers' prospect of further compensation can be based on the premise of immediate reward or long-term returns like individual growth. Cash bonuses and similar devices are used to reward desired behavior in the expectation that the rewarded behavior will be repeated. People, however, do not always respond to reward mechanisms as expected. Other factors intervene: social pressures; the sentiment that the reward is inadequate; resentment at being treated like children; the improper timing of the reward; and the individual's difficulty in clearly identifying what behavior is being rewarded.

The long-term prospect of career growth within the organization has more significance as a motivational device. It combines compensation with morale-building factors. Research done on career ladder development for nonmanagerial workers in foodservice operations clearly points to the need for motivation based on the prospect of career development for these workers. Few researchers believe that an occasional five-dollar bill will significantly alter rates of turnover, absenteeism, productivity, or indifference.

A personal growth model similar to that used by other segments of the economy is needed. People who can see long-term personal benefits as a result of their current behavior and attitudes will shape their behavior and attitudes accordingly. However, the prospect of compensation through long-term personal gain must be genuine and realizable, and must provide intermediate satisfaction if it is to be successful in motivating people.

PROTECTION   Neither morale-building devices nor compensation will be effective motivators if people believe that their well-being has been sacrificed to organizational objectives. Foodservice organizations should design a work environment that will at least be perceived by workers as unthreatening. At best, pleasant working conditions can encourage productive behavior and attitudes. (See Exhibit 3.5 for a list of environmental factors in motivation.) The Occupational Safety and Health Act (OSHA) and similar legislation require that the work place comply with certain minimum standards of protection for workers. In addition to risking punitive fines, an operation's failure to meet these health and safety standards would necessarily have a substantial negative effect on the motivation of employees.

Beyond simple compliance with OSHA, there is a vast area of opportunity to motivate workers through the design of the work environment. Without violating the law, many foodservice operations make physical demands on workers that these people find unreasonable. Supply workers may object to hauling, and service workers may object to sidework. People avoid entering the foodservice industry, or quickly leave particular operations, because of the reputation of the industry in this matter, or because of their personal experiences. Large chain operations, food contractors, or the foodservice operations of institutions and other noncommercial organizations seldom have this problem. These organizations usually create a satisfactory, if not motivating, work environment in the belief that it will increase worker productivity. On the other hand, many small companies seem as indifferent to human productivity as it relates to temperature, humidity, air flow, and work-system design as they are to the comfort of the worker as a factor in behavior and attitudes.

EXHIBIT 3.5 Environmental Factors in Motivation

Factor	Satisfying Condition	Motivating Condition
Temperature	18–21°C (65–70°F) winter 21–23°C (70–73°F) summer	Well-designed air conditioning
Humidity	40–60% relative humidity	Well-designed air conditioning
Ventilation	Ventilation that meets local codes (standards vary from jurisdiction to jurisdiction)	Well-designed air conditioning
Noise	Up to 50 decibels	Well-designed program of background music; quiet, well-maintained equipment
Lighting	15–20 foot candles for general work spaces; 30–40 foot candles for hands-on work; 50+ foot candles for paper and detailed work	Glare-free lighting; appropriately colored work environment
Uniforms	Clothing that meets sanitary codes; protective clothing for extreme temperature conditions	Attractive clothing; frequent changes of clothing; provision for replacement of personal clothing damaged on the job
Employee Facilities	Facilities that meet health standards	Air conditioned, comfortable facilities; excellent shower and bathing; area for lounging and resting
Safety	Conditions that meet safety standards	Full provision of personal safety equipment such as protective glasses and steel mesh gloves, if useful; thorough training in safety procedures; input in safety programs
Equipment	Individual-use and large equipment economically justified by production demands	Equipment designed to reduce cost in human discomfort, even if it does not directly increase productivity; excellent floors or floor matting; wheeled conveyances; work boots for wet areas; work stations adjusted to height and reach of individual worker; "customized" equipment such as mop handles adjusted to worker height

As a motivating activity, protecting has a second dimension: job security. Motivational efforts of any kind lose effectiveness in a work situation that includes frequent layoffs; unpredictable changes of shift and insensitive scheduling of work hours; irregular days off; call-ins for no work (even if compensated); unusual split shifts; surprise demands for overtime work; radically varying take-home pay because of poor staffing of workers who rely on tips for wages; and other conditions that increase workers' anxiety about their livelihood. While these practices are symptoms of an organization's ill health, they must also be recognized as causing a substantial lowering of worker motivation and loyalty. Of course, it is necessary to address the fundamental problem— faulty work-system design and organization—and not just try to correct the symptoms.

6 Evaluating   Evaluating employees at their jobs is an essential part of personnel management. A program that evaluates personnel may have several of the following goals:

• To take stock of the skills and abilities that the people already employed are contributing to the organization (also part of "Personnel Planning").
• To identify personnel problems—difficulties with particular people or situations, or organizational deficiencies—so that they can be remedied.
• To offer the worker a formal opportunity for comment on the organization and its personnel management.
• To control the personnel management processes: are efforts at increasing productivity, improving morale, and reducing turnover effective?
• To appraise the performance of the individual workers with the intent of developing or promoting them, correcting or disciplining them, or assisting them to perform their jobs better.

To successfully direct such a program of evaluation, management seeks information on the work of individuals in five areas: (1) technical skills: crafts, competencies in nonmanagement work, and managerial abilities; (2) personal skills: the ability to work well with others, ability to arrive on schedule, and ability to organize personal efforts and work habits; (3) quantitative results of work activity: number of units produced, dollar sales volume and associated costs, and quality of work expressed as a percentage of predetermined standards; (4) character traits such as loyalty and friendliness; (5) overall performance: general accomplishments, success in attaining objectives.

Different methods of evaluating result from the nature of the information being sought and from the need to introduce objectivity into the evaluation activity. Among the common methods of evaluation are ratings, interviews, and assessments.

RATINGS   Ratings forms are prepared to correspond to the technical skills, personal skills, or character traits being evaluated. Generally, these forms require that the person rating an individual quantify rather than comment, perhaps by grading the worker on a scale of 1 to 5. Sometimes the person doing the rating is obliged to check one of several statements that offer different qualitative comments such as "lacking in fundamental knowledge of this area" or "needs retraining." The essential problem with rating processes is an absence of easily communicated standards. What really constitutes merely adequate (grade 3) or outstanding (grade 5) proficiency in a manual skill? What really constitutes "acceptable" or "deficient" friendliness in a person? Often, subjective factors, notably the quality of the personal relationship between the rater and the person being rated, influence the rating results.

INTERVIEWS   Interviews are a more sophisticated, but also more costly, evaluation process than ratings. A skilled interviewer who has reviewed the worker's background, experience, test scores, performance reviews by supervisors, and perhaps job performance, discusses the job with the worker. Since the interviewer is usually a staff personnel officer, not a direct supervisor of the worker, the ratings or comments that result from the interview tend to be objective. For the same reason, and perhaps also because of the lack of specific technical knowledge on the part of the interviewer, such ratings and comments tend to be less informed as well.

Interviewing may serve a variety of purposes besides rating the worker. The interviewer's mission may be to limit and correct apparent failures in the worker's performance. It may be to allow the person being interviewed to communicate a worker's perspective to someone who can then relate individual experiences to the context of the organization. It may be to assist workers in developing themselves, meeting the challenges of the job, or finding personal counseling. In practice, the particular approach to interviewing suitable to an operation depends on what the operation expects to get from the interview.

ASSESSMENT   Assessing actual worker performance is potentially the most exact way of evaluating. Its success depends upon the validity of the standards used and on the integrity of the assessment procedure. Assessment may be based on direct observation by a group of managers who carefully prepare reports, in narrative form, on the worker's performance. Performance can be assessed over a period of time, or critical incidents and work samples can be examined as indicators of performance.

Assessment can also be a basically quantitative process. Instead of being addressed to the abilities and personality of the worker, assessment may serve to evaluate the results of the worker's efforts. These results can then be compared to a standard determined beforehand by management or by management and the worker in consultation. Or, the results can be compared to the performance of other individuals in the same work units, or to standards set up for individuals the operation is likely to recruit.

MAKING PERSONNEL MANAGEMENT EFFECTIVE

Successful personnel management depends on management's effectiveness in personnel planning, staffing, facilitating personnel development, coordinating, motivating, and evaluating. Each of these six activities is made successful by the effective execution of its composite techniques: for example, successful staffing depends on effective recruitment, selection, and induction. It is still possible, however, to improve personnel management as a total system. This can be done through organization development and the use of certain forms and devices. Organization development is concerned with improving the effectiveness of the management system. The use of forms and devices is directed toward increasing the efficiency and reducing the cost of personnel management.

Organization Development

In foodservice operations, as in all organizations, it is desirable for management to take a careful look at its own organization and its ability to meet objectives now and in the future. Management then attempts to create internal conditions that favor the attainment of those objectives by changing its organization for the better. When this process is formalized and directed at the management of people, it is known as organization development.

The organization development effort is, quite clearly, concerned with developing more effective relationships between groups of people, between managerial and nonmanagerial workers, and between units of the operation as a whole. The expectation is that a program of self-renewal will lead to greater effectiveness for the operation. Management will grow stronger in direction and purpose and will make better decisions about itself, its methods of managing people, and how these methods affect its use of technology, equipment, and other resources.

An organization development program has four phases: analysis, diagnosis, planning, and implementing. In analysis, the forces that influence intergroup and interpersonal behavior and the relationships between units of the foodservice operation are identified and described. This analysis is followed by a diagnosis which determines the factors affecting these forces. Using the information from the diagnosis, the next phase involves planning strategies for change, and finally, in the last phase, implementing these strategies. Frequently, the organization development program involves the use of external or internal consultants, often called *change agents* or organization development *practitioners.* Briefly, their role is to ensure that the appropriate analytic and diagnostic techniques are used in the first two phases of the program. In the last phases, these consultants help management develop and implement strategies for change and also help counteract the opposition that the prospect of change creates in almost any operation.

Even in this short summary, the value of organization development is apparent. While the applicability of some organization development techniques to foodservice operations today is questionable, the underlying premise of organization development has great relevance: management is increasingly capable of taking the necessary action to change conditions within its own organization in order to achieve its objectives.

Use of Forms   Some of the processes in the management of people permit a high degree
and Devices   of routinization. Rather than deal repeatedly with the same procedures and information, managers use forms and devices to make these routines efficient. Exhibit 3.6 identifies the major forms and devices used in personnel management. It also suggests some uses of these instruments and describes their data base (the information they provide or solicit).

EXHIBIT 3.6 Forms and Devices Used in Personnel Management

Name	Use	Data Base
Personnel Planning		
Job Analysis *or* Survey Form *or* Job Description	Records observations or comments on tasks involved in a particular job.	Data base varies with survey method used. Generally includes task descriptions, organizational information, personal skills and experience required.
Job Specification	Communicates what a job requires; used by operations' managers to communicate with personnel department.	Formalizes those aspects of job description that relate to attributes of the person: skills, knowledge, character traits, reliability, experience, abilities needed for interpersonal relations.
Employment Requisition	Communicates need for person(s) to personnel department from operations manager.	Includes job description and job specifications plus immediate relevant information: department, salary, job title, shift time, reason for need (termination, addition, replacement), number of people needed, authorization.
Employee Record	Maintains background and current information on employee for use in evaluation, termination, promotion, counseling.	Name, employment date, job status, birth date, sex, social security number, marital status, name of spouse, number of children, federal withholding tax information, addresses and telephone numbers, education, promotion record, skills, training record, disciplinary record, and all other personnel information.
Staffing		
Employment Application	Summarizes job-related personal, educational, and occupational information of applicant for evaluation.	Name, social security number, address, years at address, previous address, job applied for, rate of pay expected, source of information about job, prior employment by company, availability for work, skills, transportation information, conviction record, medical history, educational background, military record, prior work history, personal references.

EXHIBIT 3.6   Forms and Devices Used In Personnel Management (cont.)

Name	Use	Data Base
Patterned Interview Form	Provides the interviewer with specially designed questions and responses indicative of person operations manager has specified.	Tailored to particular job category.
Interview Rating Form	Summarizes results of interview and test scores, when used.	Can require narrative summary of interview, comments, and actions taken. Often provides basis for job-candidate quantification. Traits, skills, and so on are given grades.
Reference Check Forms	Guides checking of reference by telephone and records data; or, surveys references by mail.	Queries concerning job-related skills, information submitted on application form, character traits.
Medical Report *or* Physical Report	Used to provide information to insurance and medical plans and perhaps as a criterion for hiring when physical abilities are job-related.	Results of examination by physician, medical history, results of laboratory tests.
Payroll Authorization	Inducts individual formally into the organization; sent to accounting and payroll departments as communications device from personnel department.	Name, address, tax information, department, wage/salary, employee number, and similar business-related information. Also, overtime pay status.
Wage Statement	Used to inform employee of business details of job.	Same as Payroll Authorization data.
Labor Relations Forms	Used to inform operation's labor organization of new hiring.	See Payroll Authorization data. Also, indicates whether employee is managerial worker or not.

Facilitating the Development of People

Personnel Survey	Provides, through personnel department or operations manager, "match" of current employee with better job; identifies promotion potential, training potential.	Abstracted data from employee record: performance evaluation, aptitudes, skills, and so on.
Training Plan	Organizes training program of individual.	Varies with instructional method, largely resembles lesson plan: objectives, methods, procedures, time frame.

Name	Use	Data Base
Coordinating		
Departmental Roster	Provides unit head with information on employees in unit.	Name, address, telephone number, job, employee number, and personal information as required.
Departmental Record Card	Provides background information, usually in summary form on file card.	See Employee Record above.
Absence Report	Communicates absences of employee to personnel department, other management, accounting, and perhaps to union.	Name, date, department, employee number, absence noted/noted by.
Absence Record	Allows assessment of employee absences.	Summarizes dates of absences on continuing basis.
Tardy Report	Communicates lateness of employee to personnel department, other management, accounting for pay adjustment, perhaps to union.	Name, date, department, employee number, amount of time tardy, noted by.
Wage or Position Change *or* Change of Status Report	Keeps personnel department, other management, and accounting current on employee status.	Payroll Authorization data plus prior status indicated and new status indicated with reasons for change.
Turnover Analysis	Assesses the rate of turnover in operation.	Date, number of employees, number of new employees, and percentage new to old.
Overtime Analysis	Assesses and explains use of workers at overtime rate.	Name, job rate, overtime rate, amount, date, reason authorized.
Disciplinary Notices	Informs employee, union, management of disciplinary actions taken.	Name, date of infraction, explanation of infraction, prior actions taken, nature of this action: warning, suspension, probation, or termination.
Termination Notice *or* Removal from Payroll	Informs accounting, union, personnel department, and other management of employee termination.	Payroll Authorization information plus date of termination, date effective, and reason.

EXHIBIT 3.6 Forms and Devices Used In Personnel Management (cont.)

Name	Use	Data Base
Contract	Records agreement on performance objectives between employee and supervisor.	Specific to agreement; generally includes statement of objectives, time frame, and signatures.

Motivating

Name	Use	Data Base
Vacation Forms *or* Notices *or* Requests	Notifies personnel department, other management, or accounting of employee vacation.	Name, employee number, department, work history information relevant to vacations, last day on job and first day back.
Enrollment Form for Profit Sharing Plan *or* Pension, Scanlon, *or* Medical Plan.	Informs employee of status; communicates to personnel department, accounting, trustees of plans, etc., that employee is eligible.	Payroll Authorization data plus information relevant to benefit.
Accident Reports	Informs government and others in operation of accidents.	Forms supplied by government and/or insurance company. Reports accident, person involved, date, cause, actions taken.
Merit-increase Recommendation	Conveys recommendation for raise from operational manager to other management or personnel department.	Payroll Authorization data plus prior rate, recommended rate, and justification.
Wage-incentive Report	Informs accounting from operational manager of wage premium earned.	Payroll Authorization data, amount earned, justification.

Evaluating

Name	Use	Data Base
Rating Forms	Grades employee performance, abilities, character traits, and work attitudes.	Data base designed on company objectives, usually as a numerical rating. Sometimes structures narrative comments.
Separation Interview	Records employee's reasons for leaving.	Payroll Authorization data, date of separation, reasons for separation (common reasons usually pre-printed), comments about organization by employee.
Separation Analysis	Rates according to objectives for effective management of people.	Summarizes separation interviews for given period.

Chapter 4
The Marketing
System:
Part I

A foodservice operation converts foodstuffs or raw materials into prepared food items. By processing foodstuffs into finished products, the foodservice operation adds value, or worth, to the raw materials. The foodservice operation that is not compensated for both the cost of the raw materials and the value added to them through selection and processing soon cannot function. Commercial operations go out of business; noncommercial operations are shut down or are reorganized. Thus, the ability to produce a product—even a quality product—is not enough to ensure business success.

To gain adequate compensation, the foodservice operation must match its product with a market—a sufficiently large group of consumers who are willing to buy or use the product. It is the marketing system that fits the product of the foodservice operation to the needs and desires of consumers. In order to match products with markets, the marketing system adds further value to the product. The marketing system determines and designs a product that meets market demand; it makes consumers aware of the product. The marketing system makes the product available at times and places convenient to consumers, and makes possible the transfer of ownership of the product from the foodservice operation to the consumer. This transfer of ownership is utimately responsible for the inward flow of income needed to sustain commercial (and some noncommercial) foodservice operations.

In this view of marketing as the link between product, market, and revenue, the term "product" has a broadened definition. A foodservice operation's products are more than just its food. They also include service, decor, table appointments, credit policies and the operation's prestige as well as any other characteristics designed to produce consumer satisfaction. An example may help to make this definition clear. An engaged couple dining at an expensive continental restaurant are buying more than just the food served. The pair is also purchasing an esthetic experience, a romantic interlude, a secluded table, service from deferential waiters in formal attire, status associated with the restaurant's reputation, the opportunity to mention at a later date that they have eaten at the restaurant, plus the ability to charge the whole experience on a credit card.

How well an operation's total product satisfies consumer expectations is the key to marketing success. In commercial operations, the marketing system is judged effective if product sales in the long run exceed costs, and is judged outstanding if the operation makes the maximum profit possible under its operating conditions. In noncommercial operations, the marketing system is effective if clients are satisfied.

In both commercial and noncommercial operations, the marketing efforts of the operation consist of four parts: market research, menu planning, service, and promotion. These components interlock to gather information about the market, to develop products and make them available, to increase the power of the product to satisfy the needs and wants of consumers, and to sell and deliver the product to the consumer.

Market research provides a flow of information about the market area that is used in marketing decision making and planning. Market research identifies customer or guest demands for the commercial operation and client needs for the noncommercial operation.

Menu planning creates, develops, and prices the primary product of the foodservice operation—its food items. Menu selection is based on the consumer preferences identified by market research.

Service does two things. First, it provides the distribution channel by which the product reaches the consumer from its place of production— be it a miles-away centralized food assembly line preparing prepackaged food for vending machines or a close-at-hand kitchen, a few steps from the dining room, preparing elaborate French cuisine. Second, service creates the derivative product of the foodservice operation—all that accompanies the food offered. The derivative product thus includes service style, atmosphere, serviceware, decor, lighting, and so on. It is derived from both the menu—the primary product—and consumer preferences identified by market research.

Promotion informs consumers about the product in order to stimulate demand and emphasize the product's value. Finally, promotion is responsible for selling the product.

These four parts make up the marketing system. This chapter will cover market research, while the next chapter will treat promotion. Menu planning and service, though subsystems of marketing, are so complex that they have been designated as systems in their own right. The menu-planning system is discussed fully in Chapter 6, while the service system is treated in detail in Chapter 11.

CURRENT PRACTICES IN MARKETING

Different foodservice operations stress different parts of the marketing system. A vending company may emphasize the distribution aspect of service. A limited-menu hamburger chain in a very competitive environment may devote more attention to promotion. An independent restaurant may emphasize development of unique products—both food and atmosphere. A noncommercial operation serving the continuing client may emphasize market research in order to plan more effective ways to satisfy client needs.

From a historical perspective, the American foodservice industry first went through a phase of intensive emphasis on menu planning—the era of the great chefs and the 400-item menu. This phase was followed by a period that emphasized service to the needs of the growing market of urban workers: a time when cafeterias and coffee shops were continuously opening in urban centers. When the availability of advertising media, especially radio and television, increased, the foodservice industry switched to an emphasis on promotion, or selling, as a primary marketing activity.

At the present time, there are indications that the industry's marketing approach is becoming more balanced. Industry leaders in sales volume may be opening a new restaurant every day, but they are also spending unprecedented sums on advertising, conducting market research in order to plan operations with almost assured market acceptance, streamlining their service activities, and working continuously on developing better primary and derivative products. Smaller enterprises, at least the ones that have shown rapid growth, also exhibit patterns of integrated market activity.

On the other hand, some operations and even whole segments of the industry still seem to place disproportionately heavy stress on particular marketing activities. One area, in particular, seems to be ignored, especially by smaller firms: market research that leads to planning and development of a capacity to adapt to future changes. Because of the expense, few small enterprises have carefully profiled their potential consumers and fully assessed the economic and competitive environment in which they expect to operate. A fairly high rate of business failures of restaurants in the first year of operation and a relatively low rate of return on investment (as compared to other types of enterprises) seem symptomatic of this negligence. When a restaurant fails "for lack of working capital" (as the obituary usually reads), there has been a substantial error in judging how quickly the operation would be accepted by the market. Likewise, the passing of a once-successful restaurant seems to betoken ignorance of the changing needs of its market at a time when the restaurant had the economic resources to plan effective adaptations.

While market research is frequently ignored, the promotion activity of advertising seems to be overemphasized by many foodservice operations. Advertising is seen as a total marketing program when in fact it is only a part. Some new restaurants use advertising to stimulate a "crank-up boom" which, far from giving them a good start, deals them a blow from which they may not recover. Such advertising may attract a great number of customers with varying expectations that cannot possibly be satisfied by a single restaurant operation. For many of these customers, the food and service products offered are unsatisfactory. They do not return. The operation must then reassess its marketing approach, if it still has the economic resources to mount another program.

Some restaurant operators spending 3 or 4 percent of sales revenues on advertising would be hard-pressed to demonstrate the relationship of their advertising expenditures to their present success. There is a tendency to not want to upset the magic formula that seems to have worked in the past. Some of them learn too late that last year's magic has lost its effect.

MARKETING CONCEPTS

As foodservice operations recognize that marketing is increasingly vital to success, they are adopting a marketing-oriented approach to doing business. A marketing-oriented approach views the foodservice firm as a set of interrelated activities organized to generate outputs that satisfy consumer needs and return a reasonable profit to the producer.

This marketing orientation—which must permeate the entire organization—is based on the belief that (1) the direction of a company's planning, policies, and operation is determined by the market; (2) profitability is achieved by satisfying the needs and wants of the market; and, (3) coordination of all the company's activities is necessary to meet this goal of serving the market profitably.

Thus, the transition to a marketing orientation results in an even greater emphasis on systems. The integration and coordination of marketing activities, which, in turn, are meshed with the organization's overall goals, benefits from a systems "state of mind" on the part of managers. To make wise decisions, the marketing manager must consider the whole, not just the part. Will an increase in the price of coffee—though justified—change the consumer's perception of the prices of all the other items on the menu, thus causing a loss of sales? Will adding a dessert menu decrease customer turnover so that sales of higher-priced items are sacrificed? Will an unexpectedly large response to a price-off coupon find the supply system understocked on that item and force the purchasing system to obtain supplies at a higher-than-usual cost?

The marketing program is a series of decisions in these and other areas. The effectiveness of these decisions determines the effectiveness of the marketing program. A systems approach stresses not only the need for coordination of all the tools for marketing, but it also provides an orderly, fact-based framework for dealing with marketing problems under conditions of change and uncertainty.

Marketing managers responsible for the optimum performance of the system are concerned with setting marketing objectives, interrelating the marketing system with the other systems of the organization, and dealing with the limits imposed on the system from other sources. The next sections of this chapter will discuss each of these topics.

Specific Objectives of the Marketing System

Specific objectives of the marketing system must be consistent with the operation's general goals. Marketing systems of foodservice organizations may vary somewhat in their objectives, but most of them focus on one or more of the following:

1. *To satisfy customers, guests, or clients*   The primary aim of the marketing system is to provide patrons with the food and service they want.

2. *To analyze, influence, and increase consumer demand*   Marketing activities in successful foodservice organizations seek to determine consumer needs and desires, develop products to meet these needs and desires, and to develop and maintain a demand for these products.

3. *To identify and exploit opportunities*   Most foodservice companies face the inevitable choice of improving their operations or gradually fading from the market. The marketing system is the regenerative system of the foodservice organization. It identifies new opportunities for customer, guest, and client satisfaction (for example, there are no good restaurants in this part of town, or the employees of that industrial park have no place to eat lunch). The marketing system—through market research—provides early warning of impending change in the operation's market and outlines plans to meet such change.

4. *To gain competitive advantage*   To deal with a foodservice organization's competitive environment, the marketing system establishes a series of specific strategies. The marketing system may be geared to a strategy of differentiation, consolidation, expansion, or consumer awareness.

• An operation may seek to establish a *difference* between itself and its competitors in the minds of consumers. Limited-menu restaurants on main thoroughfares frequently set this as a strategy for their marketing systems.

• An operation may want to *consolidate* or solidify its relationship with existing patrons to develop a regular clientele. Traditional, family-oriented restaurants frequently follow this strategy.

• An operation may seek to *expand*—to gain a larger market share by increasing the number of people attracted to the operation. Restaurants whose fixed costs are rising frequently espouse this strategy.

EXHIBIT 4.1   Marketing Successes and Failures as Related to Objectives

Objectives	Successes	Failures
To satisfy customers, guests, and clients	University and college foodservice operations introducing limited-menu restaurants, health food menus, salad bars, and so on, to replace cafeteria stereotypes.	General unresponsiveness by some commercial restaurants to consumer demands for nutritional information, truth-in-menu, and so on.
	Military foodservice operations introducing flexible meal plans, alternative dining facilities, and so on.	Limited abilities of health care facilities to do more than sustain clients.
	Widespread use of salad bars in commercial restaurants.	Lack of variety and value in products offered by most recreational foodservice operations.
To analyze, influence, and increase consumer demand	Success of hamburger chains in displacing the frankfurter as the number-one small-meal snack item.	Inability of school lunch programs to persuade students to eat nutritionally balanced meals.
	Dramatic increase in restaurant wine sales.	Inability of traditional restaurants to manipulate menu mix (number of high-profit items such as stews sold in comparison to low-profit items such as cuts of beef).
To identify and exploit opportunities	Success of a number of small chains in developing theme restaurants catering to needs of the newly significant, 20–40 year old, middle class, college-educated, white-collar market.	Lack of interest by commercial restaurant operators in the opportunities offered by the growing population of older and retired persons.

• An operation may seek to make potential patrons *aware* of its existence. Newly opened restaurants often follow this marketing strategy.

Exhibit 4.1 suggests that there have been efforts by individual operations to achieve at least some of these objectives. This exhibit also offers examples that seem to indicate either an ignorance of the contribution of marketing or an inability to achieve these marketing objectives.

Interaction of the Marketing System with Other Systems   The marketing system interacts substantially with the other systems of the foodservice organization. It sets strategies for gaining consumer satisfaction that must be supported by all the other systems. It assists in charting future courses of action to keep the foodservice company in tune with its markets and thus sets changes in motion that ripple through-

Objectives	Successess	Failures
	Success of limited-menu restaurants in offering some ethnic cuisines; Italian and Mexican food, for example.	Lack of interest by commercial restaurants in opportunities offered by culinary minorities: dieters, people on therapeutic diets, people following religious dietary regimens.
	Increased use of central commissary systems by all types of restaurants.	Inability of traditional restaurants to develop satisfactory alternatives to labor-intensive processes such as table service (except for salad bars).
To gain competitive advantage	Ability of some restaurant enterprises to carve out a significant market share wherever they open units.	Failure of many independent restaurants to establish competitive differences, develop regular clientele, or grow in market importance.
	Expansion of limited-menu restaurants to include other meal opportunities.	Failure of many restaurant operations to plan for large-scale entry of major limited-menu chains into smaller markets.
	Controlled and successful expansion of a number of restaurant chains.	Failure of business reorganization of a number of chains that overexpanded.

out the other systems. It provides data for decisions made by managers of the other systems through the information-gathering tool of market research. As the revenue-producing arm of commercial and some non-commercial operations, it supports the other systems financially.

Exhibit 4.2 shows how marketing plans are coordinated in the overall functioning of an organization geared to meeting consumer needs. It is apparent from this exhibit that the marketing system is the company's chief link with its consumers. In contrast to behind-the-scenes systems such as production and purchasing, the marketing system as planner of menu items, distributor and seller of products, and communicator and gatherer of information is the most public system of a foodservice firm and thus "represents" it in the eyes of the consumer.

EXHIBIT 4.2   Integrated Functioning of Marketing Within the Organization

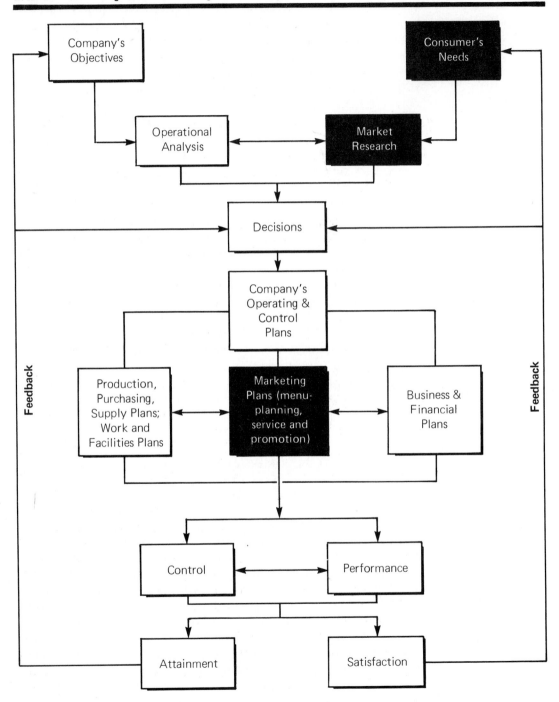

MANAGEMENT AND MARKETING

In small owner/operator foodservice operations, general management and marketing are inseparable. No distinct marketing department exists. The owner/operator performs and supervises the essential marketing functions. The owner/operator, through day-to-day familiarity with the organization, makes changes to meet consumer needs. If enough customers request a certain menu item—and costs and quality are acceptable—the item is placed on the menu. If the decor—part of the derivative product—is becoming shabby and affecting the image of the restaurant, the owner/operator, perhaps with the aid of a freelance interior designer, plans a refurbishment of the operation. If luncheon trade is declining, the owner/operator may design several luncheon "specials" to attract customers from the surrounding office buildings, write and prepare a simple printed handbill, and hire temporary help to distribute these handbills to potential patrons as they are entering their work places in the morning.

In noncommercial operations—a foodservice facility in a hospital, for example—the director or chief dietitian may perform some marketing functions and delegate others. For example, market research (an examination of patient records) may reveal a need for patient meals with certain ethnic or religious considerations taken into account. A dietary aide from the foodservice department may interview patients to record their reactions—good and bad—to hospital meals. A dietitian educator in the foodservice department may "promote" classes in nutrition education for expectant mothers or in behavior modification of eating habits for diabetics. All of these activities exhibit a marketing outlook even though no formal marketing structure exists.

In large companies—chains in particular—marketing departments, under the management of a vice-president or executive of equal stature, exist and grow. The marketing executives participate in high-level management planning and policy making, and direct a department that has responsibility for the full range of marketing activities and the authority to see that they are carried out.

Whatever the structure of the foodservice marketing system—formal or diffuse—management skills are necessary to its successful functioning. The management process, as applied to marketing, includes setting objectives, planning a marketing program, selecting people who will perform marketing tasks efficiently, organizing the efforts of these people, and directing the actual operation of the marketing program. The marketing system is a partner to the management system in directing the foodservice operation toward its goals.

The marketing system must support the decisions of the management system and in particular must function in accordance with the competitive stance, financial targets, industry position, and change orientation decided upon and actively pursued by management.

Competitive stance   A foodservice firm's position in regard to its competition has direct implications for the marketing system. Top-level managers may take an entrepreneurial posture, thus viewing the marketing department as the means by which sales volume and profits are increased. Aggressive advertising, a policy of expansion, and emphasis on product development are signs of this approach. Top-level managers may take an administrative stance, thus viewing the marketing system as the means by which the efficiency of present efforts is increased. In this view, marketing is used to fine-tune and consolidate an operation.

Financial targets   A foodservice organization's profit goal is of great importance to the marketing system. It affects the volume of business that is sought and the costs that are allowed.

Industry position   A foodservice company defines its place in the industry in terms of size, major function (multi-unit hamburger chain, contract feeder, independent restaurant, and so on), and quality and price levels. This definition determines the scope and size of the marketing system. A marketing department with a $10-million-a-year advertising budget, a separate market research group, and a formal management committee for new product development varies greatly from a marketing department of a gourmet restaurant chain, serving the highest quality products and catering to a select group of patrons.

Change orientation   A conservative foodservice firm may adapt reluctantly to changing conditions while marketing-oriented foodservice organizations expect change to occur and are able to make rapid shifts in marketing procedures and policies, in specific and overall objectives, and in marketing strategies to meet these changes.

WORK AND
MARKETING
The work system designs the operation's physical facilities and plans and coordinates the flow of physical tasks required to move raw materials from purchasing through supply and production to the consumer.

The marketing system influences the work system because marketing strategies affect decisions about the number and kind of foodservice outlets, space allocations for production facilities, and the capital investment in equipment. In addition, the existing work system of a foodservice operation may limit marketing activities. New products with high acceptance by the operation's patrons cannot be marketed unless they can be produced efficiently. This fact is widely ignored by thousands of operations that expand their product lines for marketing reasons without considering that their work systems are incapable of efficiently producing the added item—be it a Chinese, Mexican, char-broiled, barbecued, delicatessen, or health food.

PURCHASING AND
MARKETING
The marketing system contributes to efficient purchasing by identifying consumer preferences for certain food products. Decisions about buying mild or salty cured ham, different brands of bourbon, choosing prepared

baked goods or selecting flour for baking should be based on an assessment of consumer preference. Purchasing contributes to marketing effectiveness by obtaining raw materials that expand the arena for menu planning and by cost-effective buying that provides the operation with the most latitude possible in making pricing decisions.

SUPPLY AND MARKETING

An accurate forecast of demand for specific items and an accurate forecasting of volume—both of which are based on information provided by the marketing system—increase the efficiency of the supply system. Unduly large inventories of products incurring inventory and storage costs need not be maintained if usage can be projected accurately.

PRODUCTION AND MARKETING

An effective marketing system can fine-tune production to meet consumer preferences. Different versions of the same food item can be of equal quality but still vary in flavor, texture, presentation, appearance, or portion size. Only market information allows the kitchen staff to decide how much red pepper sauce belongs in the beef stew; whether frankfurters take sauerkrant or chili garnish; or whether doughnuts should be light or chewy.

The marketing system can also provide information that allows economical production to be scheduled. Accurate and complete market data can be the basis of judgments about the quantity and selection of items to be prepared and of the number of employees to be scheduled.

BUSINESS AND MARKETING

The foundation of all business and financial decisions about the creation and maintenance of a foodservice enterprise is an assessment of the viability of the enterprise in its business environment. The marketing system provides initial information that assures management that the business is feasible. The marketing system then provides information for decisions about pricing, capital investment, and financing.

Marketing comes under the influence of business-system decisions that allocate resources. In successful foodservice operations, the marketing and business systems are mutually supportive: effective marketing provides sufficient revenues to allow more extensive—and perhaps more effective—marketing. In less successful operations, increased marketing efforts might be too costly at the current level of sales. This dilemma frequently confronts operations that have not properly assessed the cost of market acceptance or the time required to reach desirable levels of sales. The problem is resolved either by rare good fortune or by a painful financial restructuring.

CONTROL AND MARKETING

The control system evaluates the performance of the foodservice organization—including the marketing system—and provides feedback to management so that it may effect necessary changes needed to keep the firm on track. An important tool for the control of the marketing system is the marketing audit—a systematic and critical appraisal of the marketing system—its objectives, policies, organization, procedures, and personnel.

Accordingly, a marketing audit should examine these aspects of the marketing system:

Objectives   Are objectives being met? If the management of a chain of family restaurants wishes to become the undisputed market leader in this category, are indications of meeting this objective found in an analysis of sales volume as compared to competitors? Are objectives clearly stated? "To increase sales volume" is a general statement. Should this same family restaurant chain restate this objective in more specific terms, such as "to broaden our market base and thus increase sales volume by creating menu items and promotions that appeal to children"?

Policies   Are marketing policies consistent with objectives? If this same family restaurant chain mentioned above wishes to appeal to senior citizens, does it have a policy of offering them a discount? If service personnel are expected to make point-of-sale suggestions in order to increase check averages, is training in this technique a matter of company policy?

Organization   Is the marketing system capable of achieving its objectives? Would advertising campaigns be more effective if carried on by an outside agency? Is the marketing system limited unnecessarily by another system in the organization?

Procedures   Are the procedures involved in implementing a step-by-step marketing program logical and effective? Has adequate market research preceded a decision by a Southern-based company to expand to Northern cities? Should a print advertising campaign be conducted simultaneously with a radio advertising campaign to increase the effectiveness of both? Are particular marketing strategies effective? Is a restaurant redesign planned to create a more "homey" atmosphere effectively resulting in increased customer satisfaction and in increased customer return rates?

Personnel   Is successful attainment of marketing objectives used as the criterion for evaluating marketing personnel?

Limits on the Marketing System

The marketing system must achieve its objectives within the current limitations on market activities. Constraints can be imposed by economic conditions, market dimensions, competition, or the public environment.

ECONOMIC CONDITIONS

Economic conditions can affect demand to the extent of preventing profitable market ventures. Marketing efforts aimed at increasing demand can be severely hampered by high unemployment, low or declining disposable income, and the threat of layoffs.

MARKET DIMENSIONS

Market size always imposes a limitation on the marketing activities of foodservice operations; most foodservice operations have a definite geographical market area. Few consumers outside this market area can be expected to frequent the operation.

Another market dimension also has to be acknowledged, although it is not as readily defined as market size: the socio-economic dimension of the market. Most *existing* foodservice operations have already established themselves as appealing to groups of consumers who, in addition to geographic location, can be characterized on the basis of occupation, income level, educational background, family status, and so on. Effective marketing outside this group is possible, but difficult, and may be dangerous to the operation's financial health.

The difficulty stems from the increased resistance of other groups to the marketing effort. The danger comes from the possibility of alienating the existing market. For instance, a fine steak house decides to add a number of low-priced entrees in order to attract young married couples in the neighborhood. But these people associate the restaurant with the stodgy "establishment" types who they suppose frequent it, and they resist the operation's marketing efforts. Present patronage declines since customers or guests feel uncomfortable with the new image the operation is presenting. A family restaurant trying to upgrade its market would have the same problem. Obviously, new restaurant operations should elect to appeal to whatever group of consumers seems to offer the most potential.

COMPETITIVE LIMITS   The effect of competition on marketing activities varies considerably. Competition can be an advantage when competitive promotional activities stimulate a general demand for the products the operations offer. The first two Mexican limited-menu, take-out/take-in restaurants (each started by different companies) in a New England city will probably prosper more quickly because of their combined advertising efforts. However, competition becomes a problem when the operation cannot establish any difference in the minds of consumers between its products and those of similar operations. It is extremely difficult for another limited-menu, take-out/take-in restaurant to offer hamburgers in an area where a major hamburger chain has already been established. Even the giant limited-menu restaurant chains avoid this kind of confrontation. A leading hamburger chain has yet to introduce fried chicken; a leading fried-chicken chain has made only tentative efforts to introduce hamburgers. A second leading hamburger chain has backed off from the costly battle and is investigating totally new products instead.

PUBLIC ENVIRONMENT   Public sentiment or the public environment in which the foodservice operation functions can also limit marketing activities. Federal legislation, for example, prohibits monopolization of markets, unfair competition, and deceptive advertising. State and local regulations regarding advertising, trade practices, billboards, and truth-in-menu can also restrict marketing activities.

Both state and federal agencies regulate franchising. Securing a franchise through payment of fees to public officials for concessions in parks, vending outlets, and food concessions in public buildings may violate local statutes, federal law, and the Security and Exchange Commission's regulations for publicly traded companies.

The community's standards of good taste and fair play, although not necessarily codified, can also limit marketing activities. The use of nudity in advertising, the aggressive sale of alcoholic beverages, or competitive activities that are seen as predatory can invite social condemnation that tends to offset whatever financial benefit is gained.

MARKET RESEARCH PLANNING

Market research is the systematic assembly and analysis of facts relevant to any marketing or marketing-related problem. Because it provides information from which decisions about creating and running a foodservice operation are made, market research is a key tool in high-level management and marketing decision making. Well-founded decisions require accurate information from well-planned market research.

The quality of an operation's market research thus has a critical impact on the success of the operation. Those foodservice operations that have achieved outstanding success without a planned program of market research were either established during a period of less rigorous competition and consumer demands or are blessed with management capable of amazing feats of intuitive judgment. Neither of these bases for operating can, in the absence of market research, promise success in the future. Today, except for foodservice operations created as playthings by millionaires or founded by people befuddled by dreams of riches and the taste of their own apple pie, market research planning must precede the actual planning of the operation or even the decision to plan. Any other course of action is based on speculation.

Even in already-established operations, problems arise because of lack of well-planned market research. We see the evidence in the business failures of even well-financed and well-promoted restaurants; in menus that have become a collage of assorted enticements as the operators scramble to find out what consumers really want; and in the continued offering of food items that consumers no longer want—for example, the obligatory boiled potato with fish.

It might be argued reasonably that the cost of professional market research is beyond the means of many independent restaurant owners. Two answers might be suggested. If operators cannot afford market research, they really cannot afford to gamble by opening or operating a restaurant that may cost three or four thousand dollars a seat. In addition, much market research can be done by the operators themselves, using either primary research techniques or secondary sources.

The types of market research will be discussed later in this chapter; here we will examine the planning process as it relates to market research investigations. Though no two market research tasks are ever exactly alike, the planning steps of (1) defining the problem, (2) securing internal data, (3) finding secondary data, (4) collecting primary data, and (5) interpreting research findings can generally be applied to most market research projects.

Defining the Problem   The first step in any market research project is definition of the problem. The problem may be identified by someone within the marketing department or by someone from another area of the organization. For example, the management of a major doughnut chain wished to expand its product line to attract lunch business but did not want to introduce a product that would change its image. The market research problem was to find out what particular product would be compatible with the doughnut chain's primary image. Or, at the suggestion of an energy conservation consultant, the management of another foodservice firm wished to stop automatically serving water to each patron as a conservation practice. The market research problem was to find out consumer reaction to such a possible policy and assess its impact on sales volume. The marketing students of an Arizona university defined the problem for their student union's foodservice facility. A class project to survey campus eating habits and food preferences led to a change from cafeteria style to a fast-service operation featuring Mexican food and to a complete redesign of the interior—both decor and equipment.

Here are some typical problems that might be identified for market research investigation.

- Why is the image of the operation confused in the consumer's mind?
- Do any new opportunities exist for customer, guest, or client satisfaction?
- Why has the operation not been attracting the consumers who constitute its major market?
- Why is the competition gaining an increasing market share?
- Why do present promotional activities have no effect on demand?
- Is the operation's present market shrinking in size?
- Is there a market for present products at higher prices?

Since resources seldom permit an operation to research all problems at once, priorities must be established. Those problems that immediately menace the operation's survival are necessarily researched first; those opportunities that offer the greatest return on investment or effort are dealt with second; and so on.

Securing Internal Data

After the problem has been clearly defined, a market researcher explores the data available inside the company. An examination of company records may provide some insight into the problem. Sales records, financial data, check averages, inventory records, proportion of business done at breakfast, lunch, and dinner, and so on, may be explored. Previous market research investigations conducted by the company may contain useful facts. The researcher also can interview others in the company who may provide information or opinions of value. For example, useful information about the effect of future price increases may be gained by examining the volume-price relationships of past periods. Insights into consumer attitudes might be gained by talking with service personnel.

Finding Secondary Data

The next step in the market research procedure is to assemble and analyze secondary data, or previously published information. The use of secondary data has two advantages: it is (1) easier to obtain and (2) less expensive to secure than primary data (information gathered directly from the people who make up the market). If a market research problem must be solved quickly, secondary data is used almost exclusively. If costs are a factor, secondary data may be relied on for reasons of economics.

These advantages are offset by two disadvantages: (1) the information in secondary sources may be obsolete or (2) it may be difficult to apply to the problem at hand. For example, Bureau of Census population data are collected every ten years, and toward the end of the ten-year period, the demographics of a particular area may have changed drastically. Even if up-to-date and well-documented, city-wide demographic surveys may be difficult to apply to a traditional family restaurant opening in a single neighborhood of that city. Or, as another example, let us say that a trade association in the liquor industry researches and publishes consumer liquor preferences. What specific implications (if any) does the increased consumption of light bourbon whiskey on the part of a particular market segment have for the menu of a foodservice operation?

Despite these reservations, foodservice operators find that secondary research can be quite useful and that secondary sources for market research are numerous.

Data from the federal *Bureau of the Census* provide useful information on population, business, and housing. The *Census of Population* provides a count of all the residents of the United States by state, county, city, and metropolitan area, and, in major cities, by census tract and by city block or blocks. Age, sex, race, citizenship, educational level, occupation, employment status, income, and family status are also gathered. The *Census of Housing* reports housing information such as type of house, number of rooms, year constructed, and race of occupants. The *Census of Business* is organized by county and by large city. It presents data regarding retail and wholesale trade and includes information on foodservice operations. Such facts as the number of particular types of operations, employment figures, total sales, and legal form and organization are presented. The multi-volume federal census reports may be found in large libraries.

The Department of Commerce also produces digests of federal government statistics such as the *Statistical Abstract of the United States* and the *Survey of Current Business.* These publications are available at minimal cost.

State and local government sources provide reports of planning commissions, zoning boards, highway departments, and other agencies that must justify public projects in terms of the population they will serve. In some cases, parts of these reports may be of use to the foodservice market researcher.

Commercial publications offer information on general economic characteristics of particular market areas. For example, *Sales Management* magazine publishes its "Survey of Buying Power" each year. It lists population, income, effective buying power, and retail sales for cities with populations over 10,000. Annotated bibliographies (summaries of sources of information) are also published six times a year in *The Marketing Information Guide.*

Surveys from advertising media, such as newspapers, magazines, and radio and television stations, give information about the market served by each kind of medium. A newspaper, for example, is eager to demonstrate to potential advertisers such as restaurant operators that the number of people who read the advertisements in that newspaper and are thus attracted to their establishments is significant.

Foodservice suppliers often collect marketing information about their products to use as a sales tool and will share this information with foodservice operations who are prospective buyers.

Restaurant associations and other foodservice industry trade associations frequently commission primary research. For example, the National Restaurant Association has published market research studies such as "Consumer Attitudes and Behavior in the Foodservice Marketplace," "Selected Impressions of Full Service/Tablecloth Restaurants," and so on, as part of an ongoing program of market research. The NRA—along with a group of large foodservice companies—also participates in the CREST or *Chain Restaurant Eating-Out Share Trends* survey. The survey tracks expenditures and behavior in the commercial segment of the foodservice industry. In this study, about 10,000 families who reflect the U.S. Census record their restaurant experiences in a two-week period for each of the four quarters of the year. The results provide statistical information on customer behavior. Summaries of these reports are available to NRA members.

Private firms, such as the A.C. Nielsen Company, conduct market research, publish their findings, and make them available on a subscription basis. For example, a Nielsen report on "Nutrition: Consumer Beliefs and Practices" might coitain useful information for an investigator confronted with a research problem concerning menu planning.

Professional journals directed toward college and university, health care, school, and military foodservice operations often publish market research data.

Collecting Primary Data

When the secondary data is not complete enough or if more data are required, the foodservice market researcher must collect primary data. Three methods of gathering primary data are used: observation, survey, and experiment.

Observation is simply watching people in action. This research method requires a trained, detail-conscious observer. Observation may be used to check the traffic count at a potential location for a restaurant. It may be used to determine the area from which customers are attracted. For example, an investigator may list the numbers on the license plates in the parking lot, and the addresses of owners may be traced through license bureaus. A group of observers may investigate the service and courtesy of restaurant personnel by "acting" as customers.

Survey methods seek information by mailed questionnaires, by telephone, and by personal interview. Data are gathered from a limited but representative number of people (a sample). In contrast to observation methods which record *what* happened, survey methods can explore opinions and motivation.

The mailed questionnaire allows the researcher to collect information at a reasonable cost. Deficiencies of the mailed questionnaire include the slowness of the process, the lack of an easy way—outside of a follow-up study—to probe the more interesting responses, and the tendency of many people to discard mail questionnaires rather than answer them. Mail questionnaires, however, guarantee that every person in the sample is asked the same questions in the same way.

Telephone surveys are used when a quick response is needed. Telephone surveys are more flexible than mailed questionnaires, since follow-up questions may be asked. Questions must be asked, though, that invite short responses since respondents may not wish to be kept on the phone for more than a few minutes. Bias may creep into the sample since many people may refuse to respond, may not be at home when the interviewer phones, or may have unlisted telephone numbers.

The personal interview is the most time-consuming and expensive of the survey methods but can provide the highest quality of information. The interviewer can modify questions to clear up any confusion in the mind of the respondent or to obtain more complete answers. However, bias can be introduced into the personal interview method through inadequate training of interviewers or outright interviewer cheating as when interviewers answer the questions themselves or fail to interview the designated respondents. A panel is a type of personal interview in which a representative group of people agree to provide information on a repeated basis.

Some restaurant market researchers have had great success stopping customers who have just come out of their restaurant and interviewing these consumers with a quick, five-to-ten question survey. The meal experience is still fresh in the respondents' minds, and often respondents offer interesting impromptu observations on the restaurant that are not solicited in the survey questions.

The experimental method is the least used, slowest, and most expensive of the survey methods. The experimental method is most often used by large foodservice companies that are test-marketing new products. For example, a budget steak house chain may have made a preliminary decision to introduce a seafood salad at lunch in order to expand business at that time of day. Certain company stores in representative areas are chosen to offer the seafood salad on a test basis. If customer reaction is favorable, the product is adopted throughout the chain. In this method, a small group of stores represents the entire chain, and the results in these stores allow the marketing manager to predict—on the basis of actual sales—the acceptance of the new product.

Interpreting Research Findings   Whatever research method or combination of methods is chosen, the results must be tabulated, interpreted, and presented. The ease with which data can be tabulated and interpreted depends a great deal on the design of the questionnaire. It will be far easier to report the results of this question: "Do you think the service in this restaurant is excellent, good, adequate, or poor?" than it is to report the results of this question: "What do you think about the service in this restaurant?"

Once the data is tabulated, it can be analyzed. Conclusions can be drawn and recommendations made. This report of data and conclusions should be presented in a written document to be used as a basis for final decision making.

MARKET RESEARCH ACTIVITIES

Market research is the first of the four marketing activities. Because the aim of market research is to furnish as many facts as possible upon which to base decisions, it must precede menu planning, service, and promotion. Market research is the essential beginning step in a successful marketing program.

Market research itself is made up of four research activities that seek information in four different areas. These research activities are *market analysis, consumer analysis, product analysis,* and *sales analysis.*

Market analysis examines the size, location, characteristics, and general nature of markets. In commercial operations, this type of analysis aims to identify market areas with population, economic, and other kinds of characteristics that indicate the potential for high levels of profitability. In noncommercial operations, market analysis is less complex. For example, in a grade school, pediatric hospital, or prison, the market is to an extent predetermined.

Consumer analysis investigates the characteristics of consumers, including attitudes, motivations, and reactions. This kind of analysis attempts to pinpoint specific groups of consumers within the defined market area.

Product analysis focuses on identifying products that can satisfy both consumer wants and needs and business criteria.

Sales analysis examines the potential profitability of the operation in its particular market.

Market Analysis   Market analysis provides information about the area a foodservice operation serves or intends to serve. If conducted by an existing foodservice operation, market analysis attempts to describe—often quantitatively—the resources of the operation's market in order to provide information to improve the operation and to meet changing market conditions. If conducted as part of the planning for a new foodservice operation, market analysis attempts to describe the characteristics of the market area to see what kind of opportunities are available or to see if the market population and resources meet the criteria established by the potential foodservice operator. The prospective foodservice operator may be willing to open any type of restaurant that has a profit potential, or the market may be researched to determine if a significant number of people meet the operation's criteria for ideal patrons. The first approach is used by entrepreneurs who are willing to modify their preconceptions to meet market realities. The second approach is commonly used by foodservice chains entering new markets.

Market analysis seeks data relating to population (income, education, occupation, age, sex, eating-out expenditures, race, ethnic background, number of persons in family, and other factors); competition (direct and indirect—for example, a pizza restaurant competes not only with other pizza restaurants but also with all other foodservice operations that are within its price and quality range in the same area); economic factors (employment and unemployment, wage rates, and so on, as well as economic potential—whether, for example a certain area is in the process of rejuvenation, is declining, or is maintaining the status quo); location of facilities that may generate business (present and future office developments, convention centers, industrial parks, medical facilities, shopping centers, and so on); and, for operations in the planning stages, legal information relevant to market limitations (zoning ordinances, building codes, liquor laws, and so on).

Information for market analysis can be gained from many sources: Bureau of Census population reports, local bankers, the area chamber of commerce, regional and local planning commissions, and field offices of the U.S. Department of Commerce. The yellow pages of the phone directory will provide a list of competing eating and drinking establishments. Auto tours of the area can be made at different times of the day to determine traffic flow, and, in the process, personal observation can be made of housing (value and age), numbers of children, industrial areas, and so on.

In the planning stages, market analysis will give a clear, but general, picture of the area in which a foodservice operation wishes to do business. It allows identification of the most probably profitable areas and rejection of unsuitable markets. For ongoing operations, market analysis points out strengths that can be exploited and weaknesses that must be countered through the marketing program.

Market analysis gives an overall picture of the market area. In order to satisfy consumer wants and needs, more precise information about the consumer is needed.

Consumer Analysis

Consumer analysis zeroes in on information regarding consumers in a distinct market area while market analysis compiles demographic information. Consumer analysis attempts to profile particular consumers on the basis of attitudes, preferences, buying behavior, motivations, and so on.

Frequently, market researchers for foodservice operations classify people into groups on both demographic and behavioral bases. Such groups, really subparts of a market, are called *market segments*. The assumption is that these groups have characteristics in common so that what they want or need in a foodservice operation can be deduced. Thus, the successful retail foodservice operation does not usually market its product to everyone. Rather, it offers a product tailored to a specific group of consumers or market segment. For the foodservice industry, market segments frequently identified with specific, unique wants and needs are family travelers, teenagers, gourmets, college students, office workers, female shoppers, businesspersons, singles, young marrieds, and so on.

As an example, business travelers are a market segment in a broader group that is based on occupation. If business travelers are part of the operation's present or potential market, then it could be assumed that if they behave in a way consistent with their role as business travelers, they will have certain needs and wants that can be satisfied in specific ways.

The exact nature of these needs and wants and the methods of satisfying them can be determined by primary research methods or by comparison with data presented in secondary sources. An operation could, for example, make use of the National Restaurant Association's published results of a total of 1,048 personal interviews with business travelers in ten major U.S. cities. Exhibit 4.3 presents part of the questionnaire used in this survey when it was conducted in Chicago. According to this survey, the business traveler most often chooses to eat evening meals when away from home in atmosphere/specialty restaurants (moderate to very expensive restaurants with full bar service and moderate to elaborate decor and service). The NRA-sponsored survey also included a life-style questionnaire, part of which is shown in Exhibit 4.4. On the basis of this inquiry into psychological traits, the market research company conducting this survey offered comments on the motivation of the business traveler:

> The strong preference for atmosphere restaurants lends support to the notion that he (the business traveler) is self-indulgent and willing to treat himself to a special dining experience when he is away from home. He may actually see it as a small reward for working hard and for being away from home in the first place.*

An effort was also made in this survey to integrate objective characteristics such as age with the motivational and behavioral factors. The survey results characterize the business traveler as a college graduate (73.1 percent of the respondents) between the ages of twenty-five and fifty-four (84.7 percent), and so on.

In ongoing operations, consumer analysis can be conducted through a survey of customers or guests. Exhibit 4.5 suggests some items of information that might be sought. If designed, administered, and evaluated properly, the consumer profile will provide significant information about the operation's most frequent patrons and eliminate speculation or guesswork about the nature of the operation's customers. Consumer profiles may be conducted for each location within a chain and also for lunch, dinner, and, if necessary, breakfast.

Product Analysis   The market research activities of market analysis and consumer analysis identify the characteristics of a significant group of people that can be served by the foodservice operation. However, such analysis cannot identify the particular products—both primary and derivative—that will satisfy the needs and wants of these particular consumers. It remains for product analysis to provide the information about consumer preferences and responses to specific food products and the settings in which they are

---

* Edward J. Mayo, *The Restaurant Habits of the Business Traveler*, National Restaurant Association Consumer Attitude Survey Series (Chicago: National Restaurant Association, June 1976) p. 27.

EXHIBIT 4.3 Portion of NRA Questionnaire on Business Travelers

Respondent Name: _____   Date: _____

Hotel Name: _____   Interviewer's Initials: _____

City: _____   Code #: _____

I. Trip Characteristics

1. What is the purpose of your trip to this city? a. Primary business _____   b. Business and pleasure _____

2. How much time will you have spent in this city during this trip? _____ Days _____ Nights

3. How much time will you have spent away from home during this trip? _____ Days _____ Nights

4. How did you arrive in this city?   a. Air _____   c. Train _____
                                         b. Auto _____   d. Bus _____

5. Do you have access to a car while you are in Chicago on this trip? _____ Yes _____ No

6. Approximately how far away from home are you? _____ Miles

7. How many people are in your travel party? _____ (Number)

8. Approximately how many overnight trips have you made to this city during the past twelve months? _____ (Number)

9. Approximately what percentage of your work time do you spend on out-of-town, overnight business trips? _____ (Percent)

II. Eating Habits

1a. What type of eating establishment did you have dinner in last night?

     a. Atmosphere/Speciality (moderate to very _____   e. Take-out (no seating, inexpensive to _____
        expensive restaurant; expensive food,   moderately priced)
        decor, service; cocktail service)
                                                                 f. Did not eat at a restaurant _____
     b. Cafeteria (self-service, moderately priced) _____
                                                                 g. Did not eat this meal today (please _____
     c. Coffee Shop _____   think, then, about your noon meal
                                                                    today and then answer this question
     d. Family type (e.g., family steak restaurant, _____   and all subsequent questions with
        pizza house)   reference to the noon meal)

1b. What is the name of this restaurant? _____

1c. Did this restaurant have mainly an ethnic menu? _____ Yes _____ No

1d. *(If YES)*, was it?   a. French _____   d. Mexican _____
                            b. German _____   e. Greek _____
                            c. Italian _____   f. Oriental _____
                                      g. Other _____

1e. Had you ever eaten at this particular establishment before? _____ Yes: Approximately how many times? _____
                                                                _____ No

2. Do you normally prefer to eat this meal in the same type of establishment when you're away from home?
      a. Yes _____   b. No _____   c. Like Variety _____

3. With how many other persons did you have this meal? _____ (Number)

4a. Did you pay for your own meal?   _____ Yes _____ No

4b. Did you pay for anyone else's meal? _____ Yes _____ No

From The Restaurant Habits of the Business Traveler, prepared by Edward J. Mayo for National Restaurant Association Consumer Attitude Survey Series. National Restaurant Association, Chicago: June 1976. Reprinted by permission.

EXHIBIT 4.4 Portion of NRA Questionnaire to Business Travelers

National Restaurant Association
1976 Travel Study

Name _____   Code _____

City _____

Directions: Listed below are a number of statements, some of which deal with eating out and restaurants and some of which deal with general life-style factors. For each statement listed, we would like to know whether you personally agree or disagree with the statement.

After each statement, there are five numbers from one to five. The higher the number, the more you tend to disagree with the statement. The lower the number, the more you tend to agree with the statement. The numbers 1–5 can be described as follows:

1. I strongly agree with the statement.
2. I generally agree with the statement.
3. I neither agree nor disagree.
4. I generally disagree with the statement.
5. I strongly disagree with the statement.

For each statement, please circle the number that best describes your feelings about that statement.

(After you complete the questionnaire, please place this form into the attached stamped, self-addressed envelope and mail.)

Statement	Strongly Agree				Strongly Disagree
1 I prefer to order a la carte rather than order a dinner.	1	2	3	4	5
2 I prefer a service charge be automatically added to my bill rather than having to tip.	1	2	3	4	5
3 I like to try new and different menu items.	1	2	3	4	5
4 I prefer a self-service salad bar to being served a salad at the table.	1	2	3	4	5
5 I usually tip a fixed percentage of the bill regardless of the service I get.	1	2	3	4	5
6 Atmosphere is just as important as the quality of the food in selecting a restaurant.	1	2	3	4	5
7 I love to eat.	1	2	3	4	5
8 I usually look for the lowest possible prices when I shop.	1	2	3	4	5
9 Information I get about a product from a friend is usually better than what I get from advertising.	1	2	3	4	5
10 I have annual physical check-ups.	1	2	3	4	5
11 If a new restaurant opened in town, I would probably be among the first to try it out.	1	2	3	4	5
12 My days tend to follow a definite routine, such as eating meals at a regular time, etc.	1	2	3	4	5
13 I exercise regularly.	1	2	3	4	5
14 I enjoy most of my business trips.	1	2	3	4	5
15 Sometimes I like to do things on the "spur of the moment."	1	2	3	4	5
16 I would like to take a trip around the world.	1	2	3	4	5
17 Most people are in too much of a rush.	1	2	3	4	5
18 I like fast-food restaurants.	1	2	3	4	5
19 When I must choose between the two, I usually dress for fashion, not for comfort.	1	2	3	4	5
20 I often wish for the good old days.	1	2	3	4	5
21 I like to be considered a leader.	1	2	3	4	5
22 A party wouldn't be a party without liquor.	1	2	3	4	5
23 I would rather spend a quiet evening at home than go to a party.	1	2	3	4	5
24 I like to pay cash for everything I buy.	1	2	3	4	5
25 I love the fresh air and out-of-doors.	1	2	3	4	5
26 I follow at least one sport very closely.	1	2	3	4	5
27 I enjoy a cocktail before dinner.	1	2	3	4	5
28 I often check prices, even for small items.	1	2	3	4	5
29 I eat more than I should.	1	2	3	4	5
30 No matter how fast our income goes up, we never seem to have enough.	1	2	3	4	5
31 I often seek out the advice of my friends regarding which brands to buy.	1	2	3	4	5
32 I like to try new and different things.	1	2	3	4	5
33 I feel uneasy when things aren't neat and organized.	1	2	3	4	5
34 I just can't relax when eating out.	1	2	3	4	5
35 I prefer to use a credit card rather than cash when eating out.	1	2	3	4	5
36 Business takes me away from home more often than I'd like.	1	2	3	4	5
37 I am an impulsive individual.	1	2	3	4	5
38 I'd like to spend a year in some foreign country.	1	2	3	4	5

From The Restaurant Habits of the Business Traveler, prepared by Edward J. Mayo for National Restaurant Association Consumer Attitudes Survey Series, National Restaurant Association, Chicago: June 1976. Reprinted with permission.

EXHIBIT 4.5 Items for a Consumer Profile Survey

About Consumers

Age of income earners in household

Sex of income earners in household

Number of persons in the family

Occupation of working members of household

Total family income

Place of residence of family

About Consumers' Visit to Your Operation

Type of trip: individual, husband and wife, family

Origin of the trip (home, work, shopping, and so on)

Reason for coming to the foodservice operation

Amount of time needed to travel to the operation

Frequency of visits to the operation

About Consumers' Eating Out Habits in General

Amount usually spent on eating out

Different requirements desired in restaurant serving breakfast; serving lunch; serving dinner

Restaurant usually patronized by entire family, by husband and wife, or by individual (how decided on)

Expression of likes and dislikes for existing restaurants

served. This information is needed to develop a menu (discussed in Chapter 6) and to create an atmosphere and service system (discussed in Chapter 11) that will appeal to the target market segment.

In practice, foodservice operators frequently omit product analysis under two conditions. In the first case, they model their product on the products of another successful operation that is currently satisfying the same target market segment. One attraction of the franchise foodservice operation to the franchisee is certainly the proven formula for satisfying the needs and wants of a defined market segment. There is a certain logic in suggesting that if a market segment is big enough in population, there is room for another similar operation. But problems occur with this approach when the size of the segment has not been assessed well or when it has been identified poorly. Problems also arise when mistakes are duplicated; when the business basics of the two operations are not the same; when novelty and innovation were major reasons for success in the first operation; and when the derivative product—the atmosphere, for example, cannot be duplicated. However, this method can work, and when it does, product analysis as a formal research activity is not absolutely required. In the second case, product analysis is less important when a restaurant develops "organically," as when the operator comes from the market segment to which the restaurant will appeal and has tastes similar to those of the market segment.

In most operations, however, the real opportunity does not lie in copying the competition or in playing personal hunches. If so, then critical information about consumer likes and dislikes in regard to the operation's product or proposed product must be gathered. Thus, the objective of product analysis is to provide information about consumer preferences that will be used to determine the foodservice operation's concept—the definition of itself that it wishes to convey to its target market. The concept of a foodservice operation is made concrete through its primary product—food items—and its derivative product—serviceware, decor, atmosphere, lighting, and so on. Exhibit 4.6 shows a restaurant concept— somewhat exaggerated for effect—built around a wide market segment seeking both privacy and adventure. Product analysis is used to determine if this concept or some variation of it is acceptable to the target market.

Product analysis is concerned with both the food preferences and the environmental considerations that together make up the consumer's meal experience.

FOOD PREFERENCES   Despite many inexpensive means of finding out what consumers want, there is considerable evidence that in the absence of product analysis, foodservice operations are wrongly second-guessing consumers' likes and dislikes. Exhibit 4.7 offers some results from a British survey of restaurant operators and their customers. The restaurant operators were asked to forecast preferences of their patrons—revealing the assumptions on which they based their menus. A comparison of these forecasts with actual consumer preferences shows some significant disparities. American restaurateurs fare no better. A comparison of consumer preference polls with menu censuses describing what is actually offered in American restaurants reveals significant problems.

Product analysis often is conducted prior to the opening of a foodservice operation. Usually, a professional marketing research firm is engaged to interview a carefully selected sample of the market segment to elicit information on menu items. Questions used in the interview must be subtle enough to evoke genuine responses indicative of future behavior. Other research techniques used include focus group interviews, psychodrama in which the respondents simulate buying behavior, and panel testing which uses trained tasters to evaluate food items. For example, college and university foodservice operations often screen new menu items through student taste testers.

EXHIBIT 4.6   A Foodservice Concept Statement: The Tree House

Market Segment: The Tree House has broad market appeal. Its unique construction and concept make it the restaurant to see. The appeal of its mood makes it the restaurant to return to again and again.

Construction: Basic structural elements are also the decor. Stripped, stained, and varnished tree trunks linked with hidden steel beams support the three basic levels constructed of rough-hewn planking. Niches and hollows are created by building up from each of the levels, using cross-cut tree trunks as platforms and dark, stained wood paneling as dividers. Railings on "bridges" and stairs are varnished saplings bolted together.

Decoration: Vertical interior supports give the impression of a vast tree above, thus establishing the dominant decor. Naturalness is emphasized. Visible fittings and lighting are of black iron. Black iron bottle-glass lanterns seemingly "tacked" to the walls emphasize the authenticity of the concept.

Market Perceptions/Impressions: Alone with somebody special, in a special place. Safe. Protected. A rough-hewn niche for two. The conventional restaurant has few tables where people can be alone with each other. In the Tree House, every table is a private table, a retreat, a shelter. This is a restaurant that people love to love. Visit after visit reveals new dimensions. Unique perspectives are provided by the massive branches and small hollows that turn the Tree House into a natural sculpture of flowing lines and subtle coloration. The atmosphere seems to summon a deep primordial recollection of the glowing fires and grilling meats that once comforted our ancestors.

Serviceware: Dishes of rough wood slabs with brown earthenware inserts. Glassware of heavy bottle-glass. Mugs of brown earthenware. Wood-handled forks and spoons; modified hunting-knife steak knives.

Accessorization: Tabletops equipped with wood or earthenware salt and pepper shakers, and ashtrays. Heavy earthenware serving vessels, seemingly handcrafted; some designed to fit into wooden holders. No tablecloths but guests given giant napkins of homespun-type cloth.

Uniforms: Woolen knit jerkins in assorted earth colors cinched by broad leather belts; with dark green trousers.

Food: Mulled cider, ale, mead; Hunter's stew; Roast rack of lamb; Forest green salad.

In ongoing operations, product analysis of food preferences is conducted by talking with customers to determine what their likes and dislikes are through comment cards, through tabulation of guest checks to maintain a popularity index of menu items offered, and through actual trial testing of new menu items.

For comparison purposes, a considerable amount of secondary research is available on consumer preferences in food products. For example, the

EXHIBIT 4.7   Foodservice Operator Market Assumptions in the Absence of Market Research

First Course Choice		Second Course Choice		Vegetable Choice	
(Percent)					
Soups		Meat		Potatoes	
(a) customers	46	(a) customers	42	(a) customers	78
(b) caterers	71	(b) caterers	60	(b) caterers	63
Melon		Poultry		Peas	
(a) customers	17	(a) customers	26	(a) customers	29
(b) caterers	4	(b) caterers	10	(b) caterers	50
Fruit juice		Mixed grill		Brussels sprouts	
(a) customers	14	(a) customers	21	(a) customers	26
(b) caterers	3	(b) caterers	12	(b) caterers	19
Hors d'oeuvres		Fish		Cabbage	
(a) customers	13	(a) customers	4	(a) customers	5
(b) caterers	4	(b) caterers	1	(b) caterers	12
Shellfish		Shellfish		Cauliflower	
(a) customers	5	(a) customers	3	(a) customers	15
(b) caterers	2	(b) caterers	1	(b) caterers	10
Pâté				Green beans	
(a) customers	4			(a) customers	15
(b) caterers	2			(b) caterers	7
				Carrots	
				(a) customers	8
				(b) caterers	5
				Asparagus	
				(a) customers	11
				(b) caterers	3
				Broccoli	
				(a) customers	6
				(b) caterers	2
(a) What customers want					
(b) What caterers believe customers want					

(From "The British Eating Out." A Report from Britain's National Catering Inquiry. Sponsored by Smethursts Foods Limited.)

federal government has conducted numerous preference surveys of military personnel. A foodservice operation whose consumer profile parallels the profile of the young soldiers surveyed—one that serves construction workers on the project site or athletes at a training camp, for example —might find this material useful. Commercial foodservice operations have more limited opportunities to use secondary market research. In addition to some surveys prepared by trade associations, trade magazines have published the results of professional polls. Unfortunately, these results are categorized on the broadest of demographic and sociological criteria—age, occupation, and region of the country—and it is easy to draw too many conclusions from the results.

ENVIRONMENTAL
PREFERENCES

Just as the market dictates the food items that the operation may successfully offer, so too it also dictates the environment or setting in which it is served. An English pub can no more be imposed on a market segment than the people in that segment can be force-fed steak-and-kidney pie. In designing a restaurant to create a particular environment, preferences of consumers must be sought regarding the following items:

Name
Furnishings: style and spacing
Serviceware
Wall covering and color
Lighting: type, level, and color
Background music: selections and loudness
Staff: uniforms, age, social class, sex
Food accessorization
Menu design and language
Staff manners and quality of service
Table linens (or the decision not to use them)
Portion size (especially of drinks)
Floor coverings and color
Interior signs
Artwork and decorative elements
Reservations policy
Entertainment
Temperature and humidity control
Space utilization (open or divided into small areas)

It is somewhat easier to manipulate these items to satisfy the expectations and desires of a market segment than it is to translate consumer characteristics into food items. Often, people have already revealed the things they prefer. Certainly, a market segment that buys jazz records, small foreign cars, corduroy and tweed sport jackets, the *New Republic* magazine, and Danish modern furniture has suggested the restaurant atmosphere that it will find pleasing: a French bistro, or perhaps an interior garden.

It should also be noted that when a foodservice operation elects to astonish a market segment with novelties and spectacular effects—antique automobiles hung from the ceiling or interior waterfalls—the life cycle of the product is shortened. Thus, especially in operations with innovative environments, product analysis must be conducted repeatedly to see if the concept is still appealing to the market segment or if its impact is waning.

Product analysis of environment preferences is not always necessary when foodservice operations elect to provide a dining atmosphere that is essentially neutral. They do this because they expect to attract customers from market segments with radically divergent tastes, and also because market research suggests that a neutral decor has little impact on the consumer's repeated patronage. Few people can even remember the color of the tableware of their favorite restaurant.

Sales Analysis   Up to this point, market analysis has examined the general market area, consumer analysis has profiled the people of the particular market segment, and product analysis has identified the menu items, atmosphere, service, and price levels that will satisfy the market. It is now necessary through sales analysis to determine if the operation can achieve a sufficient sales volume to satisfy its business objectives. Is the foodservice operation—well-defined though it may be from the consumer's perspective—feasible when the operation's potential sales are related to construction costs, operating costs, and return-on-investment objectives? If investment objectives cannot be achieved, it may be necessary to abandon the project, or target another market segment. The financial factors involved in a decision to abandon or alter a product are treated in Chapter 12, "The Business System." Suffice it to say here that the operation usually expects to break even at a realistic sales volume.

Sales analysis is concerned with using research techniques to estimate how frequently the people in the market segment will patronize the foodservice operation. Thus, it is possible to project the total number of people who will patronize the establishment in any particular accounting period. By relating this information to data on how much consumers are willing to spend for the product, a sales volume figure can be projected.

It is also possible to use information from another market area as the basis for the sales forecast. Large foodservice companies frequently use this method. They rely on their experience with the same product offered to a parallel market segment. Thus, historical data and current data can be examined in order to offer several different forecasts: an optimistic forecast, a normal forecast, and a "worst-case" forecast. A very conservative company may undertake a project only when the worst-case forecast predicts a good return.

Sales forecasts can also be pegged to general economic forecasts (of business activity or discretionary income) if these factors have been shown to be accurate indicators in prior applications.

Without historical data, as in the case of a proposed operation, the sales forecast is on much weaker ground. Generally, in targeting the market segment, some criteria have been applied that relate to the sales forecasts for that segment. There are foodservice industry rules-of-thumb that suggest that it takes a market segment of a certain size to support a particular kind of restaurant. The foodservice operator, in targeting a market segment, might need to identify 50,000 people in that segment. Competition is a certain consideration when this method is used. The way the market segment will be divided among competitors determines what any one of them can forecast as a market share. Frequently, this leads to still another consideration, the cost of promotion to gain market share. This cost influences the decision about the financial potential of the endeavor.

Sales forecasts, which form the basis for budgets prepared by the business system, are also useful in establishing the level of costs. On the strength of the number of expected patrons, a new foodservice operation estimates opening costs for construction, equipment, food products, labor, utilities, and so on. The costs of these materials often vary with the quantities purchased, and the quantities purchased are related to the sales volume that has been forecast. These costs are then used to calculate simulated operating statements to project the break-even point, return on investment, cash flow, and other business information. After building in some margins for an increase in costs and for unforeseen expenses, the operator can decide if the return is worth the effort.

In an ongoing operation, sales analysis can be researched to forecast sales trends as well as costs of sales, advertising, promotion, and service and thus to show the profitability of certain products or product areas.

MAKING MARKET RESEARCH EFFECTIVE

A number of basic guidelines for making market research effective can be identified:

• Market research must be recognized as fundamental in planning foodservice operations.

• Market research methodology must be rigorous. The costs of guesswork are prohibitive.

• Professional assistance is imperative if the foodservice operator does not have market research capabilities within the organization.

• If the methodology of market research seems unimpeachable, the results should be accepted, even if those results run counter to the operator's intuition, tastes, and business instincts.

• Market research must be conducted continuously. No operation is so firmly established that it is not vulnerable to fundamental market changes.

• Market research must be used in operational planning. Market research can indicate how many people will frequent the operation during any planning period; therefore, staffing, purchasing, and production should all be based on this forecast.

Chapter 5
The Marketing System: Part II

This second chapter on the marketing system covers *promotion,* the branch of marketing that tells people about an operation. Promotion directs information about the operation's food (developed through *menu planning*) and *service* at the market segment targeted by *market research.* Promotion is essentially a kind of communication—a transfer of information from an operation to its customers, guests, or clients.

The aim of promotion is to expose potential consumers to an operation's products and services and to get them to respond positively to that exposure. The response sought by commercial foodservice operations is increased consumer demand for the product or service, which in turn will increase or maintain profits. The response sought by noncommercial foodservice operations is consumer acceptance or appreciation. Both of these responses depend on consumer satisfaction with the product or service being promoted. Promotion is critical in the competitive world of commercial foodservice, though it is also becoming increasingly important in noncommercial operations as the trend toward concern with consumer satisfaction continues.

However important promotion is to the success of most operations, it should be recognized that promotion has only a limited ability to influence consumers. Attractive and informative promotion cannot compel people to buy a product that is inconsistent with, or inappropriate to, their needs and desires. Promotion activities can only stimulate demand and foster appreciation in a target market. If no significant segment of the market finds the product desirable, then the product is not promotable. Promotion cannot simply create a market segment that will perceive a particular product or service as desirable; it can only help people to define their needs and desires and suggest that a particular product or service can satisfy them. An operation depends on market research to find out whether or not such a demand exists. Thus, promotional planning begins with thorough market research.

PROMOTIONAL PLANNING

Market research directs the planning of promotion efforts by determining where promotional opportunities lie. Market research must identify the market segment's motivation for buying, its buying attitudes and practices, as well as the market segment's source of information about foodservice operations. Market research also determines how the market segment is influenced in deciding what to buy and projects the cost of the promotional effort.

Promotion can only be as good as the market research on which it is based. Just as an operation cannot sell a product whose creation was based on erroneous market research about the kind of food a market segment wants, an operation cannot promote a product successfully if its promotion campaign is not based on sound market research about how to appeal to these consumers.

Because influencing consumer behavior is not an exact science, it is difficult to predict what makes promotion effective. No magic formulas exist for planning successful promotion campaigns—just some practical guidelines. After using market research to determine how to promote, most promotion programs are planned in these five steps, each of which will be explained in the sections that follow: (1) formulating objectives for promotion, (2) developing the promotion message, (3) allocating funds for promotion, (4) selecting promotion activities, and (5) preparing promotion materials.

Formulating Objectives for Promotion   Managers develop promotional objectives for the particular promotional opportunity at hand. These objectives reflect what the operation hopes to gain from its promotion campaign. As the first step in promotional planning, promotional objectives set the tone and pace of the promotion effort. Most promotion campaigns have one or more of the following objectives:

1. *To make the market aware of the product*   Promotion may simply tell consumers in the target market that the product exists. Newly opened foodservice operations often use promotion for this purpose.

2. *To assert the fundamental value of the product*   Beyond simply making potential consumers aware of the product, promotion can explain what makes a product good or desirable. Foodservice operations use promotion for this purpose to attract members of the market segment who are new, who are slow to change their dining habits, who have tried the foodservice operation and discontinued their patronage, or who simply need reinforcement of a product's continuing value.

3. *To identify the product as a means of satisfying existing wants or needs*   Beyond asserting the value of the product, promotion can suggest how the product's particular value can satisfy a consumer's particular needs. Promotion may do this by teaching consumers to use the product

as a means of attaining something they want: social status, a stimulating emotional experience, or just a good nourishing meal. All foodservice operations use promotion for this purpose, but it is most effective when the operation or the product is new, or when the operation wishes to change the image of itself or its product, perhaps by identifying with a new or different consumer need or desire.

4. *To establish competitive differences*   Promotion can suggest that a product has more value, and consequently a greater ability to satisfy consumer wants or needs, than similar products marketed by competitors. Foodservice operations carving a market niche—attracting a share of the market—use promotion for this purpose.

Developing the Promotion Message   The promotion message must contain the information that will influence demand in such a way that the promotional objective is achieved. What information about the foodservice operation or its products will cause the market to alter its behavior in the desired fashion? If the promotional objective is to assert the value of the product, then the promotion message must contain information establishing the product's value. If the promotional objective is to establish competitive difference, then the promotion message must convince the market segment that the product is superior to or different from similar competing products. If the promotional objective is to satisfy particular consumer wants or needs, the promotion message may, for example, identify the product with desirable upper-class social values, or may emphasize its convenience.

The particular promotion message employed depends on the particular promotional objective. Not all features of a foodservice product or establishment can be promoted at the same time. The message must assert a *specific* market benefit. Messages with mixed appeals can appear confusing to consumers. The best promotion message is generally one with a short (easily digested and remembered), strong, and singular appeal.

Allocating Funds for Promotion   The funds available for promotion depend upon the general forecast of sales and expenses for the whole operation. Though an operation should of course not spend more on promotion that it can expect to gain in return, it is difficult to isolate the impact of promotion on sales and profits. Few foodservice operations have sufficient confidence in their ability to forecast demand to base their promotion budget on such forecasts. Though forecasts are of course considered, in practice budgets are developed by other methods.

Promotion budgets are often determined as a fixed percentage of sales, using as a guide the operation's own sales history, published industry standards, or the expenditures of a principal competitor. Industry standards for promotion budgets range from one-half to four percent of sales. Some foodservice operations determine their promotion budget by establishing a promotional cost-per-unit of the item being sold. For example, a hamburger chain may determine that it should spend two cents on promotion for every hamburger it expects to sell.

The size of the promotion budget also depends on the scope of promotional objectives. If an operation wishes to promote a new product, or to change its image, it may require a more extensive promotion campaign and consequently more funds to support such a campaign. If an operation has gained a sufficient number of steady patrons and uses promotion simply to remind them of the value of its products, then substantially less money would be required for promotion.

Of course, the sum budgeted for promotion may also be completely arbitrary or may merely represent whatever money is available. Obviously, such methods are not very sound ways of deciding on promotion budgets.

Selecting Promotion Activities

Foodservice operations engage in three kinds of promotion activities: advertising, sales promotion, and merchandising. These activities differ in the way they transfer information to potential consumers.

Advertising is any paid, openly sponsored message communicated by media such as newspapers, television, direct mail, billboards, magazines, and the like.

Sales promotion includes publicity, special offers, and all direct personal selling which is conducted somewhere other than the operation. Sales promotion differs from advertising in one of two ways: either it is not paid for or it does not entail a mass communications medium. For example, even though publicity entails a mass medium, it is classified as a sales promotion tool because publicity is not bought.

Merchandising includes all efforts to stimulate sales used within the operation, such as personal selling by dining room personnel, use of dining room displays, and the like.

Specific methods of advertising, sales promotion, and merchandising are chosen on the basis of their appropriateness to the market segment, the promotional message, the funds available, and so on. The goal in selecting promotion activities is to gain the greatest benefit with the amount of money available. Advertising, sales promotion, and merchandising will each be discussed in detail further on in the chapter.

Preparing Promotion Materials

The final step in planning a promotion campaign is the actual preparation of the materials to be used in particular promotional activities. Such preparation includes actually writing the copy for television, radio, or print commercials; selecting or creating artwork or videotapes for displays, presentations, or advertisements; and planning merchandising demonstrations and choosing accompanying props. The preparation of promotional materials includes all the technical work necessary to render the promotion message in the chosen medium.

The planning of promotion campaigns culminates in the selection of appropriate promotion activities and the suitable preparation of materials. No matter how well-thought-out an operation's promotional objectives, promotion message, or allocation of funds, if promotion activities are not selected and developed with great thoroughness and care, there is little chance that the promotion campaign will prove fruitful. The following section of this chapter discusses the different kinds of promotion activities.

PROMOTION ACTIVITIES

Foodservice operations generally follow a pattern in their reliance on different promotion activities, for they use promotion differently at different stages in their life cycle. These different stages reflect the operation's evolving relationship with patrons and potential patrons. An operation's choice of promotion activities changes as its promotional objectives change, since different ends require different means.

On opening, foodservice operations engage in intensive and extensive promotion activities. A very wide net repeatedly is cast to capture the market segment and any other people who have not been targeted but to whom the operation might appeal. This can be considered the "pioneering" stage. The pioneering stage is usually dominated by extensive advertising campaigns, because the operation's promotional objective is simply to make people aware that it and its products exist, and advertising provides the most exposure.

Once the operation has identified itself to the market, its promotion activities can be directed to specific, limited, objectives. At this point, the operation is probably contending with competitors for the market and has reached the "competitive" stage. The operation's general promotional objective at this stage is probably to establish competitive differences and thus carve a market niche.

In the competitive stage, an operation often emphasizes sales promotion, frequently accompanied by supportive advertising. Sales promotion usually involves nonrecurrent selling efforts that are not usually a part of the promotion routine. An example might be a local pancake house hosting a pancake-eating contest, or a national hamburger chain sponsoring a visit from the chain's cartoon character mascot and giving away cups with pictures of the mascot on them to all purchasers of soft drinks. Such unusual methods are more arresting, and can thus help draw consumers away from similar competitors. The advertising used during this stage is more pointed, reflecting the operation's more clearly focused objectives, rather than being aimed at the general exposure sought in the pioneering stage.

After the competitive stage—the period in which promotion is perhaps most effective—the operation has consolidated its market. It ceases to make substantial gains through promotion activities. Promotion may still be necessary to sustain profits by meeting competitive pressures, but does not result in a radical upsurge of long-term profits. At this point, the operation turns to promotion activities that develop its market, such as personal selling by dining room staff. This is called the "retentive" stage.

In the retentive stage, merchandising is stressed though sales promotion and advertising continue to be important. An operation in the retentive stage of its life cycle has already established a steady patronage and reputation and need not concentrate efforts simply on attracting consumers. Such an operation instead directs promotion efforts at people who are already inside the establishment. Through merchandising, the operation both appeals to and successfully sells to these people. The operation's promotional objectives are no longer geared to general exposure or dramatic attempts to beat out competition. Promotion may now assert the fundamental value of its products and services and establish how these products and services are especially satisfying to consumers.

Of course, specific promotion activities may be undertaken at any phase in an operation's life cycle—there is always a need to "pioneer" to new people in the market segment. The domination of these phases by particular promotion activities is not a set formula for a long-term marketing program, but simply a general observation on the current use of these particular promotion activities by actual foodservice operations.

In order to select the promotion activities appropriate to the operation, the operation's manager must be familiar with the different promotion activities available. The three following sections will cover the different kinds of advertising, sales promotion, and merchandising useful to foodservice operations.

Advertising   Management decisions about advertising in foodservice usually concern the choice of medium. A medium is any means of presenting the advertisement to the potential consumer, such as newspapers, billboards, radio, and the like. The combination of media chosen is called the *advertising mix*. A manager must select the advertising media that best suit the operation's promotional objectives. In deciding on the advertising mix, a manager should consider these features of media:

• *Appropriateness to the promotional message*   A billboard would be inappropriate to a complex and lengthy message. A direct mail letter would be better suited to such a message.
• *Cost*   The cost of reaching a member of the market segment is a first concern. This cost per person is figured as the total cost of the advertising divided by the number of market segment members reached. Cost considerations also include the cost of preparing materials for par-

ticular media as well as the cost of the time or space needed for the advertisement.

• *Effectiveness in eliciting response*   Some media are more effective than others in getting people to act on the basis of an advertisement. A given advertisement may have a low cost of exposure, in that many people in the market segment will see it, but a high effective cost because few will respond to it.

• *Flexibility*   Some media limit the format of the promotional message, or limit how and when it can be prepared.

• *Consumer attitudes*   The attitude of particular market segments toward certain media must also be considered. A restaurant seeking to establish a "luxury" image may not want to advertise by distributing handbills on the street. Some market segments may associate television advertising with suspect, overpromoted products or services. A certain newspaper may be an unacceptable medium for advertisements that identify a foodservice operation's product with social values opposed to those upheld in the paper's editorial content or projected by the newspaper in general.

• *Life span*   Different media offer advertisements different life spans. Some media are suited to immediate messages, others to messages that must be repeated, and still others to messages that should be "durable" (looked at again and again).

• *The advertising mix of competitors*   It may be strategically desirable to extend the "battle" for the market segment to include a media battle. An operation might use the same media a competitor uses, hoping to win patrons with superior advertising as well as with a superior product. This strategy is of course undesirable if a competitor's resources are too great. Instead of risking the loss of potential patrons' business because of decisions based on the quality of advertising rather than the quality of the products or services, the operation should seek another medium.

Not only must managers compare the features of particular media, they must also bear in mind the possibility of a limited environment, which may make desired media unavailable or unaffordable. The location of the operation imposes one kind of environmental limitation on the choice of media. A restaurant that wants to advertise on the radio may find that locally there are only country and western radio stations and that its potential customers do not usually listen to country and western music. Instead, its target market listens to a classical music station that broadcasts from a city 100 miles away whose advertising slots are too expensive and are broadcast over too wide an area to be a cost-effective medium for the restaurant.

The relatively small budgets of many foodservice operations may preclude the use of certain media, notably television. Some foodservice organizations have budgets too small to interest professional advertising agencies in preparing and placing their advertisements. In effect, this rules out advertising in certain media that require professional quality materials.

Perhaps the greatest limitation on foodservice advertising occurs because many operations appeal to highly select market segments. Advertising media may reach too many market segments. A restaurant can hardly advertise in a city-wide newspaper and still hope to make its promotion cost-effective if its legitimate market lies in a small neighborhood. In the absence of a neighborhood newspaper or its equivalent, the operation's advertising is limited to such media as direct mail, handbills, its own signs, and the like.

Exhibit 5.1 summarizes some general advantages and disadvantages typically experienced by foodservice operations in their use of specific advertising media. The following sections will examine each of these media, concentrating on how they satisfy different advertisers' needs.

NEWSPAPERS Newspapers are widely used for promoting foodservice operations. Newspapers differ from one another in the number and kind of readers they attract. A national newspaper like the *New York Times* is read throughout the country. Aside from restaurants located in New York City, a restaurant must have national appeal to advertise successfully in the *Times*. Perhaps a restaurant in a major tourist area could justify advertising in the *Times*.

Another national newspaper, the *Wall Street Journal,* offers a more selective readership. Restaurants in business centers anywhere might consider placing advertisements in the *Journal*. Local newspapers (neighborhood, small town, or free shoppers' papers) offer an even greater degree of market segmentation. Newspapers generally supply prospective advertisers with circulation data that can reveal how well the readership of the paper corresponds to an operation's target market. It is also possible to test newspaper advertising through the use of coupons. Or, an operation can have such advertising audited by specialized firms that will survey, by telephone or interview, samples of the readership to assess the effectiveness of the operation's advertising in a particular newspaper (or any designated medium).

Several types of newspaper advertisements are used by foodservice operations. *Display* advertising, the most common, may include graphics, headlines, and a lengthy text message. *Classified* advertising generally consists of only copy (text) and is published in a special section of the newspaper. Restaurants in a particular area sometimes cooperate to advertise in a classified restaurant directory—almost a published group of business cards. *Reader* advertisements resemble the newspaper's copy, but the publisher frequently demands that they be set in a different style and bear the word "advertisement." Restaurants frequently use

EXHIBIT 5.1 Advantages and Disadvantages of Advertising Media for Foodservice Operations

Medium	Advantages	Disadvantages
Newspapers	Format and nature of message are highly flexible. Gains immediate exposure. Advertising can be placed just prior to publication. Offers intensive coverage in market area; many people read newspapers. Different cost structures are available from different newspapers.	Reproduction quality is poor. Newspapers are read quickly. Life of advertisement is short. Coverage of a particular newspaper may encompass too many market segments. Competitive advertising may appear on the same page. Small advertisements tend to be lost in the mass of print.
Magazines	Readership data provide ability to isolate market segments. Reproduction quality is usually good. Advertisement generally has long life; it may be read several times. Magazines offer special services to advertisers, such as including the advertiser's own preprinted materials.	Format is limited by magazine size and standards. There is usually a long lead time between the placement of the advertisement and its exposure. Magazine advertisement is usually expensive (per unit bought).
Direct Mail (including personal letters and mailed advertisements, circulars, and announcements)	Can be personal: a direct communication to a single person. Can be scheduled to meet the advertiser's needs. Complex and lengthy messages can be sent. It is possible to test direct mail by limited mailings.	The cost per person contacted is relatively high (but this must be considered in light of the possibility of great selectivity in sending mailing pieces). Mailing lists may be difficult to obtain for foodservice market segments; they tend to be stale. Because of wide use of direct mail by a variety of companies—some with products of dubious worth —customers may resist direct mail approaches.
Television	Provides impact on several levels: sight and sound. Offers extremely wide coverage. Lends itself to repetitive short messages. Format is flexible, within confines of the medium—anything from cartoons to print can be used.	It is expensive on a cost per unit basis. Coverage may be too broad for foodservice. TV advertising is generally conceived of as an interruption. TV advertising may be associated with huckstering. Materials are difficult and expensive to prepare.

Medium	Advantages	Disadvantages
Television (cont.)	Has prestige possibilities by association with quality programming.	Local television stations may lack basic research data on audience.
Radio	Impact is immediate. Presentation is highly flexible. Lends itself to repetitive advertising. Can isolate market segments. Enjoys wide use by consumers (in car, home, or office).	There are frequently too many stations to choose from. The message is short-lived, and unavailable for reference. Market data may be unavailable.
Outdoor (including billboards and signs)	Advertising can occur at point of sale. Has high visual impact. Can be seen again and again. Advertising can have long life.	Lacks flexibility in format. Message must be brief and simple. Preparation of materials is expensive. May be associated with environmental pollution. Zoning and other regulations restrict its use.
Point of Purchase (including advertising cards, indoor signs, table tents, and so on)	Materials are inexpensive, and often free from suppliers. Will be read several times. Finds customers in the buying mood.	Tends to compromise image of fine restaurant. Can be confusing if used too extensively. Message must be brief.
Transportation (including sign cards in trains and buses, advertising panels on trucks, and sign boards in transportation facilities)	Costs are low. Will be read several times. Lends itself to repetitive advertising. In advertisements within transportation vehicles, message can be complex.	Competes with other advertising directly. Format is limited. Coverage cannot always isolate desired market segments.
Directories (including the *Yellow Pages*, and travel guides)	The consumer is usually already looking to buy. Directories may isolate market segment. May offer prestige of endorsement by appearing in credit card directories.	Usually, there is a long lead time between placement of advertisement and its exposure. Competitive advertisements may appear with the advertisements of an operation. Market may not be selective. An operation tends to be stereotyped by the other advertisements or listings.

this type of advertising to republish favorable restaurant reviews or to personalize the operation by offering the readers of the paper cooking or gastronomical information presented in the form of a newspaper "column."

Newspapers may offer the opportunity for color advertising or the inclusion of advertising in magazine supplements. They may even provide the opportunity for the restaurant to prepare its own supplement to be included in the newspaper.

MAGAZINES   Magazines can be an effective advertising medium for foodservice operations. The essential problem for foodservice advertising is that many magazines are published for and distributed over a wide area. Thus, though a restaurant's magazine advertising may be reaching exactly the kind of people to whom the operation wishes to appeal, the overwhelming majority of these people may not live in the restaurant's market area. National magazines have attempted to deal with this problem by publishing regional, even local, editions. Foodservice operations can advertise successfully in these editions of national magazines, or in magazines with only regional or local circulation and appeal (such as the flourishing city magazines like *Chicago* or *Washingtonian*).

Three types of magazines are generally used by foodservice operations: *Consumer* or *general* magazines, *tourist* or *visitor* magazines, and *trade* or *business* magazines. Consumer or general magazines, which may be local or national in circulation and of limited (a stereo magazine) or general (a news magazine) appeal, frequently run editorial material related to leisure activities. They hope to attract associated advertising on this basis. Tourist or visitor magazines are largely concerned with leisure activities. They offer the traveler specific information about entertainment and dining. While obviously effective at isolating the market segment, they have the disadvantage of presenting numerous competitive advertisements. Trade or business magazines are directed to persons employed in a specific industry or profession. Only operations in places that attract conventions or in areas where the industry is located can effectively advertise in such magazines.

Many magazines accept display and classified advertising. Some have sections devoted to the presentation of small display advertisements by restaurants. Many magazines offer color printing, high quality reproduction of photographs, and such special services as the insertion of return postcards and advertising materials.

DIRECT MAIL   Within the rather generous limits of postal law, a considerable variety of advertising materials can be sent through the mail. Some problems, though, present themselves in direct mail advertising for foodservice operations. Appropriate mailing lists are difficult to develop and maintain. The names and addresses of members of a restaurant's market segment may not be readily available if the target market consists of selected interest groups drawn from the general population. A restaurant catering to executives in a downtown district may have few problems. Prospective patrons can be addressed by title and by company name researched from the telephone directory or chamber of commerce listings. A restaurant catering to junior employees and clerical help has much greater difficulties. Lists purchased from companies that sell mailing lists tend to be too broad. Only when the foodservice operation can obtain an effective list does the fairly high cost of preparing and sending advertising materials seem justified. For instance, a health food restaurant in a small town might obtain an effective list from a local health food store or weight reduction group. Consumer resistance to direct mail advertising is a second major problem. Unless people receive a typed letter bearing their full name, they tend to disregard direct mail advertisements. The widespread use of direct mail advertising has led people to classify all mail that is not personalized as "junk" mail.

Foodservice operations mail six types of advertisements, called *mailing pieces:* (1) the personalized letter; (2) display advertising materials, called *folders,* which fit in standard business envelopes; (3) broadsides, which are large display advertisements that unfold as posters; (4) their own menus, with or without some accompanying message; (5) circulars, which are brief messages usually printed on one side of a sheet; and (6) mailing cards, which are postcards, often very attractive, bearing brief reminders or announcements.

TELEVISION   Television advertising is usually described as either network or local. Network advertising is broadcast by one of the three major networks on all the stations affiliated with it during the time periods when programming is the network's responsibility. In effect, network advertising means national coverage, a low cost per person (usually expressed as cost per thousand persons), and the possible prestige of being associated with good programming. Several major foodservice companies use network advertising extensively, even more than major auto companies do. They may also develop commercials called *spots* which are a special kind of network advertising broadcast in particular geographic market areas for specific promotional objectives rather than shown on all the network stations in the country as regular network advertisements are. This method is called "national spot" advertising.

Local advertising is part of the program of the local station. Some franchise foodservice organizations may supply their local units with television advertisements, but many foodservice operations develop their own commercials for local broadcast. Some sponsor entire programs, using several commercials.

Television stations, at least the larger ones, can supply program ratings, audience distribution studies, share of audience studies, and other data that allow the foodservice operation to determine the approximate cost of reaching specific market segment members. Television advertising rates are usually based on the number of people the specific program will reach. Necessarily, the foodservice establishment must relate this information to the market segmentation of the viewing audience. Typically, television advertising is most useful in reaching the large social and economic middle class, as this group has the heaviest viewing pattern and most television programs are created with it in mind.

Almost any advertisement within the bounds of the Federal Communications Commission regulations and local standards of decency and taste as interpreted by the station can be broadcast. But successful television advertising requires the kind of technical expertise and polish that most foodservice operations can get only with the aid of an experienced advertising agency. Without professional help—and sometimes even with it—local foodservice advertising tends to lack focus, and consequently fails to communicate effectively the intended promotional message.

RADIO Radio advertising is also classified as local or network, including national spot. There are two different types of radio, FM (frequency modulation) and AM (amplitude modulation) transmissions. FM signals are generally received in a smaller area than AM signals are. Each station's effective coverage will depend on the type of transmission and the amount of operating power it has.

Radio stations can be classified as local (15 to 25 mile reception range radius), regional (25 to 100 miles), or clear channel (100 miles or more). Larger, more powerful radio stations usually have extensive data about their audiences which can be related to the foodservice operation's objectives in reaching its market segment. Smaller stations may lack such research data, but they tend to be closely identified with specific audiences which may correspond to the market segment targeted by a particular foodservice operation. Without doing extensive research, it is quite possible to assume correctly that a rock and roll station's listeners are unlikely to be potential patrons of a gourmet restaurant but probably include many hamburger and pizza customers.

Many areas of the United States that lack any other appropriate means of advertising for foodservice operations have at least one radio station. Hence, radio is a common advertising medium for foodservice. Radio commercials are frequently prepared by the station or by local advertising agencies. As radio is used daily by almost everyone, it provides a fairly low-cost way of reaching potential and actual customers.

OUTDOOR

For foodservice operations, two major types of outdoor advertising are used: billboards and the operation's own signs. Both types can be quite effective if the limitations of outdoor advertising are recognized. In both, the message must be brief and must make an immediate, comprehensible impact.

For foodservice operations that depend on attracting motorists, outdoor advertising may be the primary means of promotion. The essence of the operation must be communicated in the few seconds that the sign is visible to potential patrons as they drive by. Franchise operations have an obvious advantage here because their programs of national advertising cause the motorist to immediately associate a billboard or the sign of a restaurant with messages stored from other advertising. Other operations try, with some success, to communicate a single important message like value for the money, family dining, bargain prices, or huge portions. Conspicuous, large, and colorful outdoor advertising may, however, be associated by some market segments with undesirable qualities: tawdriness, commonness, and ecological or esthetic pollution.

POINT OF PURCHASE

Point-of-purchase advertising is used widely in the foodservice industry. Such advertisements occur at the point of purchase—when the customer is inside the establishment ready to order—and communicate by printed or graphic means virtually any kind of promotional message. A representative list of point-of-purchase materials used in foodservice operations includes the following: *table tents* (colorful, durable folders that show graphics and copy promoting particular products and made to stand up in the center of a table setting); *advertising displays* (anything on which a word or picture promoting a product can be printed, such as wall clocks, mobiles, rubber change mats, door mats, and light-cord hangers); and *indoor signs* (window signs, banners, super-graphics, posters, lobby signs, and elevator signs).

Much of this material can be obtained free from companies or organizations with an interest in promoting the products depicted or named, or can be prepared or purchased with a subsidy from such companies or organizations. Typical point-of-purchase advertising materials available in this way are promotional boards for fruits, vegetables, or beverages, and exhibits from liquor companies, manufacturers of convenience items, beer producers, and the like.

TRANSPORTATION

Transportation advertising can be placed on the inside or outside of vehicles. Such advertising suits the promotional objectives of many foodservice operations because it combines low cost, flexibility, and some degree of market segmentation.

Advertising on the outside of transportation vehicles is used less frequently because the unit cost is relatively high. Bus, train, taxi, and some truck companies will attach a display sign to their vehicles as a means of raising revenues.

Advertising inside transportation vehicles is quite common and is found in buses, some trains, and some taxicabs. These vehicles are fitted with panels that hold advertising cards of various sizes. Since the customer is exposed to the message for fairly long periods of time, readership rates and recall rates are both high. Inside transportation advertising of this type is relatively inexpensive (figured per thousand persons reached) because the transportation companies consider the fee charged for it as added income, not as a primary source of revenue. A number of advertising agencies specialize in the preparation, placement, and servicing of transportation advertisements.

Advertising within transportation facilities is also generally included in this category. Restaurants are frequent advertisers in airports, bus terminals, and rail stations. Display posters, standing displays, and electric signs are commonly used in such advertisements.

DIRECTORIES   The classified section of the telephone book (usually called the *Yellow Pages*) is the best known directory used by foodservice operations. It is possible to purchase listings or display advertising in this book. Some telephone directories also offer advertising classified by restaurant category (French, Italian, fast-food) as well as alphabetical listings in the restaurant section.

A number of national directories of foodservice establishments and associated hospitality enterprises are also available. Some of these publications are, in effect, critical guides to restaurants and do not accept paid advertising. Others will accept paid display and classified advertising as well as simple listings.

Credit card companies publish directories of their business members, which include many foodservice organizations. They may also advertise locally to promote the use of their cards, and may list or describe member restaurants in such advertisements.

Directory advertising is evaluated on the same basis as other advertising media: cost to reach the market segment, expressed in cost per thousand persons.

Sales Promotion   As stated earlier, sales promotion in the foodservice industry includes direct personal selling that takes place somewhere other than the operation, publicity, and special offers.

PERSONAL SELLING   Personal selling involves the direct communication of the operation's promotional message to a potential consumer by a representative of the operation. As such, it offers limited possibilities for most foodservice organizations. But in *social catering, convention sales,* and *contract feed-ing,* three important areas of foodservice, personal selling is very often necessary and does pay off. *Social catering* for banquets, weddings, parties, and social affairs of all kinds is sold by direct presentation to the prospective client. Often the sales effort is aided by audiovisual ma-terials, printed brochures, sample menus, catalogs, tours of the estab-lishment, and the like. Foodservice operations in the hospitality industry that offer banquet and business meeting facilities for *conventions* sell their services directly to consumers the same way that social catering companies do. *Foodservice contractors* that seek to serve the customers, guests, or clients of another enterprise first must sell to that sponsoring enterprise. Successful selling efforts in bidding for institutional feeding contracts are extensive, well organized, and elaborate. The presentation by a foodservice contractor to a major hospital or school system may require several hundred hours of preparation and research. Frequently, the written proposal is as long as a hundred pages. The actual presenta-tion can take a day and involve several sales executives of the contracting company. Companies seeking to place vending machines, coffee service concessions, or foodservice concessions in recreational facilities, parks, or public buildings make similar presentations, though of course on a smaller scale. Since personal selling is costly, such efforts frequently follow other promotional activities, such as media advertising, direct mail advertisements, trade show displays, telephone solicitation, and the like.

PUBLICITY   Publicity is an indirect effort to stimulate sales, largely by simply making the public more aware of the operation. The objective is to create news that will merit coverage by newspapers, magazines, or radio and tele-vision stations. Since publicity is not paid for, and since each of these media has its own business objectives and obligations to its audience, whatever is presented must be genuinely newsworthy. Something un-usual, exceptional, or special about the operation should be the focus of a publicity effort.

The news may be inherent in the operation or created specifically for the purpose of publicity. If a restaurant wins culinary awards, is visited by famous people, or serves the largest or the most of something, these events are inherently newsworthy for local media and have not been created specifically for promotional publicity. Foodservice operations can also plan special publicity efforts in hopes of attracting attention. By holding cooking competitions or eating contests, or by publicizing the purchase of a $10,000 bottle of wine, an operation can generate in-terest in itself. By sponsoring a public service event such as an anti-litter campaign or a Christmas party at a veteran's hospital, an operation can gain publicity as well as provide personally satisfying experiences for the employees involved.

SPECIAL OFFERS Foodservice operations sometimes promote themselves by offering consumers immediate, exceptional reasons for patronage. Most often promotion of this type is directed at stimulating new patronage on the theory that the operation will then sell itself to the consumer, who will return. These offers can be made in three ways: by giving away samples of products, by offering a special gift or partial gift, or by offering a discount.

Many foodservice operations with numerically large market segments may give away samples of their products to passersby in their market area. Such free samples might be bits of pizza, mini-hamburgers, fried chicken, miniature cones of ice cream, or tiny cups of soup. Some kind of advertising material, such as a printed napkin, may be given to the passerby with the product, and signs may identify the operation and its location.

Offering a gift or a partial gift, called a *premium*, is another common promotional device of this sort. A specially imprinted attractive glass may be offered free with the purchase of a beverage. Or, the operation may offer a quality thermos bottle at a discount to stimulate coffee and doughnut sales. A good premium promotion usually results in an immediate upsurge of sales; it is necessary, however, to evaluate its enduring effects, for often the premium rather than the operation's products attracts the customer. In an effort to promote the special offer, it may have been necessary to stress the value of the premium, and consequently important promotional messages about the operation and its products were obscured.

Discounts are offered in a variety of ways. A foodservice operation may include money-off coupons in its advertising. It may advertise a cash discount of 10 percent. Frequently, restaurants will offer two meals for the price of one, either through independent advertising or as part of a club that sells ticket books to its members. A promotion offering two entrees for the price of one may be made with the expectation of making a profit on the other items the customer may order. Some operations offer discount books; the customer pays in advance for ten meal tickets but receives eleven or twelve. Other operations punch cards until the patron has bought ten meals and then offer an eleventh free.

Discounts pose several problems. The customer taking advantage of the discount may not be a new customer at all. Some customers who take advantage of the discount may be able to afford the restaurant only at the special price and will not return. Discounts may change customers' favorable impression of the operation: some customers may feel that the restaurant has been cheapened by offering discounts. Certainly, discounts may occasion feelings of regret in those customers who have patronized the restaurant before the discount was instituted, as well as in those customers who took advantage of it and are aware of its ending. Such feelings of regret may change their attitudes toward the operation.

Merchandising   Merchandising attempts to stimulate or maintain profits through promotion within the foodservice establishment. Merchandising efforts may be geared toward these specific objectives:

• Establishing an atmosphere in which patrons are made to feel more welcome, more comfortable, or more satisfied through their interaction with restaurant employees. An operation can establish an important competitive difference on the basis of these intangibles.

• Influencing customer buying decisions to the mutual benefit of the customer and the operation. This objective may be satisfied simply by suggesting particularly outstanding dishes, but could include attempting to sell customers additional food or drink (thus increasing checks) or influence them to select dishes with a greater cost-profit ratio or "special" dishes that cannot be used for the next day's meals. Customers' food choices can also be influenced so that work on production stations is balanced; if production is efficient, patrons get their food faster.

• Promoting products or services of the operation other than those that the patron is immediately enjoying. Social catering, other meal opportunities, the use of catering facilities, take-out products, and so on are often promoted in this way.

These objectives can be achieved by particular merchandising techniques such as sales management, menu merchandising, food displays and samples, and personal selling in the dining room.

SALES MANAGEMENT   Sales management is the selling of the operation as a whole. More than anything else, successful sales management involves instilling staff with an attitude of warmth and accommodation toward the patron. Sales management aims to create a personal relationship between the operation and its patrons, even on their first visit; this goal involves thoughtful services and sensitivity to the patrons' wants and needs that go far beyond simply serving them food with adequate efficiency.

Sales management strives to establish a competitive difference based on intangibles, which can be the most important role of merchandising. Frequently, foodservice operations cannot distinguish themselves in any other way. Consider a restaurant that wishes to increase or maintain its market share while competing with other operations that are similar to it—say, one of a string of hamburger restaurants on a highway or one of a cluster of luncheon restaurants on the main street of a small city. Competitive difference can only be established by favorably changing the market segment's perception of some aspect of the restaurant. A problem is created since the restaurant shares the same market segment, the same product and prices, and the same labor pool with other similar operations. Lowering prices, the obvious solution, will not result in sufficient increased volume to maintain, much less increase, profits.

In such a situation, the only factor that can favorably change the market segment's perception of the restaurant is the personal contribution of the employees. They must be perceived as friendlier, more willing to please, and more accommodating than competitors' personnel. This is where sales management comes in. Though sometimes employees that are in contact with consumers make this contribution spontaneously as an extension of their personalities, more often it is an attitude instilled by successful sales management. The selling of the operation is as important as the sale of food or drink.

Managers of operations serving continuing clients also practice sales management. Several of the dietitians on the staff of a large health care foodservice operation may devote themselves to interacting with patients. The managers of a contract foodservice operation may devote a good part of their time to furthering good relations with their client company and its employees.

Sales management techniques vary, but many approaches include the following:

• Selecting employees on the basis of personality and attitude, as well as on skill.

• Training employees in consumer relations, courtesy, proper address, and positive service attitudes.

• Employing hosts or hostesses whose principal function is to greet patrons and make them feel welcome or remembered.

• In operations serving the continuing client, basing meals on ethnic menus, or sponsoring special food events such as "roaring twenties" parties or food festivals.

• Offering special customer accommodations such as table telephones so that a market segment composed of business people can receive calls, lockers for shoppers, and special menus, booster chairs, and toys for small children.

• Extending personal attention by providing particularly desired products (for example, a certain steak sauce) or special tables, by having personnel greet patrons by name, or by offering food gifts on special personal occasions.

• In commercial operations, giving special parties and food festivals free for regular customers, or at a price approximating actual costs.

• Mailing patrons birthday and anniversary greetings or small food gifts.

MENU MERCHANDISING   An operation's printed menu or menu display can be used as a promotional device. The design of the menu can define the operation's image. An elaborate, obviously expensive menu suggests social prestige or luxury. A cute, colorful menu may be associated with inexpensive family dining. If the foodservice operation has thematic decor, the menu can mirror it. Narrative text written on the menu may actually contribute to the operation's image by giving its history or offering a message from the proprietor. The menu can also contain advertising for other services of the operation. Frequently, the back panels of the menus of foodservice operations associated with lodging establishments are used to promote other features of these establishments.

Some foodservice operations attempt to use descriptive language to promote menu items. The consumer is attracted by enticing descriptions of those food items that the operation particularly wishes to sell, such as dishes that the operation expects will help establish competitive differences, or items with a high cost-profit ratio, especially side dishes. On occasion, color photographs are used on the menu for the same purpose.

Menus can be designed to allow the inclusion of other merchandising materials called *tip-ins* if they fit into special slots in the menu and *clip-ons* if they simply are clipped to the top of it. Use of tip-ins and clip-ons gives the operation some flexibility in its promotional activities, for different items can be featured at different times, thus sustaining customer interest in the operation through this variety of offerings.

As with any other promotional device, the cost of menus must be compared with their impact on profitability. While negative reactions to the menu—it may be dirty or illegible—always endanger sales, positive reactions to an elaborate or extravagant menu do not necessarily increase sales. Thus the use of the menu as a merchandising device should not be made overly important. Regular patrons tend to be less affected by the menu each time they visit the operation. Some may refuse any menu at all, as they have come to the operation with their order in mind. In a luxury restaurant enjoying a regular clientele, a simple, elegant, and inexpensive menu with spare use of lavish language is probably more effective than any elaborate, expensive, and dramatically worded menu. But selective use of menu merchandising does have a legitimate place in foodservice promotion.

FOOD DISPLAYS
AND SAMPLES

Attractive food displays serve both to stimulate sales of specific food products and to enhance the meal experience. Placing an attractive display of appetizers, wines, baked goods, or desserts near the entrance to a restaurant can increase the sale of these items and convey an impression of good living. In self-service restaurants, the appearance of the food offerings is directly related to their sales.

Foodservice operators can display food in several ways, including:

- Dessert carts in the dining room.
- Refrigerated display cases.
- Visible wine cellars.
- Carts for main course items or for soups.
- Salad bars.

- Tableside preparation and display cooking.
- Preparation tables for the dining room.
- Food used in decor, such as fruit baskets or lobster tanks.
- Window displays of raw ingredients, like fine meats, or of products cooking, like ribs grilling or chicken broiling on a spit.

A foodservice operation may offer samples of food in an effort to stimulate the sale of the food item or as a method of generally increasing customer satisfaction. Many foodservice operations have been successful in promoting wine sales by first offering customers samples of house wines. Others offer free cheese bars, appetizers, or desserts, either to entice customers or to control customer flow in and out of the dining room. Customers held in a bar with complimentary food until tables are available will be more content and more likely to order drinks than those held in a waiting area. Customers invited to have complimentary coffee or dessert in another area of the restaurant release tables for other customers at peak dining hours.

Sampling can also help promote the sale of unfamiliar items. Patrons are reluctant to try food for the first time; they do not wish to order a dish they may not like. Sampling relieves them of this problem and helps overcome general resistance to exotic foods which may be very profitable for the foodservice operation.

PERSONAL SELLING   Foodservice personnel serving tables or waiting on counters can increase sales through their contact with consumers. In most instances, suggestive selling techniques are used. The foodservice employee counsels, suggests, reminds, and assists the consumer in making decisions about what to order. Frequently, management has targeted specific items for personal selling efforts, such as cocktails, wine, appetizers, side dishes, desserts, and daily specials. The foodservice worker finds some opportunity in conversation with the patron to mention or describe these items. Frequently, foodservice workers are trained to suggest certain items in tandem with the customer's order of complementary items. An order for pie is immediately followed by the employee's suggestion of having ice cream with it. A suggestion of french fries follows a hamburger order; Roquefort dressing follows salad; onion rings follow steak.

Management has two primary responsibilities in the area of personal selling: training personnel and providing them with incentives. Specialized techniques can be suggested for profiling patrons and promoting the items they are likely to buy. Management can suggest that service personnel match celebrating couples with a champagne sale or match large parties with baked Alaska for dessert. Some operations train their personnel to interpret body language—nonverbal communication by facial expression or body movement—so that employees can sense what kinds of products patrons are likely to buy and gear their sales efforts accordingly.

Incentives motivate employees to sell. "Bottle bonuses" for wine sales or a commission on food sales gives employees a stake in the promotional effort. As another incentive, an operation may compensate an employee for selling an item that is profitable for the operation but less expensive than other items, and therefore reduces the total check on which the employee's tip is based. The outstanding sales effectiveness of particular employees can be rewarded by assigning them to shifts and stations where there is a greater opportunity to earn gratuities.

MAKING PROMOTION MORE EFFECTIVE

Certain strategies and guidelines are used by successful foodservice operations to make promotion efforts more effective. These considerations are the result of valuable experience and should be borne in mind when embarking on or revamping a promotion campaign. A list of these strategies follows and can be used by any foodservice organization to make its own promotion program more successful:

• *Promotion activities must be seen as communications processes.* The promotion method used must be chosen with consideration of the information that is being communicated and of the problems and obstacles that may arise from the audience's understanding of the chosen means of communication.

• *Promotion activities must be evaluated and controlled.*   Specific promotion activities—for example, newspaper advertising—can be evaluated by market research methods such as surveys, questionnaires, and so on. The overall cost of promotion has to be related to an operation's measurable returns: an increase in sales, profits, market share, or the like.

• *Professional assistance is usually worth the cost.*   Preparation of advertising copy for newspapers, magazines, television, and radio and the development of accompanying pictorial or graphic materials require special training and talents. For truly effective promotion, the foodservice operation must either employ individuals with these abilities, as major foodservice companies do, or hire outside consultants, such as advertising or promotion agencies, to provide the necessary expertise.

• *Promotion messages must be based on substance.*   People discern misleading claims in foodservice promotion much more quickly than they do in the promotion of other products. Consumers are much more familiar with the basic qualities of food. Because of their geographically limited markets, most foodservice operations must rely on repeat business and word-of-mouth advertising as well. Misleading claims and general deception can quickly damage the reputation (and profitability) of a foodservice establishment.

• *Promotion activities must not intrude upon the patron's enjoyment of the meal.*   Advertising materials and merchandising techniques used within the restaurant should not disturb or interrupt the patron's enjoyment of the meal.

• *The best promotion message may be conservative.*   People are suspicious of foodservice advertising that seems "too good to be true"; they look for the catch. More modest claims of quality, uniqueness, superiority, and value tend to be interpreted as more likely to be true. The consumer generally feels that "you get what you pay for."

• *The most effective promotion messages deal with the sensuous enjoyment of food and the social prestige associated with certain foods or food rituals.*   Food is a special product, imbued with meanings and significances that make responses to it more intense and emotional than responses to many other products. Food is sold most effectively by appealing to this level of motivation. The symbols appropriate to the target market's value system must be included in the promotional message.

• *Promotion activities must be considered an integral part of the marketing system and not a substitute for the other elements.*   Market research, menu planning, and service must be successfully developed to ensure that patrons will return once they have been influenced by promotion to try a foodservice operation.

• *Promotion activities must be considered in the context of the total foodservice operation.*   A number of foodservice operations have successfully promoted themselves out of business by influencing demand so well that they were unable to serve consumers satisfactorily. The too-rapid expansion of a restaurant chain because of the effectiveness of its promotion can so weaken its financial structure that the least downturn in demand threatens the life of the enterprise.

• *Having a good product is the best promotion.*   It is less expensive to keep a current patron than to find a new one. By offering good food and service, and by continually finding new ways to improve its food and services, an operation can well satisfy consumers and influence demand in its own favor. Having a good product to sell is the essence of successful promotion. A satisfied customer, guest, or client is an operation's best means of promotion.

Chapter 6
The Menu-Planning
System
Menu planning is the development of the choice of food, or primary product, to offer a particular operation's target market. As part of the marketing system (see Chapter 4), menu planning is built on information about consumers and products discovered through market research. Though one output of the menu-planning system is the printed menu, this system involves more than creating a list of foods to be offered and more than producing the traditional paper or signboard catalog. The menu-planning system transforms the concept of the particular operation into a set of concrete realities. This concrete end result is the menu program, which is the sum of all the individual menus a restaurant or other operation offers over a given period of time. The menu program includes not only the printed menu, but also guidelines for standard specifications, production orders, budgets, and control devices.

CURRENT PRACTICES IN MENU PLANNING

In ideal circumstances, everyone affected by the menu program—including the consumer—should participate in menu planning. Quite clearly, a contribution can be made by those people concerned with purchasing, supply, production, service, and the work system, as well as those concerned with management, business, control, and, of course, marketing.

Large contract feeders, fast-food chains, hotel chains, catering companies, and institutions certainly approach this ideal. Large foodservice businesses of any kind usually recognize the value of widespread participation in menu planning and decision making. A variety of individuals can contribute their own special talents and experience to planning a successful menu program. Later, these same people will have a stake in the success of the menu program they helped to plan.

In some large companies, such broad-based menu planning is conducted in public. Evidence of this is seen in the foodservice industry trade press which routinely reports the test-marketing of new products by large chains, customer evaluations of new products, and so on. Meal planning for public schools and public institutions may even become the subject of public debate, with contributions from a number of constituencies incorporated into the resulting menu program.

In smaller foodservice operations, and even in a number of larger ones, the participative process for menu planning is not firmly established. Often the perspective of the persons responsible for planning the menu is too narrow. For example, the menu program of a small restaurant may be planned by a chef who is an accomplished craftsperson but who does not clearly understand the importance of a market orientation or the implications of the menu for facilities or service. Or such operations may use the services of graphic artists who fail to understand that the printed menu—however attractive—may imply totally unacceptable production or service procedures. Or the menu may reflect the personal tastes of owners or managers which may differ radically from those of the operation's legitimate market or may even offend that market's sense of values.

Institutional menu programs, often referred to as *meal programs* or *meal plans* because the menu changes each day for each meal, are sometimes planned by individuals who emphasize nutrition or cost effectiveness at the expense of food acceptability. Menu-planning consultants who do not work closely with the architects planning an institutional kitchen may structure a menu program that cannot be produced effectively when the facility is finally completed. Such a situation can occur if product availability, prices, or the makeup of the market change in the time intervening between planning and completion of the facility.

Even organizations with broad-based and participative menu-planning practices may jeopardize the soundness of their program if they fail to keep menu planning ongoing and current. In a number of instances, companies with basically sound procedures have introduced new menu programs that were already obsolete because of price movements or shifts in market tastes.

One particularly restricting view of menu planning considers the menu program as a blueprint for other organizational functions like staffing, purchasing, and so on. The menu-as-blueprint idea is dangerously static because a menu developed from this rigid viewpoint probably would not be based on many of the dynamic factors needed for success. When menu planning is seen as a blueprint, the operation may not be flexible enough to respond to changing conditions.

Fortunately, the trend in the foodservice industry is toward menu-planning practices that can and do respond to change. The more widespread use of computers for menu planning has encouraged this development. A computer can perform all the operations necessary for good menu planning much more frequently and faster than a person can.

In deciding what salad to offer as one day's luncheon special, for example, a manager might successfully address all the factors necessary to make a reasoned judgment. He or she may gather current information on guest preferences, availability of produce, costs, offerings by competitors, and so on. However, the same manager would have great difficulty in applying such analysis to two-dozen menu items. Once a computer is programmed—once its tasks are defined and it is given the necessary information and instruction—it can perform the same analysis in a moment for any number of items, any number of times.

In addition to planning the menu program, a computer can produce the information and materials needed to adapt the operation's purchasing, supply, production, and service systems to modifications in the menu plan. Currently, preparing such materials is a laborious but necessary process. Consider what would happen if an operation's other systems were unaware of menu modifications such as what salad special had been scheduled: the purchasing department would not know what to buy and the production department would not know what to make. Even such simple menu modifications demand the speedy flow of information through the operation that computers can efficiently provide.

MENU-PLANNING CONCEPTS

Developing a dynamic and successful menu program is a complex task; it involves much more than following any set of "cookbook" rules. Rather, its development requires judgments based on information from external and internal sources.

Menu planners must consider the objectives of menu planning in developing their operations' menu program. They must also consider the effect of the menu program on the other systems of the operation, as well as the limits imposed on the menu program by these other systems. Additionally, they must weigh the implications of the legal limitations— truth-in-menu, food safety laws, and so on—on the menu. The following three sections of this chapter will thus cover the objectives of menu planning, its interactions with other systems in the organization, and the legal limitations imposed on it.

Specific Objectives of Menu Planning   The menu-planning system is directed toward achieving specific objectives, which can be summarized as follows:

1. *To select food items that please the customer, guest, or client and that are either profitable (for a commercial operation) or affordable (for a noncommercial one)*   The primary aim of menu planning is to create a menu program by choosing and organizing desirable food offerings while at the same time staying within the operation's budget and meeting its financial objectives.

2. *To establish standards on which other of the operation's activities can be based*   Besides identifying the foods to be offered, menu planning determines the portions to be served, the ingredients to be purchased, and the quantity and quality standards on which food production is based. Through constant appraisal of these standards, menu planning makes possible the ongoing improvement of the operation.

3. *To contribute to the operation's market image*   The menu-planning and service systems share this objective, as the two together largely create an operation's market image. Both the menu program and the service style (and accoutrements) define the operation in patrons' minds. The image that consumers hold of an operation is called the operation's *market image*. Planning the menu for a new restaurant in a highly competitive market may demand offering food items that create a strong market image and thus distinguish this restaurant from the competition. The result might be a Mexican restaurant or a restaurant that offers a distinctive signature item such as fried ice cream, broiled grapefruit, or American cheese pie. The menu then suggests a scenario for the customer's experience in the operation.

Planning the menu program for noncommercial operations may also involve the operation's image or identity as perceived by clients or guests. A boarding school might be distinguished from other institutions because of the variety and quality of its meals. A hospital might develop a reputation because it offers menu selections rather than a single-choice menu.

Interaction of Menu Planning with Other Systems   The menu-planning system affects and is affected by all the other systems of a foodservice operation; the limits imposed by the menu program on the other systems, and the constraints other systems in turn impose upon menu planning, must both be considered.

It follows then that the success of a menu program is the result of a series of compromises. For instance, the choice of a particular menu item might be a compromise between what the operation can easily produce and what it would *ideally* offer the consumer but cannot produce efficiently, or at all. The need of some dishes for tableside preparation might substantially reduce the productivity of the dining room staff. Fewer patrons could be served while service personnel prepared the item. Another dish—equally satisfactory in other respects—should replace the one requiring tableside preparation.

MARKETING AND MENU PLANNING   As defined in Chapter 4, menu planning is really a part of marketing. By using information gathered through market research, the menu program is based on a knowledge of the dominant characteristics, preferences, and expectations of customers, guests, or clients. Market research keeps menu planning abreast of consumers' changing wants and needs. For example, students' increasing interest in appealing vegetarian fare has prompted many college and university operations, as well as restaurants, to feature attractive meals of this sort.

In order to create the desired market image, the menu program must be consistent with the concept of the operation. If a restaurant has been conceived as an English pub because market research indicated that a significant number of people would patronize an English pub, then the menu program must at least be consistent with this concept. An English pub that served Chinese food might be too novel for the market to accept. A significant market may exist for one or the other, but probably not for both as part of the same operation. It is not necessary for the operation to offer unfamiliar English dishes such as bubble and squeak or finnan haddie, but it is necessary to offer items that do not confuse the patron's image of the restaurant.

WORK AND MENU PLANNING
The design of an operation's existing equipment and work system can influence the scope of the menu program. Items selected during menu planning usually must be produced or at least finished by the operation. The operation may not have the equipment necessary for certain items. For example, many school foodservice facilities do not have deep fryers and therefore cannot offer french fries. It is more common, however, to find that it is not viable for an operation to produce a particular combination of items because these items will overload pieces of equipment or work stations. For example, even if a school foodservice facility has two deep fryers it still may not offer fish and chips because two deep fryers cannot produce a large enough quantity of both items fast enough.

Menu planning, in turn, influences the design of the kitchen as well as the choice and purchase of kitchen equipment (including waste-disposal and ware-washing units). A kitchen cannot be successfully planned without some knowledge of what foods will be produced in it. It is one thing to say that a kitchen must produce pleasing meals for nine-year-old middle-class children, and quite another thing to say that a kitchen must produce a particular group of menu items including hamburgers, hot dogs, spaghetti, and chicken pot pies because they are pleasing to nine-year-olds. The second, more specific, menu plan is an adequate basis for making design decisions and equipment specifications; the first is not.

PURCHASING AND MENU PLANNING
The particular marketplace wherein the operation purchases raw ingredients may provide opportunities for, or place limitations on, menu planning. Opportunities might include abundant local fresh produce, regional specialties, skilled local bakers, or cooperative farmers. Limitations could be a short growing season, unavailability of certain products, locally high prices, or consistent spoilage and poor quality of produce shipped into the area, all of which can limit the menu program.

SUPPLY AND MENU PLANNING
The capacity of the supply system to store and preserve food items also affects and is affected by menu planning. Obviously, the menu planner

must bear in mind how well the supply system can support a particular menu program. If an operation plans to serve fresh lobster and other shellfish that must be kept alive until cooked, large saltwater holding tanks must be a part of supply facilities. If an operation has only a small deep freezer and hasn't either the space or the funds to build a new one, it may not be possible to buy and store a large enough quantity of expensive cuts of meat to economically justify their presence on the menu.

PRODUCTION AND
MENU PLANNING

The skills and availability of qualified production personnel, particularly cooks, may limit the extent and quality of the menu program. Fortunately, more and more products are being purchased with some of the labor involvement supplied by the manufacturer. Items that once involved talents beyond those of the operation's production workers or time that could not be economically justified may now be included in the menu program. A good example of such purchased labor is the widespread availability of quality baked goods at operations that do not themselves produce these goods—which take both time and skill to prepare.

The production system may also provide opportunities for developing a better menu program. The skills of the persons working in the operation should be assessed before the menu is planned. Quite possibly the vegetable cook can also make a great apple pie.

SERVICE AND
MENU PLANNING

As defined in Chapter 4, the service system is also a part of the marketing system, and as such is closely linked to menu planning. Unfortunately, the critical relationship between the menu program and the service system is frequently overlooked. For instance, a take-out restaurant may attempt to offer an item on its menu for which there is no satisfactory packaging (packaging is part of service). Similarly, a foodservice contractor may include menu items in its meal plan that cannot be transported easily and safely to the facility where they will be served. Or a traditional restaurant may offer items that are so time-consuming to eat— steamed crabs, for example—that the overall productivity of the dining room staff diminishes.

As the wages of service workers rise because of increases in the minimum wage and reduced tip credit (the amount of the minimum wage considered to be contributed by tips), more attention must be paid to the effect of the menu program on productivity in the dining room. Some operations find that they can no longer afford to offer dessert because the added sales do not compensate the operation enough to offset the increased time the service staff must spend with the patron.

Some menu items that are excellent in every other respect cannot be served economically. For instance, take the example of the complete dinner menu. While the food cost of the appetizer, soup, side dishes, and dessert included in the complete dinner may be small, these additional courses may be impossible to serve economically if 15 to 20 trips to the kitchen are needed to serve each party ordering such a dinner.

The service system can offer opportunities to menu planning as well as impose limits on it. In the proper circumstances, short tableside preparation can add immeasurably to the appeal of the menu without adding significantly to the amount of time service personnel must spend with the customer or guest.

BUSINESS AND MENU PLANNING
The business system is affected by menu planning in that the menu program helps to determine the sales, profits, and return on investment that can be expected. Menu planning also provides a basis for the allocation or budgeting of resources. Aside from the profit motive, menu planning and business are also closely linked in noncommercial operations. Success of the menu program is seen as meeting an acceptable cost per meal that is within budget limitations. Obviously, what may be included in the menu program of both commercial and noncommercial operations is always limited by financial and budget standards.

Limits on Menu Planning

Besides considering the limits imposed by interactions with other systems, the menu planner must be aware of the limits imposed on the development of the menu program by truth-in-menu requirements, the necessity of adequate food safety, nutritional requirements, and proper product identity.

Truth-in-menu requirements   The use of a printed menu, signboard, or meal program that is misleading or not truthful can invite litigation and punitive fines. Even though customers, guests, and clients may reject beef liver when it is called "beef liver," it cannot be called "calf's liver" in order to promote it. Enticing merchandising language should be used in menu item descriptions only if such language conveys an accurate representation of the appeal of these items, such as garden green peas, baby Belgian carrots, milk-fed veal, bay scallops, imported ham, and homemade pie. Likewise, if an operation represents itself as offering kosher food, that food must meet the requirements to be called "kosher."

Truth-in-menu regulations apply to claims of size as well as quality. An operation that represents itself as serving 200 gram (7 ounce) hamburgers or a foot-long hot dog must deliver a finished product that meets those standards. If the standard is based on the size before cooking, it should be stated on the printed menu. Failure to deliver any product as claimed is fraud.

Food safety   In some operations the difficulty in complying with stringent applications of food handling and food hygiene regulations may limit the menu program. Some local regulations specify that hollandaise sauce must be made no earlier than one hour before serving. If an operation cannot comply with this regulation, hollandaise should not be included in the menu program. No production station should be so overburdened that food products fall into the 4.4–60°C (40–140°F) temperature range, which promotes the growth of micro-organisms. Shellfish should not be included in the menu if there is no reliable, approved source of them.

Nutritional requirements   Noncommercial foodservice operations may be operating under regulations that mandate nutritional values for foods. Examples of such operations are the school lunch program, health care facilities, and the foodservice facilities of penal institutions. Obviously, menu planning must comply with such regulations.

Product identity   In some localities, it is necessary to post signs publicly or to note on the printed menu that the operation uses margarine and/or nondairy creamers. Inasmuch as this information may be prejudicial to the operation's image, the inclusion of such items in the menu program must be carefully considered.

CONSUMER PROFILE FOR MENU PLANNING

In addition to information about the objectives, interactions, and legal limitations of menu planning, the menu planner must have an accurate consumer analysis based on market research which thoroughly investigates the operation's target market: who they are, what food they like, and why and how often they will patronize an operation. Good market research is essential to good menu planning.

The menu planner needs market research information focused on patrons' personal characteristics and socio-economic level. Personal characteristics that have impact on the menu program include the age, sex, activity level, and physical condition of consumers. For example, the size of acceptable portions is related to all of these characteristics. The socio-economic level of consumers includes their educational background, economic status (not necessarily related to the sum of money immediately available to spend), birthplace, occupation, and religion, all of which should be considered by the menu planner. Various surveys have indicated that eating habits can be related to any of these factors. The menu planner must know the market in order to know what to offer it.

After identifying the consumers who make up the target market, the menu planner can identify their wants and desires that relate to eating away from home. Such an investigation includes finding out how often consumers would be likely to visit the operation, what food items they prefer, and what their motives are for eating out in general. All of these things can contribute significantly to shaping the menu program.

Frequency of Use   Knowledge of how often consumers are likely to eat in an operation greatly affects the diversity of the menu. A menu program that must serve the continuing client—hospital patients, for example—must offer a wide variety of menu items. On the other hand, a restaurant that offers a single main course item can be quite successful, provided no one has to eat there every night. Thus, menu variety, as such, is not always an imperative. The need for variety depends on how often a patron is likely to visit the operation as well as how quickly particular menu items become so boring that the consumer will seek variety elsewhere.

Consider, for example, two very different operations having similar menu programs: a specialty restaurant that has only six main courses, and a boarding school that has only six different dinners per month. The second menu program is obviously flawed because it fails to consider how many times its particular patrons would be willing to eat the same six main courses. On the other hand, since the patron of the specialty restaurant is likely to choose to be an infrequent visitor, its menu program of only six main courses would probably be successful.

Food Preferences   As discussed in Chapter 4 in the "Product Analysis" section of market research activities, examination of patrons' food preferences focuses on what consumers think is attractive or tasty, what they have learned to like or dislike, and how venturesome or sophisticated they are in taste. All together this information tells the menu planner what the consumer prefers to eat.

Misconceptions about food preferences are common. For example, there is an abundance of literature on menu planning that suggests that certain foods should be served together, like cheese with noodle dishes, or that certain foods should have particular garnishes, like mint jelly with lamb. Such judgments may or may not be valid. A menu program that incorporates these or similar judgments as absolutes would be totally unacceptable in a variety of circumstances. People from many European countries do not eat mint jelly with lamb. Oriental people tend not to like cheese. On the other hand, these strictures on taste preferences might be entirely appropriate for a particular group of consumers; it is important simply to recognize that such preferences are not universals.

Good market research tells the menu planner what foods potential patrons prefer. In a surprising number of instances, it can result in a menu offering foods that the menu planner would not have chosen, but which are appealing to the target market. Food that appeals to preschool children, for example, might include peanut butter and jelly sandwiches —an item that the menu planner might not choose to eat.

Motivation   The menu planner must investigate both why consumers eat out in general and why they come (or will come) to the particular operation. A given individual's reasons for eating may vary from one occasion to another. At one moment a person may be motivated by hunger and thus value the opportunity for quick nourishment. At another moment, the same consumer may want excitement and a change of mood and would therefore value only an exotic meal experience that includes venturesome foods. Of course, what is venturesome for one consumer may be ordinary for another: Chinese food, for example, may be very novel to some people, but quite commonplace to others. Thus the menu planner must correlate information about consumers' motives with an understanding of who these consumers are in terms of their personal characteristics and socio-economic level.

Restaurant customers, lodging guests, and noncommercial foodservice clients all may be eating away from home for a variety of reasons. These various motives fall into six major categories: hunger, mood change, social needs, habit, reassurance, and role expectations. Of course, consumers may be prompted to eat by any combination of these motives.

Hunger   Certainly hunger by itself or combined with other factors is a most common motive. The dominance of this motive in a market would suggest that the menu program provide quickly served, ample portions of popular and easy-to-eat foods.

Mood change   Consumers motivated by the desire for a mood change may conceive of the meal as a form of entertainment or an escape from the ordinariness of the daily routine.

Social needs   Often, one reason for eating in a restaurant is the desire to associate with others. The menu programs for weddings, special celebrations, or business meetings must be planned with the role of the event in mind. Groups of people, even small groups, do not have the same expectations, preferences, or even eating behavior as do the same individuals when eating alone. The menu program must reflect these differences.

Habit   Habit is a very strong motive for eating, perhaps even stronger than hunger. At noon many people are motivated to eat simply because it is "time for lunch," not because they really feel hungry. In traveling familiar routes, people may have routine stops for snacks. They bring a set of expectations to these operations as to what constitutes an appropriate lunch or snack. The menu program should not frustrate such expectations. The person who for twenty years has stopped for a roll and coffee before entering a commuter train expects the station snack bar to continue to provide these items.

Reassurance   Sometimes people eat to forget personal troubles, to reward themselves, to assert their individuality or identity, or to calm their emotions. A foodservice operation that becomes the focus for such expectations must necessarily provide a menu program that is consistent with them. For the displaced New Yorker in Paris, the restaurant in an American-owned hotel may offer hamburgers and hot dogs to reduce the traveler's homesickness. For similar reasons, a health care facility might include ice cream frequently in its menu program.

Role expectations   People eating out often assume a role, consciously or unconsciously, which implies certain expectations about the meal. For example, people traveling on business generally act and eat as they think people traveling on business *should* act and eat. A foodservice operation that attracts these persons must be aware of the patron's role playing, and must satisfy the expectations about food and drink that go along with it. Don't business travelers always have big steaks? Don't people celebrating always have champagne? They might—if they have the tastes and preferences that match the role they are fulfilling.

Assessing the impact of consumers' role expectations requires the menu planner to identify the model on which the role is based. Commonly used models are movie and fiction portrayals, business superiors, "jet-setters," and society people. The implications for menu planning are clear: the menu must be geared to satisfying the expectations that accompany whatever role consumers wish to play.

ACTIVITIES OF MENU PLANNING

The activities of menu planning are really steps in the ongoing process of planning, reevaluating, and updating the menu. The first activity of menu planning consists of selecting a group of menu items, thus establishing a repertory of menu offerings from which to plan daily menus. The menu planner then must organize the menu, possibly around the meal opportunities afforded at customary meal times, or according to a strict course structure. Once organized, these menu items must be costed and, in commercial operations, priced. Exhibit 6.1 diagrams the process of planning the menu step-by-step. The operation then prints (or reprints) its menu, and prepares related materials such as standardized recipes which convey the needs of the menu program to those other systems in the operation that are responsible for buying and producing it.

Selecting Menu Items   Menus are planned by elimination. In selecting menu items, every menu planner is confronted theoretically with an unlimited number of foods that could be offered to consumers. Books of menu items, accompanied by brief descriptions, are published for the specific use of menu planners. Some of these books contain more than 16,000 menu items. In a single year, the 14 or 15 national magazines that have a food orientation publish some 7,000 recipes. While not every one of these menu items is unique, such combined sources still offer an enormous number of choices.

Of course, the menu planner cannot really consider all recipes published in the foodservice industry. The overwhelming majority of these recipes will be unacceptable to a particular operation. The planner usually begins with a tentative list of menu offerings already focused on consumer preferences and on the operation's own capacities, which can

EXHIBIT 6.1   Menu Planning Step-By-Step

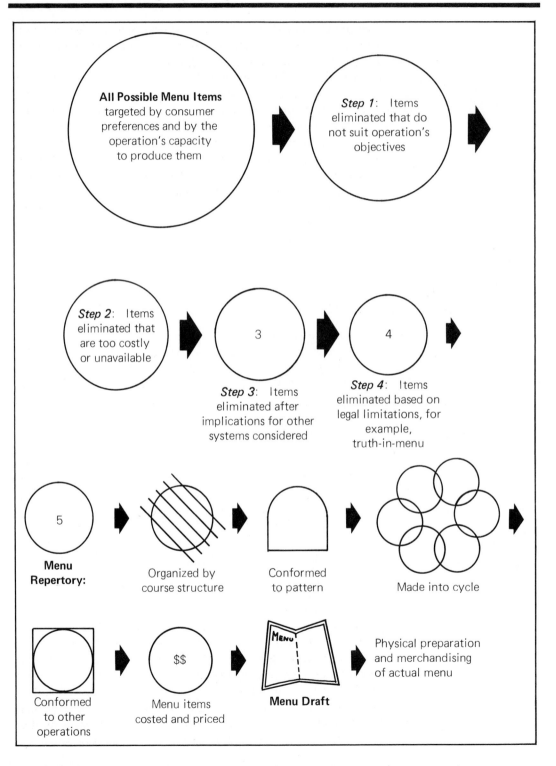

be pared down or added to. The process of planning specific menus consists mainly of applying definite criteria to this given field of possibilities and then systematically eliminating items.

Items from this field of possibilities may be eliminated because they do not satisfy the operation's overall objectives: for example, if they are incompatible with the operation's desired market image. Tentative menu offerings may be eliminated because they are too costly, or because their ingredients are not regularly available. Menu planners must consider items in light of their implications for the operation's other systems as well. For example, if production hasn't the equipment or skilled personnel needed to prepare a particular item, then the item must be dropped from the menu. Or, if certain foods require tableside preparation, then these items may be eliminated because they place too great a burden on the service system.

This final field of possibilities becomes the operation's *menu repertory,* the catalog of food items it can produce and wants to produce. With a menu repertory of several hundred chosen items, the menu planner avoids the problem of constantly introducing new items. When daily menus are planned, only the items in the repertory are considered. The person in charge of planning menus for the military service of the United States must deal with a repertory of several thousand items for which they have standardized recipes. Exhibit 6.2 presents an example of part of a repertory. Instead of creating menus from among the thousands of dishes in classical cuisine, items for particular menus are chosen from a series of basic preparations.

Organizing the Menu

Once the menu repertory has been decided upon, the menu planner must consider how to organize this group of acceptable menu offerings. At this point, certain conventions for organizing menus can be useful, at least as a starting point for planning. Such conventions include organizing the menu around conventional meal times, or according to standard course structure, set menu patterns, menu cycles, and so on. None of these conventions should be adhered to blindly, however, as they may not apply to a particular operation. The following sections describe these different conventions for organizing menus.

MEAL OPPORTUNITIES

If the menu planner chooses to organize the menu around conventional meal times, he or she is taking advantage of what the industry refers to as *meal opportunities.* A menu planner who relies on meal opportunities presupposes that the time of day and hours the operation is open dictate the nature, quantity, and type of food offerings that can be included in the menu program. In other words, an operation that is open at 7 A.M. must offer a breakfast menu, while one that is open at 11 P.M. must offer a late dinner menu.

EXHIBIT 6.2   A Partial "Gourmet" Repertory for Menu Planning

The preparations described at the left of the page are methods or styles of preparing the foods indicated above the narrow columns. Just as another operation might prepare "southern style" chicken and "southern style" pork chops, which would resemble each other because of common ingredients and cooking method, this operation will produce Bercy-style eggs, Bercy-style fish, and Bercy-style chicken which would have common preparations.

	Eggs	Fish	Mollusks, Crustaceans	Fowl	Beef	Veal	Lamb	Pork	Game	Variety Meats
Anglaise Boiled root vegetables, turned in regular shapes, with a simple butter or compound butter sauce.		X		X		X				X
Bercy Shallots moistened with white wine and reduced, finished with butter and parsley or marrow.	X	X	X	X	X	X	X			X
Chasseur Sliced or chopped mushrooms, coarsely chopped tomatoes and chopped parsley simmered in a demiglace sauce.	X	X	X	X	X	X	X		X	X
Lyonnaise Braised onions, oven-cooked peeled potatoes basted with brown stock, and demiglace sauce reduced with white wine and chopped onions, and seasoned with vinegar.	X	X	X		X	X		X	X	
Mirabeau Anchovy fillets, pitted olives, blanched tarragon leaves. Anchovy butter.	X	X	X	X	X	X	X	X	X	X

Using meal opportunities as the basis for menu organization can be both useful and dangerous. It is useful if the menu planner considers all conventional meal times for potential marketing and service opportunities, but dangerous if he or she presumes that certain items must be offered at certain times of the day and cannot be sold at any other time. Such a presumption is patently untrue; there are operations that sell an abundance of lamb chops at 7 A.M. and others that sell mountains of pancakes at 11 P.M. Certainly a conventional breakfast menu often satisfies the consumer's expectations, but there is no such thing as a *prescriptive* breakfast menu. In practice, blindly accepting this convention leads to "me-too" menus, while questioning it may lead to menus that offer the operation true consumer orientation and genuine identity. The value of analyzing what foods are offered at conventional meal times is not in the rigidity it might imply but in the flexibility it can provide the menu planner who looks at all opportunities for food sales or patron service. A summary of conventionally scheduled meals and the consumer needs they satisfy appears in Exhibit 6.3.

COURSE STRUCTURE | Until the mid-twentieth century, course structure had an important place in menu planning. The meal was considered to be a composition of different but related dishes served at different times. These dishes were called courses. A meal of 8, 10, 12, or more courses usually began with a first course that was light in fat content, texture, and taste, moved on to a climactic main course, and then diminished in heaviness to a dessert course, with various other courses in between. Viewed as a whole, the meal made an esthetic statement. These statements could be based on qualities quite apart from food qualities per se. For instance, a dinner at a private party might consist of courses made up entirely of pink food items or courses that reflect aspects of the host's life.

The items acceptable for each successive course are clearly defined. In French, the language universally used for this type of elaborate menu planning, the courses are, in order of serving: *hors-d'oeuvre froid* and *hors-d'oeuvre chaud,* cold and hot appetizers, like oysters or quiche, that whet the appetite; *potage,* soup, which can be clear or thick; *entrée volante,* small, often spicy, hot, side dishes, like curried sweet breads, that also stimulate the appetite; *poisson,* fish, though in lunch meals fish is often replaced by eggs; *relevé,* a meat dish, usually a large joint like prime rib, never served with an elaborate sauce but often served with a vegetable; *entrée chaude* and *entrée froide,* a hot sauce dish and a cold sauce dish, both heartier than the *entrée volante; rôti,* a cut of roast, game, or poultry, which contrasts with the *relevé; salade,* salad; *légume,* a vegetable; *entremets chaud* and *entremets froid,* a hot sweet dish and a cold sweet dish; *fromage,* cheese; and *pâtisserie,* pastry.

The problem is, what does the modern menu planner do with these 15 courses? Classicists among menu planners still structure the menu

EXHIBIT 6.3   Meal Opportunities

Type of Meal	Time of Day	Target Market
Early Breakfast	Before 7 A.M.	Consumers include night shift workers, service industry workers going to work, and persons on their way home. Most successful offerings, in addition to conventional breakfasts, are small steaks, chops, fish, and spicy sandwiches.
Regular Breakfast	7 to 10 A.M.	Clientele includes travelers, tourists, and persons on the way to work. Offerings may consist of anything from baked goods and beverages to multi-course meals that include fish, meat, vegetables, and desserts.
Morning Coffee Break	10 to 11 A.M.	Consumers are industrial workers, office workers, and professionals seeking light refreshment. Sales tend toward simple baked goods, but sausage and cheese would be possibilities.
Brunch	10 A.M. to noon	Patrons are travelers, tourists, and retired persons. Offerings tend to be light but interesting. They may include tropical fruits, fancy crepes, and small entree items (chicken a la king).
Elevenses	11 A.M. to noon	A formal meal in some European countries, elevenses has become increasingly important with flexible work scheduling. Often customers are those people who start work at 7 A.M. and those who wish to avoid lunch crowds. Offerings are varied, ranging from frankfurters and beer to frozen yogurt and fresh fruit.
Lunch	Noon to 2 P.M.	This is the second most important meal for most people. Offerings can vary from a slice of pizza to an eight-course meal. Anything goes, but portions tend to be smaller and the food less fatty and more spicy than are dinner items.
Midday Dinner	Noon to 2 P.M.	This is the most important substantial meal in some regions of the country (South, South-east, and parts of the Midwest, especially in rural areas) for people who then have supper at 5 P.M. It is characterized by large portions, good fat content, and multiple courses.
Afternoon Coffee Break	2:30 to 4 P.M.	Consumers are the same groups as for the morning coffee break. The baked products sold tend to be more elaborate and richer than those sold at morning coffee break.
Tea	4 to 5:30 P.M.	This interval is popular with persons who have lunched early or who will dine late. In addition to tea or other beverages, light sandwiches, cakes, hot breads, and small entree dishes such as meat turnovers are among the possible offerings.

Type of Meal	Time of Day	Target Market
Early Dinner	5 to 6 P.M.	Consumers tend to be older. Emphasis in meal offerings is on lower-priced items, low flavor profile, high eye appeal, and small portions.
Cocktails	5 to 7 P.M.	Consumers may be people who have already returned home, or people who have a considerable distance to travel and wish to avoid crowded transportation, all of whom will eat a substantial meal sometime later; or unmarried people for whom this is one of four or five small meals. Offerings tend to be spicy finger foods.
Supper	5 to 7 P.M.	This is the second most important meal of the day for people who have had their dinner at the noon hour. Food items tend to soup, one-dish meals, and cold boards of delicatessen items and cheese.
Dinner	6 to 8:30 P.M.	For most people, this is the substantial meal of the day. Expectation is to eat larger portions, more courses, more fatty foods, and to take longer in eating.
Late Dinner	8:30 to 10 P.M.	Consumers tend to be those with unusual work hours, tourists and travelers, and people influenced by continental ways. Items sold in commercial operations are usually more expensive on the average than regular dinner items. Wine is frequently consumed; and first courses are more substantial than at dinner.
Late Supper	10 P.M. to 1 A.M.	Consumers tend to be people who have eaten dinner, passed the evening at some entertainment, and are having their last food of the day. Attractive, light spicy items (such as Welsh rarebit), exotic desserts, crepes, hamburgers, and ice-cream desserts are successfully offered.
Midnight Snack	Midnight to 5 A.M.	Clientele may be the same type of consumer as the supper consumer but tends to include persons having their last of five snacks of the day, people in need of a large quantity of food (spaghetti and meatballs, pizza), and persons who miss breakfast in the morning but who like conventional breakfast foods such as ham and eggs.

around these courses, although often they include only 5 or 6. Banquet menus, as well, might consist of an appetizer, soup, fish, main dish, dessert, and cheese. An even more simplified version of this menu would include an appetizer, soup or fish, a main dish, and dessert. Cafeterias often offer at least a few representative items from each course. Restaurants usually offer items representing all of the courses so that the customer can fashion an esthetically satisfactory composition.

If each course is paid for individually, the meal is *a la carte*. The opposite of an a la carte menu is a *table d'hôte* menu, which offers a complete dinner or a group of complete dinners. Prices may vary among the dinners or the table d'hôte menu may also be *prix fixe*. A restaurant with a prix fixe menu offers a choice for most courses, but the patron pays a predetermined price for the entire meal regardless of the particular items chosen. If an operation has a menu that offers a group of dinners with a choice of appetizer, vegetable, and perhaps dessert that vary in price according to the main course, the meal is modified a la carte or combination. Though many foodservice operations use a very simplified version of the classically structured menu, it is unlikely a patron would find an establishment that classified tomato juice in the true classic sense as an *hors-d'oeuvre froid.*

For a variety of reasons, the menus of many, if not most, foodservice operations now depart substantially from this elaborate course structure. Many consumers do not want, or cannot afford, a seven-course meal. Most operations find the cost of producing the meal and absorbing the leftovers excessive. For many people, eating patterns have become disrupted and regular meals have given way to a series of snacks. Chefs having the culinary skills necessary to create these full-course meals may not be available or affordable. Finally, and perhaps most importantly, the esthetic values that this rigid course structure represents are no longer generally accepted in a dynamic, individualistic society.

Regrettably, there are some menu planners who see this sort of course structure as an imperative rather than an option. They stretch the menu program out of shape to provide soups that the operation cannot produce effectively or fish courses that languish in refrigerators. Today, patrons often want a main course with a salad or potato, or even a single food item. Even in restaurants with considerably more offerings, what amounts to a limited menu has been created by patrons who skip soup and appetizers (and perhaps desserts) and concentrate their purchases on three or four of the twenty entrees listed on the menu.

There are still some foodservice operations that find this course structure, in its most elaborate form, well accepted. The few dozen major cruise ships of a number of nationalities still offer classic menus. Exhibit 6.4 offers an example of a single day's selection from a dinner menu that might be offered aboard a cruise ship.

EXHIBIT 6.4 Specimen Classic Menu Based on "Modernized" Course Structure

Dinner

Appetizers: Table Celery · Ripe Olives · Kosher Pickle Sticks · Pickled English Walnuts · Marinated Fresh Brook Trout · Vita Herring Tidbits with Onion Rings · California Fruit Cocktail au Cognac · Cervelat Sausage · Yami Yogurt · Baja Shrimp Cocktail · Celery Victor Hugo · Sliced Egg Ravigote · Calf's Brains Vinaigrette · Antipasto Veronese · Chaudfroid of Partridge

Soups: Cream of Tomato Americaine · Consomme Risi Bisi · Chilled Jellied Essence of Tomato · Cream Vichyssoise Glacee

Fish: Broiled Swordfish Steak, Sauce Bearnaise, Fines Herbes Potatoes · Frog Legs Saute Provencale, Pearl Potatoes

Pasta: Macaroni au Gratin Albufera en Casserole

Grill: Roast Prime Ribs of Kansas Steer Beef au Jus, Creamed Fresh Horseradish

Entrees: Roast Saddle of Spring Lamb Edna May, Grilled Tomato, Squash, Currant Jelly · Lau Lau of Chicken Hawaiian, Princess Liliuokalani · Minced Veal Kidney Saute, Mushroom au Sherry · Adobo y Cerdo (Filipino Pork Stew) en Casserole ·

Vegetables: Buttered String Beans · Baked Squash · Creamed Small Onions · Steamed Rice

Potatoes: Baked Idaho · Boulangere · Princess · Fines Herbes

Cold Buffet: Assorted Cold Cuts, Italian Salami, Potato Salad · Roast Gosling, Green Apple Sauce, Celery Salad · Rack of Spring Lamb, Mint Jelly, Crabapple · Delice of Smoked Turkey, Spiced Peach, Cranberry Sauce

Salads: Heart of Lettuce · Sliced Tomato · Mignonnette · Mixed Green · French · Thousand Island · Roquefort · Low Calorie Dressings

Desserts: Devil's Food Cake · French Apple Slice · Peppermint Stick Ice Cream · Hot Fudge Sundae · Melba Jello · Small Cakes · Orange Sherbet

Cheese: Old English · Stilton in Wine · Teleme · Imported Swiss

Beverages: Coffee · Milk · Cocoa · Iced Tea or Coffee · Green or Orange Pekoe Tea · Cafe Espresso · Metrecal: Chocolate, Vanilla, or Butterscotch

After Dinner Mints   Fresh Fruit in Season

MENU PATTERNS   The idea of organizing the menu around a pattern is a useful extension of the classic course structure. A menu pattern is a framework around which each meal is planned. The pattern or framework for a group of meals might be the inclusion of certain amounts of certain food groups. As a very simplified example, each menu might be required to include a vegetable, meat, and potato. Most menu patterns have a functional basis. Many are based on nutritional aspects of food and are aimed at creating a framework for developing well-balanced meals.

In federally funded meal programs, specific foods must be included if the operation, usually a school, is to receive subsidies. The meal pattern for menu development is thus based on these items. The menu planner makes sure that at least one food that meets each of the following requirements is included in every lunch menu: .25 liters (one-half pint) whole milk; 50 grams (1.75 ounces) of meat or the protein equivalent, 200 grams (7 ounces) of vegetable or fruit or combination of the two; a slice of whole grain or enriched bread or the equivalent; and 10 milliliters (2 teaspoons) of butter or fortified margarine.

A health care institution or boarding school might want to use this same idea to ensure that clients receive the Recommended Dietary Allowances (RDA) of protein, calories, fats, vitamins, and minerals. Such an organization would probably establish a food-group pattern as a nutritional basis for planning the menu. Four major food groups, with appropriate servings, are presented in Exhibit 6.5. Using this pattern, an actual menu for the day can be constructed as shown on Exhibit 6.6.

It should be obvious that thousands of different menus could meet the requirements of the menu pattern. It is essentially a planning tool. But the concept of a menu pattern can be abused, particularly if patterns are used that have no functional basis. Someone at sometime may have decided that an operation's menu *always* should offer three juices, two soups, four main dishes, two cold plates, and five desserts. Often, it is time to see if that *always* should be reevaluated.

MENU CYCLES   For many operations, the menu program once planned is changed only occasionally. Many commercial restaurants do not change their menu programs frequently unless they expect that regular customers will find the menu "stale." Some of the most famous and successful restaurants in the United States have had virtually the same menu for years. Perhaps some slight flexibility is built into the menu by having an item or two change daily, but everything else remains constant. If the market will permit it, it is an advantage for the operation to have a standard menu program. Production, purchasing, supply, service, and management are all made simpler and more efficient. Expensive continental restaurants, ethnic restaurants, and limited-menu restaurants typically have menus that do not change greatly.

However, the American plan hotel with continuing guests, the non-commercial foodservice operation with continuing clients, and the commercial restaurant with regular customers cannot simply develop a single successful menu, produce that menu, and repeat it day after day. The consumer expects variety. If it is not provided, commercial guests and customers will limit their patronage, and noncommercial clients will complain.

Many operations find it necessary to limit the problems that constant changes in the menu program would cause. Consider the difficulties of constantly writing new specifications for purchasing items; training staff to prepare and serve new menu items; changing control standards. Faced with these problems, foodservice operations develop menu programs that allow menus to be repeated periodically. A set of menus and their accompanying specifications, production orders, training instructions, service instructions, and control forms are produced. Different menus are used daily, but the program as a whole does not change. This way of varying menus is called "menu cycling." The term "cycle" is misleading, however, since not all menu programs developed on this premise repeat in a regular, predictable fashion. The menus described below include a true cyclical menu and its variations.

True cyclical menu   A true menu cycle is a set of daily menus that repeat in a regular, predictable way. The number of menus in the set depends on the manager's estimate of how soon a menu can be repeated without the customer, guest, or client finding the menu program repetitious. For example, a health care facility serving the continuing client three meals a day for long periods of time may choose a 21-day cycle. The menu that is offered on the first day of the month will not be offered again until the 22nd day of the month, when the cycle starts over again. This facility thus must deal with 21 menus and related menu-program materials. On the other hand, a resort hotel that has an average guest stay of four days may use a seven-day cycle with some assurance that only a small percentage of the guests will stay long enough to encounter the same menu twice.

Jump cyclical menu   A jump cyclical menu offers menus that recur in a regular order but not on the same day of the week because the number of menus used is *not* a multiple of seven (the number of days in a week). Instead of using a 21-day cycle, which repeats every three weeks on the same weekdays, an operation would use a 22-day cycle, which does not. This method complicates the pattern as perceived by the consumer and limits the possibility of the consumer seeing that there is a cycle. Every third Monday is not corned beef and cabbage day.

Split cyclical menu   While consumers want variety, they do not necessarily want it if it means frequently giving up their favorite foods. Apple pie is a favorite dessert; chicken noodle soup is a favorite soup. Should they not be served more than once every 21 days? If the opera-

EXHIBIT 6.5   Functional Basis (Nutritional Requirements) of a Menu Pattern

Milk Group:

Persons over 20 years—.5 liter (1 pint). Persons under 20 years—1 liter (1 quart).

Any form of milk counts toward the total—skim milk, buttermilk, reconstituted, dried, or evaporated milk. Cheese and ice cream can be substituted for part of the milk, based on the calcium equivalent for .25 liter (1 cup) whole milk.

These foods will supply the recommended .5 liter (2 cup) and 1 liter (4 cup) levels, using calcium equivalents and .25 liter (1 cup) whole milk.

.5 liter (2 cup) milk level:
.25 liter (1 cup) fluid whole milk
16.5 cu cm (1 cubic inch) of cheddar cheese
.125 liter (½ cup) ice cream
30 ml (2 tablespoons) dried milk (in cooked dishes)

1 liter (4 cup) milk level:
.25 liter (1 cup) fluid whole milk
33 cu cm (2 cubic inch) of cheddar cheese
.25 liter (1 cup) ice cream
60 ml (4 tablespoons) dried milk (in cooked dishes)

Vegetable-Fruit Group:

Plan a total of four or more servings.

Count as serving: .125 liter (½ cup) vegetable or fruit (100 grams or 3½ ounces), or the portion ordinarily served.

Any fresh, frozen, canned, or dehydrated fruit or vegetable can count toward the four servings, but the selection should include:

1 **Good** source of vitamin C or
2 **Fair** sources of vitamin C; and
1 **Good** source of vitamin A (every other day)

tion offers three different soups and three different desserts, the problem is compounded. Sixty-three soups and 63 desserts are needed for a three-week (21-day) menu cycle. Without a doubt, some of these soups and desserts are favored by consumers over others, and it is certainly no advantage to the operation to offer them only once every three weeks. Menu planners solve this problem by splitting the menu cycle and adopt-

Sources of vitamin C:

Good sources: grapefruit or grapefruit juice; orange or orange juice; cantaloupe; guava; mango; papaya; raw strawberries; broccoli; brussels sprouts; green pepper; sweet red pepper.

Fair sources: honeydew melon; lemon; tangerines; watermelon; asparagus tips; raw cabbage; mustard greens; potatoes and sweet potatoes cooked in the jacket; spinach; tomatoes or tomato juice; turnip greens.

Sources of vitamin A:

Dark green and deep yellow vegetables and a few fruits, namely: apricots, broccoli, cantaloupe, carrots, pumpkin, spinach, sweet potatoes, turnip greens and other dark green leaves, and winter squash.

Meat Group:

Two or more servings.

Count as a serving: 55–85 grams (2–3 ounces) lean meat, poultry, fish, or meat alternatives: 2 eggs; .25 liter (1 cup) cooked dry beans or peas.

Bread-Cereal Group:

Four or more servings.

Count any of these foods as a serving: 1 slice of bread; 28 grams (1 ounce) ready-to-eat cereal; or .25–.37 liter (½ to ¾ cup) instant cereal, cooked cereal, cornmeal, grits, macaroni, noodles, rice, or spaghetti.

Plus other foods such as butter, other fats, sugars—enough to round out meals.

A menu may use these requirements to build a menu program that is nutritionally sound but that also offers variety.

ing different cycles for different parts of the menu. Soups may be repeated on an eight-day cycle; desserts may be repeated on a ten-day cycle; potatoes may be repeated on a five-day cycle, and so on. A resort hotel may offer lobster or steak on a three-day cycle, while varying other parts of the menu, in order to ensure that at least once during the average guest stay of three days a guest has a special dinner.

EXHIBIT 6.6   Two Sample Menus Based on Meal Pattern to Supply Nutritional Needs

---

Breakfast

Orange juice	Strawberries
Oatmeal with milk	Bacon and eggs
Cinnamon toast	Biscuits
Milk or coffee	Milk or coffee

Lunch

Hard-cooked egg or peanut butter and jelly sandwich	Baked ham on seeded roll with lettuce and tomato
Celery sticks, banana	Asparagus in cheese sauce
Bread (in sandwich)	Bread (in sandwich)
Milk	Milk

Snack

Cookies	Pear
Fruit punch	Chocolate milk

Dinner

Fried chicken	Beef rib roast
Carrots (fresh)	Broccoli with butter sauce (frozen)
Mashed potato	Corn on the cob (fresh)
Bread (white enriched)	Dinner rolls
Apple pie	German chocolate cake
Milk or coffee	Milk or coffee

This Sample Daily Menu is Patterned on the Food Groups in Exhibit 6.5

Random menu   This kind of menu program uses the tools of a menu cycle but does not schedule meals in any particular order. A random menu may have 21 complete meals worked out, but schedules them without adherence to a cycle.

For example, if the 21 menus and related materials are identified by letters of the alphabet, the program for the first week in January might be J, D, A, P, T, L, I. For the second week in January, it might be E, P, G, L, R, R, B. In arriving at these schedules, the manager of a resort hotel might be considering the guests' background or age, or the season of the year. The manager of a catering concern might schedule just this pattern for a banquet room that seats 100 guests after consultation with the person making each night's arrangements on price and menu preference. Production demands, employee schedules, availability of food, and cost can also be factors that help to determine the order of menu offerings for a random menu.

BALANCED   In organizing the menu program, there is usually an attempt to balance
MENU OFFERINGS   individual menus according to taste and appearance. Thus the menu planner evaluates a menu program in progress to determine whether there are too many similar items and whether some items that would give greater variety to the menu should be added. A number of different qualities of food can serve as checkpoints for such an evaluation:

1. *Flavor:* sweet, salty, sour, spicy, bland, bitter, hot
2. *Color:* red, brown, white, green
3. *Texture:* crunchy, chewy, crisp, thick
4. *Kind of food:* protein, starchy, fatty
5. *Category of food:* veal, chicken, tomato
6. *Kind of sauce:* brown, Madeira, Mornay
7. *Shape:* balls, cubes, tiny particles, chunks
8. *Moisture:* juicy, dried
9. *Preparation:* stewed, braised, fried, raw, broiled
10. *Complexity:* sauced dishes, combinations, plain

From these considerations, the menu planner can develop rules for specific types of menus. For example, one rule for a banquet menu might be that white foods should not be served with white sauces. A rule for a school lunch menu might be that Italian dishes made from noodles and tomato sauce should not be served more than once a week. A series of related menus, for instance those of a menu cycle, can be evaluated on this basis by circling similar items in the same color ink. How many sweet, or red, or stewed items are included then becomes apparent at a glance.

The idea of balance in menus certainly has validity. But applying rules that are based on the contribution of balance in taste and appearance can sometimes lead to menu programs that are defective. A notable example is the average school lunch program. If school children like spaghetti and lasagna and there are three main course selections every day, why shouldn't these children have the opportunity to eat such food more than once a week? In such circumstances, offering spaghetti or lasagna only one day a week limits the client's choice on four days of the week to foods that are seen as less desirable. Preference studies show that teenagers value crunchy foods simply because they *are* crunchy. Why give them boiled onions when they much prefer raw carrot sticks?

Similar abuses of menu balance may be seen in commercial restaurants. In an effort to fulfill his or her idea of a balanced menu, the menu planner may choose items that confuse the image of the establishment and do not sell. Many operations have items that haunt the refrigerator because somebody used them to balance the menu—that stray broiled veal chop or forlorn beet. These items may be favorites someplace, but, in general, menu planners must temper variety for variety's sake with a sensitivity to consumer preferences.

CONFORMITY TO SIMILAR OPERATIONS

Many menu programs are based on the printed menus of other similar operations. In such instances the menu planner questionably assumes that the printed menu reveals the basis for the decisions that led to its creation; that operations that are somewhat similar can use profitably the same or similar menu programs and printed menus; and that common practice is the best practice.

A printed menu does not necessarily reveal the basis for the decisions leading to the creation of the menu program. In examining the printed menu of an operation, the menu planner can make a number of objective observations: how many items are offered, whether the food is served with sauces, and so on. The planner can also make some deductions about the analyses that led to the development of the menu. There is, however, no way of discovering from the menu the capacities of the other operation's production system, its budgetary limits, sales of individual items, nor even very much about its patrons' preferences. Many menus, even the menus of successful operations, are defective. That is, if such menus had been carefully examined by their own operations, items that generate excessive costs and, therefore, should not have been included would have been discovered.

However, there is value in examining the menus of similar operations. Examination of a number of such menus would reveal the general expectations of patrons and operators alike for that type of operation. There are some common conventions that apply here. For example, it is apparent from an examination of the menus of traditional American restaurants and gourmet restaurants that the American restaurant offers portions, items, and prices that suit children, while the gourmet restaurant does not. Such a generalization can help make a decision about the menu program being developed. The menu planner must decide whether another operation is similar enough to the operation for which the menu program is being developed to warrant using the other operation's menu as a model.

Costing and Pricing Menu Items The menu program should be developed to make profits in commercial operations and to meet costs in noncommercial operations. Meeting costs or making profits begins with computing the raw food costs of individual menu items. The cost of the ingredients in recipes—hence the cost of the recipes themselves (either per portion or per batch)—is determined. The menu planner may use current prices or may attempt to forecast price movements in the marketplace, such as price fluctuations due to seasonal availability of foods, in order to arrive at an annual average cost for the ingredients of each menu item.

Once individual menu items have been costed, the concerns of the commercial and noncommercial operation diverge slightly. At this point, the noncommercial operation can estimate how much it will cost to feed the people it serves. The costs of individual menu items to be used in the menu or menu cycle are totaled. If the menu is very simple—that is, one item per meal, or one item per course per meal—and there is little or no waste, then the maximum cost of feeding one person can be determined by simple addition. If the menu offers a choice between several items that cost different amounts, then a forecast must be made as to which items will be chosen. Then total costs can be computed.

The menu planner for a commercial operation performs basically these same calculations, except that customer or guest choices may be much harder to predict, especially if complete histories of sales are not available for the menu program. Moreover, the menu planner in a commercial operation must determine prices as well as costs, and the price of an item on the menu often affects the demand for it. The tendency of people to shun items at higher prices must be related to the forecast of customer or guest choices. Price alone may determine how well certain items will sell.

The person in charge of setting prices for the menu of a commercial operation must use a pricing method that will result in satisfactory overall performance of the menu. Pricing individual items so that the menu program as a whole makes target profits is the primary goal. However, because of the complex problem of predicting the effect of price on demand, no menu pricing method can guarantee hitting target profits exactly. The following methods are widely used, with varying effectiveness.

TRIAL-AND-ERROR PRICING In pricing by trial and error, the menu is first priced by guess or by examining the menus of competitors. After a period of time long enough to show whether the operation has yielded profit or loss, adjustments are made in prices and items are removed from or added to the menu. This trial-and-error experiment continues until profits are acceptable.

Though trial-and-error pricing can lead to a well-priced menu, the operation is in quite a precarious position financially while prices are being tested. Unless an operation is solidly backed by a large amount of capital, the risk of failure during this time is great. Obviously, such a chancy method of pricing leaves much to be desired.

FACTOR PRICING   Determining prices by using a factor is better than the trial-and-error method because at least the cost of food involved is considered. The selling price of a menu item is determined by multiplying its food cost by a number called a "factor." If the factor chosen is three, then the cost of each menu item is multiplied by three to arrive at its selling price. The price of every menu item is three times its food cost, and the overall food cost is 33 percent of the menu price.

Pricing by a set factor has built-in problems. Some items cannot be priced this way with any expectation of selling them. A steak dinner costing the operation $5 may not find many customers at $15. But the operation would probably sell a great many steaks at $10 (50 percent food cost) and still make $5 per order. Though the $10 steak price is low compared to its cost, the operation makes more selling $10 steaks than it does selling the same number of orders of chicken deluxe priced at $4.50 with a 33 percent food cost of $1.50. Even though the price of the chicken is three times its food cost, the operation only makes $3 a sale, as opposed to $5 a sale for steak. On the other hand, tea, which costs an operation about two cents a cup, cannot be realistically sold for six cents a cup. The operation of course charges more and again disregards the factor.

Factor pricing involves still another problem. In determining menu prices, only food costs are considered. The cost of making chicken deluxe might be more than the cost of preparing the steak. Shouldn't this additional cost be reflected in the menu price? Thus, the factor method, which may seem very businesslike, appears upon scrutiny to be quite flawed. However, factor pricing can be used effectively when the basic cost of preparing similar menu items (such as types of pizza or hot dogs) is the same.

PRIME-COST PRICING   Pricing according to prime cost is a more sophisticated variation on factor pricing. The prime cost includes raw food cost as well as the cost of the labor needed to prepare the food and the cost of condiments and other accompaniments like bread and butter. The prime cost is then multiplied by a factor, usually a lower factor than that used in factor pricing: instead of three, the factor in prime-cost pricing might be two and one-half. The selling price that results from prime-cost pricing is more accurate than that from factor pricing because it at least reflects some production costs.

ACTUAL-COST PRICING   The actual-cost method of pricing does not begin with raw food costs and a factor, as factor pricing and prime-cost pricing do. Actual-cost pricing begins instead with a projection of all expenses except food costs and works backwards, subtracting these expenses from expected sales revenues to arrive at what raw food costs should be. The amount of projected sales revenues is designated as 100 percent, and each expense item (wages, fuel, menus, rent, and so on) is figured as a percent of sales. These percentages are totaled, and to this sum a profit percent of sales is added. Five or six percent is the average profit percent, but this figure varies depending on how much the operation must realize as a return on investment. The sum of the expenses percents and the profit percent is then subtracted from 100 percent (total sales). The resulting figure is the percent of sales that food costs must be if the operation is to make the projected profit. Thus, if expenses total 58 percent and profit, 6 percent, subtracting this sum from 100 percent sales revenue would set food cost at a maximum of 34 percent. The advantage of actual-cost pricing over the factor or prime cost methods is clear: actual-cost pricing at least relates food cost to other operating costs and, most importantly, to profits.

BASE PRICING   With the base-price method, instead of trying to project what percent of sales food costs should be, the operator prices the menu on the basis of a minimum check per customer, called the base price. Projected profits and projected expenses—including raw food costs—are added together, and this total is divided by projected patronage to arrive at the average check per customer. For example, in a given period of time, let us say a restaurant spends $300,000 in operating costs and $150,000 in raw food costs to serve 100,000 people, and wants to make a $50,000 profit. This goal requires that each patron pay $3.00 toward operating expenses, $1.50 toward food costs, and 50 cents toward profit, or $5.00 in all (the combined sum of $300,000 + $150,000 + $50,000 divided by 100,000 patrons).

Thus, menu items must be priced so that the average check is $5.00. Five dollars becomes the operation's base price, or the minimum check per customer needed for the operation to make its projected profit. In practice, this method of pricing can be used effectively in a limited-menu restaurant such as a steak house where a single item (the entree) represents the major portion of the check.

There is also another way of computing a base price. Instead of basing prices on each patron's individual contribution to sales revenue, the price is based on the contribution of each food-cost dollar. In the example above, the $350,000 of combined expenses and profits is two and one-third times the food costs of $150,000. For each dollar of food cost, the price of an item must include that dollar plus two and one-third dollars ($2.34) toward expenses and profit. Thus, if raw food cost for an item is 60 cents, the price would be that 60 cents plus two and one-third times 60 cents for profit and expenses, or 60 cents plus $1.40 for a total selling price of $2.00. This method is similar to factor pricing, but uses a much more accurately determined factor.

MAKING MENU PLANNING EFFECTIVE

Though the printed menu is the most visible result of menu planning, other related materials are necessary to implement the menu program. These materials facilitate interpretation of the menu program by people involved in purchasing, production, and control.

The printed menu lists items by name only, or includes only a general description couched in merchandising language. Even if the item is a common one like a hamburger and not a fanciful one like "seafood delight," the menu listing alone cannot be used as the basis for determining what ingredients are needed to prepare it, what size portions are intended to be, and how much each ingredient should cost. Other materials are needed to record this essential information. The *standardized recipe* is the most important device in menu planning. A standardized recipe is an exact formula for preparing a menu item; an example of one is shown in Exhibit 6.7. The step-by-step procedure detailed in Exhibit 6.8 indicates the care and exactness that recipe writing requires.

A number of other useful forms are used to monitor the success of the menu program, and are listed in Exhibit 6.9. Such aids include the *pattern worksheet* needed to analyze a particular meal in terms of the menu pattern it follows and the *scatter sheet* that counts how much of a given item is ordered over a period of time in order to measure both its popularity and its profitability.

EXHIBIT 6.7 Sample Standardized Recipe for Chicken a la King

Chicken a la King

Yield: **100 Portions**   Each Portion: **1 cup**

Ingredients	Weights	Measures	Method
Chicken, broiler-fryer, whole	45 lb		1. Wash chicken thoroughly inside and out under running water.
Water		9 gal	2. In stock pot or steam-jacketed kettle place chicken, adding water and seasoning. Bring to a boil; reduce heat and simmer 2 hours or until tender.
Salt	6 oz	9 tbsp	
Bay leaves		9 leaves	
Monosodium glutamate		9 tbsp	3. Remove chicken; skim off fat and reserve for use in Step 6; strain and reserve stock for use in Step 4; remove meat from bones; cut into one-inch pieces. Set aside for use in Step 9.
Onions, dry, chopped	1 lb	3 cups	4. Cook onions and celery in stock until tender; remove vegetables. Set aside for use in Step 9.
Celery, fresh, chopped	5 lb	3-3/4 cups	
Milk, nonfat, dry	13 oz	2-7/8 cups	5. Reconstitute milk; add to stock; mix thoroughly. Heat to simmering temperature.
Water, warm			
Chicken fat or butter or margarine, melted	2 lb	1 qt	6. Blend fat, butter, or margarine, and flour to make a cold roux; mix until smooth.
Flour, wheat, hard	2 lb 4 oz	2 qt	7. Gradually add roux to stock, stirring constantly.
Salt	3 oz	4-1/4 tbsp	
Pepper, black		2 tbsp	8. Add seasonings; heat slowly until smooth and thickened, stirring constantly.
Peppers, sweet, fresh, chopped	1 lb	3 cups	9. Add chicken, onions, celery, peppers, and pimientos to sauce; heat to serving temperature.
Pimientos, canned, chopped	14 oz	1-3/4 cups (two 7 oz cans)	

EXHIBIT 6.8   Writing Standardized Recipes Step-By-Step

Most foodservice operations use a standard form prepared to resemble Exhibit 6.7 on which the recipe information, ingredients, and procedures are entered. Follow these conventions in writing standardized recipes.

Step 1:   Write Recipe Heading

Place menu name of product in center of form being used for the recipe. Enter item classification; yield (number of servings); portion size (in weight or measure, or both); number of pans (and pan size) produced; and cooking temperature if applicable.

Step 2:   List All Recipe Ingredients in Order of Use

Items that require pre-preparation for use in the recipe are listed first so that this preparation may be done. Descriptive terms are used to clearly define the kind and form of the ingredient and what is to be done with it to make it ready for the recipe.

Descriptive terms **before** the name of an ingredient designate the kind and form of food **as purchased**, or heating or cooking required before the ingredient can be used; for example, **canned** tomatoes, **hot** milk.

Descriptive terms **after** the ingredient name designate preparation necessary to make the ingredient suitable for use in the recipe; for example, cooked turkey, **diced**; onions, **chopped**; apples, **pared**, **sliced**.

Ingredients which require that another standardized recipe be used have a reference to that recipe number in parenthesis. For example, Tomato Sauce (S-19); Pie Crust (B-78).

Ingredients that have a preparation loss or gain or are purchased in units other than those specified in the recipe are marked with an asterisk (*). This asterisk refers the purchasing department to a yield table.

Step 3:   List the Quantity of Each Ingredient

The quantity of each ingredient is given in both weight and volume measure whenever it is practical to do so. Weight alone is used for foods that are not easily measured accurately, such as meats, uncooked fish, and fresh, whole vegetables.

Volume measure alone is used for liquids such as water, broth, and milk. Volume measure alone is also used for small quantities of foods weighing less than 2 ounces unless the weight is exactly 1/4 ounce or a multiple of it, or if the metric system is used.

In some instances, quantity is indicated by number under the "measures" column instead of weight or volume, for example, "100" for hamburger rolls or "100 large" for hard-cooked eggs.

Weights are given in pounds and ounces or kilograms and grams. Fractions of a pound are not used; that is, 5 lb 4 oz (not 5-1/4 lb). Fractions of an ounce are used as needed when weights of ingredients are less than 2 lb 8 oz; for example, 3-1/4 oz, 5-1/2 oz, 1 lb 12-1/2 oz. Fractions are rounded to whole ounces when the weight of the ingredient is more than 2 lb 8 oz; for example, 2 lb 8-1/2 oz is written as 2 lb 9 oz.

Volume measures are stated in terms of standard measuring utensils: teaspoons, tablespoons, cups, quarts, and gallons or milliliters, centiliters, and liters. Fractions of quarts and gallons are expressed in the simplest terms. For amounts smaller than 1 quart, the use of a fraction in a measurement is avoided by converting any fraction of a quart to cups; for example, 1 cup (not 1/4 qt); 1-1/4 qt (not 1 qt 1 cup).

Note that in both weights and measures abbreviations are not made plural: for example, 3 lb (not 3 lbs).

Step 4:   Write Simple, Easy-To-Understand Directions and Procedures

Directions are written so that each procedure or series of closely related procedures is a separate, numbered paragraph. Groups of related procedures and the ingredients used are separated by a horizontal rule. Procedures are in the order in which they are performed.

Procedures must be written very carefully.

If a utensil is used, indicate the utensil first; for example, "In a 9-inch frying pan."

Omit descriptive terms mentioned in the recipe ingredients; use them only if there are two ingredients which might be confused.

Use verbs with definite objects; for example, "Bring *milk* to a boil."

Use imperative mood, not words like "should"; for example,"*Be* careful not to burn the glaze."

Phrase instructions to avoid the use of the words "you" or "the cook."

For cooking processes in which the time is not clearly evident, give the times. The best place is usually just after the utensil has been indicated; for example, "In a heavy-bottomed 12-quart pot, *for 45 minutes*, cook. . ."

When there is no mention of a utensil, the time statement should precede the verb; for example, "*For 5 minutes*, knead the dough."

Do not repeat the quantity of ingredient in the procedures unless only part of the ingredient is being used in that step. When two or more steps should be done simultaneously, this fact should be indicated in the first step.

Step 5:   Indicate Panning or Portioning Method

When pans of a certain size are needed for satisfactory results or as a guide in portioning, the dimensions, number of pans required, and volume or weight of food per pan are included in the directions; for example, "Pour into 4 greased baking pans (about 12 by 20 by 2 inches), about 5 lb or 2-1/4 quart per pan of the mixture."

State the serving portion in ounces. Indicate the portioning devices (disher or ladle) used to measure portions, for the dimensions of the portion; for example "Portion with No. 24 scoop; makes 100 portions," "Cut into 25 4" x 3" squares."

EXHIBIT 6.9   Useful Forms for Menu Planning

Form	Use	Data Base
Standard Recipe	Forms the base of all cost analysis of the items offered and hence of the menu itself. Serves as the basis on which production orders and food product specifications (descriptions) can be written.	Item name Category Ingredients Amount of ingredients Procedures for preparation Yield Portion size
Recipe Cost or Cost Test Form	Allows the presentation of the cost of a portion of a menu item or a batch of a menu item. Based on information from the standard recipe. Allows comparison of item cost from period to period.	Ingredients used in recipe Cost per unit as used Cost per portion as used
Portion Control Sheet	Communicates portion sizes of items on the menu. Used to maintain standards on which menu program is based.	Portion name Portion size(s)
Pattern Worksheet	To analyze and evaluate a specific menu against the pattern established. Can also be used as menu planning worksheet.	Data base depends on pattern.
Menu Precost and Abstract	Precost information presents forecast of each item's sales and its contribution to total sales, thus allowing the profitability of the total menu to be projected. Abstract data serve to compare projections with actual performance. Abstract also serves as a popularity index: what percentage of total items sold individual item constitutes.	*Precost* Item name Selling price Estimated sales Cost of item Cost percentage of item Estimated sales as a percentage of total number estimated to be sold (ratio to total) *Abstract* Number sold Total sales Total cost Cost percentage Ratio of total of each item sold to total sales

Form	Use	Data Base
Menu Cost Analysis	Treats the entire menu as a single item. Used for single-choice offerings in catering and in institutions. Data developed are similar to those of recipe cost form, or cost of items that require no further preparation. Can also be used to preevaluate menu on basis of dietary requirements, therapeutic value, and so on, before introducing other data areas.	Items to be served Ingredients by name and quantity in all items to be served Total cost of menu Cost of individual portion
Menu Performance Analysis: Scatter Sheet	Allows the items to be scored on the basis of popularity by permitting actual count of sales. Relates sales in units and in dollars to food cost so that for each item percentage of profit contribution and percentage of cost of total sales can be calculated and compared. This analysis may reveal that some items contribute considerably to costs but not to profits and their inclusion in the menu program must be reexamined.	Item Menu price Percent sold Times sold (for scoring) Total sold (number) Sales value (dollars) Percent total items (number) Percent food cost (of total of each item sold as a percent of total spent for all items sold) Percent of gross profit (total profit on each item sold as a percentage of total profit on all items sold)
Entree Mix Cost Percentage	Used as worksheet to complement menu performance analysis described above. Also used to analyze forecast menu sales.	
Meal Census	A report of the quantity of an item served and other data, the number of people or meals served, and average check.	Varies with objective Date Number served Quantity served Comparison with existing sales data from similar times is common base

EXHIBIT 6.10   Cost Test Form for Recipe Costing

Item	Vendor
Date	By

Ingredients	Size Portion	Unit Cost	Portion Cost	Adjusted Cost to Date		Adjusted Cost to Date	
				Cost	Date	Cost	Date
1							
2							
3							
4							
5							
6							
7							
8							
9							
10							
Cost Adjustments Finished Cost							
Selling Price Deduct Finished Cost Gross Profit Gross Profit Percentage							

EXHIBIT 6.11 Menu Precost and Abstract

Department _____ Meal _____

Day _____ Date _____ Weather _____

			Forecast						Actual					
Entree	Selling Price	Cost	No.	Revenue	Cost	Cost %	Ratio to Total	No. Sold	Sales	Cost	Cost %	Ratio to Total

EXHIBIT 6.12 Scatter Sheet

Date_____ Day_____ Covers_____ Cover Average _____Remarks_____

Item	Menu Price	Percent Sold	Times Sold	Total Sold	Sales Value	Percent Total Items	Percent Food Cost	Percent Gross Profit

Chapter 7
The Work

System

The work system of a foodservice operation is comprised of both the physical facilities of the operation and the work that goes on in them. The work system encompasses all that is physically involved in getting food from the delivery carton at the service door to the patron's plate—every task performed and every person, machine, and material needed to do that task. The work system is the system by which the foodservice facility is run, for it coordinates all the work activities that take place in the operation, principally in the four operating systems—purchasing, supply, production, and service.

This chapter will present an overview of the work system. It will offer a practical procedure for creating a work system whose scope entails the design of the total foodservice facility. The first half of the chapter will outline the criteria that must be considered in planning both the work system and the total facility. The remaining half will give a step-by-step plan for setting up a work system and will conclude with a section on how to improve and maintain the work system once it is operating.

Designing the work system requires thousands of interdependent decisions. Consider, for example, only the decisions involved in offering hot rolls with dinner. There are many different ways to make rolls. The restaurant could have its own baker make the rolls from bulk ingredients or from a prepared bread mix. Or the restaurant could buy raw bread dough ready to be formed into rolls and leavened, or buy raw dough already formed into rolls and ready to bake. Or the rolls could be bought already baked and ready to be browned and warmed, or already baked and browned and ready simply to be warmed. Consider the possible ways of serving the rolls. A single roll could be placed on a bread-and-butter plate and brought to the table, or a basket of rolls could be available at a salad bar or buffet. Each of these different methods of preparing and serving rolls requires different kinds and amounts of labor, space, materials, equipment, energy, and expenditures.

Somehow, the decisions concerning the preparation and service of the rolls must be integrated with similar decisions about every menu item.

Fortunately, no work-system planner must start from scratch in making these crucial decisions. Because all foodservice operations share certain common characteristics, the experience of one operation can usually be applied—in general terms—to another, and the effects of the differences between them can be properly gauged. Work-system planners have identified and analyzed certain relationships between facilities, equipment, labor, materials, and costs. The individual planner need only gather such relevant information and use it effectively. This chapter will attempt to present information that is necessary for effective planning. To begin such planning, one must know the objectives of the work system and the current practices in work-system design, including the problems in planning that now challenge the industry.

SPECIFIC OBJECTIVES OF WORK-SYSTEM PLANNING

A good work system satisfies certain objectives, and a good work-system planner must always keep these objectives in mind. Within the limiting conditions imposed on each planner's design, a work system should be designed to best achieve the following specific objectives:

1. *To ensure the smoothest and fastest work flow throughout the operating systems*   A work system must be designed to coordinate work flow in the operation. The work system should be planned to minimize lost time due to equipment breakdowns, production shortages, or problems in the service areas.

2. *To be flexible in meeting consumer demands*   Because consumer demand fluctuates constantly, the work system should be planned to accommodate different levels of volume as well as new products.

3. *To maintain product quality throughout the operation*   The work system should be planned so that product quality is preserved by proper handling, storage, holding, and preparation at every stage in the processing.

4. *To maximize space utilization*   The work system should be planned to maximize revenues per square meter, especially in operations with limited space. By minimizing space requirements for back-of-the-house work activities, customer areas can be profitably enlarged.

CURRENT PRACTICES IN WORK-SYSTEM PLANNING

Those operations, even newly constructed ones, that do not seek to attain these objectives through work-system planning have failed to recognize profound changes in the business environment. The planners and managers of such operations presume, as one might have 40 years ago, that the costs of labor, construction, equipment, materials, and energy are so low that inefficient use of them will have little impact on the operation's overall success. But no resource is cheap anymore. Given the current rise in costs, such excesses as extra employees or wasted electricity can severely hamper an operation's efficiency and profitability. The foodservice industry's sluggish attitude toward change, induced by decades of inexpensive operation, must be reanimated by better management and planning, two newly emphasized concerns which have invigorated other sectors of the economy.

Data from the federal Bureau of Labor Statistics, although incomplete, suggest that the foodservice industry is experiencing zero productivity growth. The output produced by an operation and the human work hours involved have been increasing at the same rate. This situation markedly contrasts with that of the rest of the economy, which has enjoyed an increase in output per work hour. Although the information is fragmentary, it is also apparent that many owners of small restaurants receive virtually no return on the investment of their capital. Their businesses provide only a steady job and the pride and problems of ownership.

While other factors such as weak management can contribute to these problems, poor planning of the work system is a fundamental cause. Exhibit 7.1 offers a checklist of symptoms indicating a poorly planned work system. Small, independent foodservice operations are especially likely to show some of these symptoms. Because they lack initial capital, small operators often establish work systems that require little investment in equipment but much labor. Thus, the continuing costs of production are higher than they need be. Storage is relegated to leftover space instead of being considered a valuable asset which, when planned and managed well, can help boost profits. The first consideration in selecting equipment is the cost and convenience of installation, with scant regard for how well the piece of equipment fits the particular needs of the operation.

Problems are also created by deficient work-system planning in larger, better financed operations. Like those of smaller operations, the problems of larger foodservice operations result because planners do not recognize that the work system must be designed as a whole. The need for an efficient, well-planned work system is overlooked as the owner concentrates on the more obvious, though no more important, aspects of setting up a foodservice establishment. The owner may believe that attractive dining room decor, a fine menu, high quality ingredients, top-of-the-line equipment, and an outstanding chef will somehow result in efficient food production. Work-system planning is forgotten as the kitchen is jammed into an alleyway inconveniently far from both storage areas and the service area door. Booster stations (provision areas in the dining room), employee locker rooms, food-holding equipment, custodial closets, and dish storage areas are tucked into the facility wherever they can fit. This

EXHIBIT 7.1   Checklist of Symptoms of a Poorly Planned Work System

Labor

— Frequently idle workers
— Employee complaints about working conditions
— Periods of over- and understaffing
— Considerable overtime
— Employee fatigue
— Highly paid workers doing tasks that could be performed by less skilled workers
— Frequent need for superhuman employee efforts
— High turnover and absenteeism in skilled worker categories
— Low employee morale

Materials

— Waste through spoilage
— Stock-outs and shortages
— Oversupply of products
— Poor food quality

Costs

— Unnecessarily high energy costs
— Failure to monitor expenses
— Failure to meet investment objectives despite attaining projected sales volumes

Equipment

— Infrequently used equipment
— Machine breakdowns and disruptions of production
— Work centers that include worker-contrived equipment, such as shelving made from milk crates

Facilities

— Disorder and confusion in production and service areas
— High incidence of accidents
— Violations of sanitation laws
— Only partial utilization of the space allocated for production and storage
— Lack of important design elements such as drainage for ice machines, areas for waste, ventilation for dish machines, access panels in duct work for cleaning, storage space for dining room supplies and cleaning equipment

Work Flow

— Missed production deadlines
— Inability to deliver hot foods hot or cold foods cold
— Poor food-handling procedures
— Need for constant intensive management

---

failure to recognize the importance of work-system planning burdens the operation with inefficiencies that impede operations daily.

The problems that have been built into the faulty work systems of both large and small operations have a common root. Obviously, a better approach to designing a work system is needed. The conventional method used to plan these deficient work systems does not identify and provide for all the activities of the work system. The situation of the restaurateur who considers only decor, menu, and chef is a classic example. A poor design results because planning is done in stages that assign rigid and erroneous priorities. Each succeeding stage of planning has less flexibility than the last. Such step-by-step planning precludes a comprehensive approach that could make the work system function smoothly.

In such faulty traditional planning, the manager, after receiving a feasibility study from a marketing specialist, hires an architect. The architect develops an overall plan which physically defines the facilities. Within these spatial limits, the kitchen designer arranges and chooses the equipment. Based on the kitchen organization, mechanical and electrical engineers find places for utilities, waste disposal, and ventilation. Finally, an operations specialist is confronted with a finished facility and asked to decide how to make it work best. Each specialist in the chain makes plans in relative ignorance of the problems those plans may impose on the next specialist. The contribution that each of these professions and technologies can make to the operation is limited by the planning that comes before. At worst, the final facility is fatally flawed: restaurants have been built with floors that could not support foodservice equipment or with electric outlets for equipment that uses gas. More often, the result is a traditional work system with its usual inefficiencies.

Clearly, a change in planning perspective is needed in the foodservice industry. Certain segments of the industry, notably limited-menu restaurants and health care, educational, and industrial feeding organizations, have developed a successful approach to work-system planning in which designers consider facilities, equipment, labor, and materials concurrently. This change in perspective has had remarkably good effect, for, when measurable, operations planned using this approach are more profitable and productive than comparable traditionally planned operations.

This approach is based on the industrial engineering approach to planning that is widely used in American manufacturing industries. Instead of a succession of experts contributing to the design in separate stages, everyone who can make a contribution to the efficiency of the operation participates in all phases of planning. Working together as a team, marketing specialists, architects, kitchen designers, electrical engineers, and others design the best total work system. No part of the work system is considered complete until the whole system is completed. This approach is known as the *total team, total planning,* or *industrial engineering* approach to designing the work system.

Food facilities designed this way often differ radically from traditional operations—as radically as a modern automated bakery differs from a neighborhood bake shop. For instance, traditional planners try to locate storerooms where they are convenient to culinary workers. Workers gather a few items at a time from these storage areas as the items become necessary for production. This "go fetching" may not be necessary anymore: team planners often design central ingredients rooms (that need not be conveniently close to the kitchen) in which all the ingredients for the preparation of a food item or group of items are assembled and issued as a unit to the appropriate culinary unit or work area. This change significantly reduces the time spent assembling materials for preparation and thus results in costs savings.

In light of the present need for all foodservice operations to keep operating costs down by streamlining their work systems, the total planning approach appears to be gaining influence throughout the industry. The biggest obstacles to more widespread application are its seemingly high costs and the limited number of foodservice consulting firms that specialize in all the facets of work-system planning. Unlike the large foodservice corporation which has many specialists on its staff, the individual operator must hire his own consultants. In addition to the expense, there is also the problem of managing a group of professional designers and engineers. The foodservice entrepreneur may not be able to coordinate the planning process or manage the communication problems and interpersonal relationships that are involved. The traditional method of planning remains attractive inasmuch as it spreads the cost of design over the entire construction of the project and seems to allow the entrepreneur to address one problem at a time.

The remainder of this chapter will follow the total planning approach to work-system design, which is successfully challenging the more traditional planning method.

DESIGN CRITERIA FOR PLANNING A WORK SYSTEM

The way that laws, current technology, and the operation's other systems each affect the work system yields rough guidelines for designing the work system, called *design criteria*. These criteria for planning the work system often affect the design of the entire physical facility, including buildings and grounds.

Interaction of the Work System with Other Systems   The relationship between the work system and the management, marketing, business, and control systems considerably influences the choices available in designing the work system. However, the effects of the purchasing, supply, production, and service systems—those systems whose work activities the work system coordinates—on the design of the work system are not treated here. These latter relationships are implicit throughout this chapter.

PERSONNEL MANAGEMENT AND THE WORK SYSTEM   Work systems involve people and therefore must be designed for people, and it is in this capacity that work-system planning is so substantially affected by personnel management. The work system must be designed to accommodate worker abilities, social factors, and management abilities.

Worker abilities   The work system must be planned with the human capacity for work well in mind. People can only reach so far, see so well, work so long, and move so fast. A work system that overestimates the capabilities of its prospective staff will obviously fall short of its ex-

EXHIBIT 7.2   Symptoms of a Lack of Human Engineering in a Work System

Human Capacity Required	Problem
Arm reach	Shelves that are beyond the reach of the average worker.
Arm reach	Individual work centers (for example the sandwich preparation area of an informal restaurant) that place necessary materials (such as bread and sandwich spreads) beyond the reach of the average worker.
Work speed	Warewashing systems that are designed on the assumption that the worker can load the machine as fast as the machine can process the serviceware.
Work speed	Distances between service and production areas that presume that the employee will trot from one place to another.
Strength	Control valves that require superhuman strength to turn.
Strength	Stairs that are too steep to permit heavy trays to be carried with ease.
Eyesight	Dials on machines that are too small or too complicated to be read correctly.

pected performance. Exhibit 7.2 shows some of the more common symptoms of a work system that ignores worker abilities.

The work system should not only be planned so that tasks are humanly possible, but so that tasks can be performed within the *optimum performance range* of an average person. Although a worker can reach 66 centimeters (26 inches) to pick up a plate, the average person will probably perform better if the distance is within 36 centimeters (14 inches), the normal range for one hand.

The physical conditions of work that meet basic standards of acceptability and those which tend to increase worker productivity were outlined in Exhibit 3.5, "Environmental Factors in Motivation." The work system must be planned to satisfy at least these minimum standards. Other work-system elements that directly affect worker performance such as table heights, seating construction, and flooring composition have also been researched to find out how these contribute to optimum performance. The productivity of the work system can be improved by a design that makes people's work a little easier.

If a work system is designed to include sophisticated equipment, the probable abilities of workers who will run these machines must be considered. A foodservice operation opening in a developing country must consider whether workers will know how to run even standard equipment. In both cases, the costs of construction and waste in training may seriously compromise the economy of using such equipment. An operation that draws most of its labor force from an illiterate population cannot readily use equipment that requires precise measurement unless it is automated or has nonverbal indicators of measurements, like colors or pictures. As foodservice work systems move rapidly toward a high level of technological sophistication, this matter becomes a concern of all foodservice operators. Job specifications will undoubtedly become more rigorous: not everyone can operate a sophisticated energy control system, an automated tray assembly line for hospital patients, or an automated bakery making 5,000 kilograms of bread an hour.

Work systems can also be designed to make possible the gainful employment of those with limited or undeveloped abilities, such as the physically disabled, and the emotionally, mentally, educationally, or socially disadvantaged. In most instances, these work systems can be as efficient as any other.

Social factors   At present, much of the work in the foodservice industry has a fairly satisfactory job content from the worker's point of view. Opportunities exist for creativity, personal satisfaction, socialization, individual recognition, and a variety of other nonmonetary rewards. But as the industrial engineering approach to work-system planning is applied more and more, heed must be taken of the problems that accompany this approach. Much of the work in the manufacturing industries that use this approach does not provide these opportunities. Many workers are indifferent, poorly motivated, alienated, and perhaps even hostile. Frequently, a costly loss of productivity through waste, poor quality workmanship, absenteeism, and high employee turnover results. There is little reason to assume that an assembly line in a foodservice facility will have a more positive impact on its workers than one in a shoe factory. Currently, the biggest labor problems in foodservice operations are associated with jobs that are the most industrial, such as warewashing. The possibility that these same problems will occur when other functions are industrialized—cooking, baking, pantry preparation—should be considered in work-system planning.

Foodservice organizations that operate outside of the United States—such as limited-menu restaurant chains or hotel corporations with units overseas—or with worker populations from other countries may have to deal with other kinds of social considerations. In countries where there is no running water in the homes of workers, it is necessary to include shower facilities in the work-system design. It may be necessary to adapt equipment or to use alternative equipment for tasks that have the stigma of being lowly work. Work systems planned for operations in other countries may also have to accommodate social customs such as midday rests, religious holidays and fasts, and strictures against killing animals.

Management abilities   A work-system design cannot overestimate management capabilities any more than it can overestimate worker performance. If management abilities are assumed to be greater than they are likely to be, the cost of managing the work system can seriously compromise the efficiency and profitability of the operation. Problems of this sort have often occurred in organizations that decided to open additional units. Successful owner/managers assume that they can hire a manager with the same skill, motivation, and knowledge that they themselves possess. Even though the second work system is designed just like the first, it may not function nearly as well because it requires a contribution from the new manager identical to that of the original manager. The work system may require that the manager do any job that cannot be handled by regular staff during a rush. The work system may demand a high degree of motivation from workers that is based on a long-term association with the owner/manager. The new manager obviously cannot elicit the same loyal response. The system may also require the new manager to be able to make quick decisions which require a familiarity with the operation that he or she is unlikely to have.

Obviously, a work system must change when the abilities of management change. In the situation above, it may be necessary to reexamine job requirements so that performance does not rely so strongly on a personal relationship between manager and worker. The ability of management to supervise a certain number of people effectively or to time critical activities properly must be considered in planning a work system.

MARKETING AND THE
WORK SYSTEM

The design of the work system depends on both market research and menu planning, two facets of the marketing system, because the work system must accommodate the menu and meal experience that reflects consumer preferences and expectations. Market research determines what products should be offered on the menu as well as what patrons prefer in architectural and decorative style, service facilities, parking facilities, lavatories, and noise level. Many work-system planners have seen consumers' concern with the appearance of a foodservice operation as an opportunity to identify more closely with the community. Even limited-menu chain restaurants will modify their standards to conform to the architectural style of a historic area or picturesque neighborhood. In keeping with the trend toward satisfying customers in all ways, more and more foodservice operations are introducing design features that accommodate the handicapped, such as ramped sidewalks, restricted parking areas, and special lavatory facilities.

The layout, physical facilities, and equipment of a foodservice operation must be planned specifically to produce the operation's menu program efficiently. Increasing public concern about food additives, fried foods, and truth-in-menu affects the choice of the menu program and thus the design of the work system. Too often, the work system unnecessarily limits the flexibility of the menu program because equipment needed for products that might broaden the menu appeal is omitted. Other times the work system is elaborately designed to permit the production of any kind of food, adding appreciably to construction costs and often compromising the operation's efficiency. When the menu program is finally decided upon, the kitchen may be larger and more complicated than necessary.

Too often, requirements of the menu program and the needs and expectations of the market segment are not integrated into the planning of the work system. Standard designs for a coffee shop, a 300-bed hospital, or a school cafeteria are used that fail to accommodate the information from the marketing system that should critically affect work-system planning.

BUSINESS AND THE WORK SYSTEM
The work system must be planned with crucial consideration of the business system. The business system controls the amount of money available to build and run an operation and the flow of money in and out of that operation, both of which affect the planning and the day-to-day functioning of the work system.

Before the facility is built, the planner must estimate the costs of the work system and the entire operation. Although it might be feasible to consider more than one type of operation, foodservice organizations or entrepreneurs usually test the feasibility of the kind of operation they intend to operate. If a feasibility study shows that an operation will be successful, then the projected construction and operating costs will become the construction and operating budget. Obviously, these budgets considerably influence choices in planning the work system. The work system must also include consideration of the relationship between building and operating costs and the effects of a rapidly changing business environment.

Construction costs versus operating costs   Operating costs and building costs must be balanced against one another. In some situations, it may be advantageous to trade higher operating costs over the long run for lower costs of initial construction. While small operators with limited capital often are forced to take this approach, large operations undergoing periods of expansion also often choose to take it. If the same amount of capital investment can build either ten cheaper, less efficient units which will earn $50,000 each or three expensive, highly efficient units which together will earn only $100,000, the first option is obviously the more profitable choice. The profits from the ten units can then be reinvested in them to make them more efficient.

In other situations, it may be more profitable in the long run to build operating economies into the construction of the work system, even though building costs are thus increased. Significantly lower operating costs can justify the initial investment in expensive laborsaving devices and equipment, or more durable and more costly construction materials. Backup machines, or even less efficient but more reliable machines, may be included in the work system to keep operating costs down by avoiding costly breakdowns. Booster stations in the dining room, complete with water, beverages, refrigeration, and hot-holding facilities, may cost several thousand dollars apiece to install, but each may save $10,000 in the cost of service personnel and earn the operation $5,000 in sales, just in the operation's first few years, by increasing customer turnover.

Methods of taxation and tax schedules can encourage or discourage investment in equipment and construction and thus can influence work-system planning. It may be possible for an operation to rent or lease certain equipment under extremely advantageous conditions with regard to its tax obligations. Because of such tax breaks, it is sometimes financially justifiable to rent less efficient equipment rather than buy better equipment outright.

Changing business environment   At one time, foodservice operations were planned as if they would last forever. Now, an increasing number of foodservice managers recognize that a particular kind of operation may only be viable in a particular location for a limited number of years. Less costly construction and operation may be necessary to provide an acceptable return on investment before the current work system is scrapped.

Rather than planning the work system's obsolescence, a designer can prepare for such changes in the business environment by making the work system adaptable. Of course, it costs more to build flexibility into a work system, but this expense may be justified by minimizing the economic impact of change on the operation. For example, a restaurant with full-menu table service may be planned and built with provisions for converting to cafeteria-style service should wages for service personnel rise greatly.

CONTROL AND THE WORK SYSTEM
Because of the continuous need to monitor and adjust the operating work system, provisions for such internal regulation must be built into the work system. These checks and balances are part of the control system. A traditional kitchen is organized in a defined physical space so that production can be monitored effectively. Specific personnel are accountable for material, equipment, time, and tasks. Information about operations is readily available. While this organization of the work system can be questioned on other bases, the high degree of control that it permits is desirable. Certain control functions must be considered in planning the work system, and provisions for regulating security, accountability, information flow, and standardization must be built into it.

Security   The work system must be planned with an eye to security. The need to protect the operation from theft of money, pilferage of material, or wrongful use of equipment and products can influence the placement of walls, doors, cash register stations, supply closets, storage areas, receiving doors, employee entrances, service yards, waste containers, staff locker rooms, public telephones, lavatories, and managerial offices.

Security considerations can also influence the size of facilities. The storage area in a bar may hold only ten cases of liquor because this is the largest amount that management can conveniently spot-check. The shelf in the kitchen may hold only a day's supply of towels because the availability of extra towels might encourage waste. Employee lockers may be made too small to serve as hiding places or may have transparent doors. Special security devices incorporated into the work-system plan might include television cameras, glass-walled areas, alarm systems, safes, one-way mirrors, and the like.

Accountability   The work system should have a set of automatic controls that work like a red warning light to indicate where a problem lies. When a part of the work system stops working completely, it is easy to determine why production has stopped; the cook is home sick, or the dishwasher is broken, or the lettuce has not arrived. But when a part of the system malfunctions, the cause of the problem may not be easy to find, although the existence of the problem may be indicated by a drop in the quality or quantity of production. The ability to account for such malfunctions must be built into the work system. If, for example, customers are complaining that the steaks are tough and overdone, it must be possible to track the problem to its origin. Some possible reasons for the tough steaks are poor purchasing specifications, acceptance of merchandise that did not meet specifications, poor handling in storage, improper butchering, poor food preparation, inadequate communication between service and production personnel, or the failure of service personnel to bring food to the customer immediately after it is prepared.

A work system planned to account for its problems can often avoid them because of its extra control devices. For example, the problem of tough steaks may be caused because the meat was not being used in the order that it arrived and consequently some steaks got old and tough. This problem could be corrected (and probably could have been avoided) by tagging batches of meat with the date of arrival and using them in consecutive order.

One can hypothesize hundreds of similar problems concerning everything from food cost to garbage disposal. Since no one can design a flawless work system, the planner should try to anticipate as many potential problems as possible and should make their causes easy to track if they occur. In other words, if the building cannot be made fireproof, then it should at least have smoke and heat detectors and good fire-fighting equipment.

Information flow   Management requires information so that the work system can be monitored and adjusted continuously. Sources of information and devices that facilitate the gathering of information must be built into the work system. The kitchen plan, for example, can include a clock, so that people can tell if production is on schedule.

Designated storage areas can also serve this need for information, because products can be counted there. But if food products are always *in transit* (moving from one place to another) or *in process* (being worked with), fairly sophisticated methods of gathering information are needed to find out how fast products are being used. Products and materials must be counted at some point so that supply and purchasing can be planned.

The newest cash registers can record what products are being sold. Managers can check to see what is selling at any time during hours of operation. If sales of a certain product exceed expectations, more soup can be made or more chicken defrosted. If sales are less than expected, dining room personnel can be instructed to promote slow-moving items. The waste of a daily special or perishable product might then be avoided.

Standardization   The work system should be planned to produce standardized products. The work-system design should provide for measurement at every stage of processes, uniform handling of products under a variety of work loads, preparation procedures that result in a consistent product regardless of batch size, uniform product quality without reliance on any particular individual, and uniform product flow to the consumer regardless of the number of people in the operation or the frequency with which an item is ordered.

If the necessity of such design criteria were recognized, a number of problems too common in foodservice operations could be avoided, including big slices of pie one day and small ones the next; different food on the chef's day off; excellent lasagna when it is the daily special and mediocre lasagna when it is a regular menu item; broiled lamb chops during slow times of the day and fried lamb chops when the broiler is busy; reheated french fries during slack periods; an hour's wait for a club sandwich during busy lunch periods; or beautifully garnished salads until those which have been pre-prepared are used up and then totally different salads sold under the same menu name. Consistent service and food quality and quantity are prerequisite to sustained consumer satisfaction.

Legal Limits on the Work System   All work systems must comply with the laws, regulations, and codes that cover many aspects of construction and operation. The work system design must incorporate all such regulations on construction standards, zoning, environmental impact, worker safety, work wage and working conditions, service and sale of alcoholic beverages, smoking ordinances, and food safety and handling. By affecting the design of the work system, these regulations often affect the design of the entire facility.

Construction standards   Building codes for commercial establishments and for foodservice establishments in particular may cover every conceivable aspect of construction: strength and nature of materials; construction methods; ventilation systems; lighting; fire protection; number and placement of exits; electrical and plumbing systems; size, number, and location of lavatories. In some areas, authorities must approve an operation's plans and specifications for equipment and building materials before construction begins. In other areas, authorities inspect only finished construction; the planner must know the law or run the risk of building a facility that falls short of it.

Zoning   Most areas restrict commercial construction to certain areas and limit the use of existing buildings for commercial purposes. An operation's building plans usually must satisfy zoning ordinances before construction can begin. On occasion, planners neglect details of the zoning law and complete buildings in violation of the codes. For example, a midwestern restaurant chain was obliged to seek a zoning variance after constructing a white building in a historic area zoned only for red brick construction. Another unit of a restaurant chain was required to hide its parking lot by surrounding it with a mound of grass-covered earth.

Environmental impact   On the wave of recent concern with cleaning up the environment, new laws have been passed to control exhaust, wastes, sewage, noise, litter, and traffic produced by most commercial enterprises, including foodservice operations. Work-system designers must comply with environmental regulations requiring air cleaners in ventilation ducts, processing and recycling of sewage, incineration of solid waste to produce usable steam, insulation of walls and windows, and litter-cleaning of grounds and parking lots. These concerns are new to foodservice work-system planning. Many existing operations can only comply with new environmental regulations by means of expensive renovation, if needed they can comply at all. Perhaps prudence in this area should be an added design criterion. Even if there is no existing statute in a particular community, the merits of a piece of equipment such as a char-broiler that has been under attack in other areas should be assessed with skepticism.

Worker safety   Federal law, as represented by the Occupational Safety and Health Act (OSHA), and local regulations establish many standards for safe and healthful working conditions. A planner must be familiar with those that apply to foodservice operations and to the particular jurisdiction.

Worker wage and working conditions   The design of the work system necessarily determines an operation's labor requirements. Essential planning decisions are made by comparing the cost of one method of producing a food product with another involving more labor participation. Should an operation buy potatoes already peeled or should it peel them? Does the work system require a conventional meat slicer or one with an automatic stacking device? These and hundreds of other similar decisions require basic information about such things as hourly wages, overtime pay, and employee meal allowances. The planner must also consider the likelihood of increases in wages. Since many foodservice workers receive the legal minimum wage, and since the laws of the states vary, it is possible that a work system in Mississippi would differ considerably from one in California. The implications of the law in this area are even greater outside the United States. The minimum wage laws in some parts of Canada can make certain operations with a high degree of labor involvement twice as expensive as those in the United States. On the other hand, the low cost of labor in most developing countries mandates that the work system be labor intensive, even in new operations.

If an operation has entered into a labor contract with its staff (or prospective staff), several matters critical to work-system planning may already be partially decided: job content, organization and staffing of operational units, pay scales, productivity and performance standards, minimum hours of work per shift, policy toward part-time employees, work weeks, overtime scheduling, working conditions, and facilities for employee use. The planner of a work system for a catering company must accept the fact that one bartender will serve no more than a certain number of people if that is a provision of the labor agreement.

Regulations concerning working conditions can impose a further limit on the work-system plan, though they seldom have as dramatic an impact as a labor contract. In some areas, the hours of the day during which teenagers are permitted to work may be limited. The law may require special facilities for women or may restrict work with heavy machinery to persons of certain physical capabilities.

Service and sale of alcoholic beverages   Most federal, state, county, and municipal regulations concerning service of alcoholic beverages simply govern the operating procedures of any facility with a liquor license. Some regulations, however, bear directly on such matters as the construction of bars and the number and location of entrances and exits. In certain areas, liquor signs must not be visible from the street. Regulations in some areas require establishments serving liquor to serve food of some kind or only allow liquor to be served at the bar.

Smoking ordinances   Several localities restrict patrons who wish to smoke to a defined area of the foodservice facility. Obviously, the design of the work system must take this into account.

Food safety and handling   Although state and local codes differ widely, no single area is more thoroughly and precisely addressed by law than food safety and hygiene. Such laws impose detailed design criteria. All relevant parts of the work system are affected, from physical facilities and equipment to the actual work being done.

Technological Limits on the Work System

Although there has been remarkable progress in the technology of food-service equipment and food processing, the current level of technology still limits work-system design and performance. Certain problems have been only partially solved; others have not been tackled at all by the companies supplying foodservice operations with equipment. In brief, here are 11 technological problems or deficiencies affecting foodservice design that must be considered when planning a work system.

1. Much foodservice equipment has not been designed with human engineering in mind. Thus, inefficiencies are unavoidable.

2. Any equipment maintenance and repair that can be anticipated must be considered in design criteria. Service, adjustment, and repairs for an otherwise ideal piece of equipment may not be available.

3. The quality of equipment fabrication and design may compromise the possibility of economical cleaning and maintenance.

4. The absence or inadequacy of training and instructional materials for sophisticated equipment may weigh against its inclusion in the work system.

5. Much of the equipment that is generally available for food holding and preparation also uses energy inefficiently.

6. Much useful equipment is available only with expensive features that add considerably to the cost without adding much to its functioning.

7. Several of the attractive alternatives to producing foods conventionally—such as the ready-food systems used in limited-menu restaurants—are a justifiable investment only at a very high volume of business.

8. Although there seems to be a wide variety of pre-prepared foods because of the diversity of brands, the number of products is actually very small. A work system that involves the purchase of large quantities of pre-prepared food and the reduction of labor in the operation might lead to an unacceptably limited menu.

9. Reconstitution of food products remains a problem. Although the microwave oven has proven satisfactory in many instances, methods of reconstituting full meals or products containing dissimilar ingredients are still in the experimental stages.

10. Many partial improvements in the work system require additional improvements in other parts of the work system to be fully effective: boil-in-the-bag packaging requires more widespread availability of boil-in-the-bag reconstituting equipment; equipment on wheels needs more opportunities for convenient connection to supply utilities; laborsaving equipment needs simpler and less time-consuming methods of cleaning to be cost-effective at anything other than very high volumes.

11. Foodservice equipment often lacks automatic quality control devices and instead requires the involvement of a skilled—and expensive—worker capable of exercising judgment.

The 11 problems listed above range from small but inconvenient failings to gross inadequacies in foodservice technology. All pose substantial challenges to the foodservice industry as it further develops its technological resources.

PLANNING A WORK SYSTEM

The designer begins the actual planning of a work system by gathering all relevant information. The preceding sections of this chapter have indicated the restrictions imposed on the work system by other operating systems and the legal and technological limitations that are placed on the work system. This information, called design criteria, defines the limits within which the work system must function and thus establishes general standards for planning the work system. But, for actual detailed planning, further information is needed. The planner requires in-depth data about the particular purchasing, supply, production, and service activities which are integrated in the work system. Also required is information about overall operation: volume of business (number of people served); business activity analysis (number of people served at different times); menu mix analysis (when and how much of each menu item is sold); and hours of operation.

The completeness and accuracy of this information depend on whether the designer is planning a new work system, replanning an existing work system, or planning an additional or duplicate work system (such as the second restaurant in a chain or a second service bar). Planning a new work system presents the most problems, because it is difficult to obtain all the information essential to decision making. In replanning a work system or in planning an additional one, the planner can try to improve on an existing system. In contrast, the planner of a new work system can only conceptualize a system.

Planners can get help in conceptualizing an operation from published data that show, for example, the amount of kitchen space required for a 100-seat restaurant. Or, professional planners can rely on experience gained in the course of planning other work systems; they can treat the facility to be planned as an improvement or variation on a previous one. Problems occur when a design based on published data or experience does not quite fit the new operation, but is used anyway because the critical difference is not recognized.

Planners can also conceptualize the new operation by simulation, that method used so successfully by limited-menu chain restaurants. In noncomputer simulation, the planner can simulate the work system by graphing its activities and calculating the distances between stages of the activities. Anticipated traffic flow and the appropriateness of the distances between activities can thus be assessed.

By using computers to create mathematical simulations, planners can simulate two or three alternative systems. From the computer model, planners can determine the equipment, space, and labor requirements of each alternative. But complete data are not always available nor do they always lend themselves to translation into mathematical terms necessary to make a computer model.

Usually, good planners gather information from as many sources as possible; they draw on the design criteria discussed in the preceding section, reliable published data, their own experience, and simulated models. Once this crucial information has been marshaled together, the actual planning of the work system begins. Planning involves deciding what work is to be done and how it will be done and deciding what kind of equipment is needed and how much space is needed. Then the plan must be evaluated to make sure it will work well. The following section will cover this planning process step by step. Exhibit 7.3 diagrams the six steps in planning a work system.

Deciding on Work Activities   As a starting point for deciding on work activities, the activities of a conventional restaurant might be listed. They include the following:

- Purchasing.
- Receiving.
- Storing.
- Moving products to production points.
- Pre-preparing (making ready to work).
- Preparing (cooking food, making salads, and the like).
- Holding (keeping prepared food until it is needed).
- Assembling (preparing plates or platters for service).
- Delivering (moving food to banquet or dining rooms).
- Serving.
- Cleaning (removal of waste; breakdown of work centers).

The nature of the operation being planned dictates which of these activities is relevant. A freestanding doughnut and coffee shop supplied by a bakery a hundred feet away probably requires little preparation, service, and equipment cleaning. A school lunch facility may only hold and serve food, having its food delivered from a large central commissary. If the work system of the commissary is being planned, activities such as packaging food and recovering unsold food must be added to the list.

EXHIBIT 7.3   Diagram of Six Steps in Planning the Work System

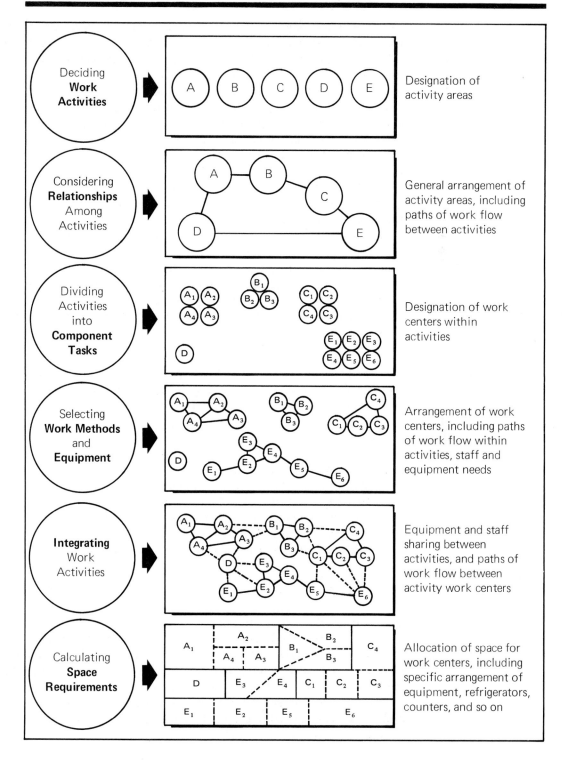

Considering the Relationships Among These Activities

Most formal methods for determining how activities are related to each other involve some kind of quantification. For example, the need for activities to be close to each other can be rated on a scale of 1 to 5. As many 5-category relationships are satisfied before any 4-category relationships are, and so on; or perhaps the highest total number of relationships, adding up category numbers, is satisfied. The amount of projected or actual traffic between two activities can also be quantified, since the density of traffic indicates an essential work relationship.

Often the relationships between work activities have implications for the rest of the system. If the relationship of one activity to another results in food being moved, materials-handling equipment is needed. If the relationship of one activity to another results in food being delayed, storage or holding equipment is needed.

As a general rule, planners try to avoid movement of products, equipment, or people that will increase total distance traveled. The relationships among activities are studied to eliminate backtracking, detours, crisscrossing, and movements of elements in opposite directions. Once the flow of materials and people has been charted, the most efficient arrangement of them is determined. Often the shortest path is the most efficient, but sometimes a longer route can eliminate handling or delay.

Dividing Each Work Activity into its Component Tasks

Each of the work activities listed above is made up of a number of component tasks. Like the activities of which they are a part, these tasks must be precisely identified and arranged according to their functional relationships. For example, baking is a way of preparing: baking can be divided up into roll and bread production, and pie and cake baking. Each of these two kinds of baking can be broken down into its component parts: roll and bread production subsumes the tasks of dough preparation, forming, and baking. Although this results in a complex hierarchy of activities that must be kept in mind, a planner must know all the work to be done if he or she is planning the way that work will be done and the facility in which it will be done. Perhaps this will be more manageable when computer programs are written for foodservice work-system planning, as they have been for rocket systems and bridge building.

Selecting Work Methods and Equipment

After becoming familiar with this level of task detail, the planner must determine how the work will actually be done and what machines will be necessary. The result should be a calculation of how persons, equipment, and materials will interact to perform each task. Though, of course, materials are an essential part of this combination, the planner's options are expressed as a formula of people and machines. For example, a decision about making 700 rolls for 500 people daily might involve choosing among these three alternatives:

1. Person/machine. This choice includes a baker—and perhaps a helper—and a number of pieces of equipment: mixer, dough divider, mechanical turnover, and the like.

2. Machine/machine. This choice would result in a fully automated roll-making system that requires minimal human supervision and preparation.

3. Person/person. This choice would include a baker and a helper using tools and small equipment to make the rolls.

Deciding among these three alternatives involves consideration of consumer, financial, personnel, management, and technological factors. Without specific operational data on pay rates, productivity, machine costs, machine availability, operating costs for machines, and union contracts, any choice is possible. Using such essential information might lead the planner to draw any of these conclusions:

- Alternatives 1 and 3 cannot be chosen because there are no skilled bakers available to the operation.
- Alternative 2 cannot be chosen because the union contract guarantees bakers the job of roll making.
- Alternative 2 cannot be chosen because the necessary equipment is too expensive or subject to breakdowns, or impossible to obtain.
- Alternative 3 cannot be chosen because the baker and helper only need to work three hours each to make enough rolls, and they will work only if each is guaranteed eight hours a day.

On the other hand, the rationale for choosing one of the alternatives might include:

- Alternative 1 is chosen: baker and machines involved justify their cost.
- Alternative 2 is chosen: machine pays for itself in six months by eliminating cost of bakers.
- Alternative 3 is chosen: labor involvement of baker and helper together is less costly per batch of rolls and per year than any alternative using machines.

It is possible to suggest other alternatives as well, such as using a part-time baker who doubles as a soup cook. It is also possible that none of the alternatives will be as inexpensive as buying the rolls ready-made from a commercial bakery.

In practice, such decisions usually do not involve so many alternatives, as a quick assessment tends to establish the two or three legitimate ones. There are simply not that many different ways of looking at inventory or arranging a service bar or getting a salad to a patron.

Integrating Work Activities   The planner may choose one of three basic approaches to integrating work activities. Activities can be arranged with a product orientation, a process orientation, or a fixed-position orientation.

Product orientation   In the food production systems of large commissaries, of limited-menu restaurants, and of large health care kitchens, activities are usually arranged with a product orientation. Breading, frying, and packaging, for example, are duplicated for every product that requires them and are arranged in order of the steps in product preparation.

Process orientation   In the food production work systems of traditional restaurants, a process orientation is most common. There is a sauce-making department, a broiling department, a steaming department, and so on. If a particular food item requires any of these processes, it travels to the appropriate department.

Fixed-position orientation   In a fixed-position orientation, all the elements necessary to produce a product—whether a cocktail or a complete meal—are assembled at one location. Neither the worker, the equipment, nor the product moves (until it is finished). This orientation is used in service bars, in short-order stations of restaurants, and in salad-making operations in commissaries.

The choice of orientation involves weighing the cost of labor in transporting the product and gathering materials against the cost of duplicating equipment and machines. The planner must also determine how well labor can be used in each of these arrangements.

Calculating Space Requirements for Work Activities   In this stage, the planner determines the amount of space that must be allocated to each activity by measuring the extent, timing, and intensity of the activity. In the course of allocating space, the planner may refine the choice of equipment and work methods and the evaluation of the relationships between activities because both have implications for the amount of work space required.

The space requirements for each activity evolve when the person/machine/material interactions are determined. For example, the most efficient method of preparing 700 hot rolls for 500 patrons implies a definite amount of storage space and a definite amount of room for counters and equipment. Collecting and integrating the plans for all work methods will define the space needed for each activity and for the total work system.

This evolutionary approach to calculating space requirements is used when the work system can be studied carefully by observation or when reliable information can be obtained. For example, much reliable research has been done on french fried potato production comparing the use of frozen french fries with french fries freshly made from raw potatoes in the operation. By applying data from these studies to the work system being planned, the designer can determine the space implications for either method.

Sometimes the calculation of space requirements is made earlier in the planning process. Some planners accept general rules of thumb for determining the size of work areas. For example, some planners may believe that the service area of a restaurant should take up 60 percent of its total area. Other planners use standards that give specific measurements. Authors of these standards may claim, for example, that a restaurant serving 400 meals a day needs 8.5 square meters (90 square feet) of vegetable and salad preparation area.

Planners sometimes allocate space on the basis of a set of assumptions: for example, french fries will be produced from frozen french fries; disposable single-service dishes will be used; canned products will be purchased once a week, and so on. On this basis, space allocations can be made: so many cubic meters of freezer space needed to hold 50 cases of frozen potatoes, no floor space needed for a potato peeler, and so on.

The value of this approach depends on the validity of the assumptions. For example, the assumption that customers in a luxury restaurant will best be served if they are seated is valid. It can be proven, if necessary, by interviewing customers in the market segment. From this assumption and a knowledge of how many patrons will be seated at a given time and the anticipated size of parties, the amount of space needed can simply be computed from the size of the tables, the amount of space a seated person occupies, number of aisles, and so on.

Some assumptions that form the basis for space allocation decisions are questionable. Must college and university foodservice operations be self-service? Must limited-menu restaurant customers leave their cars to order and receive their food? Must frozen french fries be prepared in a deep-fryer? Some foodservice operations are successful in defying these common assumptions.

When assumptions are not critical, they can serve as a reliable basis for space allocations. For example, the planner of an operation that has room for a large service yard (where trash and garbage containers are kept for removal) without limiting parking facilities or creating an eyesore, can simply assume that there will be enough room to store waste regardless of its treatment or disposal method. The planners for a restaurant on the seventeenth floor of a skyscraper cannot make the same assumption; they must calculate storage space for waste as they would for any other work activity.

Evaluating the Planned Work System This phase in planning is devoted to adjusting the total work-system design in order to provide a facility that, as a whole, achieves the objectives of maximum operating profits, maximum efficiency, minimum human cost of production, continuity, flexibility, optimum product quality, maximum space utilization, and smooth work flow throughout the other systems of the operation. The facility must still meet the design criteria that relate to its interaction with the other systems and the limitations of technology and the law.

To simplify the procedure, most planners establish priorities for their review of the design of the work system. Certain objectives are given first priority, others are grouped in a second category, and so on. The priorities that are assigned reflect the impact that problems or missed opportunities will have on the eventual functioning of the work system. Ensuring that the work design provides for all the activities envisioned is of major importance. A conventional restaurant, for example, does not function effectively without a storage system, a storage system does not work without a receiving area, and a receiving area needs receiving equipment.

Most planners develop a checklist that reflects their priorities. Exhibit 7.4 offers a checklist that includes many items that might have high priority in a given operation. The planner then attempts to correct any deficiency identified through review of the checklist. Some typical planning strategies that have helped solve common problems in design are described below. It is not suggested that these are the ultimate answers to the problems of a particular operation.

Worker travel time   Reducing the amount of time a worker spends gathering materials, finding equipment, waiting for equipment, and delivering the finished product increases efficiency. Work centers should be supplied as completely as possible with raw materials, tools, equipment, and a place for the finished product. Dining room service efficiency, for example, has been improved by introducing well-stocked booster stations into the dining room.

Materials handling   Improving the handling and movement of raw materials and finished products makes a better, more efficient work system. Foodservice operators improve materials handling by using mobile storage modules or cabinets, conveyors for transporting products and serviceware, and mobile equipment. Consolidating production by making larger batches and consolidating handling operations can also improve the efficiency of materials handling.

Equipment flexibility   Much equipment today is mobile, which facilitates both its maintenance and general sanitation and its efficient use in different work systems. Likewise, equipment which combines several different operations, such as a food processor which also grinds, blends, or prepares dough, is popular because such machines save on equipment purchases and space. Multipurpose equipment of this kind eliminates the need to move certain products during processing. The same concept is applied in other ways, in modular interchangeability of pans and racks used in cooking, storing, and serving; dishwashing racks that

EXHIBIT 7.4   Priority Checklist for Evaluating the Planned Work System

Are all conceivable activities/functions incorporated into the work-system design?

Parking for guests, employees, and service help from outside companies

Waste disposal and holding area

Utility storage area for gas and oil tanks

Management and supervisory work space

Training and instructional space; storage for materials

Parts and reserve equipment storage

Supply storage

Music system

Custodial closets

Special preparation areas to meet dietary requirements; e.g., kosher cooking

Special service areas to meet needs of particular customers; e.g., no smoking

Control of forms and devices

Security

Capacities and capabilities to meet volume demands and pace of business

Does the work system meet sanitation and safety standards?

Physical construction

Equipment operations

Working environment

Food handling and hygiene

Operating procedures

Provision of emergency equipment, first aid equipment, fire prevention

Personal safety equipment and hazard protection equipment

Do work methods accomplish functions at lowest overall cost?

Efficient utilization of machines specified

Mandated idle time for workers minimized

Pace and order of tasks to be done encourages smooth production

Capacities of equipment adequate for business

Nature and quality of materials cost-effective for work method

Maximization of human contributions: work designed for maximum human productivity

Work methods permit effective management activities

Is product quality optimized?

Food-handling procedures

Work methods related to product characteristics

Equipment processing

Adequate skill levels of human element

Quality control of product at all stages of production possible

Appearance of food preserved or improved

Measurement devices and equipment provided

Does the work system have minimum negative impact on the environment?

Appearance
Noise
Pollution
Waste
Traffic flow in neighborhood
Community standards of design

Has the work system been made as efficient as possible?

Elimination of activities that duplicate functions
Order of work designed to be most efficient
Worker abilities considered
Movements of products, equipment, and persons reduced to a minimum
Distribution of work corresponds to relationship among activity spaces
Dense work flows are made as short as possible
Minimal detours, delays, backtracking, and zigzagging
Tasks distributed to worker categories on most cost-effective basis
Combination of activities or work processes when possible
Activities' costs justified by contribution to total system

Has space been used efficiently?

Cubic space above and below work stations and equipment well utilized
Minimum of corridors, empty areas, dead-end corners, internal walls
Adequate aisles
Effective positioning of doors
Ample in-process storage capabilities
Space utilization provides for future adaptability
Conservation and effective use of floor space
Multipurpose uses of space exploited when possible

Has the work system been designed for people?

Employee facilities
Employee satisfaction with job content
Physical conditions that encourage productivity and high morale
Employee satisfiers such as lounges and food facilities provided

Can the work system operate efficiently?

Ease of maintenance and cleaning
Low operating costs for energy
Backup capacity built into system when possible

permit washing and storage; and storage carts that can be integrated with production centers.

Motion economy   Work systems are often evaluated for their ease of integration with human capabilities, which results in equipment and tools that are easy to use. Tools are often designed for special applications or with the special needs of particular workers in mind. Small equipment such as tables, holding carts, and can openers is often located at each separate work station, even if this results in some duplication.

Standards   In matters of safety and sanitation, foodservice operators often rely on the evaluations and judgments of objective groups. For example, the equipment standards of the National Sanitation Foundation (NSF) and the safety standards of Underwriters Laboratory and the National Safety Council are used widely. Such reliance tends to ensure the adequacy of the work-system design in these areas.

Automation   The use of more automatic equipment usually improves the overall efficiency of the work system. For example, deep fryers which program the cooking process and remove the fried product when it is done save on labor because they do not require a worker's attention and judgment. The modern warewashing machine with a power pre-wash, power wash, and power rinse automates a large part of the warewashing process and also lessens the need for human participation and judgment.

Open facilities   Removal of interior walls and barriers permits more flexible use of space, allows sharing of equipment and personnel between activities, and saves space by eliminating walls, aisles, and corridors. Open facilities also simplify supervision and control. In some instances, particularly in limited-menu restaurants, this concept has been extended to merging service and production areas so that kitchens become visible extensions of dining areas.

Interrupted facilities and work processes   Work-system efficiency is sometimes improved by dividing the traditional foodservice work system into its component activities and determining the cost effectiveness of each. This effort is directed to shifting work away from the operation to more efficient producers. For example, instead of constructing ten complete work systems of integrated activities ranging from purchasing to service in ten different units, a chain restaurant may construct a central commissary that distributes to ten small satellite work systems within each of the units. The central commissary may be more efficient in purchasing, storage, pre-preparation, and assembly. The satellites hold food, and serve it. The preparation of a menu item using convenience foods follows the same principle and makes manufacturing more efficient. On a more modest scale, the idea of interrupting the work system can be applied within an operation: work can be centralized efficiently. For example, all preparation that precedes cooking—the portioning of ingredients and the gathering of equipment for food production—can be centralized in a single activity area or ingredient room.

IMPLEMENTING THE WORK-SYSTEM PLAN

The design of the work system must be translated into exact layouts, procedures, and specifications that will become the actual functioning work system. The work-system plan is implemented through detailed layouts or blueprints of the physical facilities; equipment specifications; materials specification, operating procedures; and job specifications.

Detailed Layouts The detailed layout of an operation consists of a large set of blueprints that describe, within the space allocated to each work activity, the mechanical support systems that make that activity, and the work system as a whole, operate. These mechanical systems include ventilation, heating, air conditioning, utilities, plumbing, and others. Earlier phases of the planning process consider the implications of these systems for the cost of the entire work system; this phase deals with specifics of construction.

A rather complex series of engineering and construction decisions must be made if alternative ways of providing for the mechanical needs of the work system are to be evaluated. Factors which enter into such decisions include initial costs, operating costs, mechanical efficiency, ease of cleaning, ease of maintenance, simplicity of operation, and continuity of operation.

Equipment Specification In the course of planning the foodservice facility, planners determine standards for equipment performance and make cost estimates. The final choice of equipment remains to be made. For example, the planner may have to choose among several dishwashing machines that each produce 600 clean dinner plates an hour and cost roughly $1,000. To make this choice, the planner lists requirements in areas such as safety, ease of maintenance, operating costs, ease of cleaning, complexity of operation, availability of parts and service, construction features, appearance, materials, compactness, and environmental impact.

These requirements are formalized into written equipment specifications. Exhibit 7.5 is a sample specification. Note that only critical specifications are usually mentioned. If compactness is not important, for example, the equipment specification will not include dimensions. After specifications have been written and issued, the final choice of equipment is made on the basis of what is available.

Materials Specification Although many materials or particular foods are decided upon by the purchasing, production, and service systems of the operation, the work-

EXHIBIT 7.5   Sample Equipment Specification

Item No. 7—One (1) Refrigerated Salad Dressing Pan

Unit shall be of length as shown on plan x 55 cm (21 inches) wide x 5 cm (2 inches) deep constructed of 16 gauge stainless steel with all horizontal and vertical corners welded and coved on a 2 cm (3/4 inch) radius. Counter top shall be turned down 2.5 cm (1 inch) around entire perimeter of pan interior, provided with thermal breaker strips to prevent condensation on counter top. Corners of turndown shall be welded.

Provide cold pan with serpentine copper cooling coils, 5 cm (2 inches) thick polyurethane insulation and No. 18 gauge galvanized sheathing over bottom and sides of pan.

In addition, provide a 2.5 cm (1 inch) diameter brass chrome-plated waste outlet extended to spill over floor drain and a chrome-plated brass swivel gooseneck faucet, with hot and cold water controls.

Compressor shall be of horsepower as shown on plan, air-cooled type, complete with thermostatic control valve, dehydrator, expansion valve, toggle switch and necessary tubing for simple hookup on job to refrigerant coils and cold pan. Compressor to set on approved anti-vibrators and noise eliminators.

Compressor shall be set within a housing of No. 18 gauge stainless steel, constructed as hereinbefore specified and as shown on drawings. Housing shall be fully lined with .65 cm (¼ inch) thick rigid asbestos, over a coating of "carbozite," to prevent heat transmission to adjacent areas. Front of housing shall be provided with a removable No. 18 gauge hinged louvered access door. Louvers shall be die-stamped. Provide chrome-plated pull handle and rubber or neoprene gaskets to prevent metal-to-metal contact.

Although quite detailed, this equipment specification has been preceded by preliminary specifications covering standards, workmanship, materials, motors, and electrical connections which apply to this item and others. The final layout and specific mechanical plans are also part of the specification.

system plan may imply certain materials specifications. If a planner decides to use disposable single-use serviceware in order to eliminate the need for a warewashing machine, the kind of serviceware to be used is established already. A decision about the best way to produce french fries, which results in limiting storage space and eliminating the need for a potato peeler, implies that the operation will not specify raw unpeeled potatoes. If the planner includes no vegetable-washing facilities, this indicates that processed vegetables and salads will be used.

Since the planning of foodservice operations often precedes construction by several years, the implications of the work-system plan for product specification must be summarized in some fashion. The planners and the persons who manage the facility may never meet. Unless planners write down their ideas in the form of specifications or a narrative, inefficiency may result.

Operating Procedures   The relationships between fundamental elements of the work system—physical facilities, equipment, people, and materials—must be decided if the system is to be put into operation. The people who are introduced to the work system cannot know what to do unless they are told. A very conventional work system may need only simple instructions or operating procedures (this is where the rolls for dinner are heated one hour beforehand; this is where the spices are kept; this refrigerator holds dairy products; the first fryer is for cooking potatoes and the second is for fish only, and so on).

When the work system is complex, or innovative, more detailed procedures are required. Model staffing tables are sometimes needed for different levels of operation. They would be accompanied by complete descriptions of the tasks of each individual involved and by a plan for integrating individual efforts to produce the requisite number of meals.

Job Specification   After the work system has been planned, job specifications—descriptions of the skills, knowledge, and abilities of staff personnel—must be written. Chapter 3, which deals with personnel management, covers the techniques involved in this task, and discusses the crucial effect of the design of the work system on job specification.

MAKING THE WORK SYSTEM MORE EFFECTIVE

Although the planner attempts to incorporate flexibility into the work-system plan, to anticipate future needs and changing costs, and to choose durable equipment and construction materials, the foodservice industry is changing so rapidly that obsolescence and deterioration of the work system can only be prevented by active management.

In addition to the management of specific work-system activities in purchasing, supply, production, and service which are covered in their own chapters, management of the work system must include programs for work-system renewal, preventive maintenance, and cost-effective operation.

Systems Renewal   It is always possible that the decisions that were fundamental to the work-system plan were based on inaccurate or incomplete information. Unless the work system duplicates a system that has been carefully studied, some defects are likely. Even if the work system was planned to realize its fullest potential, changes occur between planning and implementation. Work systems can be improved through refinements in work methods and in the use of labor, materials, and equipment.

IMPROVING
WORK METHODS

A manager with a systems-renewal orientation seeks to identify present work methods that require improvement and improve them by eliminating or simplifying work steps, consolidating work processes, or introducing new materials or equipment. Savings on costs is always the criterion for improvement. Once the costs of development, training, and equipment acquisition have been repaid in a reasonable amount of time by increased operating economies, the new method should be less expensive than the prior method. Exhibit 7.6 is a cost-assessment form that might be used to determine whether a new work method is worthwhile.

A manager may use formal work-study techniques to identify and quantify the interactions in a work system. Much research has been done on work-study techniques by other manufacturing industries, and the industrial engineering approach to work-system planning has brought many of these techniques to foodservice operations. However, it is often difficult to justify the use of costly techniques that are likely to produce only small improvements for the operators and owners of modest enterprises. The fundamental problem with applying some of these techniques to foodservice operations is that they presume repetitive, evenly paced work with a limited, defineable task content; they also presume the possibility of deferring or accelerating work to make the process more efficient. Most foodservice operations demand that a worker perform many different kinds of tasks (compared to a worker on an auto assembly line) and that production be related directly and immediately to demand. Thus, the kind of detailed study of set tasks done in most manufacturing industries is not always helpful to a study to improve foodservice work methods.

Some industrial work-study techniques have been successfully applied to foodservice operations. Instead of focusing on individual tasks, those techniques that have found widest application have been directed toward larger concerns, such as the flow of work or materials through the operation, the design of efficient work centers, and the positioning of activities in relation to one another. A summary of techniques that are useful in these areas follows.

Flow process analysis   The work done on processing a particular product is studied with special attention to the steps taken by a worker or the stages of product completion. The objective is to identify what stages are productive work and which are wasted time and to eliminate time-consuming transportation, inspection, delay, and storage steps by a change in sequence or in the whole process itself.

Activity analysis   While flow process analysis studies all the activity involved in producing a particular product, activity analysis studies one kind of activity done over and over on many different products. Activities are analyzed generally on the basis of the percentage

EXHIBIT 7.6 Cost Assessment Form for Method Improvement Analysis

Department _____ Date _____ By_____

Procedure Studied: _____

Work Done By: _____

Equipment, Tools: _____ Classification: _____ Rate: _____

Comparison

Present Method			Proposed Method		
Step by Step	Standard Time	Cost	Step by Step	Standard Time	Cost
1.			1.		
2.			2.		
3.			3.		
4.			4.		
5.			5.		
6.			6.		
7.			7.		
8.			8.		
9.			9.		
10.			10.		

Cost	Cost
Labor: _____	Labor: _____
Materials: _____	Materials: _____
Misc: _____	Misc: _____
(Energy) _____	(Energy) _____
Total _____	Total _____

Estimate of Savings

Cost of Old Method _____

Less Cost of New Method = _____

X

Yearly Repetitions _____

=

Annual Savings _____

Cost of Change

	Acquisition	Annual
Equipment	_____	
Installation	_____	
Training	_____	=
	First Year	Yearly

Total Cost _____

Savings First Year

(Annual Savings Less Cost of Change First Year): _____

Annual Savings

(Annual Savings Less Annual Cost): _____

or

Change "Pays for Itself" _____ Months

of total time spent on transportation, actual production, and preparation for production, or cleaning after production. The objective is to reduce the time spent in activities that are not immediately productive. Exhibit 7.7 is a sample activity analysis form.

Time and motion analysis   In this type of analysis, fundamental work procedures of individuals are studied and movements of parts of the body, principally hands and feet, are identified. The objective is to eliminate those movements that waste energy either because of work habits that do not conform to the principles of motion economy or because of work centers and procedures that are poorly designed.

Travel analysis   In this kind of work-study analysis, the number of trips between points (pieces of equipment, for example) or the aggregate distance traveled over a period of time between points is studied so that relationships between equipment or activity areas can be established, and flow densities (the amount or frequency of traffic between points) can be measured. The result is the arrangement of equipment that either conforms to a hierarchy of critical relationships or minimizes dense work flows.

Equipment analysis   The use of a piece of equipment by a worker or workers is analyzed in terms of the amount of time the machine spends in production, being cleaned, being prepared to work, idling without work, and so on. The objective is to use the machine as fully as possible.

IMPROVING MATERIALS USE   Techniques of value analysis deal with the materials used in the work system. The manager attempts to identify items for which the operation is buying more quality or features than it needs. For example, the operation may be purchasing whole stuffed olives and then chopping them for a salad garnish when cheaper olive pieces, called salad olives, are available. Value analysis as it relates to other systems in the food-service operation is discussed in Chapter 2, "The Management System: Part I," and Chapter 8, "The Purchasing System."

IMPROVING LABOR USE   Dramatic successes in work-system renewal are often due to better use of labor. Labor use may be improved by scheduling workers at times that correspond to high and low points in the production cycle. Work may be better distributed among individuals or among crews of workers. Studies of labor may lead to a reordering of work sequences, creation of more effective job definitions and job structures, or further investment in equipment to enhance the work efforts of individuals or work groups.

Preventive Maintenance   All elements of the work system can deteriorate. If deterioration continues unchecked, it eventually causes costly disruption of work or expensive repairs. The logic of preventive maintenance is quite simple:

EXHIBIT 7.7   Productive Vs. Actual Restaurant Employee Labor Hours

Department and Activity	Production Time Per 100 Customers	Actual Time Per 100 Customers	Performance Index
Direct Labor	Labor Hours	Labor Hours	Percent
Meat and Vegetable:			
Preparing meat and vegetables			
Cooking			
Filling orders			
Cleaning stations			
Walking loaded			
Walking empty			
Miscellaneous work			
Unavoidable delay			
Nonproductive			
Total (or average) meat and vegetable preparation			
Salad:			
Preparing salads			
Assembling salads			
Cleaning stations			
Walking loaded			
Walking empty			
Miscellaneous work			
Unavoidable delay			
Nonproductive			
Total (or average) salad preparation			
Warewashing:			
Washing dishes			
Washing pots and pans			
Wrapping silver			
Cleaning stations			
Walking loaded			
Walking empty			
Cleaning kitchen			
Cleaning dining room			
Miscellaneous work			
Unavoidable delay			
Nonproductive			
Total (or average) warewashing			

Department and Activity	Production Time Per 100 Customers	Actual Time Per 100 Customers	Performance Index
Direct Labor (cont.)	Labor Hours	Labor Hours	Percent
Customer service:			
Walking loaded			
Walking empty			
Serving customers			
Clearing table			
Setting up tables			
Picking up orders			
Miscellaneous work			
Unavoidable delay			
Nonproductive			
Total (or average) customer service			
Bar:			
Filling beverage order			
Making change			
Walking loaded			
Walking empty			
Washing glasses			
Clearing bar			
Miscellaneous work			
Unavoidable delay			
Nonproductive			
Total (or average) bar			
Total (or average) direct labor			
Indirect Labor			
Store:			
Storeroom attendants			
Housekeepers and repairpersons			
Managers			
Total (or average) indirect labor			

it is less expensive to routinely care for the parts of the work system than to replace them during a crisis. Each part of the work system—physical facilities, equipment, and people—must be protected from misuse or overwork and requires a particular program of preventive maintenance.

PREVENTIVE MAINTENANCE FOR PHYSICAL FACILITIES

A preventive maintenance program for physical facilities usually includes routine cleaning, repair of structural elements such as walls, ceilings, floors, and parking areas, and the periodic renewal of protective structures and coatings.

Preventive maintenance procedures must necessarily be directed toward the materials used in the construction of the facility. Some typical maintenance activities are sealing and waxing uncarpeted floors; painting woods and metals that are exposed to the elements; repairing parking lots and walkways; maintaining door hinges and closures; resurfacing and renewing roofs; protecting carpeting by matting; using curtains, tinted glass, and other light screens to prevent decorative materials from fading; cleaning walls, carpets, and wall coverings; promptly removing stains and repairing minor damage; and replacing grout and resetting tiles .

Preventive maintenance is necessary to prevent deterioration of the facility that could lead to building code violations, loss of patrons, and lawsuits stemming from injuries on the premises.

PREVENTIVE MAINTENANCE FOR EQUIPMENT

Specific preventive maintenance routines for equipment are often described by the manufacturers. Most involve routine cleaning to prevent accumulation of dirt that impedes functioning or reduces efficiency. In many cases, routine lubrication of moving parts is necessary, as is a periodic adjustment of parts which tend to vibrate loose.

Most maintenance procedures are fairly simple. If they are not, servicing by trained technicians is available. It is management's responsibility to ensure that preventive maintenance activities are scheduled and performed on a routine basis.

PREVENTIVE MAINTENANCE FOR PEOPLE

The performance standards for labor always must be maintained or improved. Otherwise, the work system's efficiency is compromised: decisions about work methods, the use of pre-prepared products, and the productivity of person/machine systems are distorted.

Two areas, described at length in Chapter 3, which deals with personnel management, can be considered human preventive maintenance: training and motivating, especially by morale building.

Cost-Effective Operation

Management attention to sanitation, safety, waste handling, and energy conservation can both increase profitability and result in smoother operation of the work system.

SANITATION   The economic benefits of sanitation programs are many:

- Reduced maintenance and equipment replacement costs.
- Increased worker morale with resulting increase in productivity.
- Avoidance of punitive fines for sanitation violations.
- Maintenance of product quality and improved use of products.
- Less waste and general negligence as employees follow management's example.
- More efficient food control.
- Improved community relations.

Sanitation programs should include training personnel in sanitation procedures, communicating sanitation standards and regulations, providing adequate supplies and equipment, and structuring jobs to provide adequate time and personnel for sanitation activities. Management must direct such a program by emphasis on the importance of sanitation to increase employee awareness and effectiveness, and by supervision and inspection.

SAFETY   Programs to ensure safety fulfill management's moral and legal obligation to provide a safe working environment for employees and a safe dining situation for patrons. They also provide economic benefits:

- Reduction of accidents which disrupt production.
- Reduced insurance premiums.
- Lower cost of training personnel to substitute for injured workers.
- Lower cost of compensation to employees in the form of paid leaves of absence for work-related injuries.
- Reduced damage to equipment and facilities.
- Greater employee morale and increased productivity.
- Relative freedom from risk of unfavorable publicity.
- Improved community relations.

Safety programs in most operations include frequent safety self-inspections; employee training programs; communication of safety rules; formation of employee committees to promote safety; incentive programs for safe operations; provision of personal safety equipment; warning signs and painted indicators on all hazards; and management supervision to ensure safe equipment operating procedures.

WASTE HANDLING   Waste handling is an important foodservice management concern. The cost of processing and removing the gaseous, liquid, and solid wastes produced by foodservice operations is increasing, while public concern about pollution and ecology limits the choice of disposal methods.

Unless waste, and especially solid waste, is removed quickly from the operation, work-system productivity, sanitation standards, and employee safety standards are compromised. Three approaches are used in increasing the efficiency of waste handling: limitation of wastes, recycling, and more sophisticated handling techniques.

Limitation of waste material   Pre-preparation of products outside the operation—in central commissaries or in the purveyor's or supplier's facilities—eliminates vegetable trimmings, meat scraps and fat, packaging and single-use containers. It is possible to envision circumstances in which the cost of eliminating this kind of waste will equal or exceed the cost of buying the products pre-prepared.

Recycling   Some operations have successfully processed the by-products of food production into usable and sometimes saleable products. For example, animal fats and bone can be ground into pet food; fat can be sold to rendering companies which make it into soap. Other operations have installed incineration equipment that burns food by-products and packaging materials cleanly and thereby produces usable steam. Waste water is captured and reused while the heat from waste hot water is conserved and used.

Sophisticated waste-handling techniques   Industrial engineers have explored alternative methods for the handling of solid wastes that involve less labor on the part of the operation and the companies with which it contracts for waste handling. Among these are compacting, incinerating, pulping, and reducing waste to meet local codes in order to put it through the sewage system.

ENERGY
CONSERVATION

An energy conservation program begins with the work-system plan. Energy conservation considerations in planning the work system include:

- Using nonfossil energy sources such as the sun.
- Incorporating work methods that level out peak energy demands by shifting certain activities to off-peak hours.
- Generating energy as a by-product of cooling public areas or computer facilities.
- Using construction techniques and materials that retain energy.
- Choosing heating, cooling, and ventilating equipment to obtain maximum efficiency.
- Installing automated or computer-controlled heating, ventilating, and air-conditioning equipment.
- Purchasing energy-efficient equipment.
- Utilizing energy-recovery systems.

This list contains only a few examples of areas where energy conservation may be effected in good work-system planning. After the facility is built, an ongoing energy conservation program should include employee training and careful management of energy utilization.

Employee training   Much energy is wasted by employees who simply continue work habits developed during periods of inexpensive energy. It is necessary for management to discourage this by training, example, punishment, and rewards. Such practices as preheating equipment before it is needed; cooling, heating, and lighting areas in which there are no people; wasting hot water; and cooking at unnecessarily high temperatures must be eliminated.

Managing energy use   Several approaches to better management of energy use have been suggested. An energy audit and review with representatives of utility companies may qualify the operation for lower rates or a more cost-effective method of metering. Increased managerial emphasis on the maintenance of equipment can improve operating efficiencies and reduce overall energy costs. Alternative methods of food production can be designed to utilize existing equipment that is more efficient, such as the steam cooker.

Chapter 8
The Purchasing
System

It may be stretching things a bit to say that the fortunes of any foodservice operation rise or fall with the success or failure of its purchasing system. As long as the purchasing system operates efficiently, supplies flow freely, service proceeds smoothly, and consumer demands are met. But if the machinery falters—or grinds to a halt—even for a short time, confusion reigns. It follows, then, that the role of the food buyer is no mere cog in the machinery of the foodservice operation. It is an active force that sustains the entire system.

This chapter deals with the scope and challenge of the food buyer's task. It defines and describes the elements of effective purchasing and points to the practical application of standards and concepts in the buyer's daily routine.

PURCHASING CONCEPTS

Each year the foodservice industry uses more than 100 billion pounds of food. For every million hamburgers its customers, guests, and clients consume, someone first had to buy the ingredients of those hamburgers. Purchases in the foodservice industry might range in scope from a few handfuls of exotic mushrooms for use in a gourmet restaurant to carloads of flour for a pizza chain. Yet, despite wide variations in production and clientele, all purchases for foodservice operations make similar demands on the purchasing agents of those operations.

Purchasing management techniques do not vary greatly with either the type of operation or the product being purchased. Every food buyer —whether the purchasing agent for a hospital or the owner/operator of a small restaurant—must create a functional purchasing system that will supply the quality and quantity of food the operation requires at a cost it can tolerate.

The challenge to the food buyer is to fulfill the production needs of the operation within an ever-changing market—meeting cost standards, yet satisfying the consumer. The key to successful purchasing lies in the ability to meet this challenge rather than in an encyclopedic knowledge of the 8,000 varieties of apples or the minute details of grading standards for chickens. Information about a particular product can easily be researched when and if the buyer encounters the need for the product. Although successful purchasing does involve familiarity with product specifications, it is hard-won knowledge about the people the operation serves, its menus, its production system, and the market situation that provides the key to success in purchasing.

Specific Objectives of the Purchasing System

The purchasing agent is not simply an individual who is knowledgeable about food, because the purchasing system affects the entire foodservice operation. Through careful and expert purchasing, a sufficient supply of raw materials is procured, the financial objectives of the operation are met, and the standards for quality of the menu program are maintained. The four specific objectives of the purchasing system are as follows:

1. *To fulfill the needs of the supply system*   The fundamental objective of purchasing is supply. This goal of supply holds true whether purchasing is an individual responsibility or is shared by an entire purchasing department. Foodservice operations are similar to factories; without raw materials neither type of operation can produce anything. In periods of shortages or production crises, the assurance of an adequate supply takes precedence over price and quality considerations. The effect of a lack of hamburger rolls on a hamburger chain, for example, is surely more calamitous than paying more than usual for the rolls or accepting rolls that do not quite meet the operation's standards for quality.

2. *To meet financial objectives and increase profitability*   The purchasing system is responsible for the smooth and orderly flow of raw materials into the operation within the bounds of the operation's general financial objectives. Once this continuous supply is ensured, the matter of increased profitability through better purchasing can be considered. Often the people involved in purchasing can make notable contributions to the profits of the operation through cost-efficient purchasing. By either seeking out better prices on items whose prices fluctuate or buying a less expensive quality of certain foods, the purchasing agent can cut food costs considerably. Such internal economies raise profits directly, unlike other attempts at increasing profits, like expanding the business, that raise costs as well as profits, involve more risk, and require a much greater effort to effect. If smart purchasing causes food costs to drop from 30 percent to 29 percent of gross sales, that one percent savings is added directly to profits, bringing the percent of profits up, for example, from 6 percent to 7 percent of gross sales. In a restaurant that does $500,000 of business a year, that extra one percent adds $5,000 to the net profit, pushing profits up from $30,000 to $35,000 a year.

However, in his or her enthusiasm to cut food costs and hike profits, the purchasing agent must not compromise the quality of the operation's food. Lower food costs should not lead to lower consumer satisfaction.

3. *To determine the best values for food products*   A reduction in expenditures or the stabilization of expenditures in the face of rising prices sometimes may be achieved by shopping for the best possible price. More frequently, however, purchasing effectiveness lies in obtaining the best possible value. This might involve purchasing a different product, one that would yield cost economies in utilization. Or it might involve buying a different quality of product—for example, a lower grade of cauliflower that costs less per pound. Such a product would be adequate, and more economical per portion, for making cream of cauliflower soup. However, it is possible that buying a better quality chicken base—more expensive per pound—for this same soup would be more economical per portion because less of the base would be used in the soup's preparation. Finding value or cost-efficiency in the marketplace calls for considerable skill and experience. Shopping for value requires a total managerial perspective, knowledge of food production, perseverance, and creativity.

4. *To provide useful information on products to the entire operation*   To be effective, any purchasing system should serve as a conduit for information to the overall foodservice operation. The persons involved in purchasing have the opportunity to learn about new products, to discuss production systems with sales representatives who are familiar with many different operations, and to visit suppliers and producers who may be achieving production economies in new ways. It is not unusual for the food buyer to acquaint production people with a product than can effect a considerable savings: dehydrated onions and soy extenders are two examples. A food buyer might also inform production of better methods for hospital tray assembly learned from equipment sales representatives or from visits to a plant that makes preportioned dinners for airline feeding.

Current Practices in Foodservice Purchasing   Foodservice operations in the United States purchase thousands of different products each year. A single small restaurant might have a product list (the commercial equivalent of the "shopping list") of 400 or 500 items. If alcoholic beverages are included, stocking the bar could add another 200 or 300 items to the list.

Different operations of course purchase different items. But for every operation, differentiation between products purchased in quantity or that represent considerable sums spent and those that are of minor importance is a necessary part of the purchasing process. While the supply of every necessary item must be assured, cost-cutting is most productively directed to those items that represent major expenditures or major handling efforts. Little is achieved by saving 20 percent on the cost of canned pineapple if only one case a year is purchased. On the other hand, saving a fraction of a cent on every pound of lettuce used may be of dramatic importance to a restaurant chain that features a salad bar.

Exhibits 8.1 and 8.2 offer a reasonably accurate picture by quantity and dollar value of the food purchases of the foodservice industry as a whole. However, individual operations and types of operations will depart from these figures. Food buyers must thus be aware of what product categories are important to their particular operation.

According to a comprehensive survey of purchasing in the foodservice industry, the number of products in each of the 16 major food groups depicted varies considerably. The vegetable group consists of many individual items, whereas the beverages group has relatively few. Despite the number of items in a group, a low number of products together accounts for 50 percent or more of the total quantity or dollar value of each group. In 6 of the 16 major food groups, as few as two individual food items accounted for 50 percent or more of the quantity and dollar value. And, in all but one major food group, at least 50 percent of the quantity and dollar value was explained by fewer than 6 products.

At the time the survey was conducted, fresh whole milk was the leading dairy product, accounting for 52 percent of the dairy group's total quantity and 32 percent of its dollar value. Cheese and ice cream also contributed substantially to total purchases. In the fats and oils group, more solid shortening than butter was purchased, but butter led the group when dollar value of purchases was considered. Solid shortening accounted for 25 percent of the quantity; butter accounted for 33 percent of the value.

The influence of higher cost items in the major food groups is clearly evident for flour and cereal products. Whereas flour accounted for 44 percent of the group's quantity of 1.2 billion pounds, it represented only 25 percent of the dollar value. Conversely, prepared mixes containing flour accounted for one-quarter of the value but for only 18 percent of the quantity. For bakery products, the major item was hamburger buns, both in quantity and in value. Other principal items were pie and white bread.

Ground beef contributed substantially to the total quantity of beef, accounting for 44 percent. However, because of its higher unit cost, steak was first in value. But ground beef was a close second with more than 30 percent of total value. Roasts accounted for 13 to 14 percent of both quantity and value. Ham was the most important item in the group of other red meats; it represented 20 to 30 percent of both quantity and dollar value.

In the poultry and egg group, broilers and fryers, fresh eggs, and turkey accounted for all but 11 to 14 percent of quantity and value. Broilers

EXHIBIT 8.1   Foodservice Industry Use of Food by Quantity

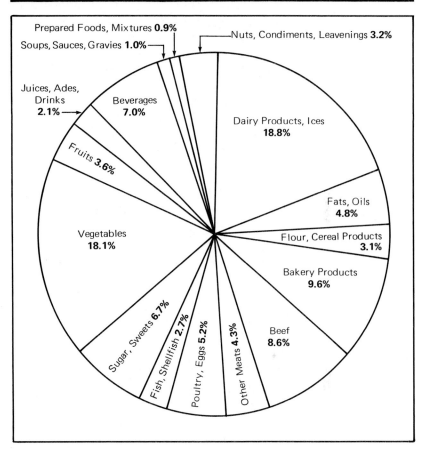

(After Statistical Bulletin No. 476, "The Foodservice Industry: Type, Quantity and Value of Foods Used." United States Department of Agriculture. 1970.)

This graph shows sixteen major food groups and the percentage of total quantity purchased in each group.

and fryers alone represented 41 percent or more of total quantity and value.

Shrimp was the foremost item on the list of fish and shellfish products. Lobster, though fourth in quantity, was second in dollar value of purchases, accounting for 18 percent of the total. The chief product in the sugars and sweets group was beverage fountain syrup. White sugar was also of consequence, accounting for 21 percent of the quantity and 13 percent of the value. With only 6 percent of the quantity, candy was second in value, accounting for 18 percent.

EXHIBIT 8.2　Foodservice Industry Use of Food by Dollar Value

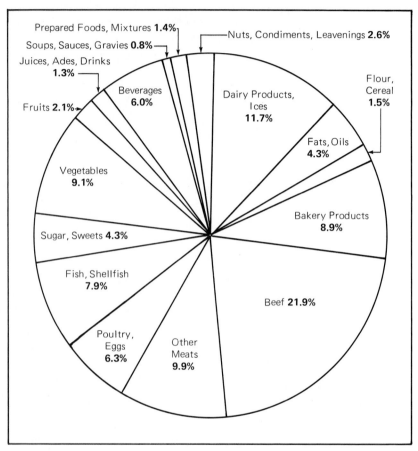

Prepared Foods, Mixtures **1.4%**

Nuts, Condiments, Leavenings **2.6%**

Soups, Sauces, Gravies **0.8%**

Juices, Ades, Drinks **1.3%**

Flour, Cereal **1.5%**

Beverages **6.0%**

Dairy Products, Ices **11.7%**

Fruits **2.1%**

Fats, Oils **4.3%**

Vegetables **9.1%**

Bakery Products **8.9%**

Sugar, Sweets **4.3%**

Fish, Shellfish **7.9%**

Beef **21.9%**

Poultry, Eggs **6.3%**

Other Meats **9.9%**

(After Statistical Bulletin No. 476, "The Foodservice Industry:　Type, Quantity and Value of Foods Used." United States Department of Agriculture. 1970.)

This graph shows sixteen major food groups and the percentage of total dollar value for each group.

Vegetables represented 18 percent of the total quantity and about 9 percent of the cost value of all foods received. Prominent items within the group were potatoes, lettuce, onions, tomatoes, and green beans. No single item stood out in the fruits group, although melons and apples were major contributors to quantity; and oranges, lemons, and peaches were not far behind. No item represented more than 13 percent of the cost value of purchases in this group.

In the juices, ades, and drinks group, more than one-half the quantity and dollar value was attributed to orange juice and tomato juice. Orange juice alone represented 45 percent of the value of purchases and 34 percent of total quantity. In the beverages group, soft drinks accounted for almost two-thirds of the total quantity. Cola drinks represented 44 percent, twice as much as fruit-type soft drinks. However, roasted and ground coffee beans together were the foremost item of the beverages group in value, representing 46 percent of total purchases.

Soups as a single food item accounted for about 310 million of the 390 million pounds attributed to the soups, sauces, and gravies group. Sauces and gravies represented about 17 percent of both value and quantity. In the nuts, condiments, and leavenings group, catsup and pickles were principal items in value and quantity of purchases. Catsup accounted for 24 to 30 percent of both value and quantity. Nuts and peanut butter ranked second in value and fifth in quantity.

The Food Buyer's Job As the purchasing responsibility becomes greater or the purchasing procedure becomes more complex or more difficult, the food buyer tends to become a specialist. In small operations, those with annual sales of less than $100,000 or the noncommercial equivalent, the manager is often the food buyer. In larger operations that have a manager but few other professional workers, the owner might do the buying.

Only in very large operations having a more formal and necessarily larger management structure does buying for foodservice needs become the primary job of one individual or of a group of persons. In large hotels, for example, the food buying may be done by a *purchasing agent* operating from the office of the food and beverage director or, perhaps, from the office of the hotel comptroller. Food buying for the client-service segment of the foodservice industry (hospitals, universities, and institutions) may be consolidated with other types of purchasing in a central buying office. Multi-unit foodservice operations frequently have a central buying department that handles most of the purchasing. In such operations, each individual unit purchases only the highly perishable products. Even then, the choice of supplier might be subject to the approval of the central department.

In large, traditionally organized, independent restaurant operations, the purchasing and supply systems are managed by the *steward* or *chief steward*. Some operations maintain a *chef/steward*, who is responsible for purchasing, supply, and production.

With the movement of the foodservice industry toward a greater degree of business sophistication, several other titles have emerged. An operation may employ a *food buyer* and also a *liquor buyer*. In some operations, the *food production manager* or the *food operations manager* has assumed the administrative duties of the chef and in this role buys food. In some schools and health care facilities, the dietitian or several dietitians might buy the food.

Despite this diversity of titles and the diversity of roles these titles imply, some generalizations about the job of food buyer are still possible.

In addition to having similar responsibilities, all of these food buyers must function as part of a larger organization if they are to be effective. Clear definitions of responsibility must be established. The food buyer's activities must not conflict with those of the central purchasing agent, the chef, unit managers, dietitians, suppliers, or other management or purchasing personnel. To prevent such conflict, responsibilities for overall purchasing or for the establishment of purchasing product categories must be precisely defined. It is more important to place the responsibility for every purchase somewhere than it is to make purchasing the total responsibility of one individual or one department.

If an observer were to study the job of a food buyer or purchasing agent, the results of such observation might be the list of activities shown in Exhibit 8.3. Besides performing these tasks, often the food buyer also must organize and manage the purchasing department, supervise the supply system, assist in the development of purchasing policy, and coordinate purchasing activities with the rest of the operation's management.

In sum, the purchasing job involves functioning at two levels: the routine administrative level suggested in Exhibit 8.3 and the managerial level mandated by the objectives of purchasing and the many decisions and judgments necessary to the maintenance of an effective purchasing system.

Any of the activities listed in Exhibit 8.3—processing requisitions, buying, expediting, accounting, clerical work, communications—can become a full-time job. Thus, as operations increase in volume, the purchasing function can require several people. The largest operations—namely, the major foodservice contract companies and large chains—have foodservice people whose job titles roughly correspond to the activities listed in Exhibit 8.3: purchasing agent, buyer, traffic manager, accounting clerk, clerk, and secretary. Their departments are managed by a director of purchasing, or a vice-president of purchasing, who is responsible for policy formation, forecasting, planning, and other executive activities.

In summary, the role of the food buyer in the modern foodservice operation is constantly growing. What once might have been a routine job now is often a great challenge. The special problems that foodservice operations encounter today have enhanced the importance of the people responsible for the acquisition, administration, control, and distribution of raw materials. More and more, the success of the overall operation centers on the skill and dedication of the food buyer. As foodservice operations strive to adapt themselves to the changing business environment, the food buyer comes increasingly to the forefront. The new consumer awareness is a case in point. Consumers now demand "truth-in-menu" and products free of preservatives or other additives.

EXHIBIT 8.3   Activities of the Food Buyer

General Activity	Examples	% of Time Spent
Processing requisitions and requests	Routing requisitions Checking accuracy Comparing requisitions with projects	5
Buying routine	Placing orders Obtaining quotes Selecting vendors Checking samples Talking with sales reps	40
Expediting	Confirming delivery Inquiring about overdue shipments Preparing operation to handle product Communicating with production	30
Accounting functions	Adjusting invoices Authorizing payments Negotiating adjustments	5
Clerical functions	Maintaining supplier lists Updating price sheets Filing product information	5
Communications	Refining specifications Reporting to management Maintaining supplier contact	15

Today, the ability of the food buyer to find genuine milk-fed veal or natural apple juice might well contribute to the success of the foodservice operation. This and many other current issues such as the rise in commodity prices, the energy crisis, increasingly sophisticated consumer food preferences, and environmental concerns touch the food buyer and make the job both challenging and increasingly important.

PREPARATION FOR EFFECTIVE PURCHASING

Sending an order for food products to a supplier is one of the final steps in the purchasing process. That order must be correct, representative of the operation's needs, and cost-effective. Obviously, ordering calls for much forethought, preparation, and management.

Before making decisions concerning an order, the food buyer must know and apply the foodservice operation's standards, or *specifications,* for the products involved. The buyer must also adhere to existing purchasing guidelines or *policies.* The food buyer must also have a written request for purchase, or *requisition,* from the production department. Following this procedure, the food buyer knows exactly what is wanted (from the specifications), how to get it (from the purchasing policies), and how much of the product is needed (from the requisition). Preparation for purchasing thus involves: (1) developing standards for purchasing; (2) establishing a purchasing policy; and (3) determining current product needs. Each of these aspects of the purchasing process will be dealt with in detail in the following pages.

Developing Standards for Purchasing

Foodservice operations do not necessarily seek the best—the cream of the crop or the top of the line—in their purchasing. Rather, each operation requires products that are most suited to the intended use. Once the suitability of a particular quality of a particular product has been demonstrated, this quality becomes the operation's standard for purchasing. Every time that product is needed, the quality specified is sought. In food production, cooking times, yields, and formulas are all based on that standard quality. Menu pricing and cost control also may require a certain standard—a consistent quality—from which the food buyer does not deviate. Consumers may come to expect a certain quality that represents value for them in the finished products.

For a food buyer to accept anything less than this standard would probably result in merchandising problems, waste, and complaints. Buying products with quality above the standard probably would result in unanticipated costs and reduced profits. The marketplace is ruthlessly fair, and products of higher quality do cost more.

In establishing standards, the food buyer is faced with two problems: how are the standards to be determined, and how shall these standards be expressed and communicated once they are established?

DETERMINATION OF STANDARDS

The determination of the purchasing standards for a foodservice operation is based on the suitability of the food products to that operation. This determination involves four steps: (1) consumer preference assessment; (2) development of recipes for the items the operation offers; (3) value analysis of products used; and (4) yield analysis of products used.

Consumer Preference Assessment

The importance of understanding the preferences and desires of customers, guests, and clients was discussed extensively in Chapters 4 and 6. Therefore it need not be stressed here. We must keep in mind that the main result of consumer preference assessment is the operation's food offerings—its menu. The selection of menu items is subject to the limitations imposed by costs, available facilities, personnel, equipment, business factors, and the price patrons will pay. Obviously, the menu should represent the tastes and desires of the people served by the operation. If there are spareribs and rhubarb pie on the menu, it is because the customers want them—and also because the operation can produce them at an acceptable cost.

However, in order to establish adequate purchasing standards, the food buyer needs more information about consumer preferences than is indicated by an operation's menu. The food buyer may need to know, for example, that the people the operation serves prefer particular spices in seasoned vegetables. They might prefer light or starchy baked goods. Or perhaps they might want white vinegar and white vinegar only for their french fried potatoes. It is a fact that people in some parts of the United States are accustomed to margarine; prefer the taste of frozen, rather than fresh, fish; and think that a hot dog without chili sauce is only half a hot dog. Other people want hot dogs that are made from beef flavored with garlic, sandwich rolls that are crusty, and cheddar cheese that is bright orange. Small wonder that consumer preference spawns an odd assortment of questions. Should cheesecake be made from cottage cheese or cream cheese? Should the operation use brown or white eggs? Should dinner rolls be hot and yeasty, or cold and sweet?

The menu as such does not reveal the particular food qualities the consumer prefers. To determine this aspect, the food buyer might discuss consumer preferences with managers of local supermarkets, newspaper food editors, or food buyers for noncompetitive foodservice operations. Eating in the facilities of competitive operations, in community halls, and in schools certainly would offer clues to local preferences. Once the food buyers have some idea of the possible alternatives, they can ask neighbors, locally hired employees, and even people on the street about their food preferences. Formal surveys, such as those reviewed in Chapter 4, also are sometimes desirable.

Development of Recipes

With consumer preferences in mind and the menu in hand, the food buyer and other individuals involved with the management of the food-service operation must develop a recipe for each menu item offered. There are few published recipes that the management team would find immediately acceptable. Rather, each recipe must be individually considered and evaluated from a variety of perspectives:

- implications for production, the work and equipment involved in making the recipe.
- implications for service, the work and equipment involved in serving that particular version of the dish.
- costs of production.
- taste and general acceptability of the dish to consumers.
- availability of the products the recipe requires.

Various recipes are tried and modified until an acceptable recipe is developed. Even the recipe for a simple item—a glass of tomato juice, for example—must be developed. How much should be served? Should it be served with lemon or lime, with parsley or crackers, or nothing at all?

During this developmental process, a variety of products might be tried. It may be that dehydrated onions solve a certain production problem in making onion soup. Or perhaps the taste of frozen okra in chicken gumbo proves to be more acceptable than that of canned okra. Thus, through the process of recipe development, the suitability of certain products is established while other qualities of the same products are rejected.

Value Analysis

Let us assume that a satisfactory recipe has been developed; it tastes good; the kitchen can produce it; the recipe works every time anyone tries it; and the measurements are accurate. It has been recorded on a standardized recipe form like that shown in Exhibit 6.7 in "The Menu-Planning System." Only one more step is necessary before these recipe ingredients can be accepted as the operation's standards for purchasing. Each ingredient must be examined. Can another product, almost the same but slightly different and less costly, be substituted without affecting the quality of the menu item? Getting the answer to this question requires value analysis.

It may be that the product used in developing the recipe had qualities that were unnecessary for the satisfactory preparation of the dish, but which added to the cost. Is it necessary, for example, to have absolutely perfect-looking apples to make apple pie? Table quality apples are much more expensive than those with slight and removable blemishes on the peel. Can the same product (for example, a frozen pie) be bought with some of the kitchen work already done, thus saving production costs? Using frozen apples already prepared for pie filling might allow the foodservice operation to produce a comparable pie less expensively. Exhibit 8.4 suggests a number of ways a product used in a recipe can be examined to determine if it is the best value for the operation.

The results of the value analysis should be incorporated as a purchasing guide in the standardized recipe. The ingredients described now can become the operation's standard of quality.

Yield Analysis

Standards of quality only partially fulfill the operation's need for standardization. The recipe development process and the development of quality standards make apparent certain relationships between the product as it is used and the product as it is purchased. It takes more than 400 grams (14 ounces) of raw fresh green beans to produce four 100-gram (3.5 ounces) portions of cooked green beans. It takes more than 200 grams (7 ounces) of prime rib of beef to produce one 200-gram steak. The exact relationship between the product as purchased and the product as served can only be determined by actual measurement or testing. The objective here is to develop a standard set of conversion factors that relate portions served to market units. Although tables such as the specimen conversion table shown as Exhibit 8.5 are helpful, they do not indicate the exact quality of the product being analyzed, nor do they fully explain the preparation procedure. Two individual operations using the products they can actually obtain and their own particular preparation procedures may obtain substantially different results.

A yield test form can provide a model for recording yield analysis. The test itself can be performed at any one stage in the product's utilization, or it can be done at several different stages. If the yield of a prime rib were being analyzed, a yield test at the time of butchering (butcher's test) and a yield test after cooking (cooking test) might both be conducted. Once the yield analysis has been done, it can be presented, along with similar information for other products, as a conversion table. The conversion table is used primarily for determining the operation's current needs for products. If the operation should need 100 portions of steak each of which has a cooked weight of 200 grams, it would be necessary to apply the appropriate conversion factor to the total to determine how much meat must be sought in the marketplace.

Yield standards can also be used as an element in the development of the quality standard for a given product. For example, it would not be unreasonable to state as part of the quality standard for fresh corn that each bushel of corn should yield at least 90 percent usable ears.

Yield standards are frequently used as a means of product evaluation. In such cases, food buyers analyze samples from different suppliers for yield to determine the exact price per portion served or used. They then choose the best value regardless of price per market unit. Prime rib of beef at $3.85 per kilogram ($1.75 per pound) is a better buy than prime

EXHIBIT 8.4   Value Analysis of Food Products: Questioning the Use of a Product

Are We Using the Right. . ?	Explanation	Example
Grade	Is the color, appearance, ripeness, and presence of defects really important?	It would be a waste of money to buy U.S. fancy grapefruit to cut into segments; the customer would not see the attractive, more expensive peel. Buy a lower grade.
Size	Some items are sold by the piece but used in some cases by another unit measure. Price quotations should be obtained on the unit measure actually used.	In making scrambled eggs, the eggs are bought by the dozen but portioned (served) by the ounce. When large eggs are 54 cents a dozen; medium, 47 cents; and small, 41 cents, the cost per pound is the same. Thus, it would be an error to buy medium eggs at 49 cents a dozen when large are 54 cents, even though the price of the medium eggs is less per market unit.
Style	Products may be offered in several sized pieces, from chopped to whole. Generally, the closer to whole the product is, the more expensive it is.	Olives may be purchased whole, but they also may be purchased as salad olives, in pieces. For making cream cheese and olive sandwiches, the use of whole olives would be wasteful.
Packaging	Wrappings, cartons, and bags can all add to the cost of a product. Is the packaging worth the price?	The operation is buying sauces in boilable bags but opening the bags and heating the sauce in a sauce pan. A sauce with a different packaging should be sought.

rib at $3.63 per kilogram ($1.65 per pound) if the more expensive prime rib yields 10 percent more usable beef steak.

COMMUNICATION OF STANDARDS
Even though the process of developing standards requires time and effort, once this task has been completed only minor revisions are necessary. A new menu item will require a repetition of consumer preference assessment, recipe development, and value analysis, but only for that single item. A new product may result in a reformulation of the recipe. But change will be gradual, and most of the basic purchasing standards of the operation will continue to be effective for a long period. They can

Are We Using the Right. . ?	*Explanation*	*Example*
Strength	When pricing competitive ingredients, the food buyer must consider how much of an ingredient is needed for the recipe in relation to how much of a comparable ingredient would be used.	An operation is using a chocolate drink mix as a flavoring in cakes. Whereas the mix is inexpensive per ounce, a great deal of it must be used to provide good flavor. Plain cocoa, although more expensive per ounce, is less expensive per use.
Unit of Purchase	Generally, the larger the unit size, the lower the cost per measure of product within the unit.	An operation is using Worcestershire sauce to make barbecue sauce and buying it in large bottles. It is available in various larger sizes, even in drums.
Uniformity	For some uses, products should have the same size and shape; for others any reasonable size will do.	An operation is using chopped tomatoes in salads and buying the presorted tomatoes that are virtually identical in size and shape. Unsorted "field run" tomatoes would serve as well.
Brand	Some brands of products are truly distinctive; others do not differ substantially from the same product made by an unknown, unadvertised company.	A food buyer finds that a less expensive product could be used successfully instead of the brand name distilled vinegar it had purchased for poaching eggs.
Specification	Specifications can be overprecise. Generally, the more exacting the specification in its departures from the bulk of products sold, the more expensive the product will be.	A food buyer finds that asking for special trim on the lamb chops he buys is costing more than does trimming the more generally available lamb chops within the operation.

be abstracted from the standardized recipes, consolidated, categorized, and codified. The final result of this effort often is an indexed loose-leaf book that is organized by product category. The categories shown in Exhibit 8.6 include, among other items, the food groups discussed at the beginning of this chapter.

Within these categories and major subdivisions, a separate page of the book treats each item. The needs of the operation for tomatoes, carrots, beef steak, ice cream, rolls and every other product are clearly and specifically described so that anyone can understand exactly what the operation requires. If the operation uses three qualities of tomatoes (one for

EXHIBIT 8.5   Model Standard Yield Table for Fruits

Fruits	Quantity* as Served	Conversion** Factor	Quantity to Buy
Apples, raw chopped		1.32	
Apples, for applesauce		1.15	
Apples, cooked, sliced		1.59	
Avocados, wedges		1.33	
Bananas, sliced for fruit cup		1.47	
Blackberries, salad garnish		1.05	
Blueberries, salad garnish		1.09	
Cherries, pitted, raw		1.12	
Grapefruit, juice		2.27	
Grapes, seeds removed		1.12	
Honeydew melon, diced		1.67	
Lemon, juice		2.33	
Orange, juice		2.00	
Orange, sections, no membrane		1.79	
Peaches, sliced		1.32	
Pears, sliced		1.28	
Pineapple, cubed		1.92	
Strawberries, garnish		1.15	
Watermelon, cubed		2.17	

*Quantity by weight
**Multiply weight of serving by conversion factor to obtain quantity to buy.

This table represents a particular operation's yield tests and subsequent conversion factors to determine quantity to buy. This table is not prescriptive. Actual yields must be determined for each operation according to production methods and the availability of products in the marketplace.

soup, one for salads, and one for stuffed tomatoes), there are three different descriptions of tomatoes in the book. Each detailed specific description is the *specification* for that quality of tomato best suited for a particular use. Exhibit 8.7 shows a sample specification for different kinds of beef roasts.

A good specification is clear and complete. It includes information that describes only the quality wanted and that, by extension, excludes other qualities. Exhibit 8.8 suggests the kind of information a specification includes and gives some examples of the descriptors that might be used to qualify these data exactly. A comparison of this table with the actual

EXHIBIT 8.6 Product Categories for the Organization of Specifications

Category	Typical Divisions within Categories
Beef	Ground meat Steak Prime ribs Meat for stewing Roasts Beef variety meats (liver, etc.)
Other Meats than Beef	Ham Pork other than ham Veal Lamb Variety meats
Dairy Products	Milk Ice cream Cheese Milk substitutes
Vegetables	Potatoes and starches Vegetables, fresh Vegetables, frozen Vegetables, canned, dried, etc. Produce, salad vegetables
Bakery	Rolls Bread Cake
Fish and Shellfish	Shrimp Fish, fresh Fish, processed Other seafood
Poultry, Eggs	Broilers and fryers Other fowl Eggs, fresh Other eggs
Beverages	Soft drinks Coffee Other beverages

EXHIBIT 8.6 Product Categories (cont.)

Category	Typical Divisions within Categories
Sugar, Sweets	Sugar Sugar substitutes Fountain syrup Other sweets
Fats, Oils	Fats for frying Fats for baking Other fats and oils
Nuts, Condiments, Leavenings	Table condiments Kitchen spices Nuts Leavenings Other condiments
Fruits	Oranges, lemons Melons Other fruits
Flour, Cereals	Rice and other grains Table cereals Flour Other cereals
Prepared Foods, Mixtures	Main-course foods Other prepared foods Prepared foods for preparations
Juices, Ades, Drinks	Orange juice Other juices Other drink products
Soups, Sauces, Gravies	Prepared soups Soup and sauce bases Gravy bases Salad dressings Other sauces
Single-service Tableware, Paper Goods	Single-service products Paper products
Cleaning Supplies	Chemicals Consumable cleaning supplies: mop heads, cloths, etc.

EXHIBIT 8.7   Specimen Specifications for Beef Roasts

Item No. 1109AR-Rib, Bone-in, Tied, Roast Ready, Special — The bone-in, tied, roast ready, special, rib is prepared from a Primal Rib—Item No. 103—Series 100. The chine bone, or bodies of the thoracic vertebrae, must be entirely removed by sawing and cutting to the point at which they join the featherbones exposing the lean meat. The featherbones must be removed and excluded. Beginning at the sawed end of the rib bones, the exterior fat covering over the entire rib must be lifted intact from over the outermost lean muscles. All of the lean muscle lying above the level of the blade bone, the blade bone and related cartilage, the small muscle below and firmly attached to the blade bone and the backstrap must be removed and excluded. The short ribs must then be removed by a straight cut across the ribs starting at a fixed point determined by measuring off 3 inches from the extreme outer tip of the ribeye muscle at the 12th rib and continuing in a straight line through a fixed point determined by measuring off 4 inches from the extreme outer tip of the ribeye muscle at the 6th rib. The fat overlying the ribeye muscle must be trimmed to a uniform level for the entire area of the seamed surface. The exterior fat covering must be returned to its natural position, except that it shall extend from the ends of the rib bones where the chine bone was removed to the sawed ends of the rib bones. Fat cover extending beyond the sawed end of the rib bones must be removed even with the ends and excluded. The exterior fat covering must be held in place by a string tying lengthwise and girthwise.

These specifications are from a series approved for meat and meat products and prepared by the United States Department of Agriculture.

specifications in Exhibit 8.7 demonstrates that each product requires only information of a certain order.

Developing complete specifications for every product and for every quality of product that an operation uses is obviously a time-consuming procedure. However, it is an investment that should be justified by long-term savings in several ways:

1. Waste and production delays are avoided when the operation receives exactly the products it requires.

2. The food buyer can compare prices from a number of different suppliers and deal with the least expensive because everyone understands the standards of the operation.

3. Price competition among suppliers is encouraged. Everyone understands on what quality quotations are being offered.

4. Value trade-offs are clear. The effects of deviating from the operation's standards are more easily determined.

5. Products that fail to meet standards after they are delivered become the supplier's responsibility if function (for example, the leavening power of baking powder) is part of the specification.

6. Adjustments with suppliers are facilitated.

Sometimes the process of specification writing can be simplified by including an existing and widely recognized standard as part of the

EXHIBIT 8.8 **Specification Data and Examples of Descriptors for Product Specifications**

Specification Data	Example Descriptors
Common name	Delmonico steak; littleneck clam
Variety	Red Delicious apple; Bosc pear
Origin	Florida grapefruit; Hawaiian pineapple
Style	Kitchen-cut green beans; peach slices
Cut (of meats)	Top round; flank steak
Trim	Fully-trimmed tenderloins; tops-off carrots; skinless hams; no more than 1/4 inch fat (roasts)
Appearance	Well-colored, no cuts, smooth (grapefruit)
Maturity	Spring lamb; yearling veal; early peas
Defects by amount	No more than 1/5 of its surface affected by discoloration (grapefruit)
Deviation by amount	No more than 5% larger or smaller (medium eggs)
Type of processing	Frozen green beans; dried dates
Pack	Rattle-pack peas; string figs
Packing medium	In heavy syrup (peaches); in soy oil (sardines)
Density of medium	Heavy syrup; light syrup; 30° Brix (peaches)
Drained weight	Ounces or grams (canned goods)
Sex	Fowl, capon (poultry); female lobster
Container	303 can; 40-ounce (1.134 kilos) package; Los Angeles lug
Size	Medium; 2 1/2" (6–7 cm) diameter; jumbo (eggs)
Count per market unit	88 oranges; 27 melons
Market unit (on which price is quoted)	Case of No. 10 sized cans of green beans; Case of 30 dozen eggs
Weight tolerance	Plus or minus 5% (30-pound or 13.6-kilo prime ribs)
Pure or imitation	Pure vanilla; imitation maple syrup

specification. There are a number of different sources for standards. It should be recognized, however, that such standards are only part of the specifications an individual operation may require. The specification excerpt given in Exhibit 8.9 from the United States standards for Florida grapefruit indicates exactly what is being specified and what is not being specified by the designation *U.S. Fancy, Uniform in Size "54" Grapefruit.*

As a means of shortening the length of their written specifications, many operations draw up production specifications using certain widely used sources of standards. These sources of standards include the following:

Specification Data	Example Descriptors
Moisture content	Not to exceed 3% (cocoa powder)
Composition (% and type)	Not less than 42% dried milk powder (cocoa powder)
Nutrition (% and type)	Not less than 16% protein
Additives (% and type)	No water added (hams); Vitamin C added (ade)
Breading (% and type)	No more than 30% cornmeal breading (prepared catfish)
Delivery condition	Less than 0°F (−17.8°C); less than 40°F (4.4°C) (frozen and fresh beef, respectively)
Bacterial count or Coliform	Not to exceed 50,000 per gram; not to exceed 90 per gram
Performance	Will produce a minimum of 14% carbon dioxide (baking powder); will disperse in 40°F (4.4°C) water (cocoa powder)
Flavoring	Vanilla sugar; mint-flavored cherries
Stability	Will not develop off-flavors in less than one year at 68°F (20.2°C) storage
Foreign material	No more than 1% foreign material (dried beans)
Yield	68% usable lean meat; 50% lean (bacon)
Packaging	Foil-wrapped potatoes; cell pack apples
Weight range	23–30 pound (10.4–13.6 kilos) prime ribs; 1–1 1/4 pound (0.45–0.57 kilos) lobsters
Feed	Corn-fed pork; milk-fed veal
Season	New crop walnuts; gas-storage applies; hothouse tomatoes
Processing/preparation	Eviscerated chickens; filleted fish; husked corn

Standards established by the United States Department of Agriculture These standards are the principal source of grade standards for dairy products; for fresh fruit and vegetables, including nuts; processed fruits and vegetables; honey; sugar products; grain; soybeans; beans; rice and peas; meats; poultry and poultry products; shell eggs; and egg products. Thus, it is possible to include such expressions as "USDA prime beef" and "Grade B broilers" in a specification. These standards also include the very important "Institutional Meat Purchase Specifications" which describe fresh beef (Series 100); fresh lamb and mutton (Series 200); fresh veal and calf (Series 300); fresh pork (Series 400);

EXHIBIT 8.9   U.S. Standards for Grades of Florida Grapefruit: U.S. Fancy Uniform "54"

Section 51.750 U.S. Fancy

"U.S. Fancy" consists of grapefruit which meet the following requirements:

(a)   Basic requirements:
    (1)   Discoloration
        (i)   Not more than one-tenth of the surface, in the surface, in the aggregate, may be affected by discoloration. (See Section 51.770 which defines discoloration)
    (2)   Firm
    (3)   Mature
    (4)   Similar varietal characteristics
    (5)   Smooth texture
    (6)   Well-colored
    (7)   Well-formed

(b)   Free from:
    (1)   Ammoniation
    (2)   Bruises
    (3)   Buckskin
    (4)   Caked melanose
    (5)   Cuts not healed
    (6)   Decay
    (7)   Growth cracks
    (8)   Scab
    (9)   Sprayburn
    (10) Wormy fruit

(c)   Free from injury caused by
    (1)   Green spots
    (2)   Oil spots
    (3)   Scale
    (4)   Scars
    (5)   Breakdown
    (6)   Thorn scratches

(d)   Free from damage caused by:
    (1)   Dirt or other foreign material
    (2)   Disease
    (3)   Dryness or mushy condition
    (4)   Hail
    (5)   Insects
    (6)   Sprouting
    (7)   Sunburn
    (8)   Other means

(e)   For other tolerances, see Section 51.761

This description itemizes accepted standards for U.S. Fancy Uniform "54" Florida grapefruit.

cured, cured and smoked, and fully-cooked pork products (Series 500); cured, dried, and smoked beef products (Series 600); edible by-products (Series 700); sausage products (Series 800); and portion-cut meat products (Series 1000).

Standards established by the Department of the Interior, Bureau of Commercial Fisheries   These standards are the source of specification information for such items as frozen fried fish sticks, raw breaded shrimp, fish blocks, haddock fillets, fried scallops, and other frozen fish items.

Standards established by the Department of Defense   These specifications can be used when the operation's standards must parallel those of the military, which tend toward superior products. Such items as bacon, canned chicken, canned ham, and hamburgers in gravy are covered by this grouping.

Standards established by the Veterans Administration   These include specifications prepared by other branches of the federal government, such as the General Services Administration, that serve federal employee-feeding facilities.

Standards established by the Department of Health, Education, and Welfare, Food and Drug Administration (FDA)   These standards are widely used. It is not necessary to describe many of the qualities of the more than 300 products for which definitions and standards of identity, quality, and fill of container have been established by the FDA because the fundamental identity and quality of the item are established by its very name. For example, there is a standard and definition for mayonnaise. The standard establishes that a product sold as mayonnaise must, for one thing, contain not less than 65 percent vegetable oil by weight; that only certain seasonings may be included without being mentioned on the label; that only certain forms of the egg yolk can be used; and so on.

Standards established by trade associations   These provisions help define the identity and purity of products, their method of manufacture, and testing procedures for determining their quality. Mention of the trade association standard as part of the specification thus includes the applicable information. A trade association for the dairy industry, for example, would adopt standards for clean milk, storage limits for butter, composition of ice cream, and so on.

Standards established by brand identification   These measures serve to short-cut the specification process if the brand consistently represents the quality the operation requires. However, suppliers may quote prices on "Brand X catsup, 6/10 cans per case" without much further elaboration.

Whether specifications are based on existing standards or are entirely created by the foodservice operation, they are useful—indeed, necessary —for effective purchasing. But the limitations of using specifications should also be recognized:

• Specifications can limit the source of supply. Some vendors may be unwilling or unable to quote on specifications because they lack the fundamental information about the products.

• Specifications tend to lead to inflexibility. The effort involved in writing good specifications makes people reluctant to write new ones. Market and production conditions change constantly, and specifications can be improved.

• Specifications may be overwritten. The specification that exceeds the operation's needs for standardization tends to limit purchasing flexibility and probably increases the cost per unit purchased.

• Specifications tend to establish the maximum quality as well as the minimum quality an operation will receive.

• Poorly written specifications tend to formalize errors that might have been corrected by the give-and-take of the marketplace.

Distribution of the specifications completes the process for developing standards. Specifications are distributed on a need-to-know basis. It may be useful to supply principal vendors with a set of the specifications for the products they supply. If this is done, specifications can be referenced to facilitate ordering. Each specification can be identified by an appropriate name or number, so that all the buyer need do when obtaining a price quote or placing an order is refer the supplier to "Salad Tomatoes" or "Spec. 5348."

Receiving personnel should have a set of specifications so that products may be checked against the operation's standards as they are received. The food production department also requires a set of specifications for their own reference.

Establishing a Purchasing Policy

Standard specifications describe the food products the operation needs, and a purchasing policy establishes the basic ground rules for getting them. An operation's purchasing policy defines what buying method is used, how vendors are evaluated and selected, and what overall purchasing strategy dominates the operation's purchasing system.

BUYING METHOD   A foodservice operation can arrange to make its purchases in a number of ways: open-market buying; sealed-bid buying; contract buying; "systems" buying; blanket-order buying; and futures buying. These are the major methods, some of which may have variations. The choice of method or methods depends on the nature of the foodservice operation, the particular products being purchased, and the market conditions confronting the food buyer.

Open-market buying   As the operation's needs occur, the food buyer purchases at the best price offered for the specified product. Often the purchases are confined to a group of vendors who meet other standards besides price. The food buyer may obtain quotations from several vendors, visit a terminal market at which vendors are located, or buy the product at a public auction.

Sealed-bid buying   In this type of buying, the food buyer, anticipating the operation's needs, asks vendors to submit written price quotations based on exact specifications. The sealed bids are opened at an announced time, often in a public session. The purchase is awarded to the lowest bidder, provided the vendor is satisfactory in all other ways. A somewhat abbreviated bidding procedure called *negotiated buying* is sometimes used instead of this sealed-bid buying. Vendors who are likely to bid are specifically invited to bid by telephone or in informal contact (rather than by public announcement), and the lowest bidder is awarded the purchase.

Contract buying   In contract buying, the food buyer anticipates the operation's needs over a specific period of time and negotiates a definite price for the specified product with just one or two vendors. The price agreed upon can be for a definite amount, or it can vary with the market price current at the time the product is shipped. For example, a contract for a beef item may be for "10 cents a pound more than the Chicago wholesale price," which is reported publicly each day. Or a contract might be for "cost plus," meaning the cost to the vendor plus a specific sum—10 cents a pound, for example—or plus a percentage markup. Sometimes the vendor is paid a monthly fee, and the operation is charged the cost of the product to the vendor. In other contracts, the vendor is paid on the basis of the number of units of the product—that is, pounds, carloads, or packages—handled.

Systems buying   As the name "systems" implies, the actual product in systems buying is only part of the services the vendor offers. Often the phrase refers to general simplification of the buying process. The vendor may maintain stocks of the product on the buyer's premises and invoice the operation only as the product is used. Or the vendor may guarantee certain delivery conditions if the buyer purchases a certain amount of the product from the vendor.

Blanket-order buying   A blanket order is a general commitment to buy either a fixed quantity of products or products at a fixed price. Blanket-order buying differs from contract buying in that the term of the commitment may not be specified. In blank-check buying, which is a form of blanket-order buying, the operation makes a commitment to buy regardless of price, specifying only quantity. This method is used in times of crisis or of short supply.

Futures buying   Futures buying is an option open to an operation whose staff is familiar with the intricacies of the commodities market. The object of futures buying is to protect the operation against price fluctuations by "hedging." Hedging is accomplished by offsetting rises or drops in the prices of basic commodities by trading futures contracts. A futures contract is an agreement to buy a certain amount of a commodity (for example, iced broilers) at a certain price at a certain future date.

An operation using a great deal of chicken—for example, a large fried-chicken chain—may contract to buy futures in chicken at the same time that it also prepares to buy the chicken it needs on the open market. If the futures market price of chicken goes up by two cents per pound and the price of chicken on the open market goes up by two cents per pound, the operation then sells its futures contracts and buys the chicken on the open market. In effect, the price increase of the chicken has been cancelled out by the profit the operation made in the futures market. If the price of iced broilers on the futures market goes down (and the open-market chicken price goes down as well), then the operation sells its futures contracts at a loss but offsets this loss by buying the chicken it needs at the cheaper price on the open market. It is important to stress that the operation *never* actually takes delivery on the commodity it agrees to buy in the futures contract. Through hedging—and careful trading—an operation uses futures buying to protect itself against price fluctuations in the products it uses, not to actually buy those products. Futures trading must be continuous to be effective since the contracts are sold by the month and are called, for example, "May soybeans."

The choice of buying method depends on the kind of operation, the type of products being purchased, and on current market conditions. Most commercial operations use open-market buying for most of their purchases. Most operations that serve the continuing client use bid buying. The difference in policy originates in the greater need for accountability in client-service operations. A system of purchasing based on written, competitive bids for precisely specified products seems to ensure the best price for an operation that is publicly supported. It also assures fairness to the vendors, who are part of that public. Unfortunately, the need for accountability also makes the procedure difficult, and only certain vendors may bid. Also, the prices quoted by vendors may reflect the expense of preparing their bids.

The cash position of the operation may be another influence on choice of buying method. A purchase by contract may offer necessary credit to an operation that has just opened. On the other hand, the enviable cash flow (the amount of cash on hand) of a large foodservice company may prompt management to undertake financial maneuvers of which futures buying is a part.

The particular product being purchased can influence purchasing method if its price does not vary considerably over a period of time. If the operation's needs remain fairly constant, there is little point in aggressively seeking better prices and new sources of supply. A contract, or a blanket order with a single vendor for this product, allows the food buyer to pay more attention to those products which do require aggressive buying. Often bread, milk, and other perishable basic items are purchased by contract or blanket order. When there is the possibility of widely fluctuating prices or radically changing supply, systems buying or a contract for a large quantity purchase may protect the operation against price rises and shortages. Operations using large quantities of canned products can sometimes profit by this sort of arrangement.

Market conditions cannot be ignored as a determining factor in the choice of buying method. Part of this picture is the attitude of major producers, manufacturers, and packers. Such vendors may be willing to deal with the operation only on a contract basis. On the other hand, small local farmers and producers, unsure of their own production and supply, may be agreeable only to cash transactions. Conditions of extreme shortage may force the food buyer to issue blank-check buying orders to reputable purveyors in order to assure a source of supply.

It should also be pointed out that if the operation is far removed from the source of supply, an elaborate contract that establishes a pipeline of continuous supply may be the only way to purchase. For example, a resort in the Caribbean area that buys from the New York market and receives its goods in a tractor-trailer truck assembled in Miami and barged to the resort must make stable, long-term arrangements with suppliers, sometimes at the sacrifice of immediate price advantages.

VENDOR EVALUATION AND SELECTION — To ensure a source of supply and a degree of reliability in deliveries, most operations select a number of vendors for each major product category. Basically, they restrict purchases, at least on an ongoing basis, to these firms. Any other procedure would invite inefficiencies that would cost more than a constant, far-reaching search for the best price would gain. There are five principal steps in vendor selection: (1) determining what the operation expects of the vendor; (2) identifying potential vendors; (3) selecting vendors; (4) establishing a working relationship with the vendor; and (5) establishing a vendor record system.

Determining What the Operation Expects of the Vendor

Price is much more of a consideration in keeping a vendor than in choosing a vendor. During the food buyer's initial contact with the vendor, it is frequently difficult to determine what that vendor's prices will be eventually. Food prices legitimately vary according to season and the availability of the product. Therefore, a vendor may quote current prices that are higher or lower than those the operation may enjoy a month later. A vendor may also offer prices that are especially attractive at the beginning of the relationship in order to secure the account. Or, the vendor may quote prices that are somewhat higher than might be anticipated later in the association because of the immediate credit standing of the operation.

Price will be a criterion in selecting vendors, but the standard will be "reasonableness" rather than best price, with significant weight being given to the other services the food buyer requires. Since the cost of these other services will eventually be reflected in the price of the products purchased, the food buyer should identify exactly what the operation is purchasing. Generally, the fewer services required, the lower the overall cost of the products.

Vendors offer a variety of services:

Credit   A vendor who will not be paid for 60 or 90 days is in effect lending the operation money for which interest must be charged in the form of higher per-unit prices. Some vendors maintain several price lists: one for cash customers; one for slow payers; one for bad credit risks.

Small orders   The vendor's cost of transporting one case of goods is the same as the cost of transporting ten. The single case must bear a proportionately higher share of transportation cost. Purchases in less than market-unit lots cause additional handling costs.

Priority deliveries   The operation may require deliveries on short notice. The vendor must charge for this service in some way.

Planning and management   Sometimes the food buyer requires the vendor to maintain inventory records, to anticipate needs, and to initiate the ordering process. This service must be paid for.

Storage   The food buyer may require that the vendor maintain large and expensive stocks of items for the operation. This occasions costs which must be passed on to the foodservice operation.

Processing   Sometimes the food buyer has specifications that are not the usual market forms of the product: special trim for meats; specially washed or sorted vegetables; fruits sorted by degree of ripeness; and so forth.

Packaging   The vendor may be asked to convert ordinary market units to other packages: repack fruits or vegetables; pack meat in polyethylene bags; and so on.

Stocking   The food buyer may place the responsibility for storing the product as it arrives in the operation with the vendor's truckers, thereby increasing the time spent on the delivery and consequently increasing its expense.

Any of these requirements may be legitimate in a specific operation's situation, but food buyers must recognize that they are seeking these services and that such extras must ultimately cost the operation something. They must decide whether the vendor or the operation can do the work more cheaply.

Identifying Potential Vendors

More often than not, the food buyer must seek the vendor. There are a number of ways of identifying vendors: consulting the classified section of the telephone book; reading advertisements in trade magazines; making inquiries to the manufacturers or producers of products for the name and address of their local distributors; calling trade associations, such as the local restaurant association or local chapter of the American School Foodservice Association; attending restaurant association shows;

contacting associates in noncompetitive or even in competitive food operations; casual observation of early-morning trucking; or placing an announcement of the operation's anticipated opening in a local newspaper. Other sources of help are local bankers and the chamber of commerce. They often are able to identify local producers.

In a metropolitan area, the vendor pool will be very large. In other parts of the United States, however, there will be only one or two suppliers. A large vendor pool can be narrowed immediately by visits to the vendor's place of business. Vendors can be eliminated readily because of poor sanitation, inadequate storage facilities, outdated materials-handling equipment, general disorder, products that largely fall below the operation's standards, lack of products, unacceptable delivery schedules, and, of course, the inability to supply the services the operation requires.

Inquiries about the vendors' business practices, general reputation, and honesty should further narrow the pool.

Selecting Vendors

After the food buyer has determined which suppliers are generally acceptable, the selection of the few vendors for each product (or product group) with which the operation will deal becomes a matter of establishing operational priorities. There are seven factors to be taken into account: (1) price; (2) delivery of the product—will it be available? (3) service to the extent the operation needs it; (4) technical assistance and know-how; (5) quality or adherence to specifications; (6) personal relations—is it easy to do business with the vendor? (7) competitive position—will the operation be an "important" account to the vendor?

It is possible to assign each of these seven factors a value that corresponds to the particular operation's needs. Price may be weighted at 50 points out of a possible 100 for one operation, whereas service and delivery might only account for 10 points each for that particular operation. For another operation, the service factor may be more important than price. An individual owner/operator may feel that an extra 2 percent markup is worth the price of such services as instant delivery, split cases, and very convenient delivery times. In such cases, the time saved the owner/operator may be more profitably applied to supervision of production personnel, marketing, and consumer relations. The extra cost may amount to a few dollars a day. Basically, this reasoning has prompted many food buyers to deal with one-stop or full-line vendors who can supply most of the operation's needs, a single invoice, a ready-made inventory ordering system, and great convenience in receiving. The additional cost of the product is offset by the savings in the cost of purchasing.

The need for technical assistance and know-how can be factors in choosing a vendor. Some vendors have a considerable knowledge of food service. A knowledgeable vendor can assist in developing production systems, making buying decisions, establishing workable specifications, arranging efficient delivery schedules, and determining the best quantities to order, all as an extension of doing business with the operation.

Personalities constitute an important but generally unacknowledged factor in vendor selection. An impersonal foodservice operation does not do the actual buying; it is still a matter of people buying from other people. Obviously, communications are facilitated if interpersonal relationships are easy and cordial.

Establishing a Working Relationship with the Vendor

Often the selection of the vendors involves a period of probation during which the operation evaluates the vendor. Also, during this period, the vendor evaluates the operation. If the relationship is satisfactory to both parties, the operation benefits. A satisfactory vendor relationship is especially beneficial in times of shortages and rising prices. Many operations of all types establish a continuing relationship with key suppliers so that price rises, shortages, and distribution problems can be anticipated by the vendor for the operation.

The food buyer can encourage a good vendor relationship in seven ways:

- Orders should be consolidated to limit the cost of deliveries.
- At least 48-hour notice of orders or order changes should be given the vendor. Daily orders should be covered by "standing orders" for a fixed amount or by contract.
- Vendor invoices should be processed promptly.
- There should be frequent meetings between vendor and food buyer to discuss mutual problems and the performance of both parties.
- Underhanded practices should be avoided. Quantities for which price quotations are sought should be the actual quantities needed; vendors asked to prepare bids should have a reasonable chance of getting the order; the privilege of getting samples should not be abused; outright vendor errors in quotations or shipments should be brought to the vendor's attention.
- Commitments to purchase, whether formal or informal, should be honored.
- Vendors who stock merchandise for the operation should be notified of closings, or of the discontinuation of the menu items involving the products.

Establishing a Vendor Record System

Just as the standard specifications for an operation must be recorded to ensure continuity of purchasing, so also should vendor information be organized. Records on *every* vendor contacted, and the active vendor records, should be coded or maintained separately to facilitate ordering.

The basic information about the vendor should include the following items:

- *Business information:* products sold—given by category, quality, and brand.
- *Services offered:* aging meat, preparing vegetables, and so on.
- *References:* business associations with other foodservice operations.
- *Delivery schedule for operation's locality:* trucking or delivery system, times of delivery, earlier stops on the route for crisis communications to driver.
- *Vendor evaluation:* results of inquiries, observations on visits to place of business.
- *Performance:* notes on exceptional performance and on failures to supply merchandise, price, promised deliveries.
- *Billing information:* invoice date and terms, credit information.
- *Purchase record:* by product, by dollar volume.
- *Rating:* updated rating by months or quarters.
- *Comments and recommendations:* reasons for doing business with the vendor or for purchasing elsewhere.

PLANNING
PURCHASING
STRATEGY

Market conditions change constantly for almost every operation: prices change; shortages occur; vendors go out of business; supplies of particular products become plentiful; credit costs increase or decrease; transportation and distribution systems become disrupted. The food buyer must have both a purchasing plan that anticipates such change and a set of clear priorities for effectively reacting to change.

The first step in planning an operation's purchasing strategies for coping with changing conditions in a particular marketplace is a full understanding of both the operation and the marketplace.

Understanding the Operation

Which items are really critical to the operation? On which items does the operation spend the highest percentage of its purchasing dollars? Which items cost the most to purchase or handle? Which items can be readily replaced by comparable items? Which specifications are critical and which are simply desirable? What are the cost implications of a change in product quality? A change in delivery schedule? What is the operation's general financial condition? To what extent are storage facilities being used? Or being underused? How long does it take to make a buying decision?

The food buyer must address these fundamental internal factors that influence purchasing activities so that the decision-making process will be speeded up when a decision becomes necessary.

Understanding the Marketplace

What is the financial condition of major vendors? How stable are the labor relations of local and regional transportation companies? When have products become plentiful or unavailable in the past? Are there seasonal price trends associated with particular major products? How much will it cost to buy in an alternative market? How much time will vendors require for orders when shortages occur? Which vendors will offer the operation priority status if supplies are limited? What kinds of crisis transportation are available? Truck rentals? Shipment by common carrier? Pickup in personal cars?

What alternative products are available? What qualities that approach specifications, but do not quite meet them, are available?

Where are national price trends in specific commodities headed? What credit is available to the operation for current purchases? For long-term inventory building?

Obviously, the food buyer must anticipate and understand changes in marketplace conditions in order to react adequately when external circumstances do change.

Purchasing Strategies

After considering the internal and external factors that can affect purchasing for a particular operation in a particular marketplace the food buyer should develop a series of plans for specific contingencies. Although it is impossible to generalize a strategy for all operations because internal and external factors differ so radically, some common approaches do exist:

1. An operation can adopt an early-warning system that will provide information from which changes in marketplace conditions can be anticipated. Commodity information from government sources and analyses of price trends in trade publications or commercial newspapers can serve this purpose.

2. The food buyer can determine the trade-offs available in the marketplace. If a particular product becomes unavailable, the buyer must know what the next best choice is as well as the best choice after that. (See Exhibit 8.10.)

3. Safety inventories can be established for items that are critical to the operation and likely to be in short supply.

4. The buyer can make sure that order lead time is long enough to allow an economical reaction to crises in supply, transportation, or vendor business conditions.

5. Critical products can be identified so that planning and effort can be devoted to obtaining them.

6. Reactions to disruption in the normal purchasing procedure can be reviewed and evaluated. The lesson of the last crisis should be applied to anticipation of the next one.

7. Anticipated price increases can be counteracted by buying more heavily than current needs demand, but only to the extent that the operation can efficiently store the product. Anticipated price decreases can be countered by reducing order quantities to the least amount that is safe.

8. Production departments can and should participate in the design of purchasing strategies so that changes are not overly disruptive.

9. Purchasing strategies can and should be recorded so that they can be applied by persons other than the originator and also so they can be evaluated.

10. Key vendors can and should be made aware of the operation's long-term needs so that they can help meet changing conditions as they occur.

Purchasing policies concerning buying method, vendor evaluation and selection, and purchasing strategies are managerial tools. They should be summarized for the information of all management in the form of a purchasing manual. The purchasing manual should be subject to constant review and revision. Such a manual ensures the continuity of communications when purchasing personnel change. Too often in foodservice operations the most hard-won lessons must be learned again and again, as a succession of food buyers must cope with unreliable vendors and crises in supply. A purchasing manual could play a pivotal role in the new food buyer's orientation to the job.

Determining Current Product Needs   Knowing from standard specifications which products the operation needs and from purchasing policies how to get them, the buyer needs only to know how much to buy.

In most operations, this critical determination is not the responsibility of the food buyer if there are other people involved in foodservice management. Yet, the success of the food buyer and the efficiency of the purchasing department depend on how accurately the operation's needs are stated. Shortages may occur in the kitchen because the food buyer did not purchase efficiently, but it is just as likely that they occur because product utilization was underestimated by someone else. A flurry of small, hence expensive, orders may be the result of disorganized purchasing or the result of the production department's failure to anticipate the operation's requirements.

The degree of difficulty encountered in accurately determining current needs varies with each type of foodservice operation. If the number of meals served remains fairly constant, as it does in many client-service

EXHIBIT 8.10 Comparative Costs of Different Cuts of Turkey

If the price per pound of whole turkey, ready-to-cook, is—	Turkey parts and products are an equally good buy if the price per pound is—						Boned Turkey Roast		Boned Turkey, Canned	Turkey with Gravy, Canned or Frozen	Gravy with Turkey, Canned or Frozen
	Breast Quarter	Leg Quarter	Breast	Drum-stick	Thigh	Wing	Ready-to-cook	Cooked			
Cents	Cents	Cents	Cents	Cents	Cents	Cents	Cents	Cents	Cents	Cents	Cents
33	37	35	42	34	40	31	58	76	74	29	12
35	39	38	45	36	43	32	61	80	79	31	13
37	42	40	47	38	45	34	65	85	83	32	14
39	44	42	50	40	48	36	68	90	88	34	15
41	46	44	52	42	50	38	72	94	92	36	15
43	48	46	55	44	53	40	75	99	97	38	16
45	51	48	57	46	55	42	79	103	101	39	17
47	53	51	60	48	58	43	82	108	106	41	18
49	55	53	62	50	60	45	86	113	110	43	18
51	57	55	65	52	62	47	89	117	115	45	19
53	60	57	68	54	65	49	93	122	119	46	20
55	62	59	70	56	67	51	96	126	124	48	21
57	64	61	73	58	70	53	100	131	128	50	21
59	66	63	75	60	72	55	103	136	133	52	22
61	69	66	78	63	75	56	107	140	137	53	23
63	71	68	80	65	77	58	110	145	142	55	24
65	73	70	83	67	80	60	114	150	146	57	24
67	75	72	85	69	82	62	117	154	151	59	25
69	78	74	88	71	85	64	121	159	155	60	26
71	80	76	91	73	87	66	124	163	160	62	27
73	82	78	93	75	89	68	128	168	164	64	27

(From *Family Economics Review*. December, 1971. Agricultural Research Service. U.S. Department of Agriculture.)

Tables such as this enable the food buyer to determine which products in the marketplace offer the best value.

foodservice operations, product requirements vary in a consistent fashion with the menu. Even if the menu offers a number of choices, a simple examination of the history of that menu will indicate how many chopped steaks are likely to be served and thus how much ground beef should be bought. However, operations that experience widely fluctuating volumes have a more difficult task in projecting utilization. In addition to forecasting which items will be served and in what relative amounts, the management must also determine how many customers are expected.

In almost all operations, the process of determining current needs is simplified by restricting the number of products for which an accurate forecast is necessary. Some items can be stocked in sufficient quantity to meet any demand that is likely to occur before another delivery can be arranged. As will be discussed in Chapter 9, "The Supply System," it is possible to establish a level to which stocks are built each time the product is periodically ordered. The operation never exhausts the supply because the total amount on hand at the beginning of the order period exceeds the amount that can possibly be used before the order is placed again. It is also possible to establish a minimum level that will prompt a reorder. When the amount on hand falls to that number of units, an order must be initiated. The amount on hand at that moment is sufficient to carry the operation until the new order arrives. In sum, the process of determining needs is reduced to a clerical procedure for the key items involved in the operation.

The number of items an operation can place on this basis depends on the operation and the products it uses. Highly perishable products such as live lobsters cannot be stocked for long periods of time, but easily stored and inexpensive items such as bread crumbs can be ordered in large quantities a few times a year.

For those items for which a determination of current needs is necessary, the procedure is fairly straightforward. The required steps are (1) menu analysis; (2) volume forecast; (3) standard recipe extension; and (4) consolidation and conversion into market units. The desired end product is a requisition that reflects the number of persons expected, what they will eat and in what quantities, and how this amount of food will actually be purchased in the marketplace.

MENU ANALYSIS   If a menu has ten items on it, the food buyer cannot assume that all ten items will sell or be chosen equally. If 100 people are served by the operation, 40 may choose beef stew; 15, chili; 5, hamburger; and so on. An examination of the sales or use of the menu items over a period of time should indicate the relative acceptance of the various items on the menu. For every 100 people who eat in the foodservice operation, a certain percentage will consistently choose each item. Once these percentages are established, management has a good idea of how many of each item will be used if 1,000 or 10,000 people are served. The particular percentage determined for each item simply has to be applied to the number of people expected. Since 40 percent of the customers chose beef stew, and 5,000 people are expected, then it is likely that 2,000 orders of beef stew will be needed. Once each item is assigned an appropriate percentage, management has a partial basis for determining the operation's needs.

VOLUME FORECAST   The second question to be addressed is how many hundreds of people are going to be served during the period for which the order is being formulated. In some operations, for some products, this period may be just one day! The question then is: How many people are going to be served tomorrow? For other operations, for example, a summer camp purchasing by bid in January, the question becomes: How many campers are expected between June and September? The period for which the judgment is being made, called the *purchasing period* or the *purchasing cycle*, is determined with several factors in mind: production capabilities, storage facilities, the perishability of the items involved, the time a vendor takes to process an order (lead time), and other operational considerations. It would not do to choose a period so long that the volume of product required during that period could not be stored in the operation or processed by the food production department. But a too-short period might require that products be delivered more frequently than the vendor could manage.

Once the purchasing period is established, volume for that period must be forecast. Health care establishments, college and university foodservice operations, and other operations that serve the continuing client can establish volume with some sureness. The persons eating the meals are already committed to having them within the operation. Only adjustments for holidays, closing, or a radical change in population will vary the number of persons expected in such establishments.

Some commercial operations, such as limited-menu restaurant chains serving hamburgers, pizza, or chicken, maintain extensive business histories. They can determine volume by comparison with comparable prior periods, perhaps with some adjustment for generally increasing or decreasing customer volume.

Traditional table service restaurants, other similar commercial operations, and those foodservice operations associated with hospitality operations have the most difficulty in coming to an accurate volume forecast. Their business is subject to numerous external factors that can influence volume—weather, advertising and promotional efforts, local events, and competitive pressures—all of which must be taken into account in making a forecast. For them, managerial judgment applied to past history seems to offer the best method for arriving at a volume projection.

STANDARD RECIPE   Once volume during the purchasing period is determined, it is a relatively
EXTENSION   simple matter to determine how many of each item will be sold. By ap-

plying the appropriate percentage from the menu analysis to the volume forecast, management can determine the number of each dish that will be sold or chosen. Depending on the management's past successes in forecasting, a more or less generous margin for error could be included to take into account unexpected customers or menu choices that do not fit within the anticipated percentages.

Knowing that 500 portions of beef stew, 250 of chili, and 150 of ham steak will be sold in the following week, the operation can make a more precise determination of its needs. It is now necessary to refer to the standard recipes for beef stew, chili, and ham steaks and determine how much of each ingredient will be necessary for 500, 250, and 150 orders, respectively. The standard recipe may be for 50 portions. If 10 kilograms (22 pounds) of beef are needed for 50 portions of beef stew, then 100 kilograms (220 pounds) are needed for 500 portions. If the standard recipe simply presents the ingredients needed in a single portion—for example, 200 grams (7 ounces) of tomato juice—then this amount is simply multiplied by the total number of portions needed. The standard recipes for the entire menu would have to be extended in this way.

CONSOLIDATION AND CONVERSION INTO MARKET UNITS The yield standards discussed earlier in this chapter now become important. The operation requires 100 kilograms (220 pounds) of beef stew meat. What is beef stew meat? How much of it has to be bought to yield 100 kilograms?

The standard specifications describe beef stew meat and all the other products the menu requires. The operation's standard yield tables, similar to the one shown in Exhibit 8.5, indicate that the amount of beef stew as served must be multiplied by the factor 1.4 to determine the amount of beef stew meat that must be purchased. Thus, for a yield of 100 kilograms of beef stew, 140 kilograms (308 pounds) of beef stew meat must be purchased. Since no loss in trimming or cooking is involved when tomato juice is served, the weight of the portion (200 grams) is multiplied by a factor of 1.0 (times the total number of people to be served).

Two further calculations remain: consolidation and conversion. The meat to be used for beef stew may also be used in another menu item— for example, in beef goulash. After the quantities to be purchased for each item have been calculated, these two quantities should be combined, or consolidated. Tomato sauce may figure in the beef stew recipe and in other recipes. The total amount of tomato sauce required to prepare the food for that purchasing period is also calculated. The result of the consolidation procedure is thus a complete product list for the period, with one line devoted to each different item.

It is necessary now to convert this product list into market units. The meat for beef stew and for other menu items that include such meat is not purchased by the ounce. If the operation is using frozen cubed beef, that item is purchased by the pound or by the 50-pound (22.7 kilograms) case. If the operation has specified "beef chuck," it is purchased by the pound, or by the piece within a specified weight range. Tomato juice is purchased in cases of twelve No. 5 or No. 10 cans. Tomato sauce is purchased in cases of six No. 10 cans, not in ounces. Thus, the entire product list must be converted to market units as stated in the operation's standard specifications. In this way communication with the suppliers is made easier.

This final list is the operation's requisition. It corresponds to the amount of particular menu items that operation will use during the purchasing period.

THE BUYING ROUTINE

Once standard specifications have been developed for the foodservice operation and a purchasing policy has been established, the food buyer's work consists largely of routine buying. The needs of the operation are assessed by means of departmental requisitions. These needs are satisfied in the marketplace by products that meet the specifications of the operation, obtained at the best price consistent with purchasing policies.

To facilitate the purchasing process, most operations use a number of different forms: requisition forms, quotation sheets, purchase orders. With such a system, the food buyer need not recreate the data base of each communication involved in the ordering process.

Ordering Routine Step-by-Step   The method of buying will determine in large part the exact ordering procedure. However, foodservice operations of all types have an established routine that resembles the one outlined below.

Receiving requisitions   Requisitions are received from operational departments and consolidated so that all of the needs of the operation are presented. In general, the only requisitions received by the purchasing department are for those items that are not requisitioned directly from inventory. However, the food buyer may receive all requisitions and route those to be filled from inventory to the operation's storage area.

Checking inventory levels   An ample stock of the products requested may already be in the operation for any one of several reasons: the food buyer anticipated the need; there is a surplus from a prior order; purchases were made in anticipation of a price rise; and so on.

Considering purchasing strategies   Is this the right time to purchase the quantity of the item requested? The cash position of the company, the marketplace situation, the order size, and many other factors influence this decision.

Soliciting quotations or requesting bids   Selected vendors are called, perhaps after the food buyer has determined what the market price should be. In some circumstances, requests for bid submission may be sent to potential vendors, or a public announcement may be made. If the items are covered by a standing order, or if for strategic reasons the buyer is only dealing with one purveyor for the items needed, this step is omitted.

Purchasing informally   Many purchases are made informally on the telephone. When the food buyer is dealing with a vendor who is aware of the operation's specifications and with whom a continuing relationship has been established, telephone purchases are commonly made.

Purchasing formally   A written purchase order may follow a verbal purchase. The food buyer may have been supplied with a form by the vendor to facilitate this process, or the operation may have developed its own standard form with copies for the accounting department, receiving area, and so on. Forms preprinted with the appropriate food items and market units are common, especially in large operations with recurrent needs.

Recording purchases   Copies of the purchase order may be sufficient record of the purchase. Otherwise, various records of the transaction must be kept. The purchasing department requires a record of the transactions as a reference and as a means of monitoring the purchase of specific products. The receiving department requires notice of the purchase to facilitate handling and to allow a comparison of the items received with the items ordered. The accounting department may require a purchase record so that the price quoted may be compared with the vendor's invoice and the amount received compared with the amount actually ordered. The production department may receive a copy of the purchase order to indicate that the requisition was processed.

Follow-up   The food buyer maintains the purchase order in an "active" file until the products are received by the operation and a receiving record has been filed with the purchase order. The active file may be maintained by date of promised delivery. If the product is not received on time, the food buyer often expedites the order. That is, he or she telephones the supplier to determine when the order will be shipped or, if it has been shipped, when it will arrive.

Useful Forms in the Buying Routine   Many written forms are used in purchasing to facilitate the buying routine. Good forms speed the purchasing process; they reduce the amount of communication necessary to complete any step in the purchasing process. The form already communicates all the unchanging information necessary to the step, and it provides a standard method for communicating the new information specific to that part of the process. For example, an operation's purchase order can be printed with the operation's billing address, shipping address, general conditions of sale, instructions to the supplier, and also provide appropriate spaces and lines for entering the vendor's address, the quantity ordered, vendor codes, item description, cost, and so forth.

EXHIBIT 8.11   Forms Used in Purchasing for Foodservice Operations

Form	Use	Data Base	
Requisition	Production or operations dept. indicates needs to purchasing or supply dept.	Production dept. Supply dept. Date/time Item Description Inventory on hand	Cost per unit Total cost(s) Approval Filling record Receiving record
Purchase Order	Purchasing dept. makes formal purchase with supplier and uses purchase order copies to notify other departments of the operation. Purchase order also serves as contract for purchase and states terms and conditions.	Name of operation Operation's billing address Operation's shipping address Supplier's address Routing (transportation) Quantity ordered Billing unit Item codes Pack/size	Description Purchase order date Arrival date Order number Freight information Price per unit Total price Conditions of sale Discount terms Purchased by whom
Purchase Record	To maintain a record of purchases of specific products: amounts ordered, price changes; to comment on the performance and price and product variations of the vendors; end use is for management information for better product purchasing.	Item name Specification number Vendor information Dates items ordered From which vendors Purchase order numbers Amount Unit prices Comments on order	
Telephone Order Record	Purchasing dept. records purchase order given on the telephone to purveyor as a matter of record to inform other depts. and to provide information for formal purchase order.	Information same as for Purchase Order	

The same information would have to be communicated if there were no purchase order, but the food buyer would need to recall exactly what should be included in a letter to a supplier every time the operation ordered anything.

The printed information on a form and the information that it requires for completion are referred to as the "data base" of the form. If the data

Form	Use	Data Base	
Invitation to Bid	Purchasing dept. describes items being purchased or offers specifications and invites potential suppliers to submit price quotes to which they are willing to commit themselves.	Operation name, address Date bid will be received Date bid is issued Date product is wanted Item name Description or specification	Quantity wanted Vendor bid price Amount on which bid is made Vendor name Vendor signature Conditions of sale Conditions of delivery
Quotation Sheet	To allow food buyer to compare price quotations from several vendors.	Name of item(s) Specification(s)	Unit of quotation Vendor(s) quotation
Inventory Order Sheet	To determine amounts of specific items to be ordered by comparing inventory level with predetermined par-level; to indicate from what vendors and at what prices items were ordered.	Name of item(s) Unit Price per unit (standing order) Price per market package	Par-level Supplier code for vendor Date of order Inventory amount Order amount
Progress Card	To maintain records of items being shipped or ordered far in advance.	Purchase order number Date of order Supplier Item(s) Specification(s)	Quantities Price Promised delivery date Record of contact with supplier
Daily Purchase List	To provide a running record of daily purchases.	Items ordered From whom Amount ordered Price per unit	Total cost Order number Delivery date
Preprinted Purchasing Guide	To inform a vendor of the amounts of a standard order wanted.	Preprinted items Preprinted units Abbreviated Purchase Order data base	

base is accurate and complete, buying becomes truly routine. Vendors and other departments in the operation that participate in the purchasing process soon become familiar with the operation's standard forms for purchasing and can quickly identify the information they need.

Exhibit 8.11 lists some commonly used forms for purchasing and describes their data bases.

Chapter 9
The Supply
System

Effective purchasing practices (discussed in Chapter 8) do not by themselves ensure a foodservice operation of the quantity and quality of products it needs. Between the time an item is ordered from the supplier and the time it is to be used by a production or operational department, the product can diminish substantially in value. It can be detoured or lost. It can become unfit for use. It can be stolen or misused. It can even be forgotten. In short, efficient purchasing practices can be negated by inadequate methods of supplying various departments with the materials needed for production and service. The person responsible for the supply system performs a vital function: the management of receiving, distribution, storage, and inventory within a foodservice operation. This chapter describes the supply system and its effective management.

SUPPLY CONCEPTS

Faulty management of the supply process—receiving, storage, inventory, and distribution—can cost an operation substantial amounts of money. Avoiding financial loss because of an inadequate supply system is a critical management concern. The profitability and efficiency of a foodservice enterprise are compromised unless a reliable and cost-effective supply system—in tune with the needs of the operation—is set up, put into operation, and maintained.

Specific Objectives of the Supply System

The manager of a foodservice supply system should identify specific objectives for the supply process. If these objectives are set, the needs and demands of the foodservice operation for certain products can be fulfilled quickly, economically, and with little or no waste. The specific objectives are three in number:

1. *To ensure a flow of materials to the production system* A properly managed supply system will be able to provide necessary items to

253

the production system as they are needed. Any delay or disruption in this flow to the production system will result in a loss of labor productivity. The baker still must be paid even though he or she may be standing idle while flour is brought in from the storeroom. In addition, if production is disrupted because of the unavailability of a product, sales will be reduced. If a foodservice operation offers strawberry shortcake on its menu and through faulty management of the supply system runs out of strawberries, disappointed patrons may forego dessert entirely when told that the shortcake is unavailable.

2. *To provide a selection of high quality products consistent with the menu program*   The supply system should be planned so that each product receives the treatment appropriate to it. For example, milk must be refrigerated, and eggs cannot be tossed into a bin. If products are mishandled, the operation in effect is paying higher food costs to make up for the waste and spoilage that occur within the operation. The operation may use products that have deteriorated because of improper storage and thereby vitiate its own standards. In addition, the operation may then become subject to legal action if its products fall below government standards for food safety. One way to avoid waste and spoilage is for the manager to determine which products are necessary to the menu program and which products are superfluous. If a manager happens upon 25 bottles of barbecue sauce cluttering a corner of the storeroom after the operation has decided to strike spareribs from its menu, the now-superfluous barbecue sauce may be the result of a lack of communication about changes that have occurred in the menu program.

3. *To maintain stocks of products as economically as possible*   Products should be handled in the most economical manner; the most commonly used products should be the most accessible so that a storeroom worker wastes no time searching for something as basic as a bag of sugar. In other words, products should be stored not only to maintain high quality, but also in a way that reflects their importance to the operation. The manager should also gather information about the supply system so that he or she can use that information to plan and to control costs. For example, the operation should not be inundated with deliveries on Mondays and need to hire part-time workers when on Tuesdays there is no work at all for the supply-system employees. The manager should also learn to interpret information received from the supply system so that each product is bought at the proper time and at an economical price, rather than at the last minute at a price disadvantageous to the operation. Finally, the manager must not commit large amounts of money to the stocking of unneeded supplies; those bottles of barbecue sauce mentioned above are not only useless but also expensive to store. Cash spent on unneeded supplies can certainly be put to better use elsewhere in the operation.

Current Practices in Foodservice Supply

A small foodservice operation that is managed by an owner/chef and which has a simple, limited menu and ample storage space probably uses an age-old supply method that is often called the *backdoor system.* This type of operation has no need for a complex supply process. In the backdoor system, the small foodservice operation is supplied by a few reliable local purveyors on a daily basis. Every morning, friendly, knowledgeable truck drivers deliver the right merchandise in the right quantities to the operation's backdoor. There it is checked by the owner and quickly placed in the storeroom by kitchen workers. High quality supplies, good handling, and careful management are ensured by the on-premises direction of the owner.

Few foodservice operations in the United States are supplied this easily. Many operations are much larger than the idealized description given in the preceding paragraph. The "backdoor" of a central commissary for a vending firm may be a receiving platform that accommodates ten tractor-trailer trucks at once. The "storeroom" of a fast-food chain may be an automated warehouse containing thousands of square feet of storage space. Several thousand items—from oatmeal to olives—may be required by a hotel foodservice operation. Shipments for a school system may be counted in thousand-pound loads. Even the supply system of an individual restaurant may process several million dollars worth of products each year.

Relatively small operations also may need a complicated supply system either because of an inaccessible location or because of distance from adequate supply sources. Thus, the supply of a remote fishing resort, a snack bar on a ski slope, or a lodge at the bottom of the Grand Canyon requires careful management. For example, a restaurant in the southwestern part of the United States which specializes in Chinese food may have to order a year ahead to ensure a supply of imported products. A gourmet restaurant in Kansas may require twice-a-week deliveries of fresh seafood from a vendor 2,000 miles away in one direction and fresh produce from another vendor 2,000 miles away in the other direction.

The immense diversity of items that many operations use also may require the creation of special storage areas. A hospital operation may require banks of refrigerators to receive pre-prepared meals. Another foodservice operation may need a temperature-controlled area to ripen melons, while still another may require space for aging beef. A seafood restaurant may install miniponds for keeping live lobsters, while a fine French restaurant may require security vaults for locking up its supply of truffles and 100-year-old cognac.

The supply challenges of a modern foodservice operation cannot be approached with the informal techniques and procedures that worked for the backdoor supply system. For most operations, a score of complexities has been introduced that make the supply system much more complicated and that demand formalized management techniques. The task of supply has become more elaborate, and subsequently, the stakes have become much higher.

ACTIVITIES OF SUPPLY MANAGEMENT

Managers of many modern foodservice operations recognize that the challenge of supply can only be met by a system that integrates receipt of product, internal distribution, and storage with the purchasing and production systems. There must be a total approach to the planning, problem solving, and decision making involved in converting raw materials into finished menu items. This integrated approach is often called *supply management* or *materials management.*

According to this view, a purchasing decision cannot be made without taking into account the cost of interest on money to pay for the purchase. Products cannot be transported within the operation without taking into account the effect of the delivery on labor efficiency in the production department. Products cannot be purchased without consideration of the availability of storage or the capabilities of the internal distribution system.

Even if various persons or departments are themselves efficient, problems occur when each part of the supply process remains separate. Large stocks of wines are purchased at a discount when the operation can least afford the cost of the carrying charges on the money it must borrow to pay for the wines. Grapefruit are scheduled to arrive when the receiving area is ready to handle them quickly but several hours after the best preparation time for the production department. Meat orders are consolidated to take advantage of reduced handling charges but without attention to the quantities of raw and semiprocessed meat already in storage.

Effective supply or materials management averts these problems by integrating and improving each part of the process. In other words, it creates a system from many previously separate supply functions. Thus, no decision is made without considering the implications for other systems within the foodservice operation.

Within a foodservice organization, supply management may be the concern of a specialist called a *materials manager.* The *steward* of a large hotel may also have this responsibility. Often, in institutions serving continuing clients, the *food production manager* is largely occupied with materials management. In other operations, the *purchasing director* also functions as the supply manager, while specific individuals within the purchasing department function as receiving clerks, warehouse workers, stock clerks, and so on. Frequently, in operations that recognize the need for efficient materials management but that cannot afford a specialist, an *assistant manager* makes supply management a priority responsibility.

Whatever the title, a supply manager has three basic concerns. Each of these concerns is examined in detail in this chapter. In brief, the areas of concern are as follows:

Inventory control   This function involves the economic storing of food and other materials to assure a continuing supply. It includes cost-benefit analysis of inventory decisions.

Materials handling   This function involves the supervision of transportation and handling within a facility. It includes the efficient planning of distribution procedures so that materials are where they are supposed to be when they are supposed to be there—and at a cost consistent with the operation's budget or profit goals.

Product control   This function involves the supervision of the safe storage, preservation, and holding of food. It includes responsibility for the efficient design and adequate capability of physical storage facilities as well as the identification and implementation of sound principles of storage management.

Inventory Control   Foodservice operations store products to meet their future requirements. These stored products are called *inventory*. The processing and sale of this inventory is the main source of revenue for a commercial foodservice operation. Since a particular operation may have large amounts of capital tied up in inventory, sound management of inventory is important.

The goal of inventory management is to provide a foodservice operation with an uninterrupted supply of necessary materials at a minimum cost. Inventory management thus involves a series of interrelated decisions regarding what items to stock, what quantities to keep in stock, what quantities to order at any one time, what timing of orders is most beneficial, and what costs are acceptable.

These decisions are sometimes difficult to make for several reasons. First, future requirements cannot always be predicted accurately. Second, production department requirements may not always be communicated clearly. And, third, marketplace conditions, including the price of the products, their availability, and the length of time it takes to obtain them may vary.

Faced with such uncertainties, a manager's tendency may be to build up inventories so that a large safety margin will assure a future supply no matter what happens. Unfortunately, in all but the smallest foodservice operations, yielding to this temptation may result in unacceptable costs. The alternative—not having sufficient inventory—is just as unsatisfactory. The operation suffers the costs of shortages, crisis purchasing, and disruption of production. In practice, then, an important part of inventory management consists of weighing the costs of having a certain amount of inventory against the costs of not having it.

The first step in sound inventory management is a careful evaluation of costs. Since individual operations vary widely in their inventory requirements, no rule-of-thumb can be applied universally. A manager must identify the actual costs for his or her own operation.

The cost of ownership of inventory includes the following:

Storage space costs   Taxes on the storage facility or land, or the proportionate share of taxes these areas should bear; maintenance on the storage space; utility costs for heat, light, refrigeration; salaries to personnel; rent or lease payments or depreciation on the building or facilities.

Equipment costs   Depreciation on equipment used to handle and distribute the inventory or the cost of leasing such equipment; fuel or utilities to run the equipment; insurance and taxes on the equipment.

Inventory costs   Inventory taxes; losses caused by spoilage, pilferage, or breakage; losses because of price declines; administrative and clerical costs; a proportionate share of overhead or general management costs.

Capital costs   Interest on the amount of money that the operation has invested in the inventory, equipment, and facilities either as interest paid to a bank, equipment company, or the supplier or the costs of losing the opportunity for other investments.

For many operations, the cost of maintaining inventory may be as much as 25 to 30 percent of the value of the inventory. For operations with rather small dollar-amount inventories, that cost may be insignificant. For example, using the 25 percent guideline, the annual cost of a constant inventory of $10,000 would be approximately $2,500. Consider, however, a large foodservice company whose many operations can generate a total inventory of millions of dollars. Their inventory maintenance cost would be appreciably higher in terms of actual dollars.

To offset the costs of inventory, it must be remembered that the ownership of inventory can have certain benefits. Savings may be realized in the following areas:

Quantity discounts   Items purchased in quantity sometimes cost less per unit.

Decreased administrative costs   The cost of placing orders, processing them, receiving merchandise, and administering the supply system should decrease as inventory increases.

Economy of scale in facilities   A facility for twice the inventory does not necessarily cost twice the amount.

Availability   An inventory can provide a hedge against unforeseen occurrences: strikes, emergency demands, price increases, changes in production or labor utilization, and shortages.

Economy in acquisition   Prices may rise on products that the operation has in inventory thus resulting in inventory "profits" in an accounting valuation.

Once the inventory cost factors are identified for a particular foodservice operation, they provide a background for further steps in the inventory management process. These factors must of course be quantified —given actual expression in dollars and cents. Then they can be interpreted to determine whether or not a certain item or a certain quantity should indeed be purchased.

INVENTORY MANAGEMENT TECHNIQUES

After basic inventory costs are identified and basic requirements are projected for a specific time period, it would seem that the questions of how much to order, when to order, and how much to inventory would become easier to answer. Unfortunately, it may be extremely difficult to answer these questions. Because of price changes in products, uneven usage, and the huge number of products that are needed, management of inventory on the basis of individual items becomes unmanageable and costly.

In practice, inventory management is concerned only with items for which there is potential significant inventory cost or cost benefit; inventory managers often rely on an extremely useful classification system called *ABC analysis,* or *Pareto analysis.* In this system, products used in an operation are grouped into three categories according to the amount spent on each category annually. For example, in a hypothetical operation, ground beef, fluid milk, and fresh shrimp may together account for more than 40 percent of the operation's purchases. This category would be called the *A-category.* Another six or eight items may account for an additional 40 percent. This category is called the *B-category.* And, finally, the remaining several hundred items account for only 20 percent of the operation's purchases. This category is called the *C-category.* The manager's efforts are best devoted to determining inventory levels and order quantities for the A-category rather than for the C-category. Even considerable success in inventory management of the C-category is unlikely to yield significant savings.

For instance, suppose spices amount to only 0.6 percent of total expenditures in an operation with a food budget of $300,000. Eliminating half the inventory of spices, or $900 worth, might result in a savings of one-sixth of this amount, or $150. Ground beef, quite obviously, is a better target for inventory control.

There are three basic areas in a foodservice operation where inventory management techniques should be applied. These areas are (1) determining when to order, (2) determining how much to order, and (3) determining the value of a discount. The next three sections of this chapter will deal with these crucial areas.

Determining When to Order

Foodservice managers use three basic methods to determine when it is time to re-order an inventoried item: (1) inspection and judgment; (2) par-level ordering; and (3) minimax.

Inspection and judgment　　In response to a production or operational need, the manager evaluates the inventory on hand and decides how much should be ordered or if any should be ordered. This decision is based on a forecast of future demand and on accurate knowledge of past use. If this information is reliable, then this method is often adequate. Operations that use an automatic data processing system for inventory control can program the computer with great accuracy to order on this basis. Unfortunately, this method of ordering is frequently used when the information on which the decision is based is not reliable. In this situation, determining when, what, and if the operation should order becomes an outright guess, more often wrong than right.

Par-level ordering　　For each item, the manager determines the average amount the operation will use between deliveries. If, for example, deliveries are made every Wednesday and orders for Wednesday must be placed Sunday night, then an inventory must be taken each Sunday and an order placed to bring the quantity in stock to the amount that represents the average use in a seven-day period.

The average amount used during a seven-day period—or for any period between deliveries—can be determined by an analysis of the operation's past use of the product. The manager surveys use for the past 52 weeks to find the average for any one week. Or the manager may choose a week in which use was above average but considered "normal." Either of these figures becomes the par-level. Sometimes the par-level is some amount less than the greatest amount needed. Holiday weekends, for example, may generate an unusual demand. In this case, the inventory for these periods should be considered separately. Sometimes, the par-level can be *above* peak use if the manager wants to provide a margin for safety.

Even if the par-level is accurate, use may still vary from week to week. Thus, the amount remaining in inventory will vary when inventory is taken each week. At no time, however, will the stock remaining after the inventory is taken be insufficient to carry the operation to the next delivery. Often par-levels are included on combination inventory/order sheets so that actually deciding how much to order is simply a clerical task. The current inventory is subtracted from the par-level amount; the result is the order.

Problems with this method of ordering occur when the levels are set poorly. A high par-level can result in excess inventory. A low par-level causes a high percentage of items to be out of stock. As conditions change, par-levels can also become stale. For this reason, inventory managers reevaluate par-level amounts by keeping a moving average of use. That is, every order period, they average the consumption for the last six order periods and compare this average with the average for the previous order period. The par-level amount can then be adjusted up or down according to changes in use.

Minimax method   In using a minimax method of ordering, the manager is trying to make the re-order process as automatic as possible. A variation of the minimax system, called the *two-bin method* of ordering, illustrates this process clearly. Two bins or bags or closets or shelves are needed. Originally, both are stocked. When one empties, the other is used to supply the operation, and an amount sufficient to refill the first is ordered. An order card can actually be placed with the product so that whoever starts the second bin automatically initiates the order. In this example, two binfuls is the *maximum* quantity the operation will have, and one binful is the *minimum* quantity before an order is initiated.

The same system can be implemented without bins by determining what should be the minimum quantity in the operation and what should be the maximum. The minimum quantity, the re-order point, is that amount sufficient to last the operation until the next delivery plus a safety stock in case of an increase in use or a delay in delivery. If the operation uses ten units a day and delivery takes eight days, then the minimum is 80 units plus the safety stock. The time between ordering and delivery is called *lead time*, and thus the formula for determining the minimum is L (lead time in days) times U (use each day) plus S (safety stock) or $L \times U + S = $ minimum. The maximum level is set in the same way that the par-level is set or by the method for determining economic order quantity discussed below.

The safety stock represents an "inventory within an inventory." If it is set too high, the inventory costs for the product will be excessive. If it is set too low, it will not be a genuine safety stock. The manager must weigh the costs of maintaining the safety stock against the costs to the operation if a certain product is unavailable at times. It may be acceptable to set the safety stock at an amount that represents an adequate supply for an extra day, two days, or three days for 90 percent of the time.

Determining Economic Order Quantity

If an operation needs 250 cases of tomato juice during the next six months, the manager can either buy them at one time and incur an inventory cost, or buy them on a week-by-week basis and incur 26 weekly buying costs in processing the purchase orders, administration, and so forth.

The cost of carrying the inventory may exceed the cost of repeated buying, or the cost of repeated buying may exceed the cost of carrying the inventory. However, if the cost of carrying the inventory is known and the cost of buying is known, it is possible to determine the number of cases for which these costs would be equal. It may be that the economic order quantity is 250 cases. While all the variables in the calculation can be presented on a graph and the economic order quantity determined from it, a general formula has been developed as follows:

$$\text{EOQ (Economic Order Quantity)} = \sqrt{\frac{CN}{IU}}$$

Where

C = Fixed cost of placing an order
N = Annual use or consumption
I = Annual carrying costs expressed as a fraction of the unit price
   (Carrying costs include interest, storage, and deterioration)
U = Unit price of the product

Applying this formula—or any others in use by general business enterprises—has difficulties for the foodservice operation. The formula is only valid if prices do not change, but only a few food products have stable prices. In many foodservice operations, the cost of buying is not known with accuracy because too many products are needed too frequently. Warehousing may not be adequate to take advantage of ordering the economic order quantity since food products, unlike coal, demand special storage conditions. Annual consumption may be difficult to determine, and use of particular products may be uneven during the year. For certain operations of sufficient size and using fairly price-stable commodities, the economic order quantity can be determined. However, in most operations of this size, automatic data processing facilitates the process.

More important, however, is the fact that any manager can make use of the concept. For example, United States Department of Agriculture surveys show that storage capacity is underutilized in many operations. If the capacity is available and already occasioning some costs, then there can be some economic advantage to increasing the order size and reducing the effort, if not the cost, of too-frequent buying.

Determining the Value of a Discount

Foodservice managers in operations of all sizes frequently have the opportunity to buy a quantity of a product beyond their immediate needs but at a discounted price. If there is adequate storage and the only inventory-associated cost that will vary is interest, the decision to buy a larger quantity at a discount hinges on whether the operation will get an adequate return on its investment by purchasing the additional inventory.

Exhibit 9.1 shows the eight steps involved in calculating the value of a discount.

EXHIBIT 9.1 Determining the Value of a Discount: Model Problem

Step 1	An operation requires 500 cases of catsup every three months at $8.00 per case
	500 X $8.00 = $4,000 (A)
Step 2	The operation may also purchase the catsup in 1,000 case lots at $7.00 per case
	1,000 X $7.00 = $7,000 (B)
Step 3	The additional investment to buy the larger quantity is B − A = C
	$7,000 − $4,000 = $3,000 (C)
Step 4	The cost of buying the larger quantity in smaller lots is calculated.
	1,000 cases X $8.00 = $8,000 (D)
Step 5	The savings achieved from buying the larger quantity is D − B = E
	$8;000 − $7,000 = $1,000 (E)
Step 6	Calculate the length of time in months the money could have been invested and multiply by the monthly interest rate.
	Months of larger quantity minus the months of the smaller quantity: 6 months − 3 months = 3 months.
	The cost of investment is 12% a year or 1% a month.
	Thus, 3 X 1% X $3,000 = $90.00 (F)
Step 7	Cost of money plus cost of catsup is equal to the total cost of investment.
	$90 + $3,000 = $3,090 (G)
Step 8	Return on investment equals the total savings divided by the total cost of the investment.
	$1,000 − $3,090 X 100 = 32% (P)

A set of hypothetical calculations showing the steps in determining the value of a discount in the purchase of catsup.

1. Since the operation does need some quantity of the product—for instance, catsup—the cost of this quantity purchased without a discount is determined. (The total cost of the smaller quantity $= A$)

2. Then the cost of the larger quantity purchased with the discount is calculated. (The total cost of the larger quantity $= B$)

3. The purchase of the larger quantity involves an additional investment, and that amount is calculated by subtracting the total cost of the smaller quantity from the total cost of the larger. (Cost of investment: $B - A = C$)

4. To determine the advantage in purchasing with the discount, the cost of buying the larger quantity in smaller lots has to be determined by multiplying the larger quantity by the unit price quoted for the smaller quantity. (The cost of buying the larger quantity in smaller lots = the unit price of the smaller quantity $\times$ the amount of the larger quantity = D)

5. The savings by buying the larger quantity is thus equal to the difference between buying the larger quantity as one lot (B) and the cost of buying the larger quantity in smaller lots (D). The savings (E) equals $D - B = E$

6. In this step the length of time in months the additional money is invested is calculated. This figure is then multiplied by the current monthly interest rate the operation must pay. This amount represents the cost of the investment (F).

7. The cost of the investment added to the actual investment then equals the total cost of the additional investment, or G. Thus, $G = F + C$

8. The savings realized (E) is then divided by the total cost of the investment (G) and that figure is multiplied by 100 to arrive at a percentage. This is the percentage return on the investment, or P.

The discount is worth taking if P is more than the operation can expect to get by investing the money gainfully for the same period.

EVALUATING
INVENTORY
MANAGEMENT

Often it is possible to improve inventory management significantly. The improvement could be signaled by any combination of the following.

1. Fewer stockouts or less costly stockouts are noted when the present accounting period is compared with an earlier accounting period.

2. The average total amount of inventory has declined from one accounting period to another. Less money is tied up in stock.

3. When compared with a previous accounting period or with industry averages, inventory has turned over more frequently. The formula for determining inventory turnovers follows:

$$\frac{\text{Total value of items issued from inventory}}{\text{Average inventory value for period}} = \text{Number of turnovers}$$

4. When compared with a previous accounting period or with industry averages, inventory investment turnover has increased. The formula for determining inventory turnover investment follows:

$$\frac{\text{Cost of goods sold during the period}}{\text{Average inventory at cost for the period}} = \begin{array}{c}\text{Number of turnovers of}\\\text{inventory investment}\end{array}$$

5. Inventories of items purchased at a discount are producing a significant return on the operation's investment.

Materials Handling   Serving just one meal can require that 1 or 2 kilograms of food, liquids, and packaging be brought into a foodservice operation. For an operation with a modest volume—a few hundred meals a day—handling a ton of products daily presents few major problems. The truckers delivering the product may place it in storage. The production workers remove it as they need it. For operations of this scale, such simple materials-handling procedures are adequate.

Inefficiencies in this area occur when the procedures for handling food used by the small operation are carried on in a larger foodservice unit. For example, in a small operation, cases of canned food may be unloaded from a truck a case at a time. This inefficient procedure does not have much economic impact because so few cases are unloaded. If the same procedure is used for a larger operation that receives hundreds of cases, the labor cost is three times greater than it has to be, since materials-handling methods are available that are three times as fast as the case-by-case unloading method.

As foodservice operations become larger, materials handling—the movement of food products within the operation—becomes a significant management concern. The goals of materials handling are to reduce labor costs, decrease the response time needed to react to the needs of the operation, improve reliability, reduce overall costs, and improve management control of this part of the supply system.

BENEFITS OF   To understand the benefits of improved materials handling, the problems,
IMPROVED   costs, and inefficiencies of current procedures have to be understood.
MATERIALS   Often the deficiencies of materials-handling procedures are hidden; they
HANDLING   are viewed as parts of other problems. A foodservice operation with materials-handling problems has some or all of the following symptoms.

- Kitchen or food production workers wait for products that are *in* the operation in order to start preparation.
- Products are handled and rehandled.
- Storage space is not fully or effectively used.
- Receiving areas become congested with products. Products that require refrigerated or frozen storage are not stored immediately.
- Checking procedures are given short shrift because receiving personnel are overburdened.
- Products are damaged in handling.

- Production workers, including highly paid craftspeople, spend at least 20 percent of their time getting the products they need to work.
- Items are received and used in large lots, but workers move these products in single units.
- On-the-job accident rates are high, especially for falls and strains.

A planned program of materials handling virtually eliminates these problems. Costs are reduced, especially indirect costs for departments served by the supply system, and management control is increased. Two additional benefits of improved materials handling may be improved employee morale because some of the more backbreaking work is eliminated and lower inventory costs because products are speeded to production departments.

GUIDELINES FOR MATERIALS HANDLING   The general methods of work-system planning as treated in Chapter 7 are equally applicable to materials handling. The flow of materials is as subject to detours, bottlenecks, and backtracking as the flow of people in a kitchen or the flow of food ingredients in a complex preparation.

Here are some additional opportunities for improving materials handling for a foodservice operation.

Use of a systems approach   Instead of viewing the materials-handling procedures of each department of the operation (receiving, storage, production, and service) as separate, the manager should look at the flow of material through the entire operation. For example, can food products be unloaded onto a piece of equipment that can be transported throughout the operation, thereby eliminating rehandling in the storerooms and rehandling again in the production department? Can materials be speeded to the production department, thereby eliminating idle time there?

Increase in size or quantity of units handled   It is more efficient to move ten cases at once by using laborsaving equipment or a better method than to move ten cases one case at a time.

Reduction in delays and holding of products   Products should move directly from a receiving area to storage and from storage to the production department. They should not be held at the receiving area or routed to temporary storage in the production area on the way to being used. Ideally, products should move directly to production, eliminating storage entirely. Thus, materials handling becomes part of the processing of products.

Use of machines not men   While not all foodservice operations can make economic use of the most sophisticated materials-handling equipment, many manual activities can be mechanized inexpensively by using some simple devices. For example, gravity is free, and inexpensive roller conveyors allow products to be unloaded from trucks; overhead rails allow meat to be placed in refrigeration; and chutes allow waste to be eliminated.

Standardization of materials-handling procedures   One objective of materials handling is the reduction of labor costs. If procedures are well planned by management, the skill level and the cost of labor involved can be reduced. Once an efficient procedure has been developed, it should be used routinely.

Planning of straight-line routes for materials movement   As much as possible, eliminate the detours and switchbacks between the receiving area and the production area.

Provision for adequate equipment   Whenever possible, existing equipment should be used effectively. Most operations have some materials-handling equipment, but it may be used poorly. Acquisition of additional equipment should be considered if the cost of purchasing and operating it is less than the cost of the procedure it replaces. Even a relatively expensive piece of equipment, an electric pallet truck, for example, can pay for itself if it speeds the unloading of trucks and the movement of food into production.

Organization of facilities to permit efficient materials handling   Storage areas should be arranged so that items used most often are the most accessible, so that moving equipment can be efficiently used, and so that equipment used for both transporting and storing can be parked.

Assignment of materials handling to the least skilled and least costly labor   Once materials handling is recognized as a distinct procedure, economies can be made by eliminating materials-handling tasks from the work of chefs, bakers, saladmakers, and so on.

Control of materials handling   Materials handling requires active management for greatest efficiency. Every aspect of the materials-handling procedure has to be evaluated on an ongoing basis. Can products be handled in their original shipping containers? Can sorting be eliminated? Can transfer from one piece of equipment to another be eliminated? Can several operations be combined?

MATERIALS-HANDLING EQUIPMENT   Any equipment an operation buys must be justified by the savings effected by using the equipment. The equipment that can make the most contribution to materials handling in a foodservice operation is not expensive. Many operations, even large ones, haul products when they should be rolling them, and handle small units when they should be handling larger lots. Equipment for these purposes is justifiable in almost any sized operation.

Of all materials-handling equipment ranging from the simple dolly to the sophisticated forklift truck, perhaps the most significant are those devices that handle pallets. A *pallet* is a wooden, plastic, or metal platform about 102 centimeters deep, 31 centimeters wide, and 15 centimeters high.

The introduction of palletization and pallet handling has had an important impact on materials-handling efficiency. Instead of handling each individual case, the entire pallet, which may hold 20 or 30 cases, is unloaded at once from the truck and handled as a unit. The pallet may be moved by a forklift truck but also by an electric pallet jack or even a much less costly mechanical pallet jack. The product can be kept on the pallet in storage and moved on the pallet to the production area. In very large operations, full pallets are stacked or placed on shelves in the storage facility. Consider the difference between handling the pallet once and having to handle each case several times as it is loaded and unloaded from hand trucks and shelves.

While not every operation can use pallet loads or even pallets loaded with several different products and while not every supplier is equipped to offer palletized products, large foodservice operations must use them to achieve efficiency in materials handling.

Other equipment can be useful in smaller operations or in complementing the handling of pallets.

Conveyors   A conveyor carries materials over a fixed route. One type of conveyor may be a moving belt that connects, for example, two work stations or the receiving area with the storerooms. Another type of conveyor may be a gravity-roller type that connects a truck bed with the receiving-area floor. Many conveyors of varying complexity are found in foodservice operations, from dish conveyors for dirty serviceware to overhead rails for moving sides of beef.

Chutes   Sometimes it is possible simply to slide materials down a slope by means of a fixed or movable chute. Frequently foodservice operations move waste materials and soiled linens in this way, but meats in a butcher shop, ice, and many other products that are not easily damaged also can be transported by gravity.

Dollies   The basic dolly is a small, wheeled platform that allows material to be rolled instead of dragged or hauled by hand. The deck of a dolly may be of wood or metal. The dolly can be rectangular, round, triangular, X-legged, or contoured. The wheels may be placed to permit tilting, steering, or turning in all directions. Using an inexpensive dolly, a single worker can move drums of detergent, garbage cans, or a dozen cases with ease.

Forklift trucks   A forklift truck is an expensive industrial vehicle capable of handling heavy, fully loaded pallets or containers with pallet-like openings at the bottom and transporting them any distance. With a forklift truck, an entire tractor-trailer can be unloaded in a few minutes and the pallets quickly stored. While obviously unsuitable for small foodservice operations, forklifts of many different types are used in central commissaries, large hotels, foodservice contracting companies, and institutions.

Freight prys   The movement of heavy equipment, for example, an ice machine, may be facilitated by using a freight pry. This piece of equipment resembles a very strong lever on small wheels. Generally freight prys are used in pairs to wheel heavy equipment short distances.

Hand trucks   Hand trucks multiply the efforts of a single person by allowing a number of cases or even a light pallet to be moved with ease. The most common and least expensive hand truck is a simply constructed, small metal platform with two wheels and an extended back that serves as the handle and support for the goods being moved. It sometimes is equipped with a lever that allows the goods to be lifted. More sophisticated models are equipped with folding extensions to the platform, belts and guides that allow the hand truck to "climb" stairs; contoured platforms and backs for barrels or drums; platforms for pallets, clamps instead of a platform, and so on.

Pallet jacks   Pallets can be moved by a much smaller device than the forklift. This device is known as a pallet jack. A pallet jack is a wheeled piece of equipment with two prongs or forks that fit into the pallet opening. A simple mechanism allows the pallet to be lifted above the ground and then moved when the handle of the jack is pulled to release the wheels.

Pallet trucks   Pallet trucks are a sophisticated version of the pallet jack. A motor provides power for the lifting action of the prongs and for movement. Most pallet trucks also allow the load to be tilted to stabilize the pallet. The more expensive pallet trucks also will lift the pallet load high enough to place it on a shelf or remove it from a truck bed.

Shelf racks or trucks; box containers   Many types of small rolling shelves, boxes on wheels, and plastic containers on wheels are used for materials handling, especially for production-area, or in-process, materials handling.

Skids and skid jacks   Skids are metal or metal-and-wood platforms that are used for transporting products and storing them. Unlike pallets that are in direct contact with the floor, skids stand either on four metal braces (a *dead skid*) or on two metal braces and two wheels (a *semilive* skid). The dead skid is moved by sliding a specialized four-wheeled jack under it, while the semilive skid is moved by a detachable jack with two wheels. Products are loaded onto the skid and then the skid is transported to the storage and production area and the jack removed. Many operations that cannot use pallets use skids because of their similar advantages.

Trucks or four-wheeled hand trucks   Many operations use a rolling metal or wooden platform with four wheels and an upright handle. Whereas in function these resemble skids, they are more expensive and cannot be easily stored or stacked.

Product Control: Food Storage and Preservation   Management of the supply system also generally includes responsibility for product control—the supervision of procedures and facilities for the storage and preservation of food within the facility.

The overall organization of the supply system will determine the storage space and storage facilities required. A traditional restaurant may have a relatively large storage facility, while a limited-menu hamburger restaurant with a greater annual volume may have virtually no long-term storage. A large hospital may store products for a year in an elaborate warehousing facility, and an equally large hotel may have storage for only a day's needs.

Supply systems may be organized as *pipelines* or as *reservoirs*. A pipeline supply system provides a continuous supply with the source of products external to the operation. Products are always in the pipeline. A reservoir contains a large product reserve within the operation, and this reserve is periodically replenished. Many factors, including the type of menu, management policies concerning inventory control, materials handling, and purchasing, and the demands of production enter into the choice of organization for the supply system. Management may even decide to compromise. It may choose a pipeline with a small reservoir, a reservoir with a small pipeline, or pipelines for some products and reservoirs for others.

The distinction between the two types of supply-system organization is important. Pipeline systems require little on-premises storage; for example, the products received by the hamburger restaurant or the large hotel are used that day. Reservoir systems require appreciably more storage; for example, the traditional restaurant may have several days' supply while the hospital may have almost a year's.

The fundamentals of managing and organizing the storage process are the same regardless of the type of operation and regardless of whether the operation has a pipeline or a reservoir supply system. These fundamentals are as follows.

• Storage facilities must meet acceptable standards for food hygiene and sanitation.
• Deterioration of products within the facility—loss of quality, value, or function—must be minimized.
• The storage facilities themselves should be easy and as low-cost as possible to operate. The labor used should be highly productive.
• Materials movement to, from, and within the operation should be efficient.
• Management must be able to readily control and administer the storage process and facilities.   •
• Storage facilities should be adequate for the needs of the operation but should not greatly exceed these needs.

PHYSICAL   Nine types of storage can be identified in a foodservice operation.
FACILITIES

1. Receiving-area storage.
2. Refrigerated storage including freezers.
3. Refuse and waste storage.

4. Dry storage for food products that do not require refrigeration.
5. Access storage in production areas. This may include refrigerated storage, frozen food storage, dry storage, and waste storage.
6. Storage for linens, cleaning supplies, equipment.
7. In-process storage for partially prepared or fully prepared food products. These products may require refrigeration or freezing.
8. Equipment storage for materials-handling and food production equipment. Some of this storage may be mobile.
9. External storage—refrigerated or not—at a public warehouse, a supplier's warehouse, and so on.

Exhibit 9.2 gives a partial list of design considerations in planning some of these areas.

The extent of space and the design of equipment for any of these types of storage depend entirely on the particular operation. Only by an examination of the needs of all the operating systems within a particular foodservice operation can *total* storage requirements and capacity be determined. The person planning the storage facilities should attempt to identify how much food and other materials will be in each of these storage categories during a particular period of time.

While rules-of-thumb have been offered for computing storage-space requirements (these are summarized in Exhibit 9.3), it is only by actually determining the space requirements for products to be stored that a manager can arrive at exact storage needs. The dimensions of each item to be stored can be found and then multiplied by the total amount of that item to be stored. Then, either the total amount of cubic meters needed or running shelf space needed can be calculated. After an allowance for aisle space, equipment space, and free space for ease of storage, the general size of the storage area can be determined.

For example, a crate of lettuce may measure 53 centimeters by 33 centimeters by 25 centimeters, meaning that it will require 43,725 cubic centimeters of refrigerator space. Fifteen crates will then require 655,875 cubic centimeters or about 0.65 cubic meters of space. A case of six No. 10 cans is approximately 48 centimeters by 32 centimeters by 18 centimeters. On a shelf 51 centimeters deep, each case will require 33 centimeters of running shelf. In 51 vertical centimeters, two cases could be stacked, allowing some room for shelving and for easy removal of the cases.

Such considerations as the amount of prepared or processed product the operation uses and how much of its production is banked against future need will affect the amount of storage capacity required. These considerations hold true even if the end product to the consumer is the same, and the volume does not vary. The same food product—beef stew, for instance—under different production conditions might be classified as follows:

1. Frozen food to be stored frozen.
2. Frozen food to be refrigerated for thawing.
3. Prepared food to be refrigerated before serving.
4. Prepared food to be frozen.

These classifications depend on whether the operation bought large quantities in excess of current needs (condition 1), bought quantities

---

EXHIBIT 9.2   Design Considerations in Planning Storage Facilities

Receiving Area

Construction	Equipment	Comments
Loading dock at least 1.83 meters (6 feet) wide protected by a roof at least 3.9 meters (13 feet) high constructed of material able to withstand loads of 1,220.5 kilograms/square meters (250 pounds per square foot) at ground level or with elevator to meet truck-bed height; with door openings to accept pallets or trucks; adequate lighting; adequate security system.	Hose outlet for cleaning; electrical outlets for equipment; stairway to ground; telephone for truckers.	Overhead rails as well as conveyors may start at loading dock.
Receiving-area floor should be able to withstand heavy loads and iron wheels —a slip-resistant floor is preferred; sanitary construction of walls (steel tile, ceramic glazed tile, painted, anti-condensation plaster); sanitary construction of area to meet codes; floor drains with traps; coved bases to allow flooding and cleaning; heavy-duty doors with kick plates; 2 to 3 watts of illumination per square foot.	Desk for administrative and clerical work; automatic indicating or beam-type scales; tables; materials-handling equipment; internal and external telephone; refrigeration for temporary holding (with doors to accommodate pallets) may be necessary; steam-cleaning equipment; fly-extermination devices.	Waste-processing equipment; refrigerated storage for garbage may also be in area.

Dry-Storage Area

Construction	Equipment	Comments
Slip-resistant, easy to clean flooring impervious to moisture, acid, grease, salt (quarry or steel tile); walls of tile, painted plaster or other impervious or vermin-proof materials; corners shielded with stainless steel to prevent damage—	Stainless-steel shelving most desirable with adjustable shelves for products and to allow carts beneath lowest shelves; dunnage racks to keep products off the floor	Area should resist encroachment of vermin; design should resist potential harborages; pipes into room should be sealed into walls;

for current needs (condition 2), prepared the product for current needs (condition 3), or prepared the product for future needs (condition 4).

GUIDELINES FOR STORAGE MANAGEMENT While specific food products may require exacting storage conditions and handling, twelve general guidelines for storage management apply widely.

Construction	*Equipment*	*Comments*
covered vertical corners preferable; door wide enough to accept pallets and trucks; ceilings which do not accumulate dust; 2 to 3 watts per square foot of lighting; temperature controlled to between 10°C (50°F) and 21.1°C (70°F); moderate air movement; floor drain and cleaning system.	if pallets or skids are not used; shelves on centers of 2.13 meters (7 feet) depending on materials-handling equipment; closed bins or containers for bulk products; scale for portioning products; desk area and equipment; materials-handling equipment.	windows are not needed; light should be limited if windows are present; one part of storage area should be dehumidified to 50 percent relative humidity.

Refrigerated-Storage Area

Construction	*Equipment*	*Comments*
Construction of refrigerated-storage area must meet standards set by the National Sanitation Foundation. Equipment capable of maintaining temperature of –23.3°C (–10°F) or below for freezing and temperature of 0°C (32°F) to 4.4°C (40°F) for refrigeration.	Refrigerator shelving of stainless steel; thermometers; materials-handling equipment.	Several temperature . zones may be necessary depending on the products being held and time or storage; humidity control may be necessary for produce.

Refuse Storage

Construction	*Equipment*	*Comments*
May have refrigerated storage to meet National Sanitation Foundation standards. General area should have impervious floors; floor drains; sanitary coving; impervious walls; adequate lighting and ventilation.	May have can-washing area with can-washing equipment; compactor; pulping equipment; steam-cleaning equipment; passive and active extermination systems.	Must be completely isolated and vermin-proof.

EXHIBIT 9.3 Rules-of-Thumb for Storage Requirements

Type of Storage Area	Volume Required per Meal Served
Receiving Area	.02–.03 square meters .22–.32 square feet
Dry Storage	.046–.092 square meters .50–1.00 square feet
Refrigerator	.014–.028 cubic meters .50–1.00 cubic feet
Freezer	.007–.016 cubic meters .25–.60 cubic feet

Accept only merchandise that is wholesome and undamaged, meets specifications, and is as represented on the delivery instrument   To implement this guideline, a knowledge of the operation's quality standards is necessary as well as the ability to recognize signs of beginning decay in food products. By implication, it becomes necessary to weigh or count items as they are delivered to assure that they are as represented. Specifications may also include acceptable delivery temperatures.

Use those items delivered first before those items delivered later This storage principle is known as "First in, First out," or FIFO. This guideline requires that a method of coding items with the date received be used. For example, cases can be marked or special tags or computer cards used.

Store food products under the appropriate conditions   Exhibit 9.4 suggests recommended storage conditions and acceptable lengths of storage time. The recommendations could be much more precise. Unfortunately, foodservice operations are unlikely to have the equipment to radically vary conditions of humidity and temperature in refrigeration. Sometimes a refrigerator with a higher-than-usual temperature (4.4°C to 7.2°C or 40°F to 45°F) is used for tropical and delicate fruits. This guideline can also include the need for ripening rooms for melons, aging rooms for beef, and so on.

Maintain perishable food products—milk, meats, cooked foods, and egg products—at a temperature below 4.4°C (40°F)   The danger zone is generally considered to be between 4.4°C (40°F) and 60°C (140°F). In storage, food products are likely to reach the temperature danger zone because of refrigerator or freezer breakdown or inefficiency due to lack of maintenance, obsolescence, or overloading, or during the transportation of the products.

Protect products from contamination   Sources of contamination may be other products both food and nonfood, water, insects, unclean storage facilities, unclean materials handling, or unclean portioning equipment. An approved program of insect and vermin extermination may be necessary.

Maintain food-storage equipment, especially mechanical equipment Refrigeration and freezing machinery require preventive maintenance if storage temperatures are to remain acceptable. It is also important to avoid overloading that will reduce overall equipment efficiency and shorten its useful life.

Keep storage facilities and receiving areas secure   It is important for the profitability of the operation and the efficiency of the supply system to prevent theft and misuse of products.

Organize storage facilities   Products should be easily identified within the facility. It should be an easy matter to locate any product or products from any shipment. Cartons should be stacked so that labels are visible. Dividers should be used between items on shelves. Shelves should be marked clearly.

Prevent mechanical damage within the storage facility   Handling practices must respect the fragility of some food packages. Frozen foods cannot be thrown into freezers; clamp trucks may damage some fragile shipping cartons; cases piled too high may topple over; bagged flour stored in an aisle may be ripped by materials-handling equipment.

Reduce access to storage areas   In order to prevent contamination and product theft, access to storage areas should be limited to those persons whose work requires them to be there. In addition, the productivity of the people involved with supply is improved. Within the storage facility there should be an effort to consolidate requests so that refrigerators and freezers remain closed as much as possible. No employee's personal belongings should be kept in the operation's storage area.

Maintain managerial control of the storage facility and the stored products by control procedures that require strict accountability for receipts, inventories, and issues   It is essential to the supply system that as products enter the operation they are identified for the benefit of other departments and that the disposition of products as they are issued to production departments be noted. Only in this way can managerial information for inventory and purchasing be accurate.

MAKING THE SUPPLY SYSTEM MORE EFFECTIVE

The supply system of a large foodservice operation can be exceedingly complicated. Even a modest traditional restaurant dealing with several hundred products and a dozen suppliers making frequent deliveries has an involved system. The manager of a supply system has two principal aids: (1) a strong supply routine for day-to-day operations; and (2) devices and forms that facilitate the management and control of the system.

EXHIBIT 9.4   General Temperature Guide for Food Storage

Food	Dry Storage (50–70° F)	Refrigerated Storage (36–40° F)	Freezer Storage (0° F or below)
Cereal Products			
Regular cornmeal; whole wheat flour	Acceptable for 60 days	Necessary over 60 days	—
All-purpose and bread flour; rice; and so on	Acceptable	Desirable	—
Canned Fruits			
Apples; applesauce; apricots; blackberries; cherries; cranberry sauce; grapefruit; grapefruit juice; purple plums; peaches; and so on	Acceptable	Desirable	—
Canned Vegetables			
Green beans; beets; carrots; corn; green peas; tomatoes; tomato juice; tomato paste; and so on	Acceptable	Desirable	—
Dairy Products			
Butter	—	Acceptable for up to 2 weeks	Necessary over 2 weeks
Cheese, natural	—	Necessary	—
Cheese, processed	—	Necessary	—
Milk, canned	Acceptable	Desirable	—
Milk, dry	—	Necessary	—
Dried Fruits			
Apples; apricots; peaches	Acceptable for 2 weeks	Necessary over 2 weeks	—
Figs; prunes; raisins	Acceptable	Desirable	—

Supply Routine   Although operations differ in their day-to-day procedures, the supply routine of many foodservice facilities—large and small—resembles the routine that follows.

   Products arrive   Products are scheduled to arrive at a time set by the operation or at least at a time the operation can anticipate. It is

Food	Dry Storage (50–70° F)	Refrigerated Storage (36–40° F)	Freezer Storage (0° F or below)
Eggs			
Shell	—	Necessary	—
Dried	—	Necessary	—
Frozen	—	—	Necessary
Fats and Oils			
Cottonseed oil; lard; olive oil; vegetable shortening	Acceptable	Desirable	—
Fresh Fruits			
Apples; peaches; pears; plums; and so on	—	Necessary	—
Fresh Vegetables			
Onions	Acceptable	Desirable	—
Potatoes	Acceptable	Desirable	—
Sweet potatoes	Necessary	—	—
Other fresh vegetables such as green beans; beets; cabbage; carrots; and so on	—	Necessary	—
Meat and Meat Products			
Frozen meats, such as ground beef; hams; pork loins; turkeys	—	—	Necessary
Cured hams and shoulders; bacon; and so on	—	Necessary	—
Other canned meats, such as beef and gravy; pork luncheon meat; pork and gravy; and so on	Acceptable	Desirable	—

important that the receiving areas do not become congested and that perishable products are placed directly in controlled storage facilities.

Products are identified and checked   After products are unloaded, they are checked against the delivery ticket or the bill of lading from the trucker and against the copy of the purchase order or specifications for the product. This check should be made in the receiving area. It is important that the quantity and quality be acceptable.

Receipt of the product is noted   Communication that the product is in the operation may not be immediately necessary, but the information is needed by the purchasing and accounting departments.

Requisitions or orders from production departments are processed Product requisitions are read, sorted, placed in some order of priority, and assigned to workers.

Orders are assembled and consolidated   The orders from the production department are assembled. In large operations, a worker may use a forklift or pallet truck to fill production orders. In others, the worker gathers orders onto rolling-shelf trucks or even into supermarket-type baskets. Since it is easier to gather all the products needed for that day from a freezer at one time, partial orders for each production department must be consolidated into a single order.

Inventory records are adjusted   The withdrawal of products from inventory is noted. If records are not adjusted immediately, then the appropriate form is left so that a notation can be made later.

Products are transported to the production department and deposited Either someone from the storage area transports the products to the production department or a runner from the production department takes them from the storage area.

Receipt of the product is acknowledged   Someone is always in charge of the product: the trucker turns it over to the storage department; the storage department turns it over to the production department; the production department turns it over to the service department.

Activities of the receiving and storage department are summarized and communicated   Summaries of items received and issued are typically sent to management and to the accounting department.

Facilitating the Supply Routine   A number of printed forms are used to facilitate the workings of the supply system. The object of using these forms is to provide accountability for products received and issued, to provide management with necessary information, and to provide an easy way of communicating production department needs to the supply system. Exhibit 9.5 lists some of the forms in use in foodservice operations and the type of information contained on them. Exhibits 9.6 through 9.8 offer some examples from this list.

EXHIBIT 9.5   Forms Used in Supplying Foodservice Operations

Form	Use	Data Base	
Physical Inventory	Provides operation with a periodic count and value of items held in stock. Used for purchasing, inventory decisions.	Type of item Name of item Physical location Item Description	Amt. of item on hand Unit(s) Unit Price Value of item on hand
Perpetual Inventory	A moment-to-moment record of the amount of an item on hand; a complete receipt and issue history.	Name of item Date and amount of all receipts Date and amount of all issues Running balance on hand	
Inventory and Purchase Record	Complete record of consumption, inventory information, and inventory-decision factors, vendor information, perpetual inventory. Used for inventory-management decision-making and for accountability.	Item name Specifications Units Location Minimax information Par-level information	Order quantity information Consumption History Vendor Comments Purchase Record by Dates and Amounts Perpetual Inventory as above
Receiving Record and Report	Identifies items as they are received; indicates distribution; establishes accountability.	Item Supplier Received Amount Received Value Number of packages received	Distribution of product Name of person receiving Total received that date
Dollar Inventory Report	Used in cash-sales department (a snack bar, for example) to reconcile product consumed with cash received.	Item Selling Price Inventory at start of accounting period Inventory at end of accounting period	Usage Value of usage Cash Receipts
Inventory Tag	Used to keep track of hard-to-mark products such as sides of beef; two-part tag is numbered on both parts.	Item name Tag number Received by Date received	Value Weight/quantity Location
Monthly Consumption Report	Used to adjust inventory levels in the par-level and minimax methods and to compute order quantities.	Item Date(s) Amounts used	Amounts used year to date Amounts used last year this month

EXHIBIT 9.5   Forms Used in Supplying Foodservice Operations (cont.)

Form	Use	Data Base	
Merchandise Receipt	Used to communicate receipt of merchandise when copy of supplier's invoice does not accompany product.	Date Supplier Item Description	Amount Value received Received by
Credit Memo	Used to request a credit from a supplier for a product returned or rejected; used to communicate need for credit to accounting department.	Operation's name and address Supplier's name and address Date Item Item Description	Quantity returned Amount returned Reason for return Signature of trucker accepting merchandise
Material Credit	Similar to credit memo but an internal document between production and supply departments.	Production dept. Supply dept. Date Item Description Quantity returned	Amount returned Reason for return Signature of person accepting merchandise
Cost and Control Sheet (Delivery Ticket Summary)	Records amounts of product purchased in various product categories and total value received for day or week. Used in institutional feeding to monitor food budgets on the same basis.	Date(s) Items received Quantities received Value received	
Daily Food Cost (Steward's Report)	Summarizes dollar expenditures of "supply system." Used to compare prior similar periods with current periods. Used to maintain a daily food-cost record.	Date Balance brought forward Issues amount Amount of direct purchases Sales today Comparative information	
Purchase Order	Copy used to communicate the receipt of merchandise; also serves as receiving record.	Name of operation Operation's billing address Operation's shipping address Supplier's address Routing information Quantity ordered Billing unit Item codes Pack/size Description	Purchase order date Arrival date Order number Freight information Price per unit Total price Conditions of sale Discount terms Purchased by whom Received by whom Comments on receipt

Form	Use	Data Base	
Requisition	Used to communicate the production department's needs to the supply department.	Production dept. Supply dept. Date/time Item(s) Description	Filling record Receiving record (In production dept.: production dept. inventory)
Receiving Ticket	Used to identify the receipt of a single item or a shipment from a single supplier.	Information similar to that of the purchase order; used on receiving ticket.	
Invoice Stamp or Ticket	A rubber stamp or small form on invoice supplied by trucker to inform the accounting dept. of either a direct payment or the receipt of the merchandise as specified on the purchase order. Preprinted in checklist fashion so that person receiving can check off appropriate comments. May also provide check points for accounting department's information.	*By receiving* Quantity verified Price verified Received by	*By accounting* Payment approved Paid by check number Date paid

EXHIBIT 9.6 Physical Inventory

Location: _____ By: _____ Date: _____ Sheet Number ____ of _____							
					Extensions		
Classification	Shelf In	Item Description	Unit	Quantity	Unit Price	Total Cost	Total Value

EXHIBIT 9.7   Cost and Control Sheet

Item		Sunday	Monday	Tuesday	Wednesday	Thursday	Friday	Saturday	Totals Qu.	Cost
Meat Beef	Q.									
	C.									
Lamb	Q.									
	C.									
Mutton	Q.									
	C.									
Pork	Q.									
	C.									
Veal	Q.									
	C.									
Fish Dried Fresh										
Vegetables Green Potatoes Root Salad										
Fruit Cooking Fresh										
Provisions Bacon Butter Cheese Eggs Lard Margarine										
Groceries Cocoa Coffee										

An example of a cost and control sheet which shows amount of product purchased in various categories for the day and the week.

EXHIBIT 9.8 Daily Food Cost

Date	*Day*	*Storeroom Balance Brought Forward*	*Storeroom Purchases*	*Total*	*Issues*	*Direct Purchases*	*Today*			*To-Date This Month*		
							Total Cost	*Sales*	*% Cost*	*Total Cost*	*Sales*	*% of Cost*
		1	*2*	*3*	*4*	*5*	*6*	*7*	*8*	*9*	*10*	*11*

Use the following to determine daily food cost:
1. Enter inventory value in column 1
2. New merchandise entered in column 2
3. Issues from requisition in column 4
4. Purchases direct to producing departments in column 5
5. Add figures in columns 1 and 2; put in column 3
6. Result is amount of storeroom inventory before making issues

Chapter 10
The Production
System
Foodservice operations traditionally have been viewed as culinary workshops to which a retail store was attached. Today, this concept of the foodservice enterprise is being questioned. As the twenty-first century approaches, the business of the foodservice enterprise has become marketing ready-to-eat food through a variety of distribution channels—dining rooms, vending machines, take-out packages, mobile carts, and so on. Food production has come to play a secondary role in many foodservice operations—in some operations it has no place at all.

The modern foodservice entrepreneur does not first build a workshop called a kitchen and then seek to market its product. Rather, having identified a marketable product, the entrepreneur tries to provide it in a way that efficiently meets both market and investment objectives. The food may be produced in a traditional kitchen, in a genuine factory, or it may simply be purchased from a more efficient producer (an outside manufacturer, processor, or commissary). The ideal food production system for any foodservice operation thus consists of those production activities that it can perform well, within the limits set by the objectives of the organization as a whole.

CURRENT PRACTICES IN FOOD PRODUCTION

The success of foodservice enterprises is measured by their prosperity in a highly competitive industry. Those organizations prosper that can produce quality products, price them competitively, and sell them at a satisfactory profit. Those operations that cannot must suffer the ultimate cost of an inefficient production system: a declining ability to compete.

There is perhaps no better example of this phenomenon than the sudden decline of the urban coffee shop as the limited-menu, take-out/take-in restaurant chains invade major cities. Marginal coffee-shop restaurants—those with high labor, material, and investment costs—do not survive the immediate decline in business that occurs when a hamburger, fish, chicken, or pizza restaurant opens nearby. A second group of coffee shops weathers the initial loss of business only to find that they cannot afford to replace worn-out production equipment at current costs. At that point their ability to compete declines. If they are not to go out of business, owners are faced with a limited number of alternatives: they can compromise the quality of their production in an effort to cut costs; they can effect full-scale reorganization of the production system in hopes of making it more efficient; or they can abandon their market segment to the limited-menu restaurant and seek a less competitive market. Even these drastic measures do not ensure success.

This scenario can be applied to other segments of the foodservice industry as well. Between 1960 and 1971, the total number of restaurants in the United States increased by 9,000. The number of limited-menu, take-out/take-in restaurants increased by 30,000 in the same period. Thus about 21,000 traditional restaurants—about 10 percent of the 1960 total—failed to adapt.

On first consideration it may seem that the success of a production system is directly related to the amount of food preparation that can be done outside the operation. Though this model for success is followed by the limited-menu, take-out/take-in restaurant, other food production models are also successful. For example, in offering a variety of broiled and roasted meat entrees, some sauced dishes, a salad bar, some side dishes and desserts, contemporary restaurants produce more on the premises than the limited-menu, take-out/take-in restaurant and less than the traditional restaurant, yet they can be as successful as the former.

These contemporary restaurants concentrate their resources on the kind of food preparation they can do well:

- Cooking meats but not butchering them.
- Assembling salad bar elements but not preparing them.
- Combining vegetable elements but not peeling, trimming, or cutting them.
- Garnishing cakes with various toppings but not baking them.
- Finishing side dishes (for example, frozen onion rings) but not preparing them.
- Baking breads but not preparing doughs.
- Preparing sauces but not preparing stocks.

Likewise, several chains of Italian restaurants successfully assemble, cook, combine, garnish, and finish menu items they offer but do not make their own pasta, pizza dough, tomato sauce, sausage, or bread dough.

Economic and marketing decisions establish the extent of the food preparation that will take place in the operation. Some foodservice organizations are successful in converting agricultural commodities such as sides of beef and flour into ready-to-eat foods. Others meet objectives

by severely limiting food preparation within the operation. One successful chain of fried-chicken restaurants finds that its production system is
most efficient if each unit prepares its menu items from whole raw chickens that are cut, marinated, breaded, and fried on the premises. Another
successful chain supplies its units with chicken ready for frying.

CONCEPTS OF FOOD PRODUCTION

The production system in foodservice establishments is comprised of all
the activities involved in the conversion of food from its commercial
market form into menu items to be served to the customer, guest, or
client. Exhibit 10.1 presents the scope of these activities and the processes and procedures involved in this conversion. Some items are prepared in just a few steps—a half of grapefruit, for example—while others
such as a roll or an order of beef stew involve several hundred steps. Although someone must prepare the consumer's order, it is the food production manager who decides at what point in the series of steps outlined
in Exhibit 10.1 the operation will assume further preparation.

Food production managers are not usually directly responsible for performing food production activities. The focus of this chapter, then, will
be on managing rather than executing these food production activities.

Specific Objectives
of Food
Production

The exact expression of objectives for a food production system varies
with each operation. The operation's competitive position, its target
market segment, and its financial and managerial resources all influence
its production objectives at any given time. In general, however, three
objectives seem primary.

1. *To arrange for and administer all the food preparation activities*
that must be performed within the operation in order to make the de-
sired menu items   The menu program dictates food production. Just
as a work order in a manufacturing plant sets in motion a series of planning, production, and packaging steps, the menu prescribes the activities
of the food preparation system. The activities undertaken will vary with
each facility, but it is the job of the food production manager to determine which preparation activities will be undertaken by the operation
and which—if any or all—will take place outside.

2. *To ensure the required level of product quality throughout pre-*
preparation, preparation, and finishing   Charged with the responsibility for the transformation of raw materials into a market-pleasing
product, the food production manager must establish food standards and
see to it that these standards are consistently met. Each operation must
establish its own relevant standards, but once established, food preparation workers must be trained to recognize and meet these standards.

EXHIBIT 10.1   Food Preparation Activities

Major Phases	Typical Activities	Typical Processes	Typical Procedures
Conversion from commercial market form into ready-to-prepare food	Cleaning	Washing	Scrubbing potatoes Soaking salad greens
		Trimming	Peeling potatoes Scaling fish Shucking oysters
	Dividing	Butchering	Breaking chucks Steaking out loins Disjointing chickens
		Portioning	Separating contents of case goods Scaling flour
	Modifying form	Particulating	Grinding meat Slicing cheese
		Shaping	Forming meat patties Cutting french fries
	Blending	Mixing	Preparing flour, baking powder, salt mixes Seasoning bread crumbs
	Modifying texture	Hydrating	Reconstituting dehydrated onions Cooking rice
		Defrosting	"Slacking" meats Tempering frozen entrees
	Unpackaging		Emptying boxes Opening and draining cans Unwrapping frozen foods
Conversion from ready-to-prepare food to menu item	Preparing	Combining	Mixing dough Preparing salad dressing
		Packaging	Wrapping potatoes for baking Trussing chickens

Major Phases	Typical Activities	Typical Processes	Typical Procedures
	Cooking	Baking	Making sheet cakes Roasting meats
		Deep frying	Frying doughnuts Frying french fries
		Broiling	Preparing steaks Toasting bread
		Water cooking	Steaming lobsters Poaching salmon Hard-cooking eggs
		Shallow frying	Griddle cooking eggs Panbroiling liver Sautéing veal Stir frying vegetables
		Concentrating	Cooking soup Making stock
		Reconstituting	Heating canned soup Warming bread
	Assembling	Mixing	Making composed salad Making derivative sauces from foundation sauces
		Enhancing	Adding almonds to vegetables Making foods au gratin Seasoning with spices Icing cakes
Conversion from menu item to food order	Portioning	Measuring	Ladling soup Dishing ice cream Cutting cakes
		Plating	Making individual salads Putting stew in casseroles
	Finishing	Garnishing	Decorating cakes Adding parsley to plates
		Heating	Browning preblanched french fries Crisping roast duck

Fundamental quality standards also include accurate forecasting of quantities needed in production and careful control of portion sizes.

3. *To conform to the principles of work-system design articulated for that particular operation*   Just as the menu authorizes what food will be produced, the plan of the work system ordains how the food product will be "manufactured." Once an efficient and effective food production process has been integrated into the entire work flow of the organization, the food production manager must administer and oversee it.

Interaction of the Production System with Other Systems   Since the activities of all the systems of a foodservice operation are interdependent, an alteration in any system ripples throughout the others. The purchasing system cannot be adapted to changes in its environment, for example, changes in food prices, without the production system being in some way affected. In a simple instance, if the purchasing agent of a large hospital, limited by a budget amount for each patient meal, proposes to purchase cubed beef instead of portioned meat patties that are more expensive per kilo, the food production system is potentially affected. It is now necessary for the food production manager to evaluate the implications of committing production personnel to grinding and portioning meat. By the same token, the food production manager may, through work study, find that the production system has the opportunity to grind and portion meat economically, if the purchasing system can supply it at particular prices relative to the cost of pre-portioned patties.

Likewise, the dining room manager of a gourmet restaurant may propose a reorganization of the dining room staff prompted by an increase in wage rates. This reorganization eliminates the possibility of tableside preparation of certain dishes. Eliminating these dishes affects marketing and menu planning; keeping them in the menu program affects the food production system which now must be charged with their total preparation.

Inevitably crises in one system affect other systems to some degree. Stock-out of a particular food product may mean a drastic alteration in the food preparation routine. It may be necessary to bake rolls when rolls are usually purchased ready to eat. The unexpected absence of key service personnel may mean a minor alteration of portioning and garnishing procedures in the kitchen.

In any of these instances, and in the thousands of others that are possible, the food production system must respond, either by appropriate anticipation or appropriate reaction. Management must decide courses of action that will provide for the most effective interactions of the systems involved.

Exhibit 10.2 suggests principal areas of interaction between the food production system and other systems. Exhibit 10.3 presents some specific decisions that correspond to some of these areas.

EXHIBIT 10.2   Interaction Between Food Production System and Other Systems

Strategic Management	Departmentalization Delegation Participation
Personnel Management	Skills Motivation Morale Training Scheduling Labor relations Compensation
Marketing and Menu Planning	Pricing Merchandising Product life Competition Product development
Work	Equipment selection and use Materials selection and use Method of work selection
Purchasing	Value analysis Make or buy Marketplace price changes
Supply	Inventory Product substitutions Timing Storage life
Service	Consumer turnover rates Division of responsibilities Communication methods
Control	Forecasting Reporting Standards Evaluation
Business	Cost volume Cost benefit Cash flow

EXHIBIT 10.3 Food Production Management Decisions Stimulated by Other Systems

Decision Areas	*Possible Decisions to be Made*
Marketing	
Price Changes	More effective production system
	Reorganization of production system for increased or reduced volume
	Reorganization of production system for different menu mix
Merchandising	Best way to increase production of merchandised items
	Minimization of loss of quality in items with declining volume during merchandising period
Product Life	Product reformulation
	Length of product life
	Product becomes uneconomical at what volume
Competition	Product development to meet competition
	Recipe reformulation for lower cost to consumer for better value image
	Evaluation of quality control procedures
Product Development	Consumer preferences translated into food items
	Maintenance of nutritional quality in products
	Cooking procedures that reduce need for food products with additives
Purchasing	
Value Analysis	Formulation of less restrictive specifications without loss of quality
	Product stage at which it is advantageous for the operation to buy it
Price Changes	Production system adaptations to rising or falling marketplace prices
Supply	
Inventory	Recipe reformulations to reduce inventory costs by narrowing products stocked
	Production scheduling to minimize inventory build-up
Product Substitutions	Contingency plans for stock-outs
Timing	Production planning to meet delivery schedules
	Production planning to minimize deliveries

Limitations on the Production System   All the systems in a foodservice organization, and even the business and social environment in which it operates, impose limits on the shape of the food production system. A food production manager discovers that the production system is constrained by a variety of factors:

• *Limited labor pool:* the unavailability of sufficient labor, reliable labor, motivated labor, or skilled labor plus low labor productivity in production and service areas.

Decision Areas	*Possible Decisions to be Made*
Storage Life	Production scheduling to use products toward the end of their storage life
	Conversion of products into forms that keep longer
	Production planning to maximize use of storage facilities

Service

Consumer Turnover Rates	Acceleration of last phases of production
	Small-batch continuous cooking programs
	Large-batch and holding programs
Division of Responsibilities	Merged systems
	Responsibility for plating, finishing, garnishing
	Sidework division of labor
Communication	Check systems
	Ordering systems
	Pickup systems

Control

Forecasting	Future labor requirements
	Product requirements
	Budgets
Standards	Yield testing
	Recipe standardization
Evaluation	Methods for evaluation and control

Business

Cost Volume	Relationships between cost of unit and total volume of production
Cost Benefit	Projected value of investment in work system modification
Cash Flow	Organization of production to accumulate or minimize stored labor

• *High cost of materials:* cost of materials for production that is high relative to the price that can be asked for the finished products.

• *High operating costs:* high costs of energy, waste removal, water, sanitation, maintenance, and other support services.

• *High investment costs:* high interest rates, high costs for construction and equipment.

• *Legal restraints:* laws and regulations that affect the food production system, such as food-handling regulations, labor utilization regulations, and truth-in-menu.

• *Technological constraints:* limited capabilities of outside enterprises to produce food products; limited capabilities of equipment.

• *Difficult market demands:* peak periods of demand during each day or week separated by periods of low demand; high consumer standards; intense need to offer competitive difference; limited product life; low consumer tolerance for delay between initiation of the order and delivery; consumer resistance to upward price changes.

FOOD PRODUCTION

However diverse the elements of food production, certain general observations can be made:

1. Good food production is ensured by following certain basic guidelines.
2. In successful operations, physical facilities for the preparation of food are based on certain criteria.
3. Food preparation equipment is most effectively selected from a process perspective.

Food Production Guidelines   Although specific procedures for preparing foods vary widely, certain guidelines for preparing food seem to be adhered to by successful food production systems. Adherence to these guidelines is usually ensured by specific rules and preparation instructions as well as by do-and-don't charts and verbal directives. A summary of these guidelines follows.

MODIFY FOODS ONLY AS NECESSARY   Food products should be modified by cooking or otherwise only as much as is necessary for the particular menu item. Color, texture, natural flavors, appearance, and other features should not be gratuitously altered by preparation procedures. For example, green vegetables such as string beans should not be overcooked, thus losing their natural color and texture.

Foods should be modified only to *increase* the ease with which they are digested. Food preparation procedures that tend to make foods more difficult to digest should be avoided. For example, eggs should not be cooked at high temperatures.

MAINTAIN WHOLESOMENESS, FRESHNESS, AND NUTRITIONAL VALUES   Only completely wholesome products should be used in food preparation. Wholesomeness should be ensured by maintaining food products at temperatures below 45°F(7.2°C) or above 140°F (60°C). For example, milk should not be kept at or above 40°F(4.4°C).

When all other factors are equal, fresh food is to be preferred to processed food. The amount of time fresh foods spend in storage is to be reduced. For example, coffee should be ground just before brewing; stocks of canned goods should be used on a first-in, first-out basis.

Food preparation procedures should be directed toward maintaining the nutritional values of food products, especially vitamins and minerals. For example, cut potatoes should be kept under refrigeration so that they do not lose vitamin C.

SET FOOD STANDARDS Responsibility for product quality and physical possession of food products should be expressly designated. For example, the roast cook should receive and sign for meat from the butcher shop before preparing it for roasting.

Portions of the same product should be consistent in all respects: quantity, flavor, appearance, garnishing, and so on. For example, the size of a serving of mashed potatoes should be exactly the same from day to day.

Precise measurement should be used for all procedures: cooking times, temperatures, determination of doneness, portioning, and so on. For example, the roasting temperature for meat should be 325°F (163°C).

MINIMIZE PREPARATION AND HOLDING TIMES Preparation procedures that can efficiently be performed before actual preparation for service should be encouraged. This pre-preparation simplifies quality control and service. For example, parsley for garnishing should be chopped before the restaurant begins serving.

Food products after preparation should be held for the shortest time possible consistent with efficiency and the maintenance of food quality. For example, coffee should not be served more than 30 minutes after it has been brewed.

PREPARE FOOD IN AS SMALL A BATCH AS POSSIBLE An increase in the volume of food being prepared at one time tends to decrease the unit cost of preparation but also decreases the opportunity for quality control, especially esthetic quality. In mass-producing products, attention cannot be given to individual differences in materials. For example, portions of roast beef should be hand-carved.

SERVE HOT FOOD HOT AND COLD FOOD COLD Specific temperatures should be related to specific products. For example, ice cream should be served at 14°F (−10°C).

MEET CONSUMER EXPECTATIONS Food products should meet consumer expectations. They should be enhanced, not altered by off-flavors or unanticipated flavors. For example, highly flavored foods, such as cabbage, should not be stored close to dairy products.

Improvement of the appearance of a product in preparation or presentation enhances the consumer's general enjoyment of the product. For example, brown baked goods by applying an egg wash; garnish plates with greens.

Food preparation should be controlled so that the end products fall within consumer desires. For example, starch-thickened pie filling should not be overcooked to the point where it will weep when cool; rolls should not be charred.

Food Preparation Facilities

Food preparation facilities must be consistent with the individual operation's work system (see Chapter 7). Specific food preparation activities taking place in the operation must be reconciled with information about business volume, production strategies, and business flow in order to arrive at functional work arrangements, space allocations, work methods, work-center design, task descriptions, and so on.

Simply taking the work-system plan of one operation and applying it to another operation is unwise. The typical take-out/take-in hamburger restaurant consists of activity areas for pre-preparation, preparation, assembling and packaging, and holding—separate areas where products are sorted, unwrapped, slightly modified and held, cooked or processed, made into customer portions and wrapped, and held at an appropriate temperature until service personnel take them. The work centers associated with these activities may be arranged in a way that in a "plan view" (as they appear on a blueprint) resembles the letters T or L or U or O. Hospital foodservice facilities, gourmet restaurant kitchens, snack bars, and other foodservice-operation preparation areas may have similar layout designs. If these layouts are viewed as prescriptive, as they are when a work-system planner wishes to short-cut the planning process, the planner is erroneously assuming that work-system designs are universally applicable. However, many work-system elements are not transferable. An examination of the physical facilities of a hamburger restaurant offers little indication of the operation's production strategy, financial limits, work methods, labor resources, market demands, or the other information on the basis of which the particular layout was designed.

Doesn't every hamburger restaurant need an area in which to grind meat and form patties? Only those hamburger restaurants that have no more efficient and effective way of presenting the cook with raw hamburger patties. The hamburger patties could be purchased preformed (fresh or frozen) or could be made by the griddle cook from preportioned fresh chopped meat, to name just two alternatives.

Though one foodservice operation's work system may not be transferable to a different operation, three general conditions apply to all operations' food preparation facilities:

1. Food preparation facilities must serve the needs of all the food preparation activities that must take place within the operation.
2. To be successful, food preparation facilities must be integrated into the total work flow of the organization.

3. Food preparation facilities must conform to accepted standards of sanitary construction, equipment installation, ventilation, and waste disposal as articulated by law and accepted as good practice.

Food Preparation Equipment   Equipment for food preparation is considered from two perspectives: (1) its role in the total process of food preparation; and (2) its function in a particular preparation procedure.

Viewed as part of the total process of food preparation, food preparation equipment includes equipment for:

storage (refrigerator)
control (scale)
processing (quick freezer)
preparation (potato peeler)
transporting (rolling cabinet)
cooking (stove)
reconstitution (microwave oven)
finishing (cheese melter)
post-preparation (steam table)
assembly (french fry bagger)
portioning (ice-cream disher)
sanitation (pressure-washer)
waste removal (compactor)

As part of an individual food preparation procedure, equipment can be identified and categorized by its role in the actual modification of foods, such as:

cleaning (salad washer)
trimming (potato peeler)
cutting or particulating (slicer)
mixing/combining (mixer)
blending (grinder, blender)
frying (deep-fat fryer)
broiling (char-broiler)
water cooking (steamer)
stewing (steam kettle)
braising (tilting skillet)
cooling (refrigerator)
freezing (freezer)
baking (oven)
texture or form modifying (dough sheeter, patty former)
warming (fudge warmer, roll warmer)

Though the larger categories based on the total food preparation process include these categories based on how the equipment actually modifies the food (for example, both "cleaning" and "trimming" are part of "preparation"), the distinction between the two ways of looking at equipment is important in selecting equipment. If the equipment is looked at as part of the total food preparation process, it is evaluated as part of an overall work system that includes other equipment, personnel, and materials. If the equipment is looked at only in terms of how it actually modifies the food, the person selecting equipment simply weighs one way of doing something against alternative ways of doing the same thing. This functional perspective is much narrower; equipment is evaluated just on the basis of its individual performance.

Using these two different perspectives to choose equipment can lead to very different choices. If the operation needs peeled potatoes to make beef stew, the larger, process perspective would lead to an examination of all possible ways of pre-preparing potatoes before cooking. If, due to marketplace conditions, the operation must buy raw, unpeeled, potatoes, the equipment and methods evaluated would include cooking the potatoes in the jacket, peeling them with a knee-action (swivel) peeler, peeling them on a hand-turned machine, and certainly peeling them in a mechanical potato peeler. If all factors are considered, including labor cost and availability, volume of business, the amount of potatoes to be peeled and when, the cost of equipment (acquisition, installation, service, and operation), and the financial structure of the company, a good decision could be reached.

On the other hand, if only the narrow functional perspective is considered, decision making is less complex: a mechanical potato peeler is more efficient (produces more peeled potatoes per hour) than any other method. The decision then becomes a matter of choosing which commercial potato peeler to buy on the basis of service contract, cost, guarantee, reputation, materials, and so on. The functional perspective may have precluded the alternative that might have been most economical for the operation: a 79 cent knee-action potato peeler with which the dishwasher (who is there anyway) could peel the necessary potatoes.

This example may seem extreme until total equipment use in functioning kitchens is analyzed. A large kitchen may have thousands of dollars worth of excellent but inappropriate equipment: ovens, mixers, slicers, microwaves, conveyor toasters, infra-quartz ovens—because equipment acquisition was not put into full perspective.

In selecting equipment, the manager is charged (1) with deciding whether the preparation should be done at all in the operation; (2) with deciding which preparation method is most economical; and (3) if the equipment is needed, with deciding on the best equipment from a functional basis. Exhibit 10.4 presents a model worksheet that outlines the decision factors involved.

EXHIBIT 10.4 Make-or-Buy Decision Factors Involved in Selecting Kitchen Equipment

Cost of Buying the Product

Annual number of units of product needed _____

Cost of ready-to-use product _____

Cost of inventory _____

Total annual cost of acceptable ready-to-use product (A) _____

Cost of Making the Product

Annual cost of materials _____

Cost of labor
  Direct _____
  Indirect _____

Inventory cost

Equipment cost
  Net purchase cost _____
  Transportation cost _____
  Installation cost _____
  Projected repairs _____
  Maintenance _____
  Insurance _____
  Operation _____

Total equipment cost _____

Total cost of making the product (B) _____

Repeat analysis for each alternative: (1) different raw materials with more or less purchased labor involvement; (2) different labor involvement inside operation; (3) different inventory cost; (4) different equipment item; (5) different net purchase cost on annual basis (depends on depreciation method). The variables can be listed as B_1, B_2, B_3, B_4, . . . B_n

Compare A and B, B_1, B_2, B_3 . . . . B_n and choose most economical alternative.

FOOD PRODUCTION MANAGEMENT

The ultimate performance of a production system depends on effective management. The simplicity of this observation should not blunt its significance. An efficient, appropriately organized production system can be compromised by managerial inefficiency. An inefficient, outmoded production system can be compensated for by excellent management. Regardless of the potential of its production system, the operation that effectively uses its labor, equipment, materials, and facilities while presenting consumers with products they want generally performs better than one that does not.

Managing a food production system requires a problem-solving approach. In order for the organization as a whole to prosper in changing conditions, the production system must also adapt to changed circumstances. The manager's role is to anticipate the necessary changes, choose a strategy and responsively alter the affected part of the production system.

The food production manager who hopes to successfully maintain the equilibrium of the food production system with its environment is first aware of the environmental factors that affect it. Secondly, the food production manager is attentive to changes in the environment and to developing trends and possible future events. The stimulus for planning can come from any quarter:

- drought in California.
- widely publicized governmental report of the contribution of dietary cholesterol to heart disease.
- consumer movements against food additives.
- proposed or actual minimum-wage legislation.
- federal, state, or local energy programs.
- prediction of uncharacteristic weather.
- entry of a new competitor into the market.

In addition to actually changing the production system, the production manager's adaptation to the problem or stimulus might also include further product development; recipe reformulation; organizational redesign; job redesign; respecification of food products; improvement in the work system; revamped communication and control devices; contingency planning for crises; training programs; and recruitment and induction of new employees with different skills.

Food Production Policies and Organization   The foodservice production manager's constant efforts to adapt the system to changing circumstances are supported by a bulwark of routine. In a sense, the manager ventures forth from a relatively secure base to manage the system as it encounters changing circumstances. The manager has time to make ongoing make-or-buy decisions, for example, because there is no need to make continual decisions on routine matters such as whether sauce cooks or fry cooks shall make the tomato sauce or when meals should be scheduled to start.

To some extent, then, the food production system is self-controlling. Production workers basically understand what their responsibilities are, to whom they are accountable, what they are expected to accomplish, and what is expected of the food production system by the organization and the public. Strategic decisions about routine matters—decisions that once made do not have to be remade—are perpetuated as the food production system's policies.

Like written policies, organization charts also help set up routine for the production department. Organization charts establish the authority of particular individuals, the responsibilities of operating systems, communication links, spatial divisions of work, spans of control, the chain of command, and so on. The manager creating or managing a formally organized production unit is confronted by various possible organization schemes that must be evaluated in light of the tasks before the production system.

Of course, even though policies have been decreed and organization has been structured, changes will still occur. The way any food production system is organized can become as inappropriate as an inaccurate specification for mashed potatoes. Likewise, policies that were functional can become as useless as a coal bin in an electric kitchen.

Traditionally, the foodservice production system's organization has been modeled on the continental or French kitchen, also called the kitchen brigade or *partie* organization. It is characterized by:

- *Strict division of labor*   Every individual has a particular, defined task, such as cleaning vegetables, making certain sauces, or preparing coffee.
- *Rigidly divided responsibility*   Definite production and management responsibilities are given to each station chef. Departmentalization is the keynote.
- *Hierarchical supervision*   Each level of authority concerns itself with the performance of the level beneath it. The chef ranks the *sous-chef*, to whom station or *partie* chefs report, who in turn are superior to their *commis,* or assistants, who in turn rank their aides and apprentices.
- *Centralized decision making*   The chef and perhaps a small group of senior chefs make all the major decisions for the kitchen.

Although this method of organization has dominated the foodservice industry for hundreds of years, many modern managers question its validity. For some production systems, a number of factors have intervened to make it inappropriate:

• Modern equipment and the purchase of pre-prepared foods have made smaller kitchen crews capable of much greater production. The traditional organization imposed on a small group is often top-heavy with administrative costs.

• Different consumer demands and the pace of business have altered the menu substantially. Rigidly divided responsibilities result in the establishment of work centers that are not fully productive.

• The modern worker tends to resent hierarchical supervision and may not be as productive in circumstances demanding continuous subordination to another individual.

• The unavailability of skilled labor for many tasks, and its costs for others, have tilted many production processes toward methods in which machines are used rather than people. Division of labor loses validity when workers must share a machine that performs diverse tasks.

• The reorientation of the foodservice industry away from production toward marketing has forced increased coordination of the production system with the service system, making the prerogatives of the chef and the authoritarian leadership style difficult to maintain.

• The size, cost, and complexity of some foodservice operations have caused the creation of managerial positions in food production not directly concerned with the preparation of food, such as food comptroller or foodservice director. This group of professionals does not readily fit into an organizational scheme based on culinary expertise.

In the foodservice industry today, the French kitchen brigade is unviable in many instances. A social catering organization or a commissary that feeds thousands of people in different outlets may require that crews perform a variety of different tasks, that a junior employee who recognizes a problem take charge, or that the function of units merge. In such instances when traditional food production system organization is inappropriate, food production management has moved toward other models:

• Away from division of labor toward the use of utility crews who perform any task required.

• Away from rigidly divided responsibility toward task orientation.

• Away from hierarchical supervision toward accountability, management by objectives, and responsibility accounting.

• Away from superior-subordinate relationships toward relationships based variously on "trust," mutual advantage, expertise, participation in decision making, parallel interests, and so on.

• Away from centralized decision making toward the development of decision-making and problem-solving capabilities in middle and lower-level management and other workers.

Strategies for
Food Production

The problem-solving approach to managing a food production system has led to the development of a number of strategies for food production. Any of these strategies can be successful if it responds to an operation's particular circumstances. Any of these strategies may be unsuccessful if it is inappropriate to the operation or incompatible with changing conditions. Unique competitive factors, market demands, and financial structure mean that each operation must seek its own best path to achieving efficient production.

MENU PROGRAM
STRATEGIES

Hamburger, pizza, fried fish, chicken, Mexican specialty, or Chinese specialty take-out/take-in restaurants, ice-cream and hot-dog stands, contemporary steak-and-salad or roast-beef-and-salad, or just salad restaurants all have solved the food production problem by limiting their product offerings. The food production systems of such restaurants rely less on specialized labor, require less investment in equipment and space, are easier to speed up or slow down in relation to demand, and are less expensive to operate because they are simpler.

On the other hand, these same operations are beginning to recognize that only a partial solution, perhaps only a temporary solution, has been found. Competitive pressures and market demands are causing them to expand their menu offerings, thus engendering in some instances the very problems the limited-menu strategy first addressed. Typically, hamburger restaurants are adding chicken, fish, dessert, or breakfast, and contemporary concept restaurants are adding sauce dishes, check-building side dishes, and difficult-to-prepare signature items.

In effect, this adaptation to changing conditions is a strategy in its own right—the full-menu strategy. An operation faced with mandated labor costs to operate its production system and a long period between peak demand periods for its present products can sometimes succeed by expanding its product line in order to increase overall profitability and productivity. Since workers and equipment are already there, additional sales of breakfast in the morning or ice cream and cake in the afternoon make a contribution to overall profitability beyond the cost of the food involved. Overall productivity of the operation is increased because there is additional volume with no increase of labor or equipment cost: each unit of production thus costs a little less.

FROZEN FOOD
STRATEGY

The logic of the frozen food strategy is simple. If a product has been completely prepared and frozen outside the operation, it makes a limited demand on the operation's production system. It simply has to be brought to the proper temperature. When the patron orders a product, it is removed from frozen storage, rapidly reconstituted, put in a serving dish, and passed to a service person.

The advantages of this strategy are apparent:

• If sufficient reconstitution equipment is provided, both high and low periods of demand can be satisfied with an almost infinite variety of items.
• Human labor involvement is minimal and nonspecialized. Anyone can take an item out of a "library" of entrees and press the button on a reconstitution device as instructed on the product label.
• Minimal equipment—compared to the equipment needed to actually make the item—is required. Thus investment costs in equipment and construction and operating costs are lower.

In application, however, this strategy has limitations:

• Although there are numerous brands of frozen entrees available, there are not very many different items. An operation has difficulty offering a menu program that truly satisfies market demands. Competitive differences are difficult to achieve with a limited array of commercial frozen food products available.
• The quality of products available may not meet consumer standards. Manufacturers of frozen products understandably strive for a flavor that pleases a great many people, but often the flavor they achieve simply displeases few.
• Freezing technologies are still imperfect. A product's texture or flavor may be altered. Reconstitution technologies remain experimental despite the bally-hoo of the equipment manufacturers. Quality control in reconstitution may still require judgment, hence skilled labor.
• The cost of the frozen food product may make its menu prices noncompetitive. What an operation saves by *not* making a product is not always offset by the amount the manufacturer must add to the cost of raw materials to cover development, manufacturing, marketing, distribution, and profit.

Other processed foods can also be discussed in similar terms. The canned-food strategy, the chilled-food strategy, and perhaps, someday, the irradiated-food strategy, or the freeze-dried food strategy—all involve a kind of pre-prepared food similar to frozen food.

Confronted by the limited availability and high cost of many frozen foods, some operations prepare and freeze their own products for later use—thereby having the advantages of ready-to-reconstitute frozen foods as well as a desirable menu program.

The principal savings to the operation lies in its being able to use culinary personnel more efficiently by scheduling them to increase productivity. Instead of alternating between periods of intense activity and waiting, the culinary worker produces constantly, making large quantities of a particular item. The operation banks or stores this labor with the product, and the labor cost per unit is less than it would be in making the product on a small-batch, sporadic basis.

In some circumstances, the operation freezing and storing its own products may face difficulties:

- The operation may not be technologically able to manufacture food products in larger volumes. Large-batch production requires different skills, recipes, procedures and equipment. In addition, the operation making its own frozen food products is faced with the technological problems of freezing foods; it is likely that the operation has much less efficient and effective equipment for freezing than a large processor has.
- While the operation may be effecting a labor savings relative to other production systems, the total cost of the product may still be more than that of the same product purchased from a food processor. The food processing worker is perhaps three times as productive as the food-service worker because of the greater capital investment of the processor. Unless the operation can justify the investment in equipment to bring its productivity to the level of the processor, the cost of its own pre-prepared foods may still exceed that of a similar purchased product.

In another variation of the frozen food strategy, the operation seeks to expand its offerings by varying a limited repertory of frozen entrees with minor add-on items (garnishes or sauces) or by offering them in combinations that make them seem like unique items. The production system is made only slightly more complex.

Unfortunately this strategy seems to demand creativity as rare and expensive as the skills the operation is trying to avoid including in the production system. The easy, cheap, anyone-can-make-food-appealing-and-different approach does not often accomplish its purpose. The consumer has penetrated the disguise of canned grapes and unmasked the frozen fillet of sole beneath its veneer of bottled sauce too often.

STORED LABOR STRATEGY   In this strategy, the operation's production needs for a period of time are analyzed to identify opportunities to produce items before they are actually needed. These opportunities can be matched with periods in which people and equipment are operating at less than full productivity. In a simple instance, an operation might be using 100 kilos of tomato sauce a day to make lasagna. Instead of making the tomato sauce each morning, it can be made in one of two ways:

1. Whenever a cook and the necessary equipment are available to make it as long as 100 kilos are available each day when they are needed;
2. In a single large batch or several batches of more than 100 kilos as long as 100 kilos are available each day when they are needed.

Alternative A presumes that the cook would be idle otherwise. Alternative B is based on the presumption that increasing batch size reduces the labor involvement for each unit made. Obviously, both alternatives can be combined in a third—whenever a cook and the necessary equipment are available, a large batch of tomato sauce is made.

Although this strategy is successful, the opportunities to implement it are less frequent than might be supposed:

• Many necessary products are perishable and must be made or used as needed, especially when demand for the finished product is irregular.
• There is a limit on the size of the batch that can be produced by the the operation because of equipment or the time available for preparation.
• Labor might not be available in units that correspond to the time it takes to produce batches of particular items. People confronted with this strategy tend to make other work to fill the "idle" time available.
• The raw materials needed for production may not always be readily available.

COMMISSARY/
SATELLITE
STRATEGY

Once marketing is accepted as the business of the foodservice enterprise, it is possible to investigate the separation of production facilities from distribution and retailing operations. An organization with several restaurants or foodservice operations that are viewed as "outlets" can manufacture products for them at one location. The advantages parallel those of any manufacturing company producing in one place and selling in others: principally, economies of scale in making large batches instead of many small ones; the use of more efficient equipment, division of labor, and assembly-line techniques; better management control and supervision; less equipment and construction investment in outlets. Against these advantages the cost of additional transportation and storage is weighed.

Even an organization with a single outlet can create a commissary. Separating production facilities from the retailing operation can be justified, for example, if the production facility will cost less to construct in some other location and if this savings is not offset by transportation and storage costs. An operation leasing prime space in a shopping mall might be able to justify producing its products in a nearby area zoned for light manufacture. The cost per square foot of land is less and the building does not have to meet the esthetic standards of the mall.

It is equally possible to create a successful commissary within an operation. Frequently, the restaurants of a hotel are served by a central kitchen, as are the foodservice operations of many universities and the nourishment stations on each floor of many hospitals.

It is also possible to create commissary/satellite relationships within the production system of the operation itself. If, for example, an operation's bakery products, fish dishes, hors d'oeuvre items, vegetable dishes, and so on, are viewed as being produced by separate production systems (following the traditional organization of the French kitchen), then these production systems could be supplied with the products that they use in common from a central source. Butchered meat, bread crumbs, pie crust dough, peeled potatoes, béchamel sauce, spice blends, chopped parsley, fancy cut vegetables, and meat stocks among other products could be centrally produced.

If the production system is extended to include aspects of the purchasing system and the supply system, other commissary/satellite relationships can be established: central purchasing; central receiving; central storage and warehousing; central portioning and assembling of ingredients and, perhaps, central tools and equipment for production runs in various departments.

Instead of establishing a commissary/satellite food production system, the foodservice organization can establish the same basic relationship with an enterprise that it does not own. The foodservice organization operates only the foodservice outlet and buys completed or nearly completed products manufactured to its specifications. In the fullest application, the foodservice organization contracts for its total production needs while performing only distribution (service) and marketing activities. A company operating machines that vend sandwiches and desserts, for example, may purchase them from another firm. Many of the foodservice organizations that supply the USDA's mammoth summer feeding program for children merely assemble prepared breakfast and lunch products purchased from other enterprises and deliver them to the sites where the children gather.

In other applications, the foodservice organization reserves some production activities, most often finishing, portioning, assembling, and garnishing. The typical ice-cream parlor makes very little of the product it sells.

Ideally, this strategy of purchasing food products on contract brings with it many of the advantages of commissary production without the need for capital investment, and also brings economies of scale without the need to use all that is produced within one foodservice organization. In application, it is subject to some of the same limitations as the true commissary/satellite strategy:

• The nature of certain food items does not permit the interrupted processing that is implied in a commissary/satellite production system. A steak, for example, would lose quality if broiled in one location and finished sometime later in another.
• The advantages of consolidating equipment and labor may be outweighed by the disadvantages of having to duplicate it at several locations. For example, ovens and broilers, and the cooks to operate them, may be idle much of the time in the satellite.

- Management and administrative needs may be multiplied and not consolidated.
- Transportation and materials-handling costs may outweigh production economies.
- Reduced job content may result in reduced overall productivity as people resist assembly-line/division-of-labor industrial techniques.
- Larger production units may be less adaptive to change.

"SELL THE SIZZLE" STRATEGY
It is possible to solve the problems of the production system by reducing the importance of the food product. If the operation can succeed in selling the "sizzle" rather than the steak, the production standards for the steak can be reduced. By implication, a less expensive production system is needed.

A recreational foodservice operation sells the excitement and fun of eating at a sporting event and can thus limit its production system to the equipment and procedures necessary to produce a minimally acceptable frankfurter. A night club sells glamour, entertainment, and alcoholic beverages and can thus organize a production system just adequate for producing simple sandwiches—sandwiches that would not sell well in other circumstances. An operation selling a novelty product, for example, a sandwich of roasted lamb loaf, yogurt sauce, and salad in a pocket of pita bread can exploit its novelty and the consumers' lack of standards for the product by preparing it relatively poorly but inexpensively.

Typically, the ultimate limitation of this strategy is the short life of the total product. The consumer becomes accustomed to the package and begins to demand substance. The operation must install a more sophisticated and expensive production system or it loses its ability to compete.

AUTOMATION STRATEGY
Some foodservice organizations have attempted to automate the food production process to achieve minimal human involvement and consequently a low production cost. Commissaries with high production volume can economically install machines that—although expensive in themselves—produce products at a low unit cost. They install the same machines that might be installed in the plant of a food processor—continuous bread lines, tunnel broilers, vegetable processing machines, breading machines, meat-forming equipment, and so on.

Several obstacles stand in the way of the automation strategy:

- The demand for foodservice products is immediate and irregular. The consumer wants food products at meal times and within a short time after ordering. An automated production system is only efficient if production can be evenly paced and economically scheduled.

• In most instances, the foodservice product does not lend itself to post-production storage. Unlike the output of an automated shoe factory, the product of automated food production cannot be warehoused to meet future demand.

• The market of most foodservice operations demands a variety of products. The production runs of an automated system would be too short (small) to be economical.

• The volume of most foodservice operations would not justify investment in an automated system. It would be idle too much of the time.

• A completely automated foodservice production system—one that would transfer raw materials from storage, modify them, and make them ready for distribution without human energy—has not yet been invented.

Certainly there is promise in the automated foodservice production system approach. After all, there are automated dishwashing systems that completely process dirty dishes loaded by dining room attendants and produce clean dishes in storage modules, and automated service systems such as vending machines and some hospital tray distribution systems. At the moment, in addition to the technological problems, progress in this area is limited by the lack of a research and development commitment from foodservice operators and equipment manufacturers, and the necessarily high cost of marketing any sophisticated new technological advance in automation.

MERGED SYSTEM STRATEGY Some activities of the food production system can be transferred to the service system. In the traditional kitchen, culinary personnel portion food items, assemble plates, and garnish them while service personnel carry the food from the kitchen to the consumer. With some success, operations have assigned service personnel to portion, assemble, and garnish orders from hot-holding cabinets and steam tables or from refrigerators and freezers. They might also be assigned to finish the food products in microwave or quartz-infrared ovens, steam refreshers, or in conventional broilers, ovens, or steamers.

In certain circumstances, this strategy offers these advantages:

• Service personnel may perform these tasks at a lower wage rate than culinary workers. Fewer dollars are spent on production and service combined. This strategy has long been used by the "diner" restaurant.

• Production workers perform more efficiently because they do not have to respond to patron orders immediately. They do not have to interrupt procedures and resume them later.

• Efficient production of single large batches may be possible, thus allowing production to be consolidated efficiently. Depending on the particular product's ability to be held after cooking, culinary workers may work only part of the time the operation is open. Certainly this situation is the case with soup-and-sandwich restaurants, salad bars, and coffeehouses offering desserts.

• Investment costs in facilities and sometimes in equipment are reduced. In the steak-and-salad restaurant the kitchen is an extension of the dining area: the area between the dining room door of the traditional restaurant and the assembly counter are eliminated. In the Japanese steak house, the food preparation area is actually part of the customer's table.

This strategy, however, may displease the operation's market segment and compromise standards of production. Holding food or allowing it to be partially produced by service personnel may lower its quality. Service personnel also may be difficult to supervise: overportioning and underportioning are common.

CADRE/UTILITY
WORKER STRATEGY

In an operation that experiences radical, irregular fluctuations in business, for example, resort hotels, recreational facilities, clubs, social catering companies, and so on, the stabilization of the production system around the human element is virtually impossible. The operation cannot afford to keep the labor necessary for its peak demand periods employed between these periods. There is neither immediate business nor sufficient opportunities to prepare for peak periods.

It is necessary to lay off workers during the period of low demand and rehire them during periods of high demand. If the food production system is traditionally organized, frequent layoffs and rehirings become impossible—skilled workers find steady work; the cost of training newly hired workers is in itself prohibitive.

In these circumstances, operations frequently develop the skills of a small group of individuals called a *cadre* to levels that are not usually necessary in an operation with a more consistent production volume. A few workers are trained in a number of different culinary specialties, in administration and supervision techniques, and in management processes so that they can provide the continuity of production in peak and nonpeak periods. Thus, the workers hired during peak periods need not have many skills and do not require extensive training. The operation can hire exactly the number of utility workers it requires for a given period and release them when the need for them is over. During nonpeak periods, the cadre, with the aid of a few necessary utility workers, can operate the production system efficiently.

Skills for Food Production Management   The success of the traditional kitchen in converting raw materials into menu items is based on the craft of the culinary worker: knowledge gained by experience or training concerning the nature of food, the capabilities of equipment to modify food products, and the results of applying specific procedures. Given a piece of beef, the competent cook knows that it cannot be treated like veal or chicken or even like another cut of beef; he or she knows what will happen to it in the steamer, broiler, or oven and the effect on it of braising, stewing, marinating, larding, or searing. Asked to produce a particular menu item, the cook chooses a method of preparation that respects the unique qualities of the raw material, the capabilities of the equipment, and the limitations of particular procedures so that the desired result is attained.

In food production systems that do not employ culinary artists, the application of the body of knowledge becomes management's responsibility. The food production manager becomes a technician—perhaps incapable of culinary handiwork but capable of effectively organizing and directing food preparation and of making the judgments necessary to attain the desired results. The craft of cooking becomes the technology of food preparation—the systematic use of basic food preparation knowledge.

In the production system organized on this basis, the change from a reliance on craft to a reliance on technology has had profound implications for the manager's activities. The manager must exercise skills in five areas:

1. *The manager must possess and apply systematic knowledge of food products*   It becomes necessary to distinguish in specification between similar products that have significant functional differences, for example, cuts of meat, since people preparing the product may not recognize the difference.

2. *The manager must plan and organize food preparation*   Precise recipe formulas must be developed. Procedures must be adapted to available skill levels and communicated so that they can be precisely followed. Craft shorthand has to be converted into step-by-step procedures that will lead the minimally skilled person to the desired result.

3. *The manager must introduce objective procedures for product quality control*   Since the persons preparing food products may not fully understand the purpose of specific procedures, it becomes necessary to establish objective standards so they can tell when food products have been sufficiently cooked, browned, whipped, chopped, and so on.

4. *The manager must purchase unavailable skills*   Purchased skills can take the form of food products that include the work of artisans more skillful than the workers of the operation. Items such as pulled-sugar cake decorations, ready-made strudel dough, and prepared soup bases may be in this category.

5. *The manager must attempt to make the technology of the production system more sophisticated*   By implication, this attempt includes the purchase of equipment that is more technologically sophisticated than the equipment specified for the traditional kitchen staffed by artisans. Equipment with automatic functions is sought such as the timed deep-fryer or the tunnel broiler so that human judgments are eliminated. Equipment capable of producing a finished product is sought, such as the automatic crepe maker and the tabletop doughnut machine, so that the need for human skills is minimized. Special-purpose equipment is sought such as the sparerib broiler or salad drier so that procedural instructions can be simplified. Often this more sophisticated equipment is laborsaving, that is, it allows production with less human involvement. As often, however, it simply places preparation within the capabilities of an individual with fewer skills, less capacity for judgment, and perhaps less commitment to the organization than the craft worker.

ACTIVITIES OF FOOD PRODUCTION MANAGEMENT

Managers of the food production system must ensure that its operation is consistent with the organization's marketing and investment objectives. The system's product must meet the market's standards; the system's performance must meet the enterprise's business standards. Market standards determine the food product's esthetic qualities, nutritional values, and healthfulness. Business standards determine the cost to the operation of the products produced.

Without management efforts directed at maintaining these standards, the food production system loses effectiveness. It contributes less to the foodservice organization than it might; it costs more than it has to.

Food production managers control deviation. They keep the food production system from producing a better product than the market wants as well as an inferior product that does not meet the market's expectations. Management restrains cost cutting that would result in a short-term increase in profitability but a long-term loss of business as well as waste and excess. Management keeps the food production system oriented to the specific task the organization has assigned it: producing a certain product at a certain cost.

Though the tasks of the food production manager may range from personnel scheduling that maintains productivity to preventive maintenance of equipment so that product quality does not deteriorate, six activities are primary: production forecasting, production scheduling, quality control, production control, materials control, and personnel planning.

Production Forecasting Forecasting how many people the operation will serve in a given period is a matter of some skill, but once the forecast has been made, determining the amount of a product that must be produced to match the forecast is a matter of mathematics. The food production manager generally follows these steps:

1. Using a menu analysis that indexes the popularity of various menu items on the basis of percentage sales, the manager determines how many orders of each item are needed to serve the forecast volume. For example, if 300 people are forecast, and menu items *A*, *B*, and *C* respectively account for 20 percent, 10 percent, and 5 percent of sales, then 60 orders of *A*, 30 orders of *B*, and 15 orders of *C* will be needed. As a formula,

$$VF \times \%M_i = N_i$$

Where VF = volume forecast
$\%M_i$ = menu percentage of an item
N_i = number of that item needed for that volume forecast

2. The manager then refers to a standardized recipe for each menu item needed and extends it to find out how much is needed. The number of portions needed is divided by the number of portions on which the recipe is based, and the dividend, called the working factor, is then multiplied by the yield of the recipe to produce the quantity of the item needed. If the recipes of *A*, *B*, and *C* are all based on 50 portions, and each recipe needs 20 kilos of raw product, then 60 portions of *A* will require 24 kilos, 30 portions of *B* will require 12 kilos, and 15 portions of *C* will require 6 kilos. As a formula,

$$\frac{PN}{PR} = W \qquad\qquad W \times YR = QN$$

Where PR = portions for which standardized recipe was developed
PN = portions needed
W = working factor
YR = yield of standardized recipe
QN = quantity needed

3. The determination in the step above may be a sufficient basis for purchasing if the item involved does not lose or gain weight significantly in food preparation, for example, breaded raw chicken for fried chicken. More often, however, there is a difference between the product as served and the product as purchased. Weight loss or gain often occurs in preparing or cooking the product as, for example, carrots are trimmed

and peeled before they are made into carrots Vichy. To determine the amount of carrots to purchase, a yield factor must be applied to the amount of carrots needed. This yield factor is determined by experiment. A quantity of a product is purchased and prepared; the purchased amount is divided by the prepared amount to give the yield factor. If 100 kilos of carrots yield 73 kilos of ready-to-cook carrots, then the yield factor for carrots is 1.37. Any amount of carrots needed multiplied by 1.37 tells the manager how much to buy to yield that amount. As a formula,

$$\frac{AP}{AS} = YF \qquad YF \times QN = QP$$

Where AP = amount as purchased
$\quad\;\; AS$ = amount as served, or as used in the recipe—sometimes called edible portion (EP), or ready-to-cook portion (RC)
$\quad\;\; QN$ = quantity needed
$\quad\;\; QP$ = quantity to purchase
$\quad\;\; YF$ = yield factor

In a complex recipe with numerous ingredients, the procedures are basically the same, except that the amount of each ingredient used in the recipe is multiplied by the working factor and then by the appropriate yield factor.

4. The final step is to convert the quantity to purchase into an appropriate market unit. In the United States, produce, for example, comes in hundreds of different market units—crates, bushels, lugs, and so on—of various weights. The quantity to purchase (in standard units) is divided by the number of standard units in the market unit to produce the number of market units to purchase. If carrots are sold in bags of 20 kilos, and 40 kilos are needed, then two bags of carrots must be purchased. As a formula,

$$\frac{QN}{U} = M$$

Where QN = quantity needed in standard units
$\quad\;\; U$ = number of standard units in a market unit
$\quad\;\; M$ = market units

This tedious procedure can be made easier by developing a table that relates all these factors. Exhibit 10.5 shows an excerpt from such a table developed for the school lunch program by the USDA.

EXHIBIT 10.5 Excerpts from Table Relating Serving Units to Market Units

Item	Purchase Unit	Wt (lbs)	Yield AS (%)	Portion Size	Amount (lbs) for 100 Portions
Asparagus	Crate	28	49	3 oz (4 spears)	29¼
Beans, lima (in pod)	Bu	32	40	3 oz	47
Beans, lima (shelled)	Lb		102	3 oz	18½
Beans, snap	Bu	30	84	3 oz	22½
Beet greens	Bu	20	44	3 oz	43
Beets, topped	Sack	50	76	3 oz	25
Beets, tops	Lb		43	3 oz	44
Blackeyed peas, shelled	Lb		93	3 oz	20¼
Broccoli	Crate	40	62	3 oz (2 or 3 spears)	30¼
Cabbage	Sack	50	75	3 oz	25
Cabbage	Sack	50	75	2 oz as slaw	16
Cabbage, Chinese	Lb		88	2 oz raw	14¼
Carrots, no tops	Sack	50	75	3 oz	25
Cauliflower	Crate	37 or 50	44	3 oz	43
Celery	Crate	60	70	2 oz raw	17
Celery	Crate	60	70	3 oz cooked	27
Chard	Bu	20	56	3 oz	33½
Collards	Bu	20	81	3 oz	23¼
Corn, in husks	Crate or bag	40		1 ear	60/crate or bag
Cucumber	Bu	48	95	3 oz raw	25
Eggplant	Bu	33	75	4 oz	33½
Endive, escarole, chicory	Bu	25	75	1 oz raw	8½
Kale	Bu	18	81	3 oz	23¼
Kohlrabi	Lb		50	3 oz	37½
Lettuce, iceberg	Carton	40	74	2 oz raw	17
Lettuce, romaine	Lb		64	2 oz raw	20
Mushrooms	Basket	9	67	3 oz	9½
Mustard greens	Bu	20	59	3 oz	32
Okra	Bu	30	96	3 oz	20
Onions, green	Crate	50	60	3 oz raw	31¼
Onions, mature	Sack	50	76	1 oz raw	7¼
Onions, mature	Sack	50	76	3 oz cooked	25
Parsley	Crate	19		(1 bu = 19 sprigs)	6½
Parsnips	Bu	50	84	3 oz	22½
Peas, green, in pod	Bu	28	36	3 oz	52¼
Peas, green shelled	Lb		96	3 oz	20

From <u>Management by Menu</u> by Lenaal H. Kotschevar. Chicago: National Institute for the Foodservice Industry. 1975.

Production Scheduling   For many foodservice operations, production scheduling is fairly routine. Production one day resembles production any other day. A small difference in the amount of production forecast may mean only a slight difference in scheduling individual workers or in assigning production tasks.

Because of constant variations in product produced, quantities needed, and supply delivery times, production scheduling for large social catering units, convention hotels, and commissaries can be much more complicated. In situations such as these, managers follow a specific planning procedure.

First the production forecast is analyzed to produce appropriate requisitions or purchase orders and requests for delivery that will ensure that the products are in the operation in time to be processed. Ideally this step ensures product delivery in ample time for processing so that the planning procedure for preparation itself does not have to be constrained by delivery times.

Second, the recipe for each menu item is analyzed to assess the equipment required; the length of time each piece of equipment will be used, including cleanup and warmup time; length of time for preparation in terms of the amount prepared; and the amount of different kinds of labor needed.

Once this information is gathered, labor, equipment, and time needs are represented on a master schedule that is used as the basis for communicating assignments to individual workers.

In effect, the production of each item is programmed so that it does not interfere with the production of other menu items by having overlapping production times in or on the same piece of equipment. Labor is controlled so that individuals have specific tasks in preparing specific food items, which minimizes the amount of time workers spend idle waiting for cooking stages to be done.

Good production scheduling is hampered more by lack of information than by its own complexity. If standards for performing particular tasks and the amount of time needed for specific equipment to cook large batches are both known, then production scheduling is fairly easy. However, the manager must still synchronize the production system with the actual volume of business as it occurs. While considering the capabilities of the food production system to produce, the processing time for the food products involved, and the amount of time they can be satisfactorily held, food production managers adapt production to consumption in several ways: by scheduling interrupted production, continuous production, small-batch production, large-batch production, bulk-batch production, and accumulated production.

Interrupted production   Food items are prepared to exactly the point in their processing at which they would begin to deteriorate and then are held until they are actually ordered by the consumer. In making a tuna salad sandwich, for example, preparation procedures would include making the salad mix, separating lettuce leaves from head lettuce for garnishing, slicing tomatoes and portioning them between sheets of waxed paper, preparing decorative garnishes of gherkins and olives, unwrapping the bread, and portioning coleslaw into cups, spooning mayonnaise from the container into a vessel at the work station, and positioning tools, equipment, and plates. The sandwich, on the command of the service person or the consumer, could be produced and plated in a very short period of time. This method has been traditionally used by the French kitchen to produce hundreds of different complex made-to-order items very quickly. It is not unusual for two individuals in a gourmet restaurant to produce 300 orders of 40 different items an hour during meal time if their setup is complete.

Continuous production   Production is almost exactly paced to consumption or at least the delivery of the product to the consumer. In a limited-menu, take-out/take-in hamburger restaurant, it is possible to determine the number of transactions that are occurring over the counter as the line of customers is served and prepare the product at a corresponding rate.

Small-batch production   If the product can be held, even for a short period, items are usually prepared in small batches instead of continuously. The process is easier to control and more consistent with the capabilities of personnel and equipment. A large order from a single group of consumers is less disruptive to small-batch production.

Large-batch production   In some instances, the only way to meet demand is to be fully prepared for it. Large resort hotels, school cafeterias, and employee foodservice facilities may have to prepare a significant number of items so that large amounts of each item are finished cooking just as they are needed.

Bulk-batch production   The operation begins with a quantity of product sufficiently large to allow some assessment of demand to be made in time to decide whether or not to prepare another batch. A limited-menu chicken restaurant may begin with 100 kilos of chicken ready to serve at noon time. If a certain number of kilos are sold, more will be prepared according to the following conditions:

• If 25 kilos are sold before 12:30 P.M., then another 100 kilos will be made immediately.

• If 50 kilos are not sold before 1 P.M., then only 50 additional kilos will be made.

• If 50 kilos are not sold before 1:30 P.M., then chicken will be made in 5-kilo batches. (The operation reverts to small-batch production.)

• If 25 kilos are sold before 12:15 P.M., then the operation begins continuous production.

This approach is frequently used by limited-menu, take-out/take-in restaurants offering an item that takes some time to prepare and by high-volume operations that cannot accurately forecast demand, for example, foodservice facilities on major interstate highways.

Accumulated production   Many cold products and some hot products are prepared in the hours prior to consumption and held at appropriate temperatures until needed. Enough production can be accumulated to meet considerable demand. This approach generally results in more efficient equipment utilization than large-batch production for the high-volume operations that use it. Accumulated production is limited by the possible deterioration of the product being held.

Quality Control   The quality of a food product has both a general and a particular dimension. The general dimension relates to the widely accepted standards for food of a culture; the particular dimension relates to the taste preferences of a specific market segment.

The distinction is important. Every food production manager in the United States can expect that customers, guests, or clients want foods free of foreign materials or insect life, want hot foods to be served at about 60°C (140°F) and cold foods at about 2°C (35°F), want chicken to be cooked to the bone and raw products to be crisp. On the other hand, a specific market segment may favor very loose porridge, fatty bacon, flaky pie crust, peppery sauces, and thick salad dressings, while another market segment may prefer thick porridge, crisp bacon, cookie-dough pie crust, mild sauces, and runny salad dressings.

General quality standards for food products are relatively easy to meet and to control. They lend themselves to communication with some precision and their attainment can often be measured objectively. Cooks can be told that the temperature of food in the steam table shall not be less than 60°C (140°F) and the temperature can be measured by anyone with an inexpensive thermometer. Exhibit 10.6 offers some of these general quality standards with an indication of those control devices appropriate to them.

Particular quality standards are more difficult to establish and monitor. Relying on the proportions and procedures stated in a standard recipe generally results in a product that approximates the standard but seldom exactly meets it. Food products are not consistent nor are cooking conditions. For example, a recipe may call for 10 grams (0.35 ounces) of thyme. Thyme can have either 1 percent or 3 percent essential oil (the source of its flavor) without it being discernably different in the package. How much thyme should be used, 10 grams or 30 grams? Another recipe prescribes that a steak should be cooked in a tunnel broiler for 3 minutes. An aged steak cooks faster than one that has not been aged as long. How does the cook know whether to set the broiler for 2 minutes or 3 minutes? Another recipe indicates that a 15 × 8 × 1 centimeter (6 × 3 × ½-inch) piece of salmon should be cooked for 2 minutes in the broiler. The broiler may be producing 60 million joules of heat or 40 million joules without the cook being aware of the difference. How long should the fish be cooked? Standard operating procedures may indicate that french fries should be fried for 3 minutes; indeed, an automatic timer may lift them from the fat after 3 minutes. But the presumption is that they were frozen and at a temperature of −10°C (14°F) when they were placed in the fryer. How does the cook compute the frying time for french fries when they are at 0°C (32°F) if the temperature difference can be recognized?

It is difficult to achieve and monitor standards of flavor, appearance, texture, and similar esthetic qualities without calling on human judgment. It becomes the food production manager's responsibility to ensure that this judgment is consistent and that individuals do not impose their own tastes on the customer, guest, or client.

To ensure this consistency, a three-point program is necessary: (1) establishment of standards; (2) contingency training; and (3) testing of product quality.

Establishment of standards   Production personnel have to become familiar with the appearance, and taste of foods that have been accepted by the market. Familiarization procedures usually consist of cooking to "standard" by each employee involved, repeated tastings, guided identification of perceptible characteristics such as color, texture, flakiness, viscosity, as well as the preparation of such appropriate aids as color photographs.

Contingency training   While food products and cooking conditions vary, they largely vary within a predictable range. Culinary personnel should be trained to recognize common variances and to know the procedural modifications appropriate to them. If 50 grams of salt does not satisfactorily season a preparation, in what amounts should salt be added? If the french fries are defrosted instead of frozen, how should the timer on the cooking device be set? If the steak does not "feel" medium done when it is pierced with a fork, how much more cooking is likely to be necessary?

Testing of product quality   The food production manager is the ultimate quality control. Responsible managers inspect and taste as many of the foods produced by their operations as possible as often as possible. It is not unusual for a manager to sample coffee from every batch, to try small quantities of every food item as it is prepared, to evaluate soft drinks, ice cream and other dispenser items several times a day, and to frequently simulate the consumer's meal experience with the food product by eating in the dining facility itself. The manager must assure the consumer of the operation's consistent food quality. In this same vein, the manager might also set up panels of employees or paid consumers to formally evaluate the production of the operation.

EXHIBIT 10.6   Objective Measurement of Food Quality

Quality Factor	Suggested Standard		Measurement Device
Doneness in meats	Rate:	52°C (126°F)	Probe-type thermometer
	Medium:	60°C (140°F)	
	Well:	82°C (180°F)	
Palatability of coffee, soup, or hot liquids	86°C (186°F)		Thermometer
Palatability of hot foods	60°C (140°F)		Thermometer
Palatability of carbonated beverages			
carbonation	2°C (36°F)		Thermometer
refreshment	63 kgs/sq cm pressure in tank		Pressure gauge
syrup	Varies*		Plastic measuring device to compare ratio of syrup to water
sugar in syrup	Varies		Brix hydrometer Refractometer
Portion size	Varies		Scales Portion scoops Measuring spoons Portion ladles
Sweetness of canned fruits	Extra heavy:	25–40°Brix	Brix hydrometer
	Heavy:	21–24°Brix	
	Light:	16–20°Brix	

Production Control

Production control procedures provide information for evaluating the performance of the production system. Control devices can record the amount of leftovers, customer returns, quality rejects, portions that are overweight or underweight, orders held beyond allowable time limits, communications errors, relate them to the total amount produced—perhaps as a percentage—and compare those percentages to the operation's standards.

Production control procedures can also provide a check on the functioning of other systems. Orders produced in the kitchen should tally exactly with orders served in the dining room as evidenced by guest check counts. The number of orders actually produced from a given quantity of raw food should exactly match the number of orders the food was calculated to supply based on recipe figures.

Quality Factor	Suggested Standard	Measurement Device
Fat in ground beef	Varies	Commercial fat analyzer
Taste of water, other qualities	Varies with use	Commercial kits
Eye appeal (color)	Varies with product	Commercial color standards: color samples against which products are compared
Lightness or volume of cakes	Varies	Commercial seed displacement device or planimeter
Tenderness of meat	Varies	Commercial hand-held penetrometers
Consistency of thick products such as batters and creamed corn	Varies	Commercial viscosimeters Consistometers
Palatability related to texture of starch gels such as puddings	Varies	Commercial "gelometers" of various types

Commercial devices are usually obtainable from scientific supply companies as listed in the classified sections of the telephone book. It is also possible to develop standards and ways of testing for product's conformity to them. For example, the lightness of cakes can be evaluated simply by measuring the height of the cake.

*Varies indicates that the operation can set its own standards and objectively test for them.

Materials Control   The menu price structure of commercial operations and the budgeting of noncommercial operations are predicated on the products being used in food preparation meeting functional standards. Although it can be the responsibility of persons concerned with purchasing or supply, only the largest foodservice organizations have laboratories equipped for such materials control. Other operations must make these determinations in the course of actual production. The food production manager frequently tests and reports the yield of cuts of meat, the drained weight of canned goods, the fat percentage of chopped meat, the shelf life of baked goods, the number of defects in produce, the percentage of cracked eggs in a case, the percentage of usable meat in corned briskets, and so on, so that purveyors can be challenged for not meeting specifications or so that decision making based on these factors can be accurate. Likewise, the total amount of money spent to produce a number of units should not increase because of spoilage, theft, misuse of ingredients, overproduction, waste, and so on.

Personnel
Planning

The food production system may present the manager with challenges related to personnel management and control. The nature of the production manager's responsibilities varies with the type of operation. For instance, the typical limited-menu, take-out/take-in restaurant has a work system based on a production strategy that reduces the worker skills needed to produce the product. The nature of this work system reduces the manager's personnel responsibilities. The number of people needed may be reduced to a formula that relates workers to the business volume forecast. Staffing can be almost as routine as ordering salt since almost anyone fits the operation's job specifications. Employees receive rudimentary training; career development is minimal in a work system that is based on easily learned skills. The manager simply coordinates, supervises, and controls personnel. On the other hand, the food production manager of a luxury hotel kitchen staffed by traditional French kitchen brigades that prepare almost all the food served must discharge a full range of personnel responsibilities.

The personnel responsibilities of managers of food production systems positioned somewhere between these two extremes vary in emphasis. In specific situations, food production managers might be concerned with the following:

- Recruitment, because they lack sufficient people to operate.
- Labor use, because of the high cost of labor relative to other costs.
- Training, because required skills are not available in the operation's labor pool.
- Motivation, because worker productivity is low due to poor worker performance (as opposed to equipment and facility limitations).
- Morale building, because of the excessive cost of turnover, absenteeism, waste, and so on, in the operation.
- Group interactions, because of the problems of coordinating units of a complex organization.
- Supervision, because workers deviate from the performance standards on which the work system was predicated.

Hence on the operational level, if the manager's expenditure of time and energy on personnel matters were examined, managers could be found working longest and hardest at such activities as recruiting part-time workers by speaking in high schools and colleges; developing schedules that maximized the use of every labor unit purchased; developing and implementing training programs, writing job and task descriptions; and so on.

MAKING THE FOOD PRODUCTION SYSTEM MORE EFFECTIVE

Paperwork in one form or another has always been necessary to an effective food production system. As early as the sixteenth century, food production managers—chefs and stewards—were producing formidable documents that included standardized recipes, procedures, purchasing guides, task descriptions, equipment lists, model banquet programs, and accounting records. Today, even with the advent of electronic data processing equipment, control procedures are still necessary to the functioning of food production systems.

Control procedures related to the maintenance of standards result in such materials as standardized recipes, yield tables, and task descriptions. They ensure the continuity of the operation; the system's performance does not have to depend on the recollection or presence of a particular individual.

Control procedures related to gathering operational data result in a variety of reports that make managerial decision making relevant to the food production system more effective.

Control procedures related to actual operations produce reports that allow the measurement and evaluation of the production system's performance in meeting objectives, achieving planning goals, complying with the law, and so on.

In some foodservice production operations, the volume of work requires the efforts of full-time administrative employees. It is not unusual for a 300-bed hospital, for example, to employ a food clerk to assist the foodservice director, food production manager, and supervising and therapeutic dietitians. The chef in a traditionally organized kitchen typically has a secretary who manages the chef's office. Even in operations with a single managerial employee for food production, administrative routine can require a great deal of time.

In specific operations, the responsibilities of food production managers for control depend on organizational boundaries. Determining current product needs can be the responsibility of the food production manager in one operation, the purchasing department in another, or the food and beverage control department in still another. Likewise, personnel management can be assigned to the management of the food production system, to general management, or to a specialized personnel department. In some smaller operations, the food production manager is also the manager of the service system and therefore must be responsible for its control routine also.

Certain standard forms and devices help make the food production system effective. Exhibit 10.7 identifies the principal forms and devices used in the management of food production.

EXHIBIT 10.7   Forms and Devices Used in Food Production Management

Form or Device	Use	Data Base
Standardized recipe	Serves as the basis on which production orders and food product specifications can be written.	Item name Category Ingredients Amount of ingredients Procedures of preparation Yield Portion size
Service/portion card or table	Standardizes post-preparation activities so that product consistency is maintained.	Menu name of item Portion size or sizes for different purposes Garnishing elements and portions Indication of appropriate serviceware
Yield table	Presents relationship between items as purchased and as served so that production can be planned effectively.	Name of item Sufficient item description to differentiate from similar items Yield factor Date of yield test
Yield test	Presents the proportions of waste and edible food in a product as purchased. Used to develop yield tables and to evaluate purchased products.	Item Item description Date of test Initial weight Weight after processing Percentage edible portion Yield factor (reciprocal) Cost extensions
Cooking-loss test card	Similar to yield test but concerned with difference between ready-to-cook weight of product and weight after cooking.	Item Item description Date of test Original weight Trimmed weight Loss in cooking Loss in cooking ratio to total weight Loss in slicing to total weight Saleable meat ratio to original weight Cost extensions
Base commodity card	Presents the cost of a product by unit of weight at the current market price and after adjustment for trim loss or cooking loss. Facilitates recipe costing and the evaluation of new recipes or recipe changes.	The information from the yield test Updated market prices Cost per ounce of edible (ready-to-cook or as served) portion

Form or Device	Use	Data Base
Recipe cost	Allows the presentation of the cost of a portion of a menu item or a batch of a menu item. Based on information from the standardized recipe. Allows comparison of item cost from period to period.	Ingredients used in recipe Cost per unit as used Cost per portion as used

Recipe evaluation	Summarized the results of testing of a recipe.	Recipe cost information
		Evaluation of
		  yield (as stated?)
		  procedures (correct?)
		  product (acceptable?)
		  portion size (adequate?)

Product scoring test	Evaluates purchased products on the basis of established criteria.	Varies with product and with operation.
Daily requisition form	Communicates needs to purchasing or supply department.	Production department Supply department Date/time Item Description Inventory on hand Cost per unit Total costs Approval Filling record Receiving record
Equipment utilization plan sheet	Presents equipment in operation, its capacities and other relevant data to allow production planning.	Equipment items Brief description Location Capacity Time to warmup or cool Time to clean
Performance standards	Allows the computation of the amount of labor time a preparation involves so that production can be planned and labor scheduled.	Product(s) produced Number per person-hour/minute How determined (average? test?)
Task descriptions	Step-by-step instructions and responsibilities related to a person's job. Facilitates communication to workers and training operations.	Differs with task but generally includes: task name, specific location associated with task, specific job titles associated with

EXHIBIT 10.7   Forms and Devices Used in Food Production Management (cont.)

Form or Device	Use	Data Base
Task descriptions (cont.)		task, equipment needed and where to obtain, and step-by-step procedures for accomplishing task.
Work assignment	Communicates the production responsibilities of particular individuals.	Name of individual Products required Quantities required Relevant recipe numbers When product is needed Delivery information
Production order or cook's worksheet	Serves as an operational plan for a period of production.	Date/day Menu items Persons assigned Recipe numbers Portion sizes Quantities needed Cooking time to start (when?)

Production order and record	Serves as an operational plan for a period of production and records results of production.	Same data base as production order plus:
		    Amount of leftovers
		    Disposition of leftovers
		    Cost of leftovers

Production control record	Same functions as above but provides the basis for evaluating production performance.	Same data base as production order record plus breakdown of any of the following items expressed in numbers and percentages of total amount produced:
		    Defects
		    Ruined in cooking
		    Returned from dining room
		    Overportions
		    Underportions
		    Held too long

Kitchen record of food served	Records the number of each menu item the kitchen passes to the service system so that this number can be reconciled with sales recorded.	Date/day/meal Menu items, listed Number of each passed to service system

Chapter 11
The Service
System

People go out to eat for more than just food. In addition to ready-to-eat food, the traditional product of a foodservice operation, the consumer seeks a secondary product of high value: frequently, a combination of convenience, psychological satisfactions, and a place to consume the food. Because of the added value of this secondary product, customers justify paying $10 for a steak dinner in a restaurant that would cost $3.50 in a supermarket or 40 cents for a cup of coffee that would cost 6 cents at home. This secondary, or *derivative*, product is the creation of the marketing system; more precisely, it is largely the creation of the marketing subsystem called the service system.

The derivative product—derived from both the menu program and consumers' preferences—involves much more than simply serving food. The derivative product includes all that increases the value of the food beyond the cost to prepare it. This increase in value includes the cost of tableware, decor, and the like, as well as the actual service of the food. The price of the same food will be much higher when served in a formal restaurant with French-style service, real linen napery, crystal glassware, fresh flowers on each table, and brocade wall coverings, than when served in a modest family restaurant. In such a case, the patron is paying as much for the derivative product as for the primary food product. Though such things as tableware and decor do not strictly contribute to the actual service of food, they are part of the service system because they are also geared to accommodate consumers by serving them in a broader sense.

In considering the operations that prosper in the highly competitive foodservice industry, it becomes clear that a service system is as important as a menu program for economic success. An operation may produce menu items that its market segment genuinely wants, but, if the derivative product is not desirable or at least acceptable as well, it will not succeed. The operation must distribute its products in a fashion that its particular market segment finds satisfactory or pleasing. Customers, guests, and clients all have a stake in the derivative product: the customer or guest buys the combination product, while the client of the noncommercial establishment experiences, evaluates, and responds to it.

CURRENT PRACTICES IN SERVICE

In considering what practices now dominate the creation of the derivative product and consequently the service system, it is essential to give due credit to the importance of both the operation's market image and the appeal of its derivative product. The market image of an establishment influences consumers in both their buying decisions and in their ultimate satisfaction with the product. An operation's intended market image partly defines how the derivative product will appeal to people.

Market Image   When an engagement ring is purchased from a prestigious Fifth Avenue jewelry store, it is enhanced and made more valuable (and probably more expensive) by its association with the store's image. It is the market image of the jewelry store that makes its product seem better than the same product bought at a more modest shop several stores away.

Perhaps to an even greater extent, the image of a foodservice operation becomes identified with its products. This market image is at least partly the projection of the derivative product of the operation and necessarily must be consistent with the appeal of that derivative product.

Frequently, the development of an appealing market image, often referred to as the foodservice operation's *concept*, contributes to its success. A concept is really the market image seen from the operator's point of view. Concepts are developed to evoke desirable associations on the part of the market segment, that is, to create an attractive market image. An operator develops a concept of the intended market image to define what the operation will be like.

In developing such concepts, foodservice organizations strive to become associated with that cluster of symbolic values they believe are important to their target market. If *modernity* is important to their market segment, then the operation must appear up-to-date and with-it. One major limited-menu, take-out/take-in restaurant chain is completely remodeling its units because market research indicates that customers associate them with big-finned cars, peg-leg trousers, and other symbols of the forties and fifties that are now largely discarded. On the other hand, another major limited-menu restaurant chain that has a modern image is creating units that depart in concept from its twenty-year-old success formula. In seeking new market segments in locations other than the nation's highways, this organization finds that it must appear less institutional to appeal to customers who tend to value their own individuality.

Because many concepts lose their appeal fairly quickly, operations frequently create concepts that can be renewed. When constructing restaurant interiors, limited-menu chain restaurants often use materials that must be replaced in a few years so that they can routinely change their interiors to something new and different.

Some restaurants have programmed changes so that market segments continue to find novelty in the meal experience. Such things as wall coverings, plantings, artwork, and service workers' clothing are changed several times a year to project a new theme. The restaurant becomes a culinary theater with a repertoire of productions. A number of major foodservice contract companies supply their in-plant and in-office foodservice units with theme packages of decorations and props. Some of these elaborate theme packages are transferred from one unit to another as a traveling show celebrating Mexico, the Roaring Twenties, or the strawberry.

The Appeal of the
Derivative
Product

While the market image is what the consumer sees in an operation, the derivative product is part of what the consumer gets out of it. It bears repeating that the two must be consistent or else run the risk of disappointing or alienating patrons who feel that the derivative product does not deliver all that the market image promises. An operation's derivative product usually appeals to patrons in one of three ways:

1. *Convenience:* The operation offers people food when, where, and how they want it.

2. *Entertainment, novelty, and fun:* The operation offers an experience other than the actual eating of the food that gives satisfaction in itself. The patron may participate in such an experience or may simply enjoy the intrigue, amusement, or pleasure the experience affords.

3. *Sociability:* An operation may offer the opportunity for shared experiences, meeting people, and feeling personally recognized, and may be especially interested in developing a regular clientele and harboring a warm atmosphere by treating patrons like "one of the family." Such operations might specialize in sponsoring occasions such as personal celebrations and business conferences.

If an operation has a market image as a fast-food place, its derivative product will no doubt be convenience. If an operation has a market image as an elegant restaurant, its derivative product will be status, which involves enjoying an experience other than the actual eating of the food.

All of the above three appeals create a substantial derivative product of some value. Operations can, however, base their appeal on having low prices because of low overhead costs, which amounts to an anti-service or an anti-derivative product strategy. Such an establishment may be in an inconvenient location, have a limited staff and closely packed dining areas, or may simply depend on doing a great volume of business at a low profit margin.

CONVENIENCE   An appeal based on convenience must aim at making the product as available as possible. One way to make a product convenient, known as the *anywhere strategy,* is to bring it to the customer. A less desirable product may be accepted by people because it is so much more accessible. Vending machines and "hawkers" in sports stands work on this strategy and sell their products because of convenience, not quality.

Limited-menu hamburger restaurants often combine the anywhere strategy with the *anytime strategy.* Food is made available both where and when the consumer wants it: outlets are numerous and open long hours. Twenty-four-hour restaurants, restaurants that serve breakfast all day or make no distinction between lunch and dinner menus, vending machines, and the like are successful because they offer products anytime.

Another way to appeal to consumers' desire for convenience is by giving fast service. Not only the hamburger or fried chicken customer but even the gourmet diner may demand instant gratification. Vending machines, limited-menu restaurants of all types, contemporary restaurants, and certain expensive restaurants catering to businesspersons at lunch or airport travelers also make speed of service a highly marketable derivative product.

Rather than simply trying to make a product as available as possible, an operation can make it available in different ways, in combination with different derivative products. In order to serve several market segments, the same operation may vary the derivative product while still offering much the same food items. There is no better example of this *multi-channel strategy* than that of the same company running several different foodservice units in a transportation terminal. All food is made in a central commissary and served in different outlets ranging from a stand-up snack bar to a tablecloth restaurant at prices that range from 125 to 250 percent of food costs. A typical large hotel may house a formal dining room, a coffee shop, a snack bar, and often one or more contemporary/atmosphere restaurants with exotic decor and cuisine. The menus of each of these different outlets may overlap considerably, but their derivative products have distinctly different appeals. A single restaurant can employ this multi–channel strategy by having different dining rooms serve different combinations of selections from the same menu and kitchen. The difference between the rooms lies in their derivative products—their decor, speed of service, seating arrangements, tableware, entertainment. The same item may be priced differently in different rooms, or patrons in one room may have to order full dinners while those in another can order a la carte.

Hospital, employee, college or university, and military foodservices use different methods of delivering food from the same kitchen to consumers, ranging from vending machines to cafeteria service to table service.

ENTERTAINMENT, NOVELTY, AND FUN

A derivative product based on entertainment, novelty, or fun offers the patron a unique and interesting experience that complements the experience of simply eating the food. A dinner theater offers just such a derivative product. The combination of the meal and entertainment offered in a dinner theater is called the *product package*. In such a package, the food is often secondary to the show, and consequently need not be outstanding to be acceptable. The food may be excellent for a dinner theater when it would be merely adequate for a restaurant. Dinner theater managers often make economic trade offs in these circumstances. If a dinner theater runs a play with six actors rather than five, the manager of the operation may decide to offer buffet service instead of table service, or tuna salad rather than crab salad, to offset the extra cost. Other examples of product packaging include an excursion on a dinner cruise steamboat, a stay in an American plan hotel which offers food with lodging, or a trip on any kind of transportation (plane, ocean liner) that includes meals.

An operation may emphasize its novelty or exoticness as a derivative product. A restaurant may be run as a stage with an elaborate set. The customers are involved in an experience that presumably differs from their ordinary routines. Both service personnel and patrons are actors on the stage. Restaurant settings include everything from the basements of medieval castles to Polynesian villages. The food may co-star in such an operation if it can be authentic, or it may simply have a small supporting part. Restaurants built around elaborate market image concepts usually rely on such a meal experience as the derivative product.

The novel experience offered as the derivative product of the foodservice operation may be the enjoyment of feeling royally served. The service system can be embellished with what the market segment perceives to be symbols of social status, elegance, and the good life. Such status symbols can include silver service, extremely diffident service personnel, flambé presentations, tableside carving, linen napery, wine stewards, foreign language menus, and very high prices. Restaurants that successfully market themselves as status symbols often charge more than $50 for an unextraordinary meal that can be had for far less elsewhere.

Less expensive restaurants such as the French soup kitchens and sidewalk cafes now popular in the United States also can appeal to patrons' desire for status and worldliness. Operators one step up from limited-menu, take-out/take-in restaurants now offer wine as part of a status appeal. Many such operations have succeeded in upgrading their decor, often with plants and paneling, to attract people who will eat hamburgers in these surroundings but would not in a working-class atmosphere of plastic laminate.

Boutique food shops use their specialized menu and supposed culinary expertise, along with an appropriate complementary atmosphere, to appeal to patrons. Consumers are attracted by the authenticity of the establishment and assume a handmade quality in foods that in fact may be mass produced. The crepes from a creperie are perceived as tasting better than crepes made on an identical machine from the same commercial mix purchased in an operation with 80 different menu items. The assertion that crepes are our only business, hamburgers are our only business, or pizza is our only business leads some consumers to the conclusion that less is more.

Foodservice operations can create an effective derivative product through an atmosphere of amusement and playfulness. One chain restaurant has service people sound a gong to announce the delivery of large ice-cream orders and then display the order by having two service people run through the restaurant carrying it over their heads on a stretcher. Service persons also hand out prize buttons to those who eat such orders. Other restaurants make amusement their derivative product by having amusing drink menus or having service people perform magic tricks. Children are frequently enticed into restaurants, bringing their parents, with fun appeals. Does the best clown really mean the best sandwich? To a child it may. In one restaurant, children's orders are brought out by a toy train. Hobby horse chairs, treasure chests of toys, and menu coloring books and puzzles are also used to appeal to children.

Many foodservice operations find that patrons enjoy being involved in their own service. Consumers have always wanted to butter their own bread, and add sugar and cream to their own coffee, and seem to find making their own salad, dishing out their own soup, cooking their own meat in fondue, and concocting their own sundaes appealing derivative products.

SOCIABILITY   Some restaurants that aim to create a warm social atmosphere as a derivative product simply concentrate on establishing good personal relationships with their patrons. Despite the availability of similar or better food at more convenient restaurants, customers may frequent a particular establishment because they feel personally welcomed there. They have been made to feel that the restaurant is "their place." This identification with the restaurant may be focused on a particular service person, a bartender, or host or hostess who is personally successful at relating to patrons. Or, the restaurant may have been successful at building the entire service system around effective human relations. Courtesy, positive attitudes, and a willingness to accommodate requests are exhibited by all personnel. Such employees, as well as effectively kept-up individual patron histories, contribute to the customer's perception of the operation as a friendly place that treats them as people and not simply customers.

A number of institutional foodservice operations have successfully personalized their services. Hospital patients are visited by dietitians who explain the meal as part of the general therapy program, solicit patient requests and comments, and sometimes take patients' food orders for the next day from a menu that offers a variety of choices. School foodservice personnel participate in classroom activities related to nutrition and meet with student menu-planning committees as part of personalization efforts. University foodservice operations encourage students to plan parties or dinner meetings around the menu items being offered.

Other foodservice operations go beyond simply establishing good personal relations and foster interaction between their patrons as well. Customers are encouraged to talk to other customers by being seated at large tables with strangers or by having to contrive their own seats and tables from a jumble of carpeted cubes. Such diverse foodservice operations as the community hall and the singles' bar use this service strategy.

SERVICE CONCEPTS

Before dealing with the service activities that all service systems entail (no matter what the appeal of their derivative product), the concepts that guide the service system must be understood. The following three sections will deal respectively with the objectives, the interactions with other systems, and the limits of the service system.

Service Objectives   As a marketing subsystem, the service system must be consistent with the objectives of the operation's marketing program, enumerated in Chapter 4. The following service objectives are derived primarily from the first objective of marketing, "to satisfy customers, guests, or clients as efficiently as possible," because service, by definition, is concerned with attending to the patron in a pleasing manner. These objectives are as follows:

1. *To make the product available to customers, guests, and clients*
The key to an operation's success may be its ability to distribute a product to locations where the product's market is found. As the distributive branch of the marketing system, the first and most general objective of service is to get the product to the consumer—either by table service, carry out, home delivery, vending machine, or whatever.

2. *To enhance the value of food by offering attractive derivative products*   In order to attract its target market segment, an operation must offer the appropriate derivative product. If the target market finds cafeteria-style service unattractive, they will not frequent the operation even if the food is good. An attractive derivative product can make a marginally acceptable food item quite appealing: certain market segments, for example, will eat hamburgers only when offered very conveniently.

3. *To project the operation's market image*   The service system, and the accompanying meal experience, must be consistent with the operation's promoted market image or else the operation runs the risk of alienating patrons by not providing them with what they anticipated or desired.

4. *To accommodate the needs and expectations of customers, guests, and clients*   A server's obligation to patrons involves more than just taking orders and serving food. If patrons expect water to be served immediately, the server must do so. Service personnel must respond to and accommodate all the patron's reasonable needs and requests, from getting extra ice or more butter, explaining menu items, providing matches, giving directions to rest rooms, to perhaps singing "Happy Birthday" with a group of service persons whenever a birthday cake is served.

Interaction of the Service System with Other Systems   It is possible to identify interactions between the service system and the purchasing, supply, business, and control systems of the foodservice organization: a change in the price of napery (the purchasing system) or the method by which it is supplied (the supply system) definitely affects the service system. But it is marketing—the system of which service is a part—and production that have the most crucial effect on service.

MARKETING AND SERVICE   Because service is really the distribution branch of marketing, marketing considerations have priority for the service system. A change in marketing objectives, the marketing mix, or marketing methods has immediate implications for service. Some typical examples of how marketing affects service follow.

Marketing Event	Service Ramifications
Advertising campaign attracts more consumers	Staff increases; delivery method streamlined to speed turnover
Marketing activities aimed at new market segment	Change in derivative product to satisfy new market segment, perhaps involving a change in service-worker attitudes or behavior or a new style of table service
New menu program	Training of personnel in proper techniques for serving new dishes
Plateaued or declining sales because market finds concept "stale"	Short-term concept changes, such as theme decorations, or the introduction of live entertainment
Marketing campaign featuring discounts	Improved efficiency in delivering discounted product in quantity
New marketing channel opens, such as take-out service	Organizing, staffing, and equipping a designated work area to efficiently accommodate take-out orders

FOOD PRODUCTION AND SERVICE

Many service activities are extensions of food production activities. Indeed, in many operations, the responsibility for portioning, garnishing, plating, and even finishing some foods is shared by production workers and service workers. In operations where food is prepared tableside, as in the currently popular Japanese steak houses, service persons are also production persons. Some typical examples of how production affects service follow.

Production Event	Service Ramifications
Change in work method	Service workers assume tasks formerly done by production workers, for example, making toast
Change in recipe	Accordingly, service workers change their description of menu item to patrons; pace of service adjusted to accommodate increased cooking time
Change in control method	Familiarization of service workers with new ordering system

Limits on the
Service System
An operation cannot offer sumptuous meals in a fantasy palace with lavish accessorization and royal service, even if this is what its market segment wants, unless its investment objectives can be met, its operating costs allow a profit, and the necessary quality of labor can be found. Limits on the service system cluster around just these three things: investment costs, operating costs, and labor availability.

INVESTMENT COSTS
The initial cost of the physical facilities, equipment, and accessories needed for service are a major consideration in deciding on a service system. Trade publications routinely report expenditures of several hundred thousand dollars to refurbish the dining areas of restaurants with fewer than 150 seats. The front area of a limited-menu, take-out/take-in restaurant often costs $100,000 to outfit. The table setting for just one person, called a *cover,* can easily run more than $100. Simple sturdy cups may cost $18 a dozen, and fancy mugs three times as much.

Obviously, the higher the initial investment in such things, the higher the break-even point—the point at which sales pay for these investment costs. It is quite common to find an established foodservice organization rehabilitated by changing service strategies because the investment costs of refurbishing the existing system are too high. The posh table service dining room in a luxury department store that has been running successfully but has become tatty may be converted into a chic buffeteria to cut refurbishing investment costs. Because the public often tires quickly of initially appealing, expensive service setups, modern foodservice entrepreneurs should be wary of investing in them. The present cost of investment in the service system has risen so high that a formerly generous budget of $50,000 may now limit an operation's service possibilities. While the operation might previously have opted for a service system based on an exotic meal experience, now it must settle for family-style service and decor.

OPERATING COSTS
Operating costs must also be considered in selecting a service system. Although expenses for energy, maintenance, and replacing serviceware and napery are important too, the cost of labor is the principal consideration.

Labor costs for service persons in traditional table service restaurants have increased considerably without a corresponding increase in worker productivity. The wages of a service worker have more than doubled in the last few years without the dollar amount of sales that result from the worker's efforts doubling.

Many service workers are now partially compensated by gratuities. They receive less than the minimum wage from the employer on the assumption that they are earning sufficient tips to compensate for the difference between the minimum wage and their pay scale. According to federal law, the employer can take advantage of a *tip credit* of up to 50 percent of the minimum wage. If the tip credit should be abolished, as it has been in several states, service systems with high labor involvement will become even less viable unless the increased cost of the operation can be passed on to the consumer. Both the general increase in the cost of labor and the possible nationwide abolition of the tip credit are prompting many foodservice organizations to seek a way of offering their market segments a desirable derivative product without involving a lot of labor.

LABOR AVAILABILITY Besides the cost of labor, the choice of a service system must also take into account the availability and quality of labor. Some service systems require a number of people, others very few: a table service restaurant and a vending machine represent the extremes. Some service systems make particular personal demands on workers: a status restaurant for example requires that the service worker be diffident, conform to a rigid grooming code, and appear in a formal uniform. In other instances, the service system depends on the worker's capacity for social interaction.

In general, foodservice organizations are having difficulty recruiting and keeping career service workers. A service system that requires trained people or a stable work force is frequently more difficult to staff than one that can be operated by part-time and sometime workers.

Likewise, there is considerable resistance on the part of people to perform service jobs they consider personally demeaning. A person embued with the spirit of American egalitarianism may resent fetching another person's food and handling another person's dirty serviceware, especially if the service system demands that the worker adopt a servile manner. In many parts of the country, it has become easier to recruit workers for informal restaurants than for more formal ones that demand a traditional patron-servant relationship. Young students, artists, and theatrical persons often can be recruited to work in restaurants that offer sufficient income because they suspend their sensibilities to the degree that their compensation satisfies them. The counter worker has no such recompense; the minimum wage buys very little attitude change.

Foodservice operations with service strategies that require service personnel capable of social interaction with customers may be fortunate enough to be located in places where the work force is naturally hospitable and charming. The foodservice operations of international hotel corporations operating in certain countries may be challenged in other ways with regard to labor, but the local people get along famously with the guests. In the United States, there are pockets of amiability (notably in the South) but in general, foodservice operators find that the work force's attitude problems are compounded by a lack of social skills.

SERVICE ACTIVITIES

The service system is complex because it must be viewed as both an operating system, like the supply or production system, and as a partial product—the derivative product that together with the ready-to-eat food the operation offers its market.

As part of an operating system, service activities include *packaging, delivering,* and *accommodating consumption.* These activities then double as products. The way a table is set (part of packaging) involves both the *activity* of setting the table properly and the *product* of the attractively set table that results.

Because the service system, as a partial product, must appeal to consumers, it must be related to market criteria. Patrons are unconcerned with how the supply system or other operating systems work, but they are concerned with the way the service system is run. It does not matter to them if a restaurant uses a conveyor belt or a forklift to unload trucks as long as the product arrives, but it does matter to them whether their meals arrive on a china plate or a paper plate. While decisions concerning other operating systems are based on economics, decisions concerning the service system must be based on both economics and market satisfaction.

Since different markets are satisfied in different ways, deciding what service system will be successful defies universal solutions. Self-service, table service, English pub, French bistro, chinaware, single-use serviceware, platter service, or plate service is no more the key to service success than pizza, duck, frozen yogurt, or cheese pie is the key to success for every menu program. Each foodservice operation is unique and must develop its own service system by choosing appropriate methods of packaging, delivering, and accommodating consumption of its products. Through *packaging,* the operation presents the product in a form convenient for sale or consumption. In *delivering,* the operation transfers the product from production to consumer. By *accommodating consumption,* the operation provides for the consumption of the products the consumer has bought or accepted.

Packaging   Packaging is based on the need to protect food, to conveniently transport it, and to conveniently consume it. Packaging in the form of coverings, accessories, and tableware frequently fulfills roles beyond simple functionality. As a kind of advertising, wrappings may bear the operation's sales message. The operation's brand identification in the form of initials or a symbol called a *logotype* may be printed on its accessories, serviceware, or napery. In addition to its functional and marketing roles, product packaging is often a good part of the derivative product. Just as consumers' perceptions and enjoyment of a perfume is influenced by the bottle it comes in—the idea of $100-an-ounce perfume in a plastic vial is inconceivable—product packaging can also influence consumers' choice and pleasure in food. Product packaging includes serviceware, accessories, napery, wrappings, and employees' uniforms. Employee uniforms are considered a part of packaging because the appearance of service persons is part of the derivative product.

SERVICEWARE   Although it is unlikely that most consumers can precisely describe the dishes, glasses, and cutlery used even in restaurants that they frequent often, serviceware is an important part of an operation's derivative product. Food may be framed attractively by the right serviceware, and colorful and dramatic service plates (the plate on the table when the customer enters), dishes, flatware and glasses can add considerably to a dining room's decor. Restaurants trying to avoid an institutional look use serviceware that cannot be mistaken for that stereotypical of hospital, school, and military foodservices. These same institutions often have similar goals, and use serviceware that is light, colorful, and stylish rather than heavy, dull, and plain.

Exotically shaped or oversized glassware is often used to make table settings eye-catching and dramatic. Glasses are available in a variety of sizes and shapes, from giant brandy snifters to fragile thimbles on 20-centimeter stems. Compared to using uncommon dishes or cutlery, using uncommon glassware is an inexpensive way to introduce style notes. Perhaps most important, glasses add height to table settings that are otherwise two-dimensional.

Advances in technology and design, and changing life-styles, have made single-use (disposable) serviceware acceptable in many middle-class homes, thereby legitimizing its use in foodservice operations catering to this market. Coated paper products that look bright and modern and plastic glassware and flatware with a satisfactory "mouth-feel" are considered appropriate for informal meals. Consumers find them attractive and, most important, sanitary. Depending on operational circumstances, single-use serviceware can be more or less expensive than permanent ware. Whatever serviceware is used must contribute to the operation's image or at least not compromise it. Will the consumer relate more satisfactorily to the operation if it uses high-style disposable glasses or the plain glass tumblers the operation could otherwise afford? Such questions require market research.

Many foodservice operations choose to narrow the role of serviceware simply to function. Plain, functional, esthetically neutral serviceware that does not impose on the food or the restaurant decor is used. The operator takes the opportunity to make visual statements to please the market in other ways: with the food itself, the restaurant concept, lighting, or dramatic accessorization.

ACCESSORIES   Unusual serviceware, especially glassware, can cause problems in use. Warewashing efficiency may be compromised by odd-sized pieces that do not fit in racks or cannot be stacked in handling and storage. Operators often choose to make effective visual statements with dramatic tabletop accessories or serving vessels. Candle lamps, candles in holders, curiosity lamps, oversized pepper mills, or vases of flowers can enhance tabletops. Attractive serving vessels include black iron or copper soup cauldrons, fancifully shaped ceramic pieces, slabs of wood resembling cross-cut tree trunks, baskets, and of course the traditional silver service of trays, oval platters, covered dishes, glass bells with silver dishes, Escoffier dishes (square, covered vegetable dishes), and stylized bi-metal frying pans with copper exteriors and tinned or stainless steel interiors.

There is no doubt that a patron offered a basket lined with a red and white checked napkin and full of raw whole vegetables reacts more strongly to this presentation than to a standard relish tray but does not necessarily eat more.

NAPERY   The use of cloth tablecloths and napkins has traditionally denoted formal dining. An operation can project luxury and status with white napery or add drama and interest to the restaurant with colored napery. The availability of crease-resistant fabrics that need no ironing has made cloth napery less expensive and more popular.

Operations using cloth napery have four alternatives: they may use crease-resistant napery and wash it on the premises; they may use traditional cloth napery and wash and iron it on the premises; they may rent napery of either fabric; or they may own their own napery but send it out to be cleaned and pressed. In weighing each of these alternatives, consumer response must be considered. Crease-resistant fabrics have been treated with resins and consequently do not have the same mouth-feel as traditional fabrics. If the operation opts to wash its own linens, the linens are not likely to be as well finished, cleaned and smoothed as those done in a commercial laundry. Commercial laundries that rent linens tend to have only a few colors and patterns available. The operation wishing to have the most dramatic napery with the best mouth-feel is likely to purchase linens made to order in special colors and patterns and have them laundered professionally.

Informal restaurants usually do not use cloth napery, but use paper, straw, or wooden place mats on attractive tabletops to replace tablecloths. Often a table scarf which is not replaced after each party dines is run down the center of the table. Paper napkins or small, brightly colored cloth napkins, usually crease-resistant, are used.

Any restaurant using cloth napkins must decide how to fold the napkin on the basis of market criteria. While there definitely are market segments that find "Viking Ship" or "Bird of Paradise" napkin folds en-chanting, others are not impressed, and some people are disturbed to think their napkin has been laboriously handled.

WRAPPINGS   Food products are wrapped to make handling easier, to preserve quality during delayed delivery, to protect against contamination, and some-times to facilitate heating. They can be wrapped in clear films, paper, foil, and foil laminates, or placed in rigid and semirigid containers of plastic, paper, foil, or plastic foam, depending on what the food is and why it needs to be wrapped.

Wrappings can serve several collateral purposes. They can display the food product and serve as the vessel from which it is eaten. Wrap-pings can also impress the operation's sales message on the consumer through print or graphics.

People's prejudices against vending machines or self-service counters can be partly mitigated by stylish non-institutional wrappings. Serving fish and chips in a mock newspaper cone is a typical example. Some Japanese restaurants offer take-out products in packaging which would dignify a birthday present; some Italian bakeries contrive tiny paper envelopes complete with string handles for 10-cent rolls.

UNIFORMS   The evolutionary relationship between restaurants and domestic eating arrangements is nowhere more apparent than in the attire of service workers. Until the last few years, service workers dressed as though they were servants in a private home. Though service persons in formal restaurants often still wear such attire, operations now seek to provide other meal experiences than enhanced domestic dining. Thus employee uniforms now vary greatly. Theme restaurants tend to have theme uni-forms. Informal restaurants allow informal dress such as blue jeans, shirts, and aprons, which attracts the personable young people they wish to employ and makes the casual young customers they wish to serve feel at home.

Delivering   The nature of the foodservice enterprise and its product can make transferring the product to the consumer, a rather minor activity in most retail establishments, into an elaborate procedure. This procedure is complicated because the service person must take the order from the consumer to the production system (usually a kitchen) and then, after a while, return with the finished product. Certain foods require different methods of delivery. The kind of food an establishment serves and the kind of seating it has, or doesn't have, to accommodate consumers greatly influence the method of delivery. The budget allotted for service is also essential in determining service method. Methods of delivering food can be classed as table service, stand-up service, and machine service.

TABLE SERVICE   When orders are taken and food is brought to the consumer's table by one or several service workers, this kind of delivery is called table service. Table service in restaurants was based originally on forms and traditions used in the homes of wealthy Europeans, and as service methods have evolved, the distinction between table service styles has been confused. The most well-known service styles are American, French, Russian, and English, though many restaurants use hybrids of these styles while insisting on calling their service a particular one of them, or simply mistakenly call their style by the wrong name. To avoid this kind of confusion, service styles shall be discussed here by their descriptive names, though the national association of each will be referred to as well.

Plate service   Plate service, or American-style service, is the simplest type of table service. The customer's order comes on the plate it will be eaten from, hence the name plate service. Because it is fast, inexpensive, and easy to learn, plate service prevails in American table service restaurants, especially the more modest ones. Service people must be accurate in taking and transmitting orders, and exhibit basic courtesy and good hygiene in handling food.

Service workers in a plate service restaurant are called waiters and waitresses and are loosely organized, each being solely responsible for serving a particular group of tables, called a *station.* When there are many waiters and waitresses, they may be supervised by a *captain,* who takes reservations, seats patrons, and transmits orders, or by a host or hostess who just takes reservations and seats people. A senior service worker called a *scrub captain* may be in charge of training and assigning work stations. Waiters and waitresses are assisted by bus boys and bus girls, who usually help clear and set up tables, get patrons water or coffee, and assist with serving large orders.

Service workers do not have to be trained in special skills. Simple skills like carrying trays and writing checks are learned on the job from other service workers. Often worker tasks may include preparation of simple items like coffee or rolls and butter, and *sidework,* work done to prepare the dining room for patrons or clean up when business is slow or when the restaurant closes.

Wagon service   In wagon, or formal French, service, food is served from a wagon or moving table called a *gueridon* that is brought flush with the patron's table. The gueridon is equipped with a small heating stove that is called a *rechaud* on which food is finished or kept warm. Sauces and some dishes are actually prepared on the rechaud in front of the patron. Cooked meats are carved and portioned on the gueridon. True French service of this kind is used less and less because the professional service people necessary for it are scarce, and few restaurants can afford the space needed to use and store a gueridon.

The service style depends on a hierarchic brigade of skilled service workers, some of whom have become common in restaurants that do not use wagon service, like the *maître d'hôtel*. The maître d' is in charge of all service activities, and can be thought of as the manager of the service system. Beneath that person, a captain or headwaiter supervises about four service stations. Each station is in the charge of a *chef de rang* who is assisted by a *commis de rang* in training to be a *chef de rang*. A *débarrasseur* is comparable to a bus person and clears away serviceware between courses. A wine steward or *chef de sommelier*, takes orders for wines and serves them, often accompanied by a *commis de sommelier*.

The tasks of the *chef de rang* and *commis de rang* in serving a table are quite specialized and distinct. The *chef de rang* takes orders, presents and collects the bill, and serves all drinks. The *commis de rang* takes orders to the kitchen, and brings finished orders out to the gueridon. The *chef de rang* prepares or finishes food on the gueridon, and serves it onto plates that the *commis de rang* will place in front of each patron.

French-style service is elaborate and expensive, and training for its personnel is lengthy. The order of service, service techniques, and the use of particular flatware with specific courses are highly defined. The required skill and grace in using serving utensils takes much training and practice. However, the hierarchy of service personnel provides excellent training on the job.

Platter service   In platter, or Russian, service, food is brought to the patron's table on a platter or serving dish. Platter service is used extensively in better hotels and restaurants, including most French restaurants, which leads to some confusion about its name. In English-speaking countries, platter service is sometimes called French service, but in France, it is always known as Russian service.

In restaurants using this service style, service personnel present the dish on a platter and then serve it onto the patron's plate. Service is slow, though faster than French, and requires a bit less skill. Platter service resembles wagon service in the organization of service workers, though fewer workers may be necessary because duties are less specialized and tasks less elaborate. Platter service is less expensive than formal French wagon service, but is still quite elegant, and for this reason is preferred by most high quality restaurants.

Family service   In family, or English, service, platters of food are placed on the table and patrons serve themselves. A member of the party may carve meat or serve soup. This service style is not common, and is used often for set menus offered on holidays such as Thanksgiving and Easter. Family service creates a more homelike atmosphere appropriate to such holiday occasions. Private clubs may also use this service style.

Mixed styles   Obviously, these service styles need not be adhered to rigidly. Many foodservice establishments combine styles, and serve different courses in different manners. Dessert carts, technically a part of wagon service, are quite common in restaurants using platter or plate service. Banquet service may be plate or platter service; the menu served is a fixed table d'hôte.

STAND-UP SERVICE Stand-up service accommodates standing rather than seated patrons, who may be in a cafeteria line, at a counter, or at a buffet or bar. Patrons may serve themselves, or be served while standing by a service worker.

Attended line   In operations using this kind of service, the consumer moves along a long case of displayed foods, as in a cafeteria, while service workers help the consumer in selecting foods and portion it onto a plate. Consumers then take their meals elsewhere to eat. Attended service requires special equipment for holding foods in the service area, dispensing beverages, and making serviceware available to consumers. Often, commercial establishments using attended service will customize standard equipment to harmonize with their decor, doing such things as mounting a dish dispenser in a wooden or mosaic-tile holder.

In traditional line service, patrons get trays and move past food stations in a line, picking up their food. In commercial cafeterias, three to five persons are served per minute, while institutional operations serve as many as five to ten per minute. Consumers take already portioned plates of food which service workers immediately replace, or service workers portion food as consumers request it. Trapping patrons in a line is sometimes believed to encourage sales; often eye-catching desserts come first. Some operations use double lines to speed consumer flow, or have enough space so that consumers can pass each other. Sometimes the line is ⊔ shaped instead of straight so people can bypass the hot station and skip from cold foods to beverages without waiting while other people ahead of them get hot food.

Consumer waiting time can be cut even more by separating food stations, and thus allowing faster access to the particular ones each patron wants. The line may be divided into several separate lines, or zigzagged or sawtoothed to the same effect. Food stations can be set up as freestanding counters or kiosks, each with its own line. This freestanding counter arrangement is called *scramble service*.

Though line service has been associated with institutional feeding, with a little imagination restaurants offering one or two items and accompaniments, for example, soup and salad, or wine and cheese, can use line service effectively to speed up customer flow without diminishing their appeal.

In the southern part of the United States, service workers often carry patrons' trays to available tables for them. This variation of attended service is called *southern line service*.

Counter service   This kind of delivery most resembles the method of a nonfood retail store. The consumer gives the service worker an order over a counter and the worker assembles and packages the order and takes payment for it. The service worker sometimes prepares food as well, as in a hot-dog stand staffed by one person, thus combining production and service tasks. In a typical limited-menu hamburger restaurant, service workers assemble orders of wrapped hamburgers and bagged french fries, but may make drinks or milkshakes as they are ordered.

If there is a waiting period between ordering and picking up food, the customer may order and pay, and then take a number that is called when the order is ready. Some operations have customers pick up orders at special pickup stations. This kind of delivery can also be used for customers in cars.

Counter service is very efficient. While it has been associated with service strategies that emphasize speed of service and nothing else, it need not be so limited in appeal. The most luxurious bar is, after all, nothing more than a well-designed and attractively decorated counter.

Buffet service   Ony at a buffet do consumers actually get all their food without the intermediary of some service worker or machine. Buffets and mini-buffets called bars present patrons with menu items which they themselves portion, put on plates, and carry away to eat. The difference between a buffet and bar lies in the extent of their offerings; a buffet presents a full meal, while a bar, such as a salad bar, cheese bar, dessert bar, or relish bar, is more limited in its offerings.

Coffee service in offices is run like a bar. In fact, the coffee area is sometimes called a buffet or bar. A foodservice contractor supplies the office with the machine, the coffee, and all other necessary supplies. Office workers not only serve themselves coffee and other hot beverages, but prepare them as well.

MACHINE SERVICE   Machines can deliver food products ranging from hot meals to ice cream. Usually such machines just transfer food to consumers, but some can prepare and process food too, though these machines are patented more often than marketed. Machines that make hot dogs and hamburgers are the most frequent targets of inventors. The most successful machine that actually prepares food items is the coffee vendor. Some machines actually grind their own beans, brew each cup of coffee, and add fresh milk and sugar if the consumer so desires.

Although vending machines are the most common kind of machine delivery, there are actually four types of machine or machine-assisted delivery: vending machines, automats, conveyor belts, and vehicles.

Vending machines   Food vending machines most often offer hot and cold drinks such as coffee, soft drinks, and milk. Machines that sell packaged confections such as candy and cake are also common. Prepared foods such as sandwiches, salads, fresh pastries, and even ice cream offered in vending machines find a much smaller market.

Vending service is almost always based on an "anywhere" strategy. While people are willing to accept a less-than-ideal product at a higher-than-usual price in exchange for having the produce when they want it, neither quality nor cost can deviate too much without loss of customers. Vending service is common in work situations because food and drink is made available to workers whenever they want it, without the disruption of work that fixed breaks and a trip to the regular dining area might occasion. Many factories have vending machines located close to almost every worker. Sometimes, only canned beverages are dispensed, as the company's industrial engineers feel that a *cup* promotes socializing that would cause workers to waste production time.

Snack machines which dispense food products such as cookies that can be kept at room temperature and those which dispense cold canned soft drinks are less expensive and technologically simpler than the machines which offer more complicated food products, such as hot or cold beverages in cups, and hot or cold foods.

Hot-beverage machines make coffee by mixing liquid concentrated, freeze-dried, or specially ground fresh coffee with hot or boiling water and with powdered or fresh milk and sugar if the consumer indicates a desire for these on the push-button selection panel. The closer the machine approaches making fresh brewed coffee, the more complex the machine must be and the more service, maintenance, and sanitizing it requires. Tea is brewed with tea bags and hot water, and is not quite as complicated. Hot-drink machines also dispense broth and hot chocolate, neither of which has the problems of coffee and tea brewing.

Most machines dispense drinks in a disposable cup that is designed not to jam, disintegrate, or burn the consumer. The best cups also feel pleasant to the mouth and convey the psychological satisfactions of a "good cup of coffee" by feeling robust in the hand and slightly warm. A perfectly insulated cup is less satisfying. Some machines allow consumers to put their own cups under the dispensing spout, thereby making the coffee seem less institutional.

Cold-drink machines dispense beverages like milk and soft drinks in cans, bottles, and cartons, as well as cups. Soft drinks dispensed into cups come from either *premix* or *postmix* machines. Premix machines hold the prepared drink in a cooled tank and dispense it into cups without further mixing. If the soft drink is carbonated, a separate tank of

CO_2 (carbon dioxide) must feed into the first tank. Postmix machines mix a syrup stored in tanks with cold water or cold carbonated water as it dispenses the drink into a cup. These machines need a source of water, either a direct connection with a water system or a reservoir and a pump. Postmix machines can use any brand of syrup in the tanks, while premix machines restrict purchases to the companies that supply the premix tanks.

Cold-food machines are like refrigerators that sell food. Cold perishable foods must be kept at a temperature under 8°C. The most common cold-food machine resembles a cupboard of glass doors in a column. The customer pays and indicates food choice on a selection panel that springs open the appropriate door. Other machines use conveyor belts arranged in a column to drop a selected item into a bin at the bottom of the machine. Cupboard machines are used to vend even caviar in Europe, and many machines there are freestanding in outdoor locations.

Hot-food machines can also be cupboard machines and must keep food heated to an internal temperature of at least 60°C. Loss of palatability is a problem in selling hot entrees and sandwiches. While a cold machine need not be serviced more than once every 48 hours (though 24 hours is the better and more common practice), hot cupboard machines must be serviced at least once every six hours. Hot-food machines that dispense heated cans of such products as soup, spaghetti and meatballs, and beef stew require less service but are more limited in appeal.

Foodservice vending machines usually are owned by a company that contracts with the proprietor of the location where the machines are placed. These companies buy processed and packaged food from their manufacturers, have them made at an outside commissary or local restaurant, or prepare foods themselves at company-owned commissaries. Accurate menu programming is necessary to reduce waste. Even in well-managed companies, food that is recovered from machines and cannot be recycled accounts for as much as 15 percent of all products offered.

Automats   The simplest automat is a battery of vending machines that offers the possibility of having a full meal. A combination of hot, cold, and room temperature food machines can offer soup, a meat casserole, salad, cheese and crackers, pastry, beer, coffee, and a candy bar. Utensils can be included in the food packages or dispensed from another machine. Batteries of machines offering such diverse products are common in libraries, factories, dormitories, hospitals, and almost any other conceivable location with a market segment that can be satisfied by an anywhere/anytime strategy. If tables, chairs, and a reasonably pleasant environment are provided, the facility is dignified by being called an automat, canteen, or automated cafeteria. Sometimes, vending batteries are installed in street-front stores but are usually attended by someone who will make change, protect the facility, and clean tables.

More sophisticated automats include reconstitution devices so that food products dispensed cold or at room temperature can be heated. Presently, the microwave oven is the most commonly installed reconstitution device, but convection ovens, infra-red quartz ovens, and even steam refreshers have been used.

Cupboard-type hot and cold vending machines and other dispensing machines have been built into the walls of dining areas. The consumer, equipped with a tray if necessary, circulates from one machine to another making selections. Both single-service and permanent ware have been used in these systems, which are true automats. They are further distinguished by being serviced from a production facility behind the banks of the machines. When a compartment or turntable is emptied, a production worker prepares additional items and fills the compartment. Product waste and deterioration are minimized.

Conveyors   The logic of materials handling talked about in Chapter 9 can be applied to the service of food. Instead of hand delivering food products a few at a time, they can be moved in bulk. Of the materials-handling equipment that might lend itself to this task, the conveyor is the most suited to serving food.

Circular conveyors or turntables that look like giant lazy susans have been used by a number of restaurants to solve the problem of easily replenishing buffets. Half the conveyor or turntable remains in the kitchen, half moves in the dining room. If the conveyor moves at about one turn every three or four minutes, consumers have ample time to make selections and assemble their plates. Production workers can replenish the buffet with fresh food as the conveyor passes through the kitchen.

Conveyors have also been used effectively to speed service in high volume facilities. In the typical cafeteria, the consumer files past the food. With a conveyor, the food moves past a number of fixed consumer stations. If the menu is limited, as it might be in a school lunch cafeteria, several conveyors, one above the other, can each offer a single item or meal at ten or more consumer stations.

Conveyors also are widely used to assist service workers. Counter service can be speeded up by a conveyor that transports food items to service stations and takes dirty serviceware back to the production area. Frequently, conveyors remove serviceware and waste from cafeteria dining rooms.

Vehicles   Vehicle service is rarely entirely service by machine, because people are needed to complete the service. The two most common kinds of vehicle-assisted service are *mobile catering* (by truck) and *cart service*.

Mobile catering trucks are really motorized counters based on an anywhere/anytime strategy. A van or truck outfitted to hold and display food is driven to a series of scheduled stops. Once parked at a stop, the driver opens the truck to display the food products, or in some cases enters the back of the van and runs it as though it were a fixed counter. Customers order and pay just as at a counter, and are then free to eat their food wherever they like. Most of the products now offered tend to be rather ordinary and slightly more expensive than comparable items in nonmobile food facilities. Customers accept these compromises, as they do with vending machines, because they value the convenience of having food delivered to remote locations such as construction sites and small factories in industrial areas. The available menu may include sandwiches, hot or cold drinks, milk, ice cream, pastries, packaged confections, and sometimes freshly made hot foods such as beef stew. In some parts of the country, mobile caterers offer Chinese and Mexican food to people at beaches or other recreational areas.

A mobile catering truck driver may own the truck and develop his or her own route, own the truck but lease the route from a commissary company, or lease both the truck and the route. Some mobile catering companies simply employ drivers who are paid a salary or hourly wage. The commissary company may own a food production facility or may buy prepared foods from outside sources and food processors, or do both.

Factories and office buildings with a large enough number of people may have mobile cart service. A cart operator develops a route through such facilities using an electric or hand-pushed cart to carry and display food products. Usually, the products offered are restricted as factories or offices large enough to support cart service are often large enough to support a restaurant or cafeteria that offers full meals. Carts generally circulate in the morning and afternoon for coffee breaks, selling hot and cold drinks, pastries, candy, and some sandwiches.

Carts can offer service fully by machine if they are motorized and equipped with an electronic device that follows a magnetic strip in the floor. They are programmed to stop at fixed stations and sound a bell tone. Either patrons are trusted to deposit appropriate sums or vending machines are used.

Accommodating Consumption

Foodservice operations must accommodate patrons' consumption of their products, either by providing an area within the operation where they can eat or by transporting the food to a place outside the operation where they will eat. Whether an establishment accommodates consumption inside or outside, the way that it does so must be coordinated with the way that the food is delivered.

ACCOMMODATING CONSUMPTION INSIDE THE OPERATION

Depending upon its service strategy, a foodservice establishment can accommodate consumption of its products by providing stand-up counters, seated counters, booths, or by various arrangements of tables and chairs.

Stand-up counters   Stand-up counters are usually used with either counter or attended line service. Consumers eat their food at narrow shelves on the walls of the dining area, at the foodservice counter itself, or at high tables, called *mushrooms* if they are round. Stand-up counters are geared to customers in a hurry, and are often used in small operations to make the most of limited space. Although in general customer checks are low, the food items themselves can be expensive. An operation with stand-up counters might sell such things as a 75-cent piece of pastry and a 65-cent cup of espresso. A luxury bar is a stand-up counter; so is an oyster bar.

Seated counters   Seated counters allow customers to sit on stools or chairs along a narrow counter which may be straight, curved in a U shape or formed around several bays where service workers are stationed. Seated counters are installed for a variety of reasons. Traditionally, they have allowed a production worker to serve customers by preparing food on cooking equipment behind the counter. In small operations, especially those owned, operated, and staffed by one or two people, this combined system is efficient.

In larger operations, most food production does not take place right behind the counter; service workers walk into a kitchen to pick food up, or it is passed through an opening between the two areas. Larger operations cannot economically justify paying a person cook's wages to serve customers, or allow minimally skilled service workers to prepare food other than beverages and desserts. Seated counters often help improve speed of service and customer flow. Service workers can deliver the food faster; customers seated at a counter often feel some increased pressure to eat quickly and leave.

Counters also accommodate single people and small parties efficiently. Unless the operation seats customers at tables with people they do not know, called *delicatessen seating*, a single person seated at a table can take three other seats out of service. Counters are attractive to customers who want to eat quickly but not alone. A number of expensive restaurants offer deluxe counter seating with upholstered club chairs and a correspondingly low counter. They accommodate the person dining alone who would prefer the relative sociability of the counter to conspicuously occupying a table for four.

Booth seating   Arrangements of fixed tables with fixed, padded benches called booths are installed for two quite different reasons. Because the booths are permanently installed, a modestly priced operation can generally accommodate more seated customers with booths than with tables and chairs. Booth seating is often more cramped than table seating; booths are the least formal way of accommodating larger groups of customers.

On the other hand, more expensive restaurants often install large booths because they promote sociability and communication among the people eating together. People appreciate the privacy and community afforded by a booth. In some restaurants, the backs of the benches are extended to the ceiling so that booths are even more private. Sometimes the front of the booth may be enclosed as well, forming a practically separate small room.

Tables and chairs   Accommodating consumption with tables and chairs is associated with service strategies that promote more leisurely dining. Customers eating in large groups generally prefer to sit at tables and usually will spend more time eating. For groups seated at a single table, the shape of the table has some influence on their perceptions of the meal experience. A round table tends to promote sociability and communication more than a square or rectangular one. Increasing the dimensions of the tables promotes leisurely dining. Closely packing tables increases the customer's dependence on the service system, which can be acceptable if service workers are truly at the beck and call of the customer.

Rows of rectangular tables appear institutional. A mixture of large and small tables of various shapes and sizes looks comfortable and informal. Table and booth seating can be used in the same operation to offer a variety of arrangements. The number of tables with two, four, or six seats depends upon market research on the size of parties that frequent the operation.

For groups of people eating together at a very large table or at several separate tables, the tables' arrangement establishes communication channels and also emphasizes status differences among group members. Large parties of friends probably prefer to sit at round tables. In business dinners or luncheons, long rectangular tables are used and arranged to indicate the relative importance of participants. Seating at the head table elevated on a platform called a dais or at the base of a U-shaped arrangement is reserved for important members of the party. Seats close to these important people have symbolic value to aspirants to prestige and power. Seating at a single table, whatever the size of the party, increases group cohesiveness.

Chairs can make a contribution to the patron's perceptions of the meal experience. Deep, luxurious chairs obviously promote leisurely dining, while small hard chairs directly promote fast customer turnover. Some operations have tried to compromise between booth or counter seating in order to maximize occupancy while still offering table seating. Chairs are affixed to tables or to table bases, which gives the impression of table seating while fully utilizing dining room space and greatly facilitating cleaning.

When consumers are waiting to be seated at booths or tables, or even at counters, they should never be kept waiting with nothing to do. This universal rule for foodservice operations has resulted in:

• The mutation of the bar from a place to drink to a place to drink while waiting.

- The development of the waiting lounge where patrons can eat free cheese, salad, and appetizers.
- The development of the waiting lounge offering movies or other entertainment.
- Restaurants that accommodate customers only with reservations.
- Restaurants that accommodate customers only at two or three definite seating times. Popular times for the first and second seatings are 7:00 and 9:30 P.M.
- The scramble service self-service restaurant organized around separate food stations selling just a few related items.
- The use of "order-takers" in limited-menu take-out/take-in restaurants. Service workers take orders from customers while they are in line and transmit them to the production system. When the customer arrives at the counter, the order is ready.
- The use of menus that include several thousand words of possibly interesting reading material concerning the history of the operation, local events, or the tourist attractions of the area.

ACCOMMODATING CONSUMPTION OUTSIDE THE OPERATION   The patrons of some foodservice operations consume the operations' products at locations away from it. This situation can oblige the service system to perform a number of either minor or considerable tasks. Consumption outside the operation is accommodated by *take-out service, hand delivery,* and *extended service,* which includes service methods that hold food without deterioration while transporting it.

Vehicle service, a kind of delivery, may seem very similar to these ways of accommodating consumption. The reason that mobile caterers and cart service are not like hand delivery or extended service is that the truck or cart of the former two methods is not just used to carry the product to a place outside the operation to accommodate consumption. The truck or cart *is* the operation, while the van that brings an order of pizza to your doorstep is not.

Take-out service   Take-out service places the fewest obligations on the service system of the three ways of accommodating consumption outside the operation. There is a difference between selling customers food in protective wrappings and offering take-out service. An operation that offers take-out service must suitably accommodate consumption of the product by packaging it in containers from which the customer can eat, by including serviceware, and by providing adequate accompaniments. Coffee and sandwiches may not permit such distinctions between these approaches; full meals and specialty items do. Some foodservice operations that specialize in deluxe take-out service, perhaps exclusive of other kinds of service, project the meal experience to the outside location. For example, sushi bars (sushi is a Japanese dish of raw fish and rice) on the east and west coasts of the United States frequently offer excellent take-out service. The customer's order is assembled in an attractive, sturdy, cardboard box, that contains, in addition to the food, a place mat, napkin, three small containers of condiments, a pair of chopsticks wrapped in paper, and sometimes an envelope of green tea leaves.

Some operations that offer take-out service provide outside picnic tables or ample parking space so that customers can eat in their cars while still allowing room for others to park.

Hand-delivery service   Hand-delivery service is an extension of take-out service. The customer calls the operation and places an order, and when the order is ready, it is carried to the customer in appropriate packaging and with necessary serviceware. Service workers may deliver food on foot but usually use cars or vans with holding equipment. The service worker may simply give the customer the order, or may accommodate the food's consumption by arranging the food on a table or desk and removing the packaging. Most foodservice operations just deliver the order, but several successful operations employ personable service workers who have definite routes during lunchtime. They take orders in the morning, assemble their orders at a commissary, hand-deliver the food to their customers, and make some effort to make the food presentation attractive. In some areas certainly, the business people who want to eat in their offices but do not want to rough it with bag lunches make a good market.

Extended service   In most foodservice operations, food is served within a few moments after preparation. Food neither loses palatability nor remains very long in the temperature zone that encourages microorganic growth. In other service situations the location of the place where the food will be eaten can occasion a delay between preparation and consumption. Product deterioration can be prevented by extending the production system or extending the service system. Operations that extend the production system transport food in a cold (6–8°C), stable state. Food products are finished with production equipment that is close to the place where they will be eaten. Thus, a hospital may transport plated entrees and otherwise assembled trays to small production facilities on patient floors called *serveries, pantries,* or *nourishment stations* where meals are heated, assembled, and served by nurses or dietary aides. Similarly, a social catering company may deliver food in insulated cabinets to a customer's home and finish production in the customer's own kitchen or with mobile cooking apparatus. Airlines and schools extend production also; both receive food from a central commissary and finish it in their own facilities.

The alternative method, also used by hospitals, social caterers, and schools, is to extend the service system by holding the product at its proper serving temperature during the period between preparation and consumption. Food products can be transported as packaged individual portions or in pans or containers holding 10, 20, or more entrees. The most common ways of doing this are by insulating products in transit to retain heat or cold, or by providing products in transit with a source of heat and cold.

Food temperature can be maintained by packing bulk containers of food in insulated cabinets or cases. Specially molded trays with insulation cores can conserve the heat of individual portions of food sufficiently to allow for a 30 or 40 minute delay between preparation and consumption. Very hot food (at least 80°C) does not fall below minimum serving temperature (60°C) during this period. Cold food also can be kept sufficiently cold to meet safety standards by using these trays.

Sometimes supplementary cooling of food in transit is provided by solid blocks of dry ice (frozen carbon dioxide—CO_2) or by snow carbon dioxide made by venting the cooled gas into the food containers. Cool temperatures can also be maintained by ice, frozen containers of chemicals, or by mechanical refrigeration devices attached to energy sources in the transporting vehicle or at the place of consumption. Hot temperatures can be maintained by having electric heating elements built into the shipping containers.

For transporting individual portions, heated or chilled discs or pellets can be enclosed in the outer layer of the specially designed serviceware that holds each portion. Safe food temperatures can be maintained this way for about an hour. Food portions in transit can also be kept hot in containers with heating devices. For example, a service worker taking hotel guests food in their rooms may use a small shelf cabinet heated with solid fuel to carry food. The hot entrees of meals assembled on individual trays can be kept hot by using special serviceware designed to allow the hot entree to rest on a miniature hot plate built into a specialized cart. Individual temperature controls allow proper temperature regulation so that cold entrees placed on the cart are not heated also.

SERVICE MANAGEMENT

Because the service system centers on the interaction between service workers and patrons, the most important part of service management is personnel management. Service personnel are in many ways a part of the derivative product; since they have the greatest contact with consumers, their behavior and attitudes can make or break a good market image. Service persons are in a sense always on stage, and the service manager must make sure they give the best performance possible.

The service manager must deal with consumers as well, as he or she constantly confronts situations created by changing populations of customers, guests, or clients. Thus, consumer relations is the second major concern of the service manager. The manager must also possess certain necessary skills and carry around in his or her head (or on paper) a checklist for service that covers all areas that make the operation ready to give the best service possible. Each of these four topics will be discussed in the following sections.

Personnel Management

The management of service workers is affected in many ways by the need for workers to interact successfully with customers, guests, or clients. Work in the service system can rarely be depersonalized as it can in the systems less visible to patrons, like production or supply. Even a hamburger becomes more of a hamburger to customers if service workers are smiling, attractive, and personable, as well as simply doing their jobs. A manager might wish that this were not so. In effect, the customer is requiring a product that frequently cannot be supplied readily at the price the customer is willing to pay. People with the personal traits desirable in service workers often do not want to work in hamburger stands at the wages hamburger stands can afford to pay. Worse, they may not want to work in luxury restaurants at fairly high remuneration because of the low prestige attached to such service occupations. These problems in attracting satisfactory service workers have been discussed earlier in this chapter in "Labor Availability." Fully recognizing the extent of the problem, foodservice organizations and managers have tried various remedies (with varying degrees of success), including:

- The use of service strategies that minimize social interactions.
- Training to improve the social skills of those workers willing to be trained.
- Recruitment among those groups of people whose attitudes toward service are at least acceptable. Frequently this means recruiting people who will not become career service workers, like students, persons working part-time to earn a second family income, and persons in the arts.
- Use of service strategies that are acceptable to worker groups and still acceptable to the market; for example, service strategies based on the meal experience rather than on status.
- Increased monetary incentives; for example, luxury private clubs with very demanding members generally provide greater compensation than other operations.
- Jobs designed to sustain worker enthusiasm; for example, career development of service workers, or provision of equipment, tools, and facilities that are pleasant as well as functional.
- Better working environments: generous locker facilities, lounges, good showers.

• Building worker dignity and morale by relaxing strict supervision of workers and allowing them more autonomy and responsibility on the job.

Beyond the inherent problems of the availability and quality of labor, the service manager must be concerned with organizing service workers and setting up policy for service workers.

ORGANIZATION OF
SERVICE WORKERS

The organization of service workers must be consistent with the quality of workers available to the operation and with the service strategy the operation employs. Service strategies that demand a high degree of interaction among employees, for example, quick service or status strategies, also require a strict division of labor and usually a hierarchal structure. Ambiguous responsibilities disrupt service; instructions given in front of consumers cannot be questioned without the consumers becoming disturbed.

In isolated units such as mobile catering and snack counters, decentralized decision making in at least some decision areas is needed to maintain efficiency. It is virtually impossible for the manager to plan for every contingency that can occur in an isolated unit. Workers should be allowed to make certain decisions themselves and should be held accountable for the results of them.

Service strategies that depend upon effective worker-customer interactions, those used in many informal restaurants, suggest work unit organization that dignifies the individual worker, specifically a de-emphasis of superior-subordinate relationships. People who are demoralized by strict supervision and discipline cannot be expected to be cheerful and charming if kept under such supervision.

During critical service periods the manager may expedite service operations by altering worker organization, and changing task assignments. For example, it is not unusual for the service manager of a dining room to move service workers from one station to another because the demands of a particular party are stressing the system.

An operation's service workers are usually divided into groups or departments based on how much interaction they have with consumers. Persons in direct contact with patrons like table service workers form one group, persons who work in the presence of patrons like service aides form another, and those persons whose work supports these activities like warewashers form a third group.

POLICY FOR
SERVICE WORKERS

The presence of customers, guests, or clients severely limits the possibility of establishing flexible policy in the service unit. The manager cannot relax dress code policy to compensate a worker for an extraordinary effort the night before. Policies in the following areas should be decided on by management or by management and service workers, and must be strictly adhered to by service workers:

- The division of gratuities among service workers.
- Sidework responsibilities.
- Service standards such as proper order of courses, the correct laying of covers, the appropriate packaging for take-out items.
- Rules related to employee and consumer health and safety.
- Dress and grooming codes.
- Procedures related to interactions with the production system.
- Procedures for writing up and collecting consumer checks.

Any managerial style can be consistent with communicating these policies and motivating workers to ensure conformity to them. The manager can sell as well as tell these policies to service workers. The manager can reward rule adherence as well as punish rule violation.

Consumer Relations   Besides developing and supervising satisfactory worker-consumer interactions, the service manager usually deals with consumers directly in quite important ways. Being in charge of the service area, the service manager necessarily works all the time in front of patrons. Often, service managers represent the operation to consumers; they *become* the operation in much the same way that orchestras are identified with their conductors. People patronize Toby's place even if the operation officially is named something else. The attention and highly developed social skills of the service manager (who may be the owner, or overall manager, as well) compensate patrons for the merely businesslike performance of other workers. Hospitals and other noncommercial operations sometimes use the same approach. The dietary aide may simply be pleasant and efficient in delivering a patient's tray; the dietitian who visits the patient personalizes the service.

Service managers often seat patrons and take reservations and are thus in charge of making patrons feel welcomed and accommodating them comfortably. It is essential for the service manager to try to pace consumer flow so that the dining room is full and yet each consumer has satisfactory service. Patrons may be kept waiting even when there are empty tables or seats if the service system is fully loaded at the moment. Seating people without being able to serve them properly is less satisfying than keeping them waiting and then accommodating them well.

Crisis management is frequently the manager's major contribution to consumer relations. Managerial intervention redeems situations that are going badly for the consumer, the service worker, or both. The problem may be either with the food product or the derivative product; the manager must try to correct it to the consumer's satisfaction. The following chart shows the kind of problems the service manager deals with in crisis management, and some possible solutions:

Problem	Possible Solution
Unsatisfactory food (even if it meets operation's standards)	Substitution of another menu item without discussion
Conflict between service worker and consumer	Completion of service by another service worker; apology by management for any inconvenience
Unsatisfactory seating arrangement or table position	Change of location and/or correction of problem (air conditioning, faulty speaker)
Excessively demanding consumers	Selective assignment of service personnel
Disorderly patrons	Minimization of disruption of other patrons' meals by reasonable, quiet, and legal means
Generalized complaints	Sympathetic listening by manager; evaluation of basis of complaints for possible correction
Altercation between patrons	Minimization of disruption of other consumers' meals, usually by transferring the disturbance to some other location

Service Manager Skills for the   Many service systems demand specialized skills of the service manager. A manager may need special skills in six areas: equipment, craft, procedures, etiquette, work systems, and safety and health.

Equipment skills   Service systems include a substantial amount of equipment, and workers must be trained to operate, maintain, and clean it. The service manager may be the only person in the operation who knows how to dismantle, clean, sanitize, and reassemble a fairly complex piece of equipment like a soft-serve ice-cream machine. In the absence of other professionals, the manager must also be able to trouble-shoot when problems occur. Service-system equipment can include warewashing machines, automated tray assembly lines, soft-serve machines, coffee-making machines, carbonated beverage systems, electronic cash registers, ice makers, vending machines, and so on.

Craft skills   Many service activities require certain manipulative skills, such as tray handling, stacking bussed serviceware, wrapping sandwiches, serving from a platter to a plate using a fork and spoon, carving, tableside cooking, mixing drinks, and so on. In order to train and supervise employees properly and help out whenever necessary, the service manager must know how to perform all these tasks.

Procedure skills   The manager must also know and communicate the operation's procedures for check writing, passing orders to the kitchen, picking up orders, doing sidework, and the like. Practices differ widely; even skilled professional service workers need specific guidance.

Etiquette skills   In some service situations, the activities are performed according to the rules of etiquette or formal manners. The service manager must teach personnel to pour from the right and clear from the left, or how to set a table so all serviceware is arranged properly according to etiquette rules. The manager may be the arbiter in disputes on such matters as the position of the oyster fork relative to the salad fork or the appropriate glass for serving sparkling red wine. The proper presentation, opening, and service of wine is necessary knowledge for the service manager of any better restaurant. On a larger scale, a service manager may need to know how to welcome titled persons, or how to manage the ritual for a formal wedding.

Work-system skills   Because the service system is a work system, the service manager must be skilled in the methods of managing a work system. The manager must know the most efficient way to accomplish whatever task confronts the system. The manager may be charged with creating assemblies for the preparation of patient trays, routing and dispatching 30 vehicles, or training 1,000 first-time employees to sell food during an international sporting event. Knowledge of work-system methods is immensely helpful to countless jobs that may face the service manager, who may have to know the most efficient way to arrange an attended service line, assemble a take-out order, drive a mobile catering route, stock a mobile service cart, move banquet food from a production facility to a function room, remove waste from a nourishment station, organize a warewashing facility, organize booster stations in the dining room, and so on.

Health and safety skills   The service manager shares the concern of all foodservice managers for public health and safety. Proper food-handling techniques are as necessary in the service of food as in its storage or production. As service managers are frequently supervising workers without prior training or experience, they must establish hygienic food-handling techniques. Service managers must teach and ensure correct methods of sanitary warewashing; sanitization of bar glasses; proper handling of butter, bread, and condiments; cleanliness and handling of ice; proper storage and holding of desserts; protection of displayed foods against contamination; sanitization of food-contact surfaces; cleanliness of dispensing equipment; cleanliness and sanitization of refrigerated equipment; and so on.

Checklist for Service　Before consumers enter an operation, the service manager should check whether or not many of the factors that contribute to the consumer's perception of the operation are up to the operation's standards. A universal service manager's checklist might consist of the following, which can of course be pared down to fit the needs of a specific service manager:

- Cleanliness of the interior.
- Amount of serviceware cleaned, polished, and available for service.
- Amount of wrapping materials in place and available for service.
- Preparation of those food items prepared by service workers, such as condiments, beverages, baked goods.
- Condition of napery.
- Uniformity and neatness of covers (laid flatware).
- Lighting level.
- Dress and grooming of workers.
- Workers' knowledge of the day's menu program.
- Workers' knowledge of ordering and service procedures.
- Worker attitudes (communicated in conversation or observed: for example, it may be learned or noted that a worker is ill).
- Music level and selection.
- Staff present and on station.
- Completion of all dining room sidework.
- Equipment available for service.
- Functioning of mechanical devices such as dispensing equipment or ice machines.
- Number, cleanliness, and accuracy of menus.
- Arrangement of dining area furnishings to be consistent with reservations.
- Readiness of the production system.
- Amount of cash on hand for making change.

Catering a social event like a banquet or wedding may demand much more of the service system, requiring the operation to deliver several hundred derivative products, from music and menus to floral arrangements, in addition to the food. A much more elaborate checklist is necessary for such an event. Typically, the service manager's plan for the event is perhaps 40 or 50 pages long and minutely detailed, full of mini-checklists for specific areas, specific instructions for particular workers, time schedules, and contingency plans in case of changing situations. Meetings, rehearsals, and previews of procedures ensure that the operation is capable of meeting the patron's standards and expectations.

Frequently the service manager for such events is called a *banquet manager, catering director, catering manager,* or *convention manager.* Service managers of operations offering recreational foodservice for sporting events, athletic contests, fairs, and festivals also make similar checklists of activities.

MAKING THE SERVICE SYSTEM MORE EFFECTIVE

Close regulation of materials and the use of various forms help make the service system more effective.

Materials Control   To ensure the efficient use of materials, the service manager should exercise control in four areas: cash, food products, packaging, and equipment.

Cash   The service manager necessarily monitors the procedure by which patrons pay their bills, and is often in charge of cash receipts from the time they are collected from consumers to the time they are transferred to the operation's bank (or business system). This responsibility can involve the service manager in cashiering procedures and in preparing bank deposits or cash disbursements.

Food products   In many foodservice operations, the guest check serves as both the patron's bill and as the record that food has moved from production to service. To ensure that all food served appears on the guest check, the service worker may give the production system a duplicate check, or kitchen check, which records what items the worker receives from the kitchen. At a set control point, a food checker also may record the transfer as the service worker leaves the production facility. In other operations, the transfer is recorded electronically. For example, the service worker of a counter system may record customer transactions on a cash register that will store this information so that it can be compared with production and cash records.

The service manager must also ensure that workers comply with portion control standards for those food products that they portion. This responsibility may include monitoring the amount of food on patient trays or serving portions of cooked food on an attended line. The managers of operations that offer free coffee with meals or unlimited bread and butter to patrons must monitor the consumption of these products as well.

Packaging   Products such as wrappings and single-use serviceware present particular control problems. They are issued to the service system but do not appear on patrons' checks. These items can be a considerable expense, sometimes costing as much as ten percent of sales revenues. Yet, employees tend to regard paper and plastic products as virtually costless. Consumption of these products must be related to sales or number of consumers. In order to introduce a measure of accountability for these items, the service manager must police employee practices with regard to personal utilization, over-wrapping, use of expensive materials for products for which less expensive wrappings or containers are supplied, unauthorized removal from the premises, and so on.

The managers of operations with permanent serviceware and cloth napery have a similar responsibility. The wide variance of serviceware breakage and loss figures among similar operations, ranging from one-half of one percent to ten percent of dollar sales, demonstrates that this area requires particular management attention.

Equipment   The equipment utilized in a service system, whether it consists of vending machines or silver platters, requires maintenance and repair, and, eventually, replacement. The management of the service system is responsible for the unit's facilities and equipment. Responsibilities vary from monitoring bulb replacement of a thousand-light marquee to periodically having copper chafing dishes retinned.

Use of Forms and Devices   The service system uses various forms to facilitate its functioning. Exhibit 11.1 presents a list of service forms, while exhibits 11.2 through 11.5 offer examples from this list. Such forms as guest checks or cash register tapes are used to compute dollar sales, and are essential to the operation's business management. The patron's check is probably the most important form generated by the service system.

Other forms of importance bear mentioning here. The *cover count, meal census,* or *meal report* records the number of patrons using the operation for different time periods: each day of the week, each meal period, sometimes even each hour of the day. This information is essential to forecast demand accurately. In many operations, particularly colleges and universities, forms such as meal-plan I.D. cards, meal tickets, or dining room authorizations are necessary to control access to eating facilities. Procedures range from simply counting I.D. cards to tallying I.D. cards with a master list to using machines that recognize voice prints or palm prints.

EXHIBIT 11.1 Service Forms

Form	Use	Data Base
Daily Sales Report or Restaurant Manager's Report	Presents information related to the operation's business activity for the use of unit management and general management.	Day/date Unit Register readings before business Register ribbon at close of business Cash sales Total: credit and cash sales Cash disbursements Reconciliation of cash sales with cash in register(s)

Cover Count, Meal Census, or Meal Report	Presents information related to the number of customers served, sometimes by time of day, meal category, or unit.	Day/date
		Number of customers
		Customers categorized by
		    time of meal
		    meal period
		    unit
		    menu choice (for example Type A lunch or a la carte lunch in a school)

Inventory:
  Linen
  Glassware
  Flatware
  Loose goods
	Controls the acquisition, use, and replacement of equipment.	Day/date of inventory
		Inventory by:
		    item names
		    item descriptions
		    item units
		      (for example, *dozens* of forks)
		Initial inventory and date
		Par-level
		Current inventory
		Order

Equipment Record	Presents information for servicing equipment, replacement, depreciation, and future purchasing evaluation.	Item name Equipment number Inventory number Location Date installed or purchased Description Purchase price Depreciation method Guarantee Date of expiration Dealer information Maintenance instructions Maintenance record

EXHIBIT 11.1 Service Forms (cont.)

Form	Use	Data Base
Consumable Inventory, Paper Goods Inventory Control Form, or Nonproductive Item Control Form	Monitors use and consumption of items that are issued to the service system but do not appear on customer checks.	Day/date Location Item name Item description Item units Initial inventory Ending inventory Consumption/utilization Sales or customer volume in that period
Sales and Booking Files: Function Files Master Cards Sales Report Forms Backlog Summaries Report of Lost Business Contracts	Used by social catering and other event-oriented foodservice operations to formally describe commitments made by and to customers, customer contacts, and the nature of the event planned.	Names and addresses of customers Salesperson making arrangements or contact Date/time of event Description of event Menu Other services to be rendered Number of guests Price and contractual information
Operational Records and Files: Function Work Order Schedules Event Resumes	Communication of instructions related to an event from the service department or unit to other operational units.	Day/date Issuing department Receiving department Communication by name of event date of event time of event location of event Specific operational instructions
Guest Check	Record of guest purchases to serve as bill; communication of guest order to production department; record of product utilization.	Name of operation Day/date Number of persons in party Service worker name or number Guest check number Items ordered Number of items ordered Amount of each item Extended amount Total

Form	Use	Data Base
Tally Sheet Recapitulation Signature Book	Record of guest checks issued to service workers so that checks returned and checks used can be compared with number issued.	Day/date Number of each check Name of service worker given block of checks Amount of check when used Return of checks unused Signature
Charge Cards, Identification Cards	Records utilization of foodservice facility by person who is not directly charged. Used by operations serving the continuing customer.	Name of person Facility Restriction Date of issue Date of expiration Photograph Signature of customer Encoded magnetic strip
Foodservice Questionnaire	Used to evaluate and improve foodservice programs.	Day/date Location Customer-related information Scoring table for food service facilities price Customer comments

EXHIBIT 11.2   Restaurant Manager's Report

Sales		
Food	*Bar*	*Sundry*

Cash Sales:
Charges:
Credit Cards: _____

   Totals:

                           Total Sales _____

House Charges		
Food	*Bar*	*Sundry*

Officers:
Employee:
Complimentary:
Walkouts:
Missed Meals: _____

   Totals   _____   _____   _____

                   Total House Charges _____

(Sales + House: _____   _____   _____
  Charge Total)

                (Grand Total:
                (Sales + House Charges) _____

Cost of Sales: Materials		
Food	*Bar*	*Sundry*

	Food	Bar	Sundry
Beginning Inventory:	$ _____	$ _____	$ _____
Add Purchases Receipts:	_____	_____	_____
Less Closing Inventory	_____	_____	_____
	_____	_____	_____
Cost	$ _____	$ _____	$ _____

EXHIBIT 11.3 Special Function Form

Function: **No.**

Date (day, month, year)

Time: **Room:**   **Number of Guests** _____

Special Arrangements:

                                                                        Flowers
                                                                Entertainment
Beverages: **Other**

Food Menu:

                                                                                            Total

Payment:

It is agreed that the undersigned will provide a minimum guarantee on the number of guests to be served 24 hours in advance of party. A variation of 5% is permitted, and the undersigned agrees to pay for all guests who attend but not less than 95% of the guaranteed number. Cash payment of charge will only be made to a cashier.

                                                            _____
                                                            Customer's Signature

_____
        Booking Party

                                    Approved by _____

EXHIBIT 11.4 Daily Cash and Check Report

Restaurant _____ _____ day   Date _____   19 ____ Hour ____

Waiter's Number	Starting Number	Next Starting Number	Checks this Period	Checks from Previous Period	Amount	Total Checks — Count	Total Checks — Void	Total Checks — Out	Nos. of Missing Checks	Paid from Register
1										**Foods** $
2										Meat
3										Fish
4										Groceries
5										Fruit and Vegetables
6										
7										
8										Eggs
9										Bakery and Pastry
10										
11										Pies
12										Coffee
13										Butter
14										Ice Cream
15										**Phone**
High checks										**Sundry**
Night checks										**Wages**
1										
2										
3										
4										
Cigars, etc.										
Totals										**Total**

Cashier

EXHIBIT 11.5 Service Worker Productivity Chart

	# Hours Worked	Total Sales	Sales per Manhour	Total # of Customers	Average Customer Sale	Comments: Re Legibility, Errors Sugg. Selling, etc.
Total for this Day's Checks						

Chapter 12
The Business
System

Money is a commodity. The business system effectively and efficiently deals with that commodity.

Managers of the business system plan for the use of money. Managers submit offers of money from outside purveyors to value analysis and endeavor to ensure the operation a supply of money when it is needed. Managers attempt to deal with the effect of external factors on the operation's money, money supply, cost of money, and possible uses of money. Managers analyze and study past uses of money in order to attain greater efficiency and effectiveness in future utilization.

In sum, the general objective of the business system is the management of money so that the organization's overall goals may be reached. Thus, the concepts and activities of money management form the focus of this chapter.

BUSINESS CONCEPTS

The contribution of the business system to the achievement of the operation's goals and the nature of business management vary with specific operations. The role of the business system in an operation that requires substantial amounts of money not readily available will differ from the role of the business system in an operation that has sufficient funds. Likewise, the role of the business system varies with the operation's overall objectives. The objectives of one enterprise, a commercial restaurant, might include expansion within its market segment, while the objectives of another, a hospital foodservice operation, would not. The business system must be geared to these differing goals.

The management of a foodservice organization develops a suitable business system on the basis of specific objectives consistent with general organization goals, with some consideration of the constraints and opportunities the external and internal environments of the operation

371

present for business system development. In other words, business systems in foodservice organizations are functional; they are created to accomplish something and, in the process, to solve actual problems.

Though business system objectives vary in their particulars, some widely applicable goals can be identified. Foodservice organizations may implement the following specific objectives as the foundation of their business systems.

1. *To create and sustain viable economic entities*   Most foodservice operations, and certainly all commercial foodservice operations, are potentially vulnerable to economic conditions that can impair their ability to acquire money, use money for specific purposes, allocate financial resources, and otherwise maintain a functioning operation. It is possible to reduce the potential impact of adverse conditions and to gain some strategic advantage by creating *formal* business organizations that are somewhat protected by law and that have some privileges. A primary objective of the business system is the creation of this bulwark.

Other internal and external conditions may thwart the smooth financial functioning of an operation. Investment money, *capital,* that the organization has converted into physical facilities and equipment, the funds (*working capital* and *revenues* from patrons), and the *profits* that the operation produces can be threatened through the frailty of managerial judgment. They can also be diminished by theft, by disaster such as fire, or by government action in the form of taxes. The business system can minimize the operation's vulnerability to these events and their effect on the operation as they occur. If this objective is realized, other business objectives may be achieved with greater ease, greater efficiency, and a reduced overall risk.

2. *To seek and develop sources of funds and investment capital* The functions of the business system in an organization include the determination of the organization's future need for money, the identification of sources of supply for the funds that the operation itself will not produce, and the acquisition of those funds on terms—price, supply, and delivery conditions—that are the best the operation can obtain. Organizations that do not need external funds, or need only small sums for short periods of time, do not emphasize this objective. For others it may be the primary function of the business system. A commercial restaurant chain seeking to expand may make the development of sources of funds a priority. A noncommercial foodservice operation, for example, a community enterprise that feeds the indigent elderly, may also establish this priority.

3. *To rank and choose among competing uses of funds*   There are always more investment opportunities than there are funds, and always more reasonable uses for funds in foodservice operations than there is money available. However, a functioning foodservice organization may

not be seeking further investment opportunities: an opportunity has already been identified and an investment made. There is a need to make the most of this investment by managing organization operating systems efficiently and effectively. The investment can be used well or wasted on the basis of decisions made in response to changing conditions facing the organization.

Much, but not all, of the performance of the operation can be evaluated in financial units—dollars and cents. The business system can contribute to the growth of the operation's capability to realize its objectives by monitoring and evaluating performance, and by identifying problems and possible solutions. By the same means, the performance of the business system itself can be monitored and evaluated with the prospect of making it more efficient and effective.

Planning as a business system activity thus has a specific goal: to weigh alternative uses of money according to criteria relevant to the foodservice organization's overall objectives.

Current Business Practices in the Foodservice Industry

The largest companies in the foodservice industry direct their business activities at achieving the three business objectives just discussed. They are successful or unsuccessful as any large company might be because of their management's acumen in such areas as marketing and production, as well as business: "Money builds foodservice companies; it doesn't manage them." However, the means by which a billion-dollar company or a chain of restaurants owned by a conglomerate with several billion dollars in sales seeks investment opportunities or develops sources of funds has little relevance to the majority of foodservice enterprises today. The financial results that a billion-dollar company's professional managers can promise to its public shareholders or corporate owners are in no way indicative of the results an owner-manager, the owners of a small enterprise, or a noncommercial foodservice sponsor can achieve.

In any but the largest enterprises, business objectives and business performance cannot be easily distinguished from personal objectives and personal performance. With the exception of the few very large enterprises, most foodservice companies, including the largest independent restaurants and most foodservice chains, are "personalized" enterprises.

The foodservice industry, despite its total size, remains an aggregation of hundreds of thousands of small enterprises with highly individualized approaches to business matters. The business objectives of a company and the way a company does business reflect the personality, needs, experience, and limitations of its owners and managers. Business objectives are tempered by personal objectives; the means employed to achieve these objectives reflect personal styles and resources.

Though highly individualized, seven typical foodservice business approaches can be recognized: minimal personal investment approach, livelihood approach, limited expansion approach, "wishful thinking" approach, professional management approach, entrepreneurial approach, and business management approach.

MINIMAL PERSONAL
INVESTMENT
APPROACH

Traditionally, the foodservice industry has permitted entry with a small amount of personal capital. Opening another type of enterprise—for example, a car dealership—requires a much greater investment. Someone with only a small sum of money and perhaps some borrowing ability could start a potentially viable business and anticipate a considerable return. Although this strategy may be successful today, success is harder to achieve. Everything connected with starting an enterprise—facilities, equipment, starting product inventories, advertising—is more expensive. Many foodservice enterprises fail because they are undercapitalized. Either the owner does not have sufficient working capital or has not made a substantial enough investment to earn market following, or the cost (debt service) of borrowed money compromises the viability of the enterprise.

Another option requiring little personal investment is a concession. The foodservice entrepreneur contracts with a club, office building, or recreational facility to operate an existing facility. A small investment suffices to equip the facility, advertise, purchase initial food products, and pay wages during the opening period.

LIVELIHOOD
APPROACH

Return on investment is only a minor objective in the livelihood approach. The owner of the operation has "bought" an opportunity to work with the expectation that the compensation received will exceed the money that could have been earned by working for another company, investing in government bonds, or some other investment vehicle. The foodservice industry traditionally has attracted persons with modest savings (or loans from their families) who are willing to subsidize foodservice enterprises with their personal labor. A person who requires $500 a week to maintain his family and has skills worth only $5 an hour is unlikely to find 100 hours of work a week. With an investment of $10,000, a foodservice operation could provide this "opportunity." If less than $500 is required for personal needs, then the accumulated surplus eventually allows the foodservice operator to enlarge the operation or purchase a more significant and profitable enterprise. Some of the most famous and successful foodservice operations were founded on this basis.

LIMITED EXPANSION
APPROACH

Most successful companies in other industries grow more profitable by selling more of their products. Each unit produced costs less to manufacture because it can be made without additional machines, labor, management, sales efforts, or overhead and perhaps with a lower cost of raw materials because of greater purchasing volume. If prices are maintained, profits increase and so does return on the original investment.

A foodservice operation does not have this opportunity. A successful restaurant cannot expect to jam more and more people into its dining room or to sell dinners at 4 A.M. In an attempt to achieve greater profitability, the operation may invest in the construction of additional dining areas or in another foodservice operation. Because of the organization's success, additional capital may be attracted for the new enterprise; it may require a very modest capital commitment on the part of the operation. The anticipated return to any investor may only be reasonable: the investment is seen as less risky than a totally new venture. The original operation thus increases the productivity of its management, kitchen, kitchen personnel, and marketing expenditures. Greater overall profits result. In the United States, numerous small chains of restaurants, sometimes called family chains, have grown on this basis. Numerous other companies have attempted expansion for these purposes but have had disappointing results. The investment was not properly evaluated, or the management of the enterprise overestimated the capacity of its human and material resources.

"WISHFUL THINKING" APPROACH   The "wishful thinking" approach represents a common problem. Lack of information concerning market factors or operating costs, lack of judgment, or changes in fundamental factors between commitment to the enterprise and the doors' opening results in an operation that cannot be profitable. For example, the investment may be $250,000; at the present level of prices to patrons, volume and costs, the operation may only produce a net profit of $5,000, or 2 percent of the sum invested. By any standard, 2 percent is a poor return for a risky investment. The owner, of course, can attempt to increase the profits by increasing the volume; by increasing prices without losing customers; and by cutting costs, but these approaches are inherently limited. Closing the doors would mean sacrificing as much as 90 percent of the investment and still might entail continued lease obligations. Most owners continue to operate in the hope of some miraculous event. Others cut their losses and reason that the $25,000 or so salvaged from the enterprise and some tax benefit occasioned by the loss might be the foundation of a more viable enterprise. Some owners seek a working partner who will see the operation as a source of livelihood and, in effect, somewhat reduce the original owner's investment and labor costs.

PROFESSIONAL MANAGEMENT APPROACH   The professional management approach is a common foodservice industry business arrangement. An organization with funds available for investment and either the need for a foodservice operation or the expectation of profits—usually the former—arranges with a foodservice management company to operate a foodservice establishment. The foodservice management company may be compensated by a share of the profits: profits it could not otherwise have earned because of lack of capital. Or it may be paid a fee for operating the establishment. Both commercial and noncommercial organizations enter into these arrangements with commercial foodservice management companies. A construction company, a real estate company, or any other company with available funds or the ability to borrow buys land and builds a foodservice operation. A foodservice company, perhaps with other operations that it owns outright or franchises, then operates the facility.

ENTREPRENEURIAL APPROACH

Frequently, foodservice trade magazines report that an individual with an "extraordinary" product and a "fantastic" concept is attempting to follow the successful path of the largest present-day foodservice companies: from a single unit to a mammoth chain in 20 or 25 years. The present unit that the entrepreneur has developed is the prototype. If a major market segment patronizes it, the entrepreneur will expand the chain. Each successive unit will presumably show increased profitability as the operation is made more efficient and as economies of scale in purchasing, marketing, and construction can be effected.

Investment capital for additional units can be acquired in several ways. The foodservice company can grow through reinvestment of profits and strategic borrowing. The entrepreneur can invite investors to become partners or shareholders. Or, the entrepreneur can attempt to sell franchises. The first two methods are relatively slow compared to franchising. If the entrepreneur can convince other people that there is the possibility of great profit potential, the chain will grow very rapidly. Individuals who wish to own foodservice businesses will invest in individual units. The franchising company receives a franchise fee, royalties on the use of its name and ideas, and the profits on equipment and merchandise it can sell the franchisor. These funds can be used to promote other franchise sales or applied to the development of company-owned units.

BUSINESS MANAGEMENT APPROACH

Another approach is careful business management; present profits are the result of a search for investments, careful ranking of investment opportunities, financial planning, and effective operations management. In sum, results indicate a fully functioning business system in which all business objectives are realized. If the performance and business practices of this operation were examined from the perspective of a conservative lending institution, the operation would be rated highly. It would offer a satisfactory return on investment, a record of sustained growth as an enterprise, and performance statistics that would demonstrate that it was soundly financed, unburdened by excessive debt, wisely utilizing its funds, reinvesting profits prudently, and so on.

The business practices of noncommercial not-for-profit foodservice operations can also be characterized on the basis of their conformity to the business management model. Not-for-profit does not mean unprofitable. While personal monetary gain is not at the basis of business activity in a noncommercial foodservice operation, business objectives remain largely the same. "Profits," the surplus of revenues over expenses, could be used to finance better future facilities, or to repay lending institutions or private lenders. If the operation produces no surplus of revenues over expenses, or even if the operation has no cash transactions, there is still the need for effective business management.

Limits on the Business System   The business activities of a foodservice operation are conducted in circumstances that cannot always be manipulated to permit business objectives to be fully realized. For example, if in developing a foodservice operation, an entrepreneur wished a 20 percent return on investment, it should be possible to determine all the costs of doing business and to fix prices at a level that will result in a net profit that in absolute terms (in dollars) will meet this objective. Often, however, numerous factors intervene that may limit this possibility. Potential limits on the realization of business objectives can be categorized as follows: (1) market factors; (2) local economic conditions; (3) national economic conditions; and (4) government regulation.

MARKET FACTORS   The opportunity to offer a group of people, a market segment, a product that it wants is the beginning of any business enterprise. It is necessary, however, to recognize that this seemingly ideal relationship between an entrepreneur who wishes to produce and a consumer who is willing to buy is limited by the productive life of the consumer's patronage over a period of time.

When a foodservice operation ceases business, a large part of the investment made in it may not be recoverable. Perhaps the building and real estate can be sold, but equipment, fixtures, serviceware, decoration, and the like have little value. An operation in rented premises, unless it can be sold as a business, is worth a small fraction of the several hundred thousand dollars it may have cost to create to the purchasers of the used equipment. It is thus necessary to think in terms of both producing a satisfactory return on investment and recovering the investment over a period of time. A person who received 10 percent on an investment for 10 years but nothing at the end of 10 years is not "even." In a bank, the same investment would have earned interest of some amount and been returned in full at the end of 10 years.

With this perspective, it is evident that a foodservice operation expected to last five years has to produce a greater net profit each year than an operation expected to last ten years for investments in either operation to be equally attractive. The productive life of the operation is in large part determined by the market. Consumers tire of a foodservice operation; competitors enter the market; fundamental costs increase. Over a period of time, net profits may diminish. While it is possible to prolong the productive life of the operation, it may not be possible to reverse the trend. The original investment decision and the other activities of the business system during operations are affected by the prospect of the operation ceasing to be profitable after some definite period of time. For example, if a five-year "life" can be projected on the basis of market research, then the initial investment must be limited to that amount that can be recovered in five years at a satisfactory rate of return.

LOCAL ECONOMIC CONDITIONS

Operations X and Operation Y are identical in all respects as franchise units of a national chain. They have equally competent managers, identical facilities, menus, virtually identical markets, and the same dollar sales. They differ in one significant respect: they are located 800 miles apart at opposite ends of an interstate highway. Operation X is a profitable operation; Operation Y is a near-failure.

Business system objectives are achieved or not achieved because of local economic conditions as well as national economic factors that affect every enterprise. It could be reasonably presumed that Operation Y was more expensive to build than Operation X: construction costs vary radically across the United States. If the net profit were the same dollar amount in the case of both operations X and Y, it would be a much smaller percentage of the larger investment in Operation Y. It may cost Operation Y twice as much as Operation X for energy. Operation Y may be in a state that has a higher minimum wage than the federal minimum wage under which Operation X functions. It may not be possible for Operation Y to take a "tip credit," that is, a lowering of wages paid to less than minimum wage with the assumption that employees will earn the difference in gratuities. Operation Y, despite the best efforts of its fully competent management, may have a food cost considerably greater than that of Operation X which may be located near a major market terminus.

If these were the franchise units of a successful national company, it is likely that Operation Y would not have been built. A feasibility study would have included a projected set of operating figures based on accurate information about costs. The unsatisfactory performance of Operation Y would have been revealed. But it is equally possible that the owners of Operation Y, while correctly discerning the market appeal of a unit like Operation X in their own locality, were quite sure that it could not possibly fail as long as the customers liked the food.

A foodservice company is especially vulnerable to local economic conditions. A manufacturing company can frequently locate its production facilities in places that offer favorable economic conditions, inexpensive energy, labor, construction, and material costs, and then sell in any market. A foodservice company generally produces in the same area in which it markets. Consider the problems of an entrepreneur who chooses to locate in a wealthy suburban community because the people living there have enough disposable income to afford gourmet dinners. The wealth of the market has generated high construction costs, high taxes, and high rentals, eliminated the possibility of finding local workers, increased the cost of food by precluding the presence of wholesalers in the area, and so on. Although the consumers are willing to spend 12 dollars for dinner, they are not willing to spend 15 or 18 dollars per person. It is likely that the entrepreneur's investment will be 25 or 50 percent less productive in this enterprise than it would have been in a limited-menu take-out/take-in restaurant in another area. For each dollar of investment the entrepreneur will receive only 25 or 50 cents when he might have received a dollar.

NATIONAL ECONOMIC CONDITIONS

Business enterprises function as parts of the economy of the United States and, to some extent, the economy of the world. As such, the achievement of business system objectives is influenced by major economic events. For example, weather conditions can result in price rises for food commodities. Government actions can result in increased rates for the funds an enterprise wishes to borrow or for the alternative investments offered potential shareholders or partners. Government policies that cause inflation may prompt or discourage capital investment. National and international political arrangements can increase the cost of production factors such as fuel, beef, sugar, coffee, and produce.

While investment decisions can initially be made with some consideration of the national economic conditions that presently affect operations—and might potentially affect operations—it is extremely difficult to predict economic events over the life of an investment. As such, foodservice operations that are dependent on agricultural commodities —that in turn are subject to the vagaries of nature and the government— are planned and operated under conditions of uncertainty that increase their risk as investments.

GOVERNMENT REGULATION

Government regulation, whether it concerns social matters or the public health, influences business activities of a foodservice operation. Obviously, in those areas of the country with less stringent construction standards, less rigorous air pollution standards, and minimal esthetic standards for building design, it is less expensive to establish a foodservice operation that meets local legal requirements. Total investment can be reduced, or some additional sums may be diverted to marketing activities, interior decoration, or operations.

Government regulation also affects business activities directly. Trade practices are regulated to discourage unfair competition, price discrimination, false and misleading advertising, and false or inadequate labeling. Large foodservice franchising companies in particular are affected by regulations and judicial rulings with respect to contractual agreements for the purchase of products only from the franchisor, and the autonomy of the franchisee unit to change the operational format and menu. In general, the law has reduced the power of the franchisor to dictate to the franchisee.

The financing of foodservice operations is also subject to a body of legislation both on the state and federal levels. Franchising activities themselves may be regulated. Financing by offering the public shares in a company or corporate bonds is strictly controlled.

Likewise, tax regulation or labor practices regulation can affect the attainment of business objectives. For example, an upward change in the investment tax credit (a reduction in taxable income for a percentage of the monies invested in new construction or equipment) encourages capital investment. Heavier taxation on investment income may cause potential investors in a foodservice operation to seek tax-free investments such as municipal bonds.

As an economic entity such as a corporation or a partnership, the foodservice operation is also subject to regulations concerning its entrance into business associations that deliberately attempt to constrain business activity and competition; such associations may be in violation of antitrust laws.

As functioning businesses, foodservice operations are subject to the general restrictions of "business law"—embodied in the Uniform Commercial Code—concerning such matters as lease agreements, contracts, sale or purchase of property, debt agreements, and so on.

In effect, compliance with these diverse regulations is expensive, although many serve to protect the foodservice organization and formalize standards that foodservice operators support. Without considering the economic impact of regulations themselves, the time required to demonstrate compliance with government standards has a definite economic effect.

MANAGEMENT OF BUSINESS ACTIVITIES

Clearly, the business-related responsibilities of the management of a foodservice organization depend on the business objectives, financial and other resources, operating conditions and problems of that organization at a particular time. It is possible to consider foodservice organizations in which business management is little more than a control function and foodservice organizations in the developmental stage in which the generation of a functioning business enterprise dominates managerial activities.

There is a rough parallel between the intensity and scope of business-related managerial activities and the stature given individuals charged with managing the business system (however it is organized). At the early stages of the development of a foodservice organization, business management is the responsibility of the entrepreneur, the person who has conceived of the enterprise and is attempting to bring it into being. At the other extreme, in operations that neither have business problems nor are seeking business opportunities, for example, a university foodservice operation or a well-established restaurant, top management is more concerned with operations or marketing, and business activities are restricted to those tasks that can be accomplished by a clerical worker or bookkeeper. Normally, business management positions and the responsibilities that go with them correspond to the nature of the operation's business objectives. A number of titles of positions and their principal responsibilities are listed in Exhibit 12.1.

While a major foodservice company involved in a full range of business activities is likely to employ individuals in all these positions or maintain divisions with all these responsibilities, smaller operations either subsume business management under general management, assign specific responsibilities to one or two managers and consider the remainder as general management, or engage in more limited business activities that only require some general management attention and control. In the typical restaurant operation, the manager, who may also be an owner, functions as the entrepreneur, financial executive, treasurer, comptroller, and business manager with some assistance from outside consultants such as accountants, tax lawyers, and corporation lawyers, the advice of bankers and insurance agents, and the aid of bookkeepers and other clerical personnel. This arrangement restricts the scope of business activities and often compromises the attainment of business objectives. There is a limit to the amount a single manager can undertake along with his or her other operational and managerial responsibilities, in addition to the likelihood that an individual will not be competent in all areas of business activity. It has to be recognized as an "expedient" arrangement—since a small operation cannot afford a full business staff—but also as an arrangement that places the small operation at a distinct disadvantage in competing with large corporations. For example, major corporations are generally aware of their future cash needs (for replacement of equipment, operating expenses, and so on), and provide for them in the most economical fashion. The management of the small foodservice operation seldom projects cash requirements. Rather, managers react to a "cash crisis" and provide the necessary money, when they can, at a cost that might have been avoided.

Although the organization of the business system in a particular operation is influenced by the realities that confront it, it is possible to suggest the guidelines that effective business managers seek to follow and to describe the business activities from which particular systems are organized.

EXHIBIT 12.1   Positions and Responsibilities in Business Management

Entrepreneur	Functional owner of the enterprise, approaching all activities with a business perspective.
Financial Executive	Manager with operational (not merely advisory) responsibilities for business affairs. In effect, the financial executive has been delegated the purely business concerns of the entrepreneur.
Treasurer	A financial executive with only some operational responsibilities (in business areas); primarily concerned with external business activities, such as providing capital, investments, insurance.
Comptroller or Controller	A financial executive with (generally) only advisory responsibilities; primarily concerned with internal business activities.

"Business" Managers
   Budget Manager
   Tax Manager
   Internal Audit Manager
   Credit Managers
	Specialists working under either the treasurer or controller in charge of specific business activities.

Accountants Data Processing Manager Information "Systems" Manager	Specialists charged with managing and controlling specific procedures of business activities, accounting, preparation of financial statements, preparation of financial statistics.
Bookkeepers Accounting Clerks Payroll Clerks	Clerical workers involved in implementing procedures related to business activities.
Cashiers Timekeepers Receiving Clerks	Clerical workers of other systems whose jobs actively involve them in recording information to be used by the business system.

Business Management Guidelines

The business management of a foodservice organization can be conducted according to guidelines demonstrated to be appropriate to many business decisions. Effective business systems generally follow these fundamentals: (1) optimization of profits; (2) limitation of risk; (3) objectivity; (4) security; and (5) control.

OPTIMIZATION OF PROFITS

Return on investment and profits should be maximized in the long term, not the short term. The objective of the organization should be to make the most profit over the life of the investment. This can result in courses of action that sacrifice immediate profits for a greater long-term profitability, for example, a decision not to raise prices because the operation's only competitor has been closed by fire; or a decision to reinvest profits in equipment so that the productive capacity and eventual profits of the operation can be increased.

LIMITATION OF RISK   To the extent possible, business decisions should favor alternatives that have the most possibility of success. If two courses of action have an equal potential return (in dollars) but one has only a 50 percent chance of success and the other a 75 percent chance, then the surer course of action should be chosen.

Unfortunately, most alternative opportunities for investment or action require that the risks involved be calculated (objectively or subjectively) and that the potential pay-outs be estimated. Financial planning and some estimation of the effect of future events on the operation are necessary. The business system, in common with other management systems, must be active—not reactive—with regard to risk-taking if objectives are to be realized efficiently.

OBJECTIVITY   Business decisions should be made on an economic basis. Personalities, personal styles, and emotions should not intrude into investment decisions, capital budgeting, or any other business activity. For example, the decision to open another unit should be economically justifiable, not an effort to "combat" a competitor; decisions about equipment replacement should be made regardless of personal conflicts with the manager of the unit that would benefit. The need for objectivity does not preclude the use of subjective judgment in making economic decisions. An entrepreneur might be able to correctly evaluate the probability of an operation's success subjectively without being able to demonstrate it objectively. It is necessary to ensure that the subjective basis of the judgment is business related, not personal or emotional.

SECURITY   It is necessary to protect the organization against events unrelated to operational activities and conditions that would reduce profitability, the value of investments, the continuity of operations, and so on. For example, the operation must be protected against theft of cash, fraudulent conversion of assets, natural disasters, and forced cessation of business activities.

CONTROL   It is necesary to establish standards with which to measure, evaluate, and correct the performance of the business system. The effectiveness of any business activity can be formally addressed with the expectation of improving performance in the future.

Business
Management
Activities

The business activities of a foodservice operation can be arranged into six categories:

- Organizing the Business Enterprise: creating an economic entity that best corresponds to the organization's overall objectives.
- Financial Planning: discovering investment opportunities; evaluating investment opportunities; developing financial plans and budgets.
- Financing: developing sources of capital for investment; managing debt.
- Asset Management: inventory control; risk management; security.
- Cash Management: providing working capital; regulating cash inflow and out-flow.
- Profit Management: pricing; cost control; tax planning and administration.

ORGANIZING THE
BUSINESS
ENTERPRISE

Business organization can take a number of legal forms. The form of business organization has several implications for the performance of business activities: it establishes where the ultimate authority for business decisions lies; it describes the limitations on the operation's business activities; it subjects the organization to particular regulations and forms of taxation that can favor or inhibit the achievement of business objectives.

Single individuals and groups of individuals developing a foodservice enterprise can choose among different forms of business association. Typically, foodservice operations are organized as individual or sole proprietorships, partnerships, or corporations. Particular variations of these forms are tailored to the needs of the business by attorneys to limit the owners' liability (risk to individuals' property beyond the funds they have invested); ensure the continuity of the enterprise after the death or withdrawal of its originators; facilitate the provision of capital at the start of the business and during operations, and minimize the impact of taxation. Exhibit 12.2 summarizes the common advantages and disadvantages of the forms of business organization.

On any of these standard forms of business organization, a franchise can be imposed. There are implications on regulation and taxation of the enterprise, and both the ultimate authority for business decisions and the operation's business activities are affected. For example, a corporation that has become the franchisee of another company by contract with the franchisor may have obliged itself to invest specific sums, buy certain equipment, maintain a certain cash balance, and certainly to pay both fees and a continuing royalty to the franchisor. Obviously, these concessions and payments will be made for some consideration that the franchisee values: financial assistance, management training, the right to produce unique products, the use of trade names and trade marks,

EXHIBIT 12.2   Types of Business Organization: Advantages and Disadvantages

Advantages	Disadvantages	Comments
Individual or Sole Proprietorship		
Low start-up costs Comparatively greater freedom from regulation Owner in direct control Minimal working capital requirements Tax advantage to small owner All profits to owner	Unlimited liability Lack of continuity Difficult to raise capital	
Partnership		
Ease of formation Low start-up costs Additional sources of venture capital Broader management base Possible tax advantages Limited outside regulation	Unlimited liability Lack of continuity Divided authority Difficulty in raising additional capital Difficulty in finding suitable partners	Several variations of the partnership are possible. The *limited partnership* which is authorized in most states permits persons to contribute capital to an enterprise and avoid the unlimited liability of general partners. However, in some states limited partners cannot manage the operation. *Partnership associations* which are permitted in some states differ from the limited partnership in that all partners have limited liability.
Corporation		
Limited liability Permits separation of owners and managers Ownership transferrable Continuous existence Separate legal entity Possible tax advantages Easier to raise capital	Closely regulated Most expensive form to organize Charter restricts business activities Extensive record keeping necessary Corporation itself subject to taxation	Two variations of the corporation are common: *Sub-Chapter S* (of Internal Revenue Code) and *close* corporations. Sub-Chapter S avoids taxation of corporate income without loss of corporate advantages but with the loss of some flexibility. Close corporations through special charter and by-law clauses, shareholder agreements, irrevocable proxies, and voting trusts, restricted transferability of shares, limited power of directors, power of veto held by particular stockholders, eliminate those attributes of the traditional corporate form which are disadvantageous to small businesses owned by a few, perhaps related, individuals. Not-for-profit organizations can also be incorporated in some states, with special charter provisions that describe and limit their activities.

continuing services, and so on. Exhibit 12.3 summarizes the advantages of a franchise arrangement and points to some of the potential disadvantages.

Some foodservice managements have no choice with regard to business organization: the foodservice operation may be part of a larger organization, for example, the foodservices of a hotel or hospital. Ultimate authority for business decisions rests with the owners or managers of the larger organization. Or, the foodservice operation may be part of a government agency, for example, a school lunch program. The ultimate authority for business decisions, however they may be functionally delegated, rests with a legislative body of government.

FINANCIAL
PLANNING
Financial planning involves the manager in three distinct areas: (1) the development of investment opportunities; (2) capital budgeting: the best allocation of limited funds; and (3) developing budgets, that is, plans expressed in financial terms.

Development of Investment Opportunities

Some investments of a foodservice organization are mandated by operational conditions. It is necessary to replace equipment that is needed for production or service; it is necessary to reorganize physical facilities to meet government standards for public and worker health and safety. Other investments are made with the expectation of improving the business performance of the organization by allowing it to earn more revenues. Investments in this category generally take four avenues: the establishment of a new enterprise; the acquisition of another enterprise; the physical expansion of the existing enterprise; and increase in the variety of products being offered.

All four alternatives require planning. It is necessary to gather relevant information, develop alternative courses of action, apply some criteria to their evaluation—including some estimation of their probability of success—and make the decision.

The discovery and development of investment opportunities usually emerges from the "data collection" phase of the planning process. An entrepreneur intending to create a new foodservice operation starts with market research and "discovers" that while a market segment would enjoy fried chicken (or a mood-changing meal experience), it is only being offered hamburgers, pizza, and frankfurters. Likewise, a corporate financial officer seeking to strengthen the capital resources of the operation gathers information on the provision of capital by accepted methods and learns of a small chain with a great deal of cash that can be purchased cheaply from owners wishing to retire.

In addition, foodservice organizations learn of investment opportunities in informal ways. Executives and even nonmanagerial employees'

EXHIBIT 12.3   Advantages and Disadvantages of Franchise Arrangements

Advantages	*Disadvantages*
1. Capital investment is frequently less than is normally called for in a comparable non-franchise business because financial assistance is often available through the franchising company.	1. Franchisor fees, prices for supplies and other charges may be too high for local operation.
2. Working capital requirements are usually similarly reduced because of financial assistance and good inventory controls.	2. Franchisee loses some independence in conforming to the national pattern of operation.
3. A proved product or service can be offered with established public acceptance.	3. With a long-term franchise agreement, it could be difficult and expensive to cancel.
4. Inexperience and limited education are less of a handicap with management assistance provided by the franchisor.	4. The franchisor's field representatives may be slow to adapt their methods to meet local conditions.
5. The better franchising companies provide management assistance on a continuing basis in financing, record keeping, advertising, marketing, and product promotion.	5. The franchisee may lose opportunities because of the need to conform to standardized procedures.
6. The franchisee can usually expect good profit margins because the whole operation is run with chain-like efficiency.	6. Franchisor may prove excellent at selling franchises and equipment to franchisees but the product may not meet market standards. Operational procedures, marketing, and so on, may be deficient.
7. The management services of a large enterprise are provided in the initial choice of location, design of facilities.	7. Franchisor may not have a viable enterprise and may go out of business.
8. There may be economic advantages because of combined purchasing, cooperative advertising, national recognition.	8. Procedures and marketing activities which benefit the franchisor (and other franchisees) may not benefit the individual operator.

heightened awareness of the organization's objectives prompts them to identify investment opportunities. The manager of a hamburger restaurant is constantly—consciously or unconsciously—looking for "potential" locations. Bankers, suppliers, other businesspersons, the creators of new products, and potential candidates for merger or acquisition can make the organization aware of investment opportunities.

Capital Budgeting

No organization or individual has enough funds or can obtain enough funds to take advantage of every investment opportunity or make every possible investment to replace equipment or improve operations. It is thus necessary to choose investments or allocate funds according to some criterion, in other words, to budget capital. Unless cessation of business activity is a reasonable alternative (bankruptcy or dissolution of the organization), those investments necessary to the continuance of the operation have first priority. If the operation's ventilation system is in violation of the law, then it must be replaced; if the roof has collapsed, then it must be repaired. If urgency and necessity do not establish investment priorities, then, in most cases, organizations rank investments or make investment decisions on the basis of their potential return to the operation.

If funds are committed to some effort or purchase, they must be borrowed or otherwise financed, or withdrawn from some other revenue-producing use. For example, a restaurant owner wishing to construct a banquet room may borrow the money needed from a bank or other lender and pay interest on the loan, or may withdraw money from a savings account where it is earning interest. The benefits the operator hopes to gain from the project must either exceed the interest that will have to be paid or exceed the interest that would have been earned. Other methods of financing which might be considered also have their costs. At a minimum, standard investments would have to meet these criteria.

If several different avenues for the allocation of funds are present (there is seldom a situation in which several are not present), and they all meet these minimum criteria, then, as would be expected, the organization would seek to fund those investments that offered the most return. It becomes necessary to calculate the benefits or return from different investment opportunities. An organization might be choosing among opportunities to schedule more advertising, purchase additional equipment to improve productivity, open an additional unit, purchase a food processing plant, and so on.

There are mathematical techniques useful in making any of these decisions. These techniques place some "time value" on money: an investment of X dollars today that returns X dollars at some time from now has effectively returned less than X dollars because in the intervening period interest has been paid on the investment or interest could have been earned on the investment. Other specific mathematical decision techniques help evaluate the tax implications of an investment: the method by which the government assesses tax can encourage or discourage specific investments. Accounting procedures can also evaluate the effect of the investment on the amount of cash the operation will have available at various times during the life of the investment.

None of these techniques deals directly with an important factor in the investment decision: uncertainty. In the simplest instance, it is possible for an entrepreneur to determine exactly the *rate of return* (by one mathematical technique) or the *payback period* (by another) of an investment in a new unit, if it can be presumed that operating expenses will be some exact amount and that revenues will be some exact amount. Likewise, a piece of equipment could be said to pay for itself in exactly so many years if its useful life, productivity, operating costs, and need for repairs could be predicted exactly. Of course, there is no way of predicting these future events with absolute surety. The entrepreneur cannot be assured that costs will not rise, that productivity of the new operation will be the same as the original, or that it will have as great market acceptance. The factor of risk has to be introduced. Some estimation of the probability of success influences the investment decision. A more risky investment should have a greater return (however it is calculated) than a less risky investment.

The probability of success (projections being accurate) is determined objectively or subjectively. Although no one would assert that the process is completely objective, a large foodservice organization with many units, because of the accuracy of its basic information, can statistically assess the risk of a new venture. An entrepreneur with no statistically validated information is likely to rely on personal judgment. The entrepreneur may also forego elaborate mathematical calculations, which are time-consuming and expensive, because their results will be based on projections that are recognized as problematical.

The entrepreneur and other managers of small foodservice organizations often arrive at some ranking of investment opportunities on a qualitative basis. The entrepreneur may try to envision the worst eventuality likely in the situation. If the worst possible scenario still has an acceptable return, the entrepreneur may undertake the venture.

Capital budgeting in foodservice cannot be as neat as the theoretical models for mathematical calculation suggest it should because of both the absence of extensive and meaningful data and the uncertain conditions that face most operations. More information gathered over a long period of time may improve this process, especially if the operation is large enough to afford to commission sophisticated quantitative analyses of the alternative opportunities for investment.

Developing Budgets

A budget presents proposed expenditures for specific items such as labor, laundry service, or liquor. It can also present projected revenues from those operational areas that produce them. Although it is possible to develop one single master budget, it is more practical to budget for specific operational areas or categories of expenses. A manager might develop a budget for sanitation and warewashing that would include such budget items as proposed expenditures for mops, rinse agent, and dish-scrapers.

As such, budgets serve several purposes in financial planning:

• Budgets are plans. The amount budgeted for sanitation and warewashing is the result of some decision process that weighed alternatives and arrived at the best course of action.

• Budgets are forecasts. The budgets prepared by operational managers are projections of anticipated expenditures. A financial planner can consolidate these forecasts and arrive at some determination of the future expenditures of the operation. Future expenditures can be compared with projected revenues and financial plans made for financing, if expenditures will exceed revenues, or investing, if revenues considerably exceed expenditures. Capital budgeting can be predicated on these projections.

• Budgets are control devices. The allocation of resources that budgets propose can be evaluated and changes made in individual budgets to respect overall organization priorities.

• Budgets are operational standards. In addition to being a forecast, budgets indicate the amount of expenditure that is acceptable.

• Budgets are evaluation devices. They allow ready review of performance by permitting comparison with the standards they establish.

The managers of an operation may prepare any number of operationally relevant budgets for these purposes. It is also customary to prepare financial budgets predicting cash-flow: the future cash position of the operation can be assessed by comparing expected receipts with expected payments at definite moments. Formal financial statements—such as profit and loss statements or balance sheets—that generally are used to report past business performance can serve budgeting purposes if the figures they present are used to project future business performance. For example, in determining whether a foodservice operation is feasible as an investment, a profit and loss statement may be projected so that estimated revenues can be compared with estimated costs and expenses. If the surplus of revenues over costs and expenses, the net profit, is not satisfactory, the investment plan must be reevaluated.

FINANCING   The creation of a foodservice operation and the expansion and continuance of an existing operation require capital: funds to be invested in the enterprise. Four methods are generally used to supply the capital needed: borrowing, leasing, equity financing, and internal financing. As a business management activity, financing implies more than the mere provision of capital. It is equally necessary to provide a sound financial structure for the enterprise without compromising either organizational objectives or the personal objectives of the operation's owners.

It is possible to supply the operation with adequate capital though ultimately to compromise its viability as a business organization. An operation may have an unsound financial structure because the terms of a loan were extremely disadvantageous to the operation. It is also possible that the entrepreneur projected profits poorly by overestimating revenues or underestimating costs. In creating an enterprise, the promoter may simply have made a faulty judgment. In expanding an enterprise, for example, from one unit to two, the entrepreneur may have presumed that market acceptance for the second unit would equal that of the first and that costs would remain constant. Depending on the terms of the financing, if the second operation is only 80 percent, or 90 percent, or 99 percent as successful (in dollar volume) as the first, there may be a problem. Likewise, depending on the terms of the financing, if costs increase only 5 percent, or 2 percent, or 1 percent, there may be a problem.

A recession, which reduces the amount people spend, or an increase in the minimum wage, which increases costs, demonstrates the fragility of the financial structure of numerous enterprises. Modest changes in revenues or costs make them unable to survive. It is said metaphorically that such events "burn out the underbrush"—presumably leaving the solidly structured financial "tall trees" standing. Seemingly successful operations do not survive. A restaurant or a chain of restaurants can be famous, jammed with customers, lauded by magazines, loved by speculative investors who want to buy stock in an apparent winner, but financially vulnerable.

An operation that is poorly financed need not collapse, but the alternatives available to its owners may not be wholly satisfactory. Faced with payments that cannot be made, the owners may attempt to refinance the operation. Another loan on different terms is made; the first loan is repaid. The second loan allows more modest monthly payments but it may be at a higher rate of interest for a longer period of time. After 15, 25, or 50 years (the time is determined by arrangement between the parties concerned), the owners may find themselves with a completely debt-free enterprise but one that has returned nothing to them during the interim period and is now at the end of its productive life with very little likelihood of producing much in the future or of being sold for very much.

The owners of the enterprise may choose to solve the financing problem by inviting other persons to join them as owners—as partners or as shareholders in a corporation. The original owners' 100 percent ownership of the enterprise is reduced by the participation of other investors. An individual who owns an enterprise and sells half either to finance its expansion or to refinance its debt now has a half-share of the enterprise and a half-share of any future gains to be made. His control of the enterprise is also diminished. Possibly, other objectives than those of the original owners intrude on plans for the operation: suppose new investors favor pocketing all profits while the original owner wishes to reinvest any surplus so that the enterprise will continue to grow.

Numerous other problems resulting from poor financing can be described. Any of the financing methods discussed below, when poorly managed, brings problems along with needed capital. On the other hand, a carefully planned and evaluated financing program based on accurate current information and sound future projections provides the capital needed for prosperity and growth without weakening the financial structure of the organization.

Borrowing

Individuals and business organizations will allow the foodservice enterprise to use sums of money in return for some consideration. The individual or organization does not share in the ownership of the enterprise or in the rights of ownership, such as the right to a share of its profits, but expects payment of interest for the use of the money lent and return of the original sum. There are two common borrowing arrangements: unsecured borrowing and secured borrowing.

Unsecured borrowing   In the various forms of unsecured borrowing, the individual or organization borrowing money agrees to pay the money back with interest, according to some agreed-upon payment schedule. Individuals, banks, investment companies, insurance companies, finance companies, and government agencies are sources of unsecured loans. The lender evaluates the enterprise's ability to meet the loan's terms by evaluating the company's present position, its future profit position, its plans for the money, the extent of its indebtedness, and the capabilities of its management according to criteria particular to the lender. An individual wishing to charge 24 percent interest on lent money will have different criteria than a pension fund or a conservative bank. There are a number of different loan instruments—accepted general forms of terms and conditions—loan agreements, promissory notes, and debentures. A *loan agreement* is a formal contract that stipulates the terms of the loan and describes the obligations of the creditor and the debtor. For example, a debtor usually agrees to pay off the interest on the loan before payments can reduce the principal. A *promissory note* is a written promise to pay a sum of money on demand or on a certain date. It is a convenient method for financing short-term debt; for example, a company may issue a note to cover the cost of new inventory items. A *debenture* is an unsecured bond backed only by the credit of the issuer. Only corporations with excellent credit can secure additional funds this way. As such, debentures are not a form of financing available to small operations run by a sole proprietor or a few partners.

The management of the enterprise borrows the money anticipating that it can be used to produce more money than it costs to borrow. The lender provides the money because it seems a productive use of funds. Although the lender has an interest in controlling the activities of the enterprise so that the loan can be repaid according to the terms and may make the loan conditional on some participation in the management of the company, borrowing leaves the enterprise's management with more flexibility than would selling of partial ownership. On the other hand, borrowing confronts the management with payments that may start immediately; lenders, unlike owner-investors, do not have to weather economic reversals with the enterprise. Overborrowing can thus severely stress an organization's financial structure by reducing the amount of money it has available for other purposes.

Secured borrowing   It may be unacceptable to the lenders to provide capital simply on the enterprise's promise to pay. Lenders may lack confidence in the future of the enterprise or in management's ability to achieve investment objectives. The loans are then made against some collateral that will be available to satisfy the loan if the enterprise cannot pay it. The most common form of a secured loan is a mortgage secured by property. If the enterprise is unable to pay the loan, then the property, which may be a piece of equipment or real estate, is sold to satisfy the loan. Equally important, this property is safeguarded against being sold to satisfy other loans until the first is satisfied. Other forms of secured loans result in *liens* against investments in other companies or in a claim on the general assets of the company in the event that the enterprise ceases to do business and assets are sold.

Another common foodservice industry method of securing a loan is the conditional sale contract: the supplier of a piece of equipment retains title to the equipment until all provisions of the sale agreement are fulfilled by the enterprise. This arrangement differs from the mortgage in that the lender retains ownership of the property until the sale is completed. It is generally easier to reclaim the property than it is to wait for the formal process of foreclosure to transfer the title of property from the enterprise to the mortgage holder.

Leasing

The value of leasing depends largely on the financial structure of the company. Obviously, it must provide a better way of financing than any other method, supply the operation with capital it cannot otherwise provide, or free capital for some more productive use for it to be worthwhile. As such, a leasing arrangement must be compared with the operation's other alternatives. The most important decision factors are the operation's solvency at various times and the impact of leasing or not leasing on taxes the operation will pay. Lease rentals are fully deductible expenses from revenues. On the other hand, the operation can, by a variety of methods with different tax implications, deduct sums of money for depreciation, the reduction in value that occurs during the life of an asset. For example, a stove bought today is worth less in a year. The difference between those two sums represents the "expense" of the stove over the year. This sum offsets some revenues, reduces the profits subject to taxes, and may make the purchase of facilities and equipment more advantageous than leasing for some operations.

There are various forms of leasing. Regular or straight leases simply provide for the rental agreement, presumably at a cost low enough to induce the enterprise to enter the agreement and yet high enough to make the investment satisfactory for the leasing company. Modified lease forms allow the enterprise to terminate the lease before it is completed or permit the purchase of the leased property at some time. Leasing arrangements are made by manufacturers, suppliers, or owners of the property or by financial institutions such as banks or specialized capital-leasing firms. In these latter instances, the operation will make all the investment decisions and simply finance the purchase through the leasing arrangement. It is also possible for an operation to sell an asset it owns, for example, land, to a leasing company and then lease it back. For example, a foodservice company that owns land and wishes to construct a restaurant can perhaps finance its construction costs by selling the land and leasing it back.

Equity Financing

The owners of an existing or proposed foodservice company may feel that they will gain if other persons invest in the operation, thereby providing it with capital but necessarily sharing in the ownership. In a simple instance, if the owners of a restaurant are receiving $10,000 a year for their investment but feel that with a $100,000 additional investment the enterprise will produce a return of $30,000, they can afford to sell a half-share to someone for $100,000. They will then receive $15,000 (one-half of $30,000) and the new investor and half-owner will receive $15,000. That their original investment was more or less than $100,000 is irrelevant: they expect to gain by reducing their ownership. Of course, the result of selling an interest in the enterprise is a proportionate diminution of control. The new owners have the same rights as the original owners to direct the business to the extent of their ownership.

For most foodservice companies, equity financing is achieved by the sale of an interest in the enterprise to friends, relatives, creditors, or patrons. The foodservice enterprise is not substantial enough to interest individuals or organizations that do not have intimate knowledge of it and its owners and do not share some enthusiasm for the venture. Other foodservice companies may attract more objective investors. The company may be large enough or in operation long enough to demonstrate strong financial performance; it may occupy a unique market position or have unique products; it may be a competitor to another company; it may allow another company to enter a new market area or provide another company with cash at a time when it needs it. The foodservice company may also be managed or owned by individuals who can succeed in "promoting" the future performance so effectively that investors are attracted by its prospects. Any of these reasons, and some others, may prompt investment by individuals, banks, insurance companies, large industrial companies, pension funds, or the general public. Numerous foodservice companies are now at least partially owned by major industrial corporations or agribusinesses. Others are "traded" at stock exchanges or over the counter. Shares in these companies are available to whoever wishes to purchase them, if there is a person willing to sell. In many instances, the original owners have retained an interest in the company, still own shares of it, or have traded their original ownership for shares of the company that acquired the enterprise.

Internal Financing

The capital needs of most enterprises already in operation are financed internally from either retained earnings or depreciation.

It is not necessary for an enterprise to directly pay its owners the surplus remaining after all other obligations, including loans, are satisfied. These earnings can be "plowed back" into the enterprise so that it may purchase equipment, expand its operations, or pursue any other investment objective. The owners are trading the present use of the money for personal purposes against some supposed greater gain in the future.

Depreciation creates another source of internal financing. A piece of equipment, for example, starts out at 100 percent of purchase value and progressively declines in value until it is worthless (or worth very little) and has to be replaced. Each year, as an accounting procedure, the amount of this decline in value offsets some profits and thus becomes available for investment. Since profits are being reduced, and the organization must pay taxes on its profits, the methods of depreciation and the useful life of the equipment are prescribed by law. It is possible, within the law, to use different acceptable methods of calculation, so that the operation realizes the full investment potential of its depreciation.

The financing of foodservice operations that are part of larger organizations such as the foodservice operations of a hotel or hospital might be considered on these same bases. Commercial operations view investment in an "internal" operation from the same perspective as any other investment: they perceive little difference between opening a restaurant in a motel and building another motel or another restaurant. Financing may be by borrowing, leasing, equity financing, retained earnings (from the larger operation), or any combination of these methods. As an investment, the foodservice operation is expected to produce a surplus of revenues over expenses that adequately compensates the parent organization.

Noncommercial operations typically are financed initially by their parent organizations. Although a hospital may use government funds and loans from bondholders to build the facility, a specific financing effort rarely is directed to the foodservice operation. Further financing requirements of the operation may be supplied by continued subsidies from the sponsoring organization or by retained earnings and depreciation. In calculating patient bills, the hospital may include a charge for "hotel services" that is in excess of the actual, immediate cost of those services. This surplus provides funds for investment in additional equipment, expansion of facilities, or replacement of equipment. The employees in a factory, although receiving meals at less than commercial prices, may be paying something in excess of costs to provide a surplus on investment.

ASSET MANAGEMENT   Asset management and financial planning in the broadest sense overlap in the area of capital budgeting. Capital is defined as an asset, that is, something of worth that the operation owns. A more limited perspective suggests activities that are more relevant to actual operations. An operation that is not seeking investment possibilities differs in perspective, if not in substance, from an operation that is involved in the development of funds to commit to new investment opportunities.

It is also possible to consider cash management as asset management: cash is an asset. However, cash requires a special kind of management to be described later.

Asset management principally concerns five areas: inventory, receivables, equipment, security, and risk management.

Management of Inventory

The use of money to buy products and store them withdraws these funds from a productive use and makes them unavailable for any other purpose. As such, an investment in inventory must be justified by earnings greater than its cost. For example, the expectation that the price will rise rapidly would justify buying as much beef as a steak house could store even if it meant borrowing money to do so.

Chapter 9 more fully discusses principles of inventory management that can be applied to maintain inventories at the minimum acceptable level.

Management of Receivables

The management of receivables is the balancing of conflicting needs: to extend credit because of marketing imperatives; to maintain solvency;

to ensure reimbursement; and to maintain and improve the operation's financial performance.

Not all foodservice transactions are in cash, although certainly the bulk of restaurant transactions are. Extending credit and making collections are important parts of business for social catering operations, commissaries, vending machine companies, and contract feeding companies. Some restaurants maintain house accounts, and other restaurants allow customers to use commercial or bank credit cards.

A large sum outstanding can present a foodservice operation with problems; it may make it impossible to meet obligations to purveyors and workers. Meeting its obligations may involve expensive short-term borrowing. In any case, even if the operation has sufficient cash on hand for its own obligations, the outstanding amount represents a loss of the opportunity to use that money during the length of time it is owed. If a company with small profit margins is owed a large sum for a long time, the interest paid on the money borrowed to pay its other obligations can eliminate the enterprise's profit or create a loss. For example, ultra-chic restaurants often extend generous credit to their upper-class patrons almost as a marketing prerequisite. Although ultimately most of the wealthy people who owe money to the operation pay, they may pay slowly. In a relatively short time, an operation can become indebted for $50,000 in food and supplies while $75,000 from good patrons remains outstanding. Although the money is collectible, the patrons cannot be badgered by the operation or a collection agency, nor can the operation sell the accounts due it, at a discount, to a third party. Yet, banks and other lenders are reluctant to finance $50,000 which is only secured by rather informal agreements with patrons. The operation's suppliers may continue to finance it by extending its credit, but their terms usually include disadvantageous prices as well as interest. Other sources of money understandably consider the loan risky and charge commensurate interest.

To avoid dilemmas of this sort, operations are careful in extending credit and careful in monitoring the amount they owe. Or, they may not directly extend credit, but may ask their patrons to seek it elsewhere. A vending company, mobile food company, or franchise company may not extend credit to the individuals who own the vending machines, trucks, or foodservice units. Rather, the company may abandon this potentially productive use of its capital and have the owner/operators seek outside financing.

Commercial restaurants may ask their customers or guests to use credit cards. In contrast to payment in cash, when a patron uses his or her credit card, the enterprise loses the use of the money for a period of time until the credit card company reimburses the operation. In addition, an operation pays a service charge of several percent (up to 7 percent) on the amount charged to the company. Since the net profit (as a percentage of sales) of the operation may be only 6 or 7 percent, a great many sales by credit card can create problems.

Equipment Management

As food production equipment becomes more sophisticated and costly, purchase decisions and replacement decisions require a business perspective as well as a work-system or production-system perspective. The acquisition of a new machine or the replacement of an old machine with a newer and better machine may reduce operating costs and ease production, but is it good business? Only if there is an overall financial gain to the operation—not just immediate gain in one area—should the purchase be made. In a simple instance, a machine that costs the operation $1,000 a month in interest, payments, and operating costs—or lost opportunity to invest the money—but saves only $500 in labor would not be a good investment.

However, decisions about equipment cannot be made by simple mathematical computation. A number of factors complicate decision making. By some method the true impact of the machine on profits must be calculated. In most instances, the underlying data for this calculation are deficient: most operations do not maintain accurate performance information about their work systems. It is also necessary to compare ways of obtaining the machine, different methods of financing, and leasing with different options. Each of these methods can have a variety of tax implications if the options for calculating tax treatment of capital investment, interest, and depreciation are taken into account. In addition, salvage value of the machine and the relative cost of replacing it now or later must be evaluated.

In sum, if the equipment is at all costly, critical estimates have to be made in several areas, and many factors have to be weighed. As this is not a problem unique to the foodservice industry—although generally the foodservice enterprise has been too small and equipment too inexpensive to encounter this problem—a number of formal methods that have been developed for use in other industries may prove valuable in foodservice equipment management. The most widely used is the method developed by the Machinery and Allied Products Institute (MAPI). Through the use of special forms and charts which have to be obtained from the institute, it is possible to measure the impact of an equipment purchase on company profits. Any method of calculation, of course, depends on accurate data.

Security Management

The assets of a foodservice operation must be protected by measures combating a wide variety of internal and external threats. There is a need for physical security such as locked doors and alarm systems; accountability such as that provided by a food and beverage control system; and security preventive maintenance such as effective check-cashing procedures. The vulnerabilities of the typical foodservice operation are presented in the list below—which is by no means exhaustive:

- employee theft of equipment or products.
- employee misuse of equipment or food products.
- embezzlement (theft of assets by a person entrusted with them).
- robbery.
- burglary.
- acceptance of bad checks or counterfeit currency.
- acceptance of stolen or counterfeit credit cards.
- theft of service (failure of a customer to pay).
- purveyor and supplier fraud (short weights on products delivered, overbilling, delivery of substandard products).
- extortion (demands for money with threats of violence).
- shoplifting.

Security management for the protection of assets is obviously not the sole responsibility of the managers of the business system, but the responsibility of every manager as a business manager.

Risk Management

Foodservice operations encounter two kinds of risk to assets: speculative risk and pure risk. Business decisions involve speculative risk that is based on some estimation of the possibility of gain and the possibility of loss during uncertain future conditions. Management, in all its dimensions, is an effort to exercise some control over the degree of speculative risk in any course of action.

Pure risk describes the possibility of occurrence of an unforeseen event that can cause only loss or no loss and no possibility of gain. Management's responsibility is to protect the operation from the harsh consequences of chance events such as fire, accidents, and theft. To ward off such consequences, the managers of companies attempt to trade a large but uncertain loss for a small but certain loss: they buy insurance (paying a premium, the small loss) to protect against calamitous events that may occasion large losses. As such, the risk is partially avoided. Exhibit 12.4 summarizes the coverage and limitations of the main types of insurance purchased by foodservice operations.

Although it is possible for a large foodservice organization to "self-insure" against losses, most foodservice organizations and most industrial companies purchase insurance against major losses from insurance companies. The choice of company theoretically is made on some evaluation

EXHIBIT 12.4   Coverage and Limitations of the Main Types of Insurance

Fire Insurance

Basic fire insurance is standardized throughout the United States.

Covers:
Fire
Lightning
Losses of goods temporarily removed because of fire

Most business extend basic coverage to other perils: windstorm; hail; explosion; riot; riot attending a strike; civil commotion; aircraft damage; vehicle damage; smoke damage.

Policy excludes:
Theft
Actions resulting from war or orders of civil authority
Negligence by the insured
Losses such as bills, money, securities, profits lost because of fire

Liability Insurance (other than auto)

Basic coverage against negligence liability in the event customers, employees, or other persons doing business are injured and demonstrate that the degree of care required under the circumstances was lacking.

Covers:
Liability judgments or other sums which the operation becomes legally obligated to pay because of bodily injury or damage to property of others that is caused accidentally.

Expenses incurred for whatever immediate medical and surgical relief to others is necessary at the time of an accident.

Costs of defending suits alleging bodily injury or property damage.

Expenses in investigation, defense, or settlement of an accident.

Costs of court bonds or interest on judgment accruing during the appeal period.

Policy excludes:
Obligations under worker's compensation laws (see below)
Damage to property of others in care, custody, and control
Liability resulting from blasting operations, from war, from the operation of state liquor laws, and
   from mishaps involving nuclear energy

Also, liability policies may limit payments to insured parties.

Automobile Liability Insurance

Basic principles of liability insurance apply to the liability of businesses that may be incurred in owning and maintaining or using an automobile. Business firms are often legally liable for the use of trucks and passenger cars even though they do not own any. This happens when an employee or a subcontractor uses a personal car on behalf of the employer.

Workers' Compensation and Employer Liability Insurance

Statutory law requires that an employer provide employees with a safe place to work; hire competent fellow employees; warn employees of any existing danger. If the employer fails in these duties, liability for damage suits—under statutory law and workers' compensation law—is incurred.

Under a workers' compensation and employers' liability policy, the insurer pays all sums the business is legally obligated to pay because of common law liability and all compensation and other benefits the applicable compensation law requires to be provided.

State law determines the kinds of benefits payable under workers' compensation policies: usually, medical care, lump sums for dismemberment and death, benefits for disability from occupational disease, and income payments.

Fidelity Bonds

Fidelity bonds protect the business against theft by employees. Requiring that employees be bonded often discourages stealing that might otherwise occur. Three types are common: *individual* covering a named person; *schedule* listing all names or positions to be covered; *blanket* covering all employees without identifying them by name or position.

Blanket bonds may have an aggregate limit that applies to any one loss or to each employee.

Surety Bonds

Surety bonds guarantee that the principal (the person or firm that is being bonded) will carry out, according to plan, the work the operation has engaged the principal to do.

Crime Insurance

Crime insurance of various kinds protects the business against criminal activities committed by persons not connected with the business. Types available are burglary insurance, robbery insurance, and various comprehensive policies that cover all risks including money lost in fire, sneak thievery, forgery, counterfeiting, and so on.

All-Risk Physical Damage Policies

This type of policy can be written to cover all perils whether named in a policy or not, instead of insuring against specific perils such as fire, windstorm, riot, and so on.

Business Interruption Insurance

Indirect or "consequential" losses are frequently more severe in their eventual costs than are direct losses from such perils as fire. Business interruption insurance (in the form of an endorsement attached to a standard fire policy) covers this situation.

EXHIBIT 12.4   Coverage and Limitations of the Main Types of Insurance (cont.)

Power Plant Insurance

The standard fire policy generally excludes explosions of furnaces, steam boilers, engines, and electrical equipment. This policy extends that coverage.

Glass Insurance

A comprehensive glass policy is advised for most firms. It provides all-risk on glass—excluding only fire, war, and nuclear destruction. Property covered includes plate glass windows, glass signs, glass bricks, showcases, glass doors, and countertops.

Rent Insurance

Several different kinds of rent insurance cover loss of real property damaged by fire or other peril. For example, if the lease calls for continued payments even if a fire makes a building uninhabitable, coverage can be obtained for this loss. *Leasehold interest* insurance covers the higher rent that has to be paid for comparable quarters elsewhere. Rental value insurance covers losses of permanent improvements made to a leased premises.

of the financial stability of the insurer, its ability to provide coverage exactly tailored to the operation's needs, and the relative cost of coverage. In practice, the choice of insurer is largely influenced by the insurance salespersons with whom the operation's management is in contact. They may be either *independent agents* representing several different insurance companies, or *direct writers* employed by a single company. It is possible for a foodservice operation to deal successfully with either type of representative. The independent agent offers the convenience of making many types of insurance available from one source, better claims representation because the independent is working for the client, not the company, and perhaps a broader knowledge of the needs of a foodservice company. On the other hand, direct writers may be able to provide more economical insurance, extra services because central administration relieves them of routine clerical tasks, and the service of specialists in reducing the risk of loss. There may be very little basis of choice for a particular operation except the subjective evaluation of the knowledge, attentiveness, helpfulness, and service of the insurance agents with whom the operation will deal.

CASH MANAGEMENT   Cash management presents special problems for business managers.

- It is necessary to provide for the cash requirements of the operation when it is opened and during its operation.

- It is necessary to use the cash the operation controls effectively.
- It is necessary to safeguard the cash resources of the operation effectively.

The activities directed toward the accomplishment of these goals include the provision of working capital; cash utilization; and the custody of cash.

Provision of Working Capital

Even a profitable foodservice operation does not always generate sufficient funds from sales to meet its current obligations. For example, a foodservice operation that has just opened has extra expenses and, likely as not, modest revenues in its first weeks. It may be necessary to build inventories, pay workers, meet payments, purchase minor equipment, and perhaps meet obligations that remain from the construction period at a time when business volume is only a small fraction of the volume the business will achieve. The operation may be subject to seasonal variations in business volume: expenses may continue while revenues slacken. The operation's patrons may be slow in paying: for example, the operation may supply a government agency with food services on contract. Payments may be subject to administrative procedures that delay them several months. If the operation is growing, funds may be needed for expansion. The sale of several more vending accounts requires that a vending company purchase additional machines; it may be possible for an operation to buy on advantageous terms, if it can pay the seller immediately.

Any of these situations can cause a need for funds from other sources than current revenues. In many instances, working capital to fulfill this need is part of the original investment in the operation. Besides financing construction and equipment purchases, the investors have planned for the cash needs of the operation and provided the funds.

Revenues and expenses can be projected and the cash flow estimated. If cash in-flow does not equal (or exceed by some comfortable margin) cash out-flow, then funds have to be provided. However, the provision of working capital from outside sources increases the cash out-flow of the operation at the time the loans must be repaid. In addition to providing working capital, an operation's management must also carefully regulate this changing in-flow and out-flow so that the operation continues to have enough cash to meet its obligations. Planning, most often in the form of a cash budget for various periods of time, is quite as important as actually providing working capital at a particular moment. There are several commonly used methods of providing working capital: trade credit, bank loans, and "commercial paper."

Trade credit   Trade credit is the credit extended by a supplier to a buyer for goods purchased. It may be made available to the operation by prearrangement at some rate of interest, but often it is made available as part of the buying transaction. For example, an operation may be billed $1,000 with terms of 2/10, net 30. If the invoice is paid in 10 days, only $980 or 2 percent less than $1,000 has to be paid. If it is paid after 10 days but within 30 days, the full sum will have to be paid. Credit has been extended for 20 days at a cost of 2 percent; on an annual basis this amounts to an interest rate of 36 percent. Sometimes the cost of credit to the seller is hidden in the price of the merchandise. Foodservice purveyors often have several price lists: one for operations that pay promptly, another, higher priced list, for those that do not.

Bank loans   Banks offer several different types of loans for financing working capital, as well as for long-term capital needs described earlier. The most common type is the simple commercial loan. The operation borrows funds for from 30 to 90 days, usually on the basis of its financial statements, and without any security. As revenues increase to meet obligations, these loans are paid. Typically, inventory and seasonal activities are financed in this fashion.

It is also possible to finance working capital with installment loans. Payments are made monthly but can be adjusted to take into account the months when inventories must be increased or the off-peak months in a seasonal business.

Frequently, foodservice operations have an understanding with a bank to provide short-term funds as they are needed so long as the total amount of the loan does not exceed an agreed-upon maximum. This arrangement is called a *line of credit*. As money is needed, management uses its line of credit at its discretion to acquire the necessary funds. The bank charges interest on the sum lent and retains the right to refuse credit if the operation no longer seems creditworthy.

Commercial paper   Large foodservice organizations with good financial reputations are able to sell unsecured promissory notes to financial institutions or specialists in this type of financial device. These notes can then be sold to other institutions or individuals. Most often they mature in three to six months.

Cash Utilization

The concomitant of providing working capital for those periods when the operation needs it is utilizing cash effectively when the operation has it. Cash planning and budgeting can reveal periods when revenues exceed current expenditures by significant sums. During these periods cash can be placed in interest-earning, short-term investments such as U.S. Treasury bills, certificates of deposit offered by banks, and the commercial paper of other enterprises.

It is also possible to use available cash to retire loans if this is in accord with the terms of the agreement and if better financing is available for future capital needs. Most obviously, it is possible to use cash to take advantage of trade discounts for prompt payment.

Cash management for effective cash utilization can have additional implications. Frequently, foodservice operations maintain several checking accounts, each with some minimum balance. Consolidation can mean that cash is freed for investment purposes. It is also possible for large operations such as national restaurant chains to make arrangements for local deposits to be centrally credited so that the use of funds for various periods of time is not lost.

Custody of Cash

Cash presents particular vulnerabilities to theft and misuse. In addition to safeguarding the money itself, it is necessary to establish accountability and responsibility for money as it is handled by the operation. Control, especially at the operational level, should include extensive procedures for monitoring the receipt of money and controlling disbursements. Most procedures provide for overlapping controls on receipts and disbursements by different individuals. No single person should have custody of money or the right to use it while, at the same time, having responsibility for controlling its custody or use.

PROFIT MANAGEMENT

Business management is not passive. Planning is necessary for the success of an enterprise and for the realization of organizational objectives. As the operation progresses from one point in time to another, it can be made to change direction. Managerial decisions based on the best information available when they were made can be altered to respond to new information about the operation and the challenges it faces.

Just as management can change production strategies, refine service concepts, or alter marketing mixes, the fundamental elements of the business system can be manipulated to improve eventual results: profits. The enterprise's investment emphasis can be changed, equipment can be sold as well as bought, and borrowing can be refinanced, but it is more likely that the enterprise's management will assess factors of profitability that are inherently more flexible: prices, costs, and taxes.

Price Management for Profitability

Profits depend on volume and selling prices, on the one hand, and costs on the other. Of these three factors, prices can be entirely controlled by the operation's management. A hamburger can be offered for $5 instead of 50 cents at the will of the operation's management, but no one can be forced to buy it at that price.

Before a pricing decision can be made effectively, information about three areas is needed:

- The effect of price on volume as determined by market research.
- The costs relevant to the item or items being sold. (Pricing on this basis was discussed in Chapter 6).
- The effect of a change in price, volume, or costs on profits.

The last area is a synthesis of the first two. As no new information is required, it is possible to determine the mathematical relationship between price, volume, and costs and arrive at precise answers by several methods. However, if the underlying information is incorrect, the answers will be imprecise and meaningless. For example, it can be said with absolute surety that if an operation has fixed costs of $10,000 (whether it operates or not) and a cost of $1 for each item it prepares, then if it can sell 10,000 items at $2 each, its total costs will equal its total revenues and it will "break even." Obviously, this purely mathematical relationship does not ensure that a single item could be sold for $2 or that costs are actually $10,000 and $1.

It is necessary to introduce these qualifications because the two methods for dealing with price, volume, and cost relationships discussed below, break-even analysis and incremental analysis, are deceptively neat. Sometimes useful for foodservice operations, they are more applicable to manufacturing companies with more accurate underlying data. Moreover, they address the price and volume of a single product: most foodservice operations sell a number of products with different costs and prices, and each patron transaction may include several products.

Break-even analysis   In the context of these qualifications, break-even analysis can show at what approximate level of sales a new product will pay for itself and begin to produce a profit. It can also indicate how far sales of an existing product can drop before the item will stop making any profit at all. It is also possible to assess the effect of an increase in costs, a reduction of selling price, or an increase in capital investment.

These determinations and the many others that could be proposed depend on a classification of costs as fixed, variable, and semi-variable. *Fixed costs* do not vary with the level of business activity. Property taxes, executive salaries, and insurance are examples of fixed costs. *Variable costs* change directly or almost directly with the volume of business activity. Examples of these costs are labor directly involved in production and materials such as food products. They tend to double, for instance, if production of a menu item is doubled, or drop to zero if there is no production. The relationship might not be directly proportionate if there is some purchasing advantage to buying large quantities of materials or some increased labor efficiency in making large quantities.

Semi-variable costs change with the level of business activity but not in direct proportion to it. Supervisory costs may be semi-variable. For example, in a small chain, only one sanitation supervisor may be needed regardless of whether two or four units are open. However, when five are open, two supervisors are required. In most break-even analysis, semi-variable costs are divided into their fixed and variable components, but they can be addressed separately.

After all costs have been identified and classified as fixed or variable, the break-even point (the point or amount of sales volume at which sales revenues just cover costs, with no profit or loss) can be found by using the following formula:

$$\text{Break-even volume} = \frac{\text{total fixed costs}}{\text{selling price minus variable cost per unit}}$$

For example, if fixed costs are $50,000, the selling price is $5, and variable costs are $3.25 per unit, then the break-even point is 28,571 units.

$$\text{Break-even volume} = \frac{\$50,000}{\$5.00-\$3.25}$$

$$\text{Break-even volume} = \frac{\$50,000}{\$1.75}$$

$$\text{Break-even volume} = 28,571 \text{ (units)}$$

Figuring the break-even point by means of this formula has the advantage of simplicity. Break-even charts—graphic forms of the same relationships—give a broader "moving" picture of business activity. They, too, show the specific break-even point, but they also show the amount of profit or loss for other levels of sales. Exhibit 12.5 presents these same relationships in graphic form.

Using the chart, the impact of a price rise, a change in volume, or a change in either variable costs or fixed costs could be determined by simply redrawing the appropriate line to represent new figures. If variable costs do not directly change with volume, then a break-even chart on this basis would show an appropriate curve instead of a straight line.

Incremental analysis   "Incremental" costs and revenues are costs and revenues that change with increases or decreases in the production level. Incremental analysis is used to determine the advisability of some change in production that will cause a change in variable costs and fixed costs (otherwise, break-even analysis could be used). For exam-

EXHIBIT 12.5   An Example of a Break-even Chart

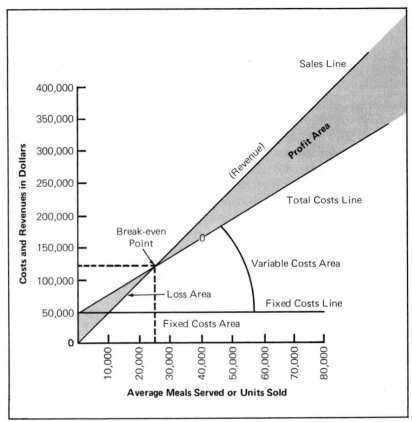

Adapted from <u>The Financial Ingredient in Foodservice Management</u> by John L. Bolhuis and Roger K. Wolff. D.C. Heath and Company. Lexington, MA: 1976. Copyright © 1976 by the National Institute for the Foodservice Industry.

ple, a restaurant might be contemplating the opening of another unit that would share some but not all of the facilities of the first unit. Or, a catering commissary may be presented with the prospect of a large order. The analytical process in the first instance is similar to that of the second. Suppose the commissary currently produces 10,000 deluxe canape platters a year. Fixed costs are $20,000 and variable costs $5 per unit: $2 for materials, $1 for labor, $1 for variable production overhead, and $1 for variable selling expenses. The platters sell for $10. The new customer wants to buy 10,000 a year at $9 per platter. A new night shift would be required to double the commissary's production as required by the new customer's order.

Costs at the original level of production are not necessarily applicable to the new level of production (20,000 platters instead of 10,000). The commissary management has calculated that the 10,000 additional platters will cost:

Variable costs per unit:

Materials	$ 2.00
Labor (including night shift premium)	2.00
Variable production overhead	1.25
Variable selling costs	0
	5.25

Incremental fixed costs:

Additional supervisors	$10,000
Power, light, heat	5,000
Other expenses	3,000
Total incremental fixed costs	$18,000

The financial results of accepting the new contract would therefore be shown as:

	Original Production	*New Order*	*Total*
Gross revenues	$100,000	$90,000	$190,000
Variable costs	50,000	52,500	102,500
Fixed costs	20,000	18,000	38,000
Total costs	70,000	70,500	140,500
Profit before taxes	30,000	19,500	49,500
Return on sales	30.0%	21.7%	26.1%

The new production would be profitable but the rate of return could not be as high as the original level of production. By this method it would be possible for the commissary management to discover that the return did not justify the contract or any other probable result of making a major change in production activity.

Cost Management for Profitability

Managerial decisions in any operational area can affect business performance. Relatively small reductions in expense factors can have a dramatic impact on profitability for most operations. Assuming that net profit before taxes is 5 percent of sales, expenses will be 95 percent of sales. A reduction in expenses equal to 2 percent of sales (from 95 to 93 percent) is a reduction of 2.1 percent in expenses but an increase of 40 percent in profits (from 5 to 7 percent).

It is simple mathematics that prompts energy conservation campaigns, aggressive purchasing, advertising audits, recipe reformulation, new procedures for dishwashing that use less rinse agent, and other similar penny-pinching devices that are inexplicable without this perspective.

Tax Management for Profitability

Every organization must pay the taxes it owes in order to continue in business. More than 50 percent of pre-tax profits may be paid by a corporation to federal, state, and city agencies to meet this legal obligation. Tax regulations, however, are not "punitive"; the intent of taxes is to raise money for government expenditures, not to punish business for prospering. There are legitimate methods under the Internal Revenue Code for limiting tax liability. In some instances, the liability is avoided entirely. The organization of a corporation as a Sub-Chapter S corporation avoids "double taxation" for its owners: earnings in the standard corporation are taxed first as corporate earnings, and then, when paid as dividends to shareholders, as income of each individual. The earnings of a Sub-Chapter S corporation are treated simply as personal income.

In other instances, tax liability is simply postponed. Taxes on earnings may eventually have to be paid, but no current tax liability exists. At the very least, this postponement provides the organization with a source of working capital that does not require interest payments or the dilution of equity. It may result in the organization's deferring taxation to a time when income will be subject to a lower tax rate.

The Internal Revenue Code contains provisions for calculating depreciation, valuing inventories, allowing for bad debts, and otherwise treating expenses that limit tax liability in a particular period. Obviously, no major investment decision can be made without considering the tax implications for the organization.

Organizations owned by an individual or a few individuals often have options that reduce their overall tax liability (as individuals and as owners of a company) in the organization and structuring of the enterprise. For example, an individual with a large taxable income from other sources who has organized a foodservice enterprise as a sole proprietorship, partnership, or Sub-Chapter S corporation can use the losses of the foodservice operation to offset taxable income. Individuals who both own and manage a corporation and who would ordinarily be subject to double taxation on earnings may avoid some corporate taxes by paying themselves large salaries or bonuses or by making generous contributions to pension plans. Reasonableness, as interpreted by the Internal Revenue Service and, ultimately, the court system, governs the use of these options.

MAKING THE BUSINESS SYSTEM MORE EFFECTIVE

To be effective, business management decisions depend on accurate information. More specifically, effective planning depends on knowing current costs and revenues and projecting future costs and revenues. Business management as an operational activity depends on continuous measurement of the operation's performance. Accurate information is also required by government agencies, the operation's creditors, and the operation's owners.

The managers of a foodservice operation—with the assistance of consultants such as accountants and aides such as bookkeepers—may spend a good deal of the time they devote to business gathering and presenting this information. As valuable as information gathering is, it should not be confused with the managerial processes. There is an important difference between elegantly presenting information and using it to achieve business system objectives and overall organizational objectives. This distinction is not always made with the vigor it merits, since the persons concerned with gathering information, measurement, and presentation and not concerned with business tend to inflate the importance of the work with which they are involved. More bluntly, a foodservice operation can have "perfect" records, books, and financial statements but be going out of business. On the other hand, an operation can have virtually no information and be prospering because of successful marketing, operations management, and intuitively excellent business management.

This argument for formal controls on the business system is financially conservative: disregarding the external demands for accurate financial information, business managers with accurate information presented in a consistent manner are more likely to make effective decisions and to correct business performance before the organization is substantially damaged.

If the methods the operation uses to gather, present, and interpret information are internally consistent—the same each time the same factors are addressed—and consistent with general business and foodservice practices, the management gains the opportunity to compare past information with current information and the operation's information with that of other organizations.

Business Routine   Numerous business system routines could be described that correspond to the objectives of a particular operation and its emphasis on the management of the business system. An operation that is growing through aggressive investment programs is likely to be much more involved with matters concerning financial planning than an operation that is not. The routine business tasks of individuals within the same organization will necessarily differ with their responsibilities. An operation's bookkeeper may be concerned with invoices from venders and preparation of payments; an operation's comptroller may be concerned with tax administration.

However the business routines of foodservice operations may differ, three distinct processes are identifiable: record keeping, accounting, and financial analysis. They differ in the level of responsibility of the persons (in a large organization) assigned to them, and in the information that they produce and the use made of it. Finally, they differ in the forms and devices used to facilitate them, and in the documents that are produced. Record keeping is a basic process of the business system. Frequently, it is the responsibility of persons on the operational level or clerical personnel. Its basic purpose is gathering and presenting business information related to operational performance expressed in financial units. Accounting, a more sophisticated process, uses the information of record keeping to measure operational performance. Financial analysis is directed toward evaluating the measurements produced by accounting so that decisions can be made.

RECORD KEEPING   The records and record keeping of a foodservice operation are often used for both business and operational purposes, serving as a means of managing and controlling the business system itself as well as a means of managing and controlling other operational systems. If there were no need to express purchases and inventories in financial terms, a need would still exist to quantify them in other units for managerial decisions related to purchasing and supply. Frequently, the financial records of a foodservice operation appear on the same forms and devices as the other records. For example, an inventory form may present the number of No. 10 cans of tomato sauce the operation has, the cost per unit of each can, and the total value of the inventory of tomato sauce.

Records related to sales, cash receipts or disbursements, payments for supplies, service or labor, money owed the operation, bank balances, and investments largely serve financial purposes. They form the basis of the more sophisticated routines of accounting and financial analysis and only tangentially serve other purposes. To facilitate these more sophisticated processes, records of this type are frequently maintained according to carefully prescribed procedures. While it is possible for someone to use the record of each discrete transaction for accounting purposes, it is more efficient to consolidate these transactions and present them on a single document, generally called a journal or report. Journals are also described as the "books of original entry"; their function is to present in one place transactions of the same kind over a definite period of time.

ACCOUNTING   The principal function of accounting is measurement of the organization's financial performance on the basis of categories that are generally accepted as relevant to the achievement of business system objectives.

Profit, various expenses, and loss are commonly used categories. They are more relevant to an assessment of the financial performance of the organization than other categories such as a measurement of the cost of producing a menu item since that cost can be expressed in financial terms. When other financial categories are of concern to the operation, specialized accounting techniques, for example, cost accounting, are used. In order for measurement to be meaningful, there must be a strict definition of both the category of expenses or revenues being measured and a strict procedure for measurement and the presentation of measurements. If there is no generally accepted meaning of "profit" or accepted way of presenting profits, accounting information would be difficult, if not impossible, to use.

Definitions and presentation methods are generally standardized for all business organizations by associations of accountants, and for specific industries by industry groups. Properly prepared accounting documents are understandable to anyone familiar with the specific definitions and procedures used. It is thus possible to use the information presented without questioning the meaning of the underlying data.

FINANCIAL ANALYSIS Measurements are made useful by comparing them with measurements of other categories of expenses and revenues. A "profit" of $10,000 offers some indication of the operation's business performance only when compared with either an expected profit, a standard that has been established, or the past performance of the operation. Likewise, any of the categories of operational performance that accounting measures can be evaluated by comparison with the operation's standards. Actual expenses for laundry could be compared with anticipated expenses for laundry, or some conception of the amount of total sales laundry expenses should represent, or prior laundry expenses.

It could also be determined whether laundry expenses or profits or any other category is increasing or decreasing. A standard could be established for evaluating the rate of this increase or decrease. Is the rate of profit increase according to plan, consistent with some conception of what it should be, faster, slower, or just the same as what it has been? In effect, the trend of certain categories of expenses and revenues is being analyzed.

Analysis can also be based on direct comparison of absolute amounts: this year's profits in dollars could be compared with expected profits in dollars, a standard expressed in dollars, and so on. But because of the interrelationships of the factors being measured, it is frequently more useful to compare relationships of measurements with other relationships of measurements. For example, expressing net profits as a percent of sales, the ratio relationship of profits and sales, allows this percentage to be compared with another similarly derived percentage. It means very little to say that an operation produced a net profit of $10,000 this year and $15,000 last year. It means more in terms of usefulness for managerial decision making and as a stimulus to corrective action to say that this year the operation produced a net profit of 3 percent of revenues and last year it produced a profit of 10 percent. Likewise, it is more meaningful to compare potential investments on the basis of the relationship of potential return as a percentage of investment than it is to compare the investments in absolute sums. Two investments could be calculated to return $5,000; one could offer a 25 percent return and the other a 10 percent return.

Since the business systems of all organizations resemble each other in significant ways, and since most accounting methods produce qualitatively similar measurements, a number of relationships of measurements have been widely accepted as indicators of financial performance. It is generally accepted that comparing profits to sales of one year with profits to sales of another year yields information that is useful for most organizations. In addition, some dozen other relationships are used as indicators to permit some objective evaluation of the operation's performance. The operation's balance sheet and profit and loss statement—two major accounting documents that present measurements of the operation's performance at a given moment (commonly, the end of a month or the end of the year)—provide basic information that is analyzed to produce ratios that can be used as indicators.

Three types of ratios are commonly developed. First, balance sheet ratios may refer to relationships between various balance sheet items. Second, operating ratios may show relationships of expense accounts to income. Third, groups of ratios may show relationships between an item in the profit and loss statement and one on the balance sheet. Exhibit 12.6 summarizes the ten most common of these relationships and indicates the performance qualities they may indicate.

Performing the arithmetic implied in each one of these relationships, such as dividing current assets by current liabilities, will result in a number: 2, 80, 55%, 35 days, and so on. It still remains necessary to establish the significance of this number by comparing it with a standard. If the standard is the goal of a managerial plan, then the comparison is immediately meaningful. If the owners of an operation wish to earn a return on investment of 10 percent and use a comparison of net profits to tangible net worth as an indicator, then the analysis becomes meaningful in determining the operation's performance. A smaller percentage of return would prompt managerial correction in a future period; a large percentage would prompt analysis so that the increase in return could be sustained. Likewise, if the results of this analysis are used to compare one year's measurements with another, the comparisons will show the state of the operation's financial health.

When the results of these analyses are compared with a standard that is based on neither a goal of a plan nor a statement of past performance but simply a conception of an acceptable quality of business performance, difficulties may occur. It may seem proper to a manager that the current assets to current liabilities ratio be 2:1 or that net profits on tangible net worth be 10 percent. Usually, typical or average figures derived from a study of many similar operations are proposed.

Standards based on typical or average figures pose several problems in the foodservice industry. Although there are some studies of foodservice operations by bank consulting firms, industry associations, and accounting firms, samples are small. There is a vast difference between suggesting standard ratios for all the steel companies in the United States on the basis of continuing studies of *all* the steel companies in the United States and suggesting standards for 500,000 foodservice operations on the basis of a study of 200 or 300 operations. Furthermore, standard ratios are average ratios: the conditions under which an operation functions can cause legitimate variations from any standard average. Because of the incompleteness of the data, both in terms of sample size and depth of most studies, the establishment of "danger points" or "marks of excellence" is also difficult. Without question, an operation that is short of working capital is more vulnerable to financial reverses than an operation that is not, but what ratio of net sales to net working capital indicates that an operation is safe? What ratio indicates that an operation is vulnerable? What ratio indicates that an operation is "too safe" and not using its working capital profitably? 5:1, 3:1, 8:1, 2:1?

By intensive and extensive study over a long period of time, it becomes possible to relate an indicator, or more realistically, several indicators, to financial performance. If one could say that 90 percent of the foodservice organizations with a 20:1 ratio of net sales to net working capital have undergone financial reorganization within six months, a ratio of 20:1 would clearly be a danger signal. Lack of basic information makes it impossible to establish this criterion or any other criteria.

Techniques for Effective Business Management The business managers of a foodservice organization can use specialists and certain standardized methods to make the business system function as smoothly and effectively as possible. Many procedures within an organization require specialized techniques and knowledge, considerable amounts of calculations, and the preparation of many documents and reports. In addition, since many procedures are governed by regulation, there is a need to conform to changes in codes and laws. The management of an organization must be aware of these changes as they occur.

For many foodservice operations, especially those which lack the resources of large corporations, effective business management is facilitated by the use of outside consultants with specialized knowledge and current information, the use of a standardized accounting method, the Uniform System of Accounts for Restaurants, and the use of standardized

EXHIBIT 12.6   Financial Ratios and the Performance Qualities They May Indicate

Ratio	Explanation	Performance Quality
Current assets / Current liabilities	A measurement of the funds (current assets) the operation has available to meet obligations is compared with a measurement of those obligations (current liabilities).	The ability of the operation to meet its obligations is assessed.
Current liabilities / Tangible net worth	A measurement of obligations (current liabilities) is being compared to what the operation owns.	The general financial condition, "strength," of the operation is assessed.
Net sales / Tangible net worth (Sometimes called turnover of tangible net worth)	The operation's sales revenues are compared to what it owns.	This relationship shows how actively invested capital is being put to work.
Net sales / Working capital (Sometimes called turnover of working capital)	Net sales are compared to working capital: assets that can be readily converted into operating funds.	This ratio indicates the operation's profitable use of its working capital and its vulnerability to creditors.
Net profits / Tangible net worth	Profits after taxes (net profits) are compared with investment (tangible net worth).	Return on capital investment is indicated.

forms and devices for record keeping and the preparation of financial documents.

USE OF OUTSIDE CONSULTANTS   Numerous individuals and organizations can offer assistance—both for a fee and without charge—to foodservice organizations in structuring the business system and in making business decisions.

Individual accountants and accounting firms with specialists in the foodservice, hospitality, or service industries can provide consulting services. In some instances, they can also provide business management counseling. Presumably, they bring the latest information on government regulations and accounting techniques to the task.

Evaluating investment opportunities and starting up a business enterprise can be facilitated by management and marketing consulting firms that specialize in the foodservice industry. Although they do not make

Ratio	Explanation	Performance Quality
$$\frac{\text{Net credit sales for year}}{365}$$ $$\frac{\text{Notes and accounts receivable}}{\text{Daily credit sales}}$$	Credit sales for the year are divided by 365 to determine daily credit sales figure, which is used to divide current notes and accounts receivable to produce average collection period.	How long money is being tied up in credit sales is shown: expressed in days.
$$\frac{\text{Net sales}}{\text{Inventory}}$$ (Inventory turnover)	Sales revenues are compared with the value of current inventories in dollars.	Relation offers some basis of comparison for evaluating inventory management.
$$\frac{\text{Fixed assets}}{\text{Tangible net worth}}$$	The amount of investment in facilities and equipment (fixed assets) is compared to the total amount of the owners' capital. Tangible net worth includes both fixed assets and current assets or working capital.	How much of the total investment is available to be used as working capital or to meet obligations is shown.
$$\frac{\text{Total debt}}{\text{Tangible net worth}}$$	All obligations (total debt) are compared to what the operation owns.	The creditor's "interest" in the operation is compared with the owner's.
$$\frac{\text{Net profits}}{\text{Net sales}}$$	Profits after taxes are compared to sales revenues.	The rate of return on net sales is indicated.

value judgments for the owners or investors of an enterprise, they can assist in interpreting information and in clarifying objectives.

Organization of a business also necessitates the services of a lawyer. Attorneys familiar with the foodservice industry can be helpful in weighing the tax implications of various forms of business organization and in creating formal organizational structure that protects the interests of the owners of an enterprise. On an ongoing basis, legal experts can facilitate tax administration, insurance administration, and the administration of those aspects of operational activities that have both business and legal implications, such as contract negotiation.

Individuals involved in offering some service to the organization frequently have expertise in particular areas of foodservice business administration. Bankers, insurance agents, real estate agents, and employees of equipment leasing firms may have experience and knowledge in areas related to their specialties. A banker or real estate agent may have participated in another operation's successful financing of a new restaurant.

No one is more expert in matters of regulation than the employees of a government agency. The Internal Revenue Service, state tax boards, and licensing agencies are prepared to counsel the owners of a food-service organization on matters that concern them. Many agencies publish detailed materials on record keeping, tax administration, payroll administration, and other business concerns.

A number of services ranging from seminars on effective business decision making to counseling by experienced executives are offered by the Small Business Administration. Other government agencies publish studies, "how-to" materials, and other informative materials.

USE OF THE UNIFORM SYSTEM OF ACCOUNTS FOR RESTAURANTS

The development of methods and procedures for administration and control of the business system is difficult, time-consuming, and expensive. Although the most effective procedures must be based on the groundwork of the operation, a general method has been developed by the National Restaurant Association. Called the "Uniform System of Accounts for Restaurants," it can become the basis of effective record keeping and accounting routine in many foodservice operations, especially restaurants. It has the additional virtue of being used widely. Operating statistics and ratio analyses developed on the basis of the Uniform System more readily allow comparison with published figures.

USE OF FORMS AND DEVICES

For every business management activity, indeed for every business decision, a specific form or device could be prepared. The same factors or decision factors are being manipulated time and time again in the management, administration, and control of the business system. It is likely that a specific operation develops standardized forms and devices for those procedures which must be performed continuously such as those procedures related to reporting operating statistics or information to the government, creditors, investors, executives, and managers. Other procedures, perhaps those concerning investments, are performed using materials developed for each instance individually. Exhibit 12.7 presents the data bases of some of the more widely used business-related forms and devices. Exhibits 12.8 to 12.10 offer some typical examples.

EXHIBIT 12.7   Forms and Devices Used in the Management of the Business System

Name of Form or Device	Use	Data Base
Forms and Devices Related to Planning		
Budget	To allocate resources, to project expenses over a period of time, to set standards.	Data base differs with specific purpose of the budget, but in general: Budget item Item expense Item expense at various points in time Comparison of actual expense with budget Variance of actual expense from budget
Expense forecasts	To communicate departmental forecasts of projected expense and revenues to business management.	Date/by Department Expense or revenue items Expense or revenue amounts Expense or revenue amounts at various points in time
Projected revenue and expense Pro forma balance sheet Pro forma income statement Cash flow projection	To project financial information in the form that actual financial information will be presented; to be able to "simulate" events in the future.	Same data bases as actual documents (see below).
Cost estimates Profit estimates Break-even analysis Incremental analysis Make-or-buy analysis	To simulate actual relationships of costs, volume, and price so that the operation's profits under various conditions are forecastable.	Fixed costs Variable costs Estimates of volume (Frequently these factors are manipulated by graphic presentation.)
Forms and Devices Related to Costs and Expenses		
Cost allocation	To fairly apportion the overhead of an operation to each product unit it produces.	Total cost of overhead or overhead by department Allocation of overhead or department costs by products Direct cost of product: materials and direct labor Total cost of each unit of product

EXHIBIT 12.7   Forms and Devices Used in the Management of the Business System (cont.)

Name of Form or Device	Use	Data Base
Cost analysis	To identify and quantify the individual cost elements in a product.	Data base differs with product being costed, but data base for a food item is typical: Name of item Portion size or batch size Amount of each ingredient used Time expended in each labor category Cost of time in each labor category Direct costs of energy Total cost of each portion or batch of product
Department expense records or reports	To communicate expenses to business management.	Data base differs with each department on the basis of each expense item. For example, food production department might report expenses for labor by category, food expenses by product category, and so on.

Forms and Devices Related to Cash

Cash reports	To account for cash received by the operation.	Date/day or period Department, station, or register Cash receipts by product category Total cash receipts Cash disbursements Over or under
Income report	To communicate total cash revenues (cash, charge, check, internal charges).	Data base of cash report with additional information related to activity by individual charge accounts, charge cards, or internal charge accounts.
"Vouchers"	To maintain records of disbursements from cash accounts.	Data base differs with particular nature of disbursement and operation but generally includes: Reference to invoice number Number of check by which payment was made Authorization for payment Date of payment Amount of payment

Name of Form or Device	Use	Data Base
Customer account ledgers, card, or statement	To maintain records of charge transactions.	Customer name Date and amount of charges Date and amount of payments Continuing balance owed Miscellaneous details about customer such as address, credit standing, and so on

Forms and Devices Related to Fixed Assets

Property ledgers	To maintain records of capital investments.	Data base is peculiar to particular item but would include purchase price, date of purchase, depreciation schedule.
Depreciation schedules	To allow calculation of depreciation of capital investments under the several methods allowed by the government.	Data differs with method but includes purchase price, useful life in years, and ultimate salvage value.
Depreciation records	To facilitate calculation of total depreciation allowance.	Data base includes current information of depreciation of each asset being depreciated.

Forms and Devices Related to Insurance

General insurance records and reports	To maintain records of the value of insured property and records of insurance coverage, claims, and so on.	Data base is related to specific items but would generally include item costs and current values, policy coverage, policy numbers, insurance agent, and so on.

Forms and Devices Related to Accounting

General ledger	To maintain records of all the operation's transactions.	Account (asset by name) Date of transaction Description of transaction Items posted: to debits to credits debit balance credit balance
Journals: payroll journal, cash journal, sales journal, and so forth	To record transactions from operationally related control documents.	Data base differs with journal and accounting method; generally includes: Date of transaction Brief description

EXHIBIT 12.7 Forms and Devices (cont.)

Name of Form or Device	Use	Data Base
Journals (cont.)		Amount of money involved Indication of the assets, liabilities, capital, or type of income affected by the transaction

Forms and Devices Related to Financial Matters

Name of Form or Device	Use	Data Base
Balance sheet	To summarize and present results of the operation's transactions during a period of time and the financial status of the operation.	Date Current assets by category Fixed assets by category Deferred expenses by category Other assets by category Total assets Current liabilities by category Reserves by category Capital (for corporations) by category Net worth Total liabilities and capital
Profit and loss statement	To present operating statistics related to the income and profitability of the operation.	Actual items differ with the nature of the operation; generally for a restaurant the following are used: Date Sales: food, beverage Total sales Cost of sales: food, beverage Gross profit: food, beverage Total gross profit Service charges Other income Total income Controllable expenses by category Profit before rent or occupation costs Rent or occupation costs Profit before depreciation Depreciation Restaurant profit Additions or deductions to restaurant profit Profit before income tax Income tax Net profit
Profit and loss schedules	To offer detailed descriptions of sales, other income, controllable expenses, rent, depreciation, and so on.	Data base differs with schedule, each is by category within each expense category.

EXHIBIT 12.8   Expenses Forecast

Estimated Expenses for Coming Year (use nearest dollar figures)

	Actual this Year	*Estimate Coming Year*
Personnel Expenses		
(Salaries, wages, bonuses)		
Executives	_____	_____
Office	_____	_____
Store	_____	_____
Salesmen	_____	_____
All other	_____	_____
Operating Expenses		
Advertising and catalogs	_____	_____
Bad debts	_____	_____
Cash discounts allowed	_____	_____
Delivery (oil, gas, repairs)	_____	_____
Depreciation	_____	_____
Donations	_____	_____
Dues and subscriptions	_____	_____
Employee benefits	_____	_____
Heat, light, power, and water	_____	_____
Insurance	_____	_____
Interest	_____	_____
Legal and auditing	_____	_____
Maintenance and repairs	_____	_____
Office supplies	_____	_____

EXHIBIT 12.9   Sample Profit and Loss Statement

ABC Foodservice Company
Profit and Loss Statement
Year Ending December 31, 19xx

	Amount	*Percent*
Total Sales	$1,605,995	100.0%
Cost of Sales		
Food (after credit for employee meals)	555,402	34.6
Gross Profit	1,050,593	65.4
Other Income	0	0
Total Income	$1,050,593	65.4%
Controllable Expenses		
Payroll	477,284	29.7
Employee benefits	39,667	2.5
Direct operating expenses	73,849	4.6
Music and entertainment	—	
Advertising and promotion	911	.1
Utilities	30,374	1.9
Administrative and general	192,630	12.0
Repairs and maintenance	24,486	1.5
Total Controllable Expenses	$ 839,201	52.3%
Income before Rent or Occupation Costs	211,392	13.1
Occupation Costs		
Rent or occupation costs	$ 140,723	8.7
Depreciation	46,628	2.9
Income Tax	11,794	.7
Total Occupation Costs	$ 199,145	12.3%
Net Profit	$ 12,247	0.8%

From The Financial Ingredient in Foodservice Management by John L. Bolhuis and Roger K. Wolff. D.C. Heath and Company. Lexington, MA: 1976. Copyright © 1976 by the National Institute for the Foodservice Industry.

EXHIBIT 12.10 **Sample Balance Sheet**

ABC Foodservice Company
Balance Sheet
December 31, 19xx

Assets

Current Assets

Cash	$21,000
Accounts Receivable	3,000
Inventory	6,000
Prepaid Expenses	3,000
Total Current Assets	$33,000

Fixed Assets

Land		5,000	
Building	15,000		
Less: Accumulated Depreciation	8,000	7,000	
Total Fixed Assets			12,000
Total Assets			**$45,000**

Liabilities and Capital

Liabilities

Current Liabilities

Accounts Payable	4,000	
Notes Payable—Current Portion	5,000	
Accrued Liabilities	1,000	
Total Current Liabilities		10,000

Long-Term Liabilities

Notes Payable—Long-Term Portion	15,000
Total Liabilities	25,000

Capital

Joe Jones, Capital	20,000
Total Liabilities and Capital	**$45,000**

From The Financial Ingredient in Foodservice Management by John L. Bolhuis and Roger K. Wolff. D.C. Heath and Company. Lexington, MA: 1976. Copyright © 1976 by the National Institute for the Foodservice Industry.

Chapter 13
The Control
System

Every foodservice organization needs an individual or group of individuals to oversee the conduct of daily business and to review performance to ensure that expectations and goals are met. Control of all of a foodservice operation's activities is one essential step in achieving profits or meeting target budgets. The control system of a foodservice operation reinforces organizational objectives set by management; it monitors, evaluates, and, if necessary, corrects performance.

This chapter will discuss what makes up the control system, explain some of the methods employed in making adjustments to current and future conditions, and present an outline of the control routine of a typical foodservice unit manager.

CONTROL CONCEPTS

Control is the process of ensuring that specific tasks are carried out and that these tasks conform to the objectives set by management. The organization of the control system must be appropriate to the structure of the particular operation. Control, unlike management, is concerned almost entirely with internal operations.

The control system is subordinate to the management system and differs from it in focus and level of activity. Management activities are directed toward the planning and formulation of courses of action consistent with the organization's objectives. (See Chapters 2 and 3). Control activities carry out these plans and monitor their success within the operation. In a small operation, both management and control are the duties of the owner/operator. However, in large foodservice chains, the unit manager is almost exclusively concerned with control of his or her unit's performance.

Specific Objectives of the Control System The control system is oriented toward performance. Through control activities, any variances from the standards of the operation can be detected and remedied. A comprehensive control system must be designed to ensure that standards are met and that no system within the operation "slips" into low-quality and wasteful performance unbeknown to management. Consistent with its support and monitoring functions, specific objectives of the control system can be identified as follows:

1. *To ensure that the operation conforms to objectives set by management*   The general objectives set by the management system are translated in detail into specific goals and tasks to be accomplished by each successive level of manager or worker. The control system ensures that the daily tasks are guided toward the achievement of these specific and general goals. In effect, control is the duty of every worker in a foodservice operation. At the heart of this day-to-day direction and determination of progress must be the consciously asked question, "Will this action help achieve the organization's objectives?"

2. *To relieve management of routine control tasks*   The control system frees the management of a foodservice operation from directing and organizing routine tasks to concentrate on major problems and on decision making. For example, a control procedure that compares bar receiving records with storeroom issue records relieves a manager from the task of immediate supervision. Or, an established standard procedure for recruiting and inducting employees saves the manager the time needed to create one for each new employee.

3. *To communicate standards and assist in their implementation*
A standard is a measurement of performance. Should an operation set a standard of producing a 10 percent return on investment or a 50 percent return? Should a worker be able to peel 10 kilos of potatoes an hour or 50 kilos?

Higher-level management sets objectives and endorses the standards that measure performance against these objectives. It is the job of lower-level management—the control system and, through it, the other operating systems—to communicate these standards to the appropriate employees. Setting a standard for the rate of potato peeling per hour would do little good unless the utility worker who peels the potatoes knows and maintains the standard.

Lower-level managers—and, through them, other workers responsible for carrying out objectives and meeting standards—also have a role in setting standards, since it is they as individuals who are accountable for failure to meet objectives and variances from standards. The control system helps determine suitable standards based on careful research and a realistic determination of what performance is possible. Any standards established should be appropriate and consistent.

Depending on what is being measured and monitored, standards can be based on:

• *An established policy or procedure*   Do operations conform to the accepted, authorized, sanctioned way of doing things? For example, have affirmative action procedures been followed in recruiting and inducting new employees?

• *A goal or objective*   Has the desirable result of the course of action undertaken occurred? For example, has the $5,000 increase in media advertising resulted in the 6 percent increase in business that was projected?

• *A comparison with past performance*   Does current performance equal or exceed earlier performance? For example, is the menu-planning system producing the profit levels it achieved a year ago?

• *A comparison with industry norms*   How does the performance of this operation compare with other similar operations? For example, does it take the same number of maintenance workers to clean the operation as it takes to clean other operations of equal size?

4. *To measure performance*   The control system is concerned with measuring the performance of the organization as a whole. Although it is also concerned with the functioning of each system individually, it controls them collectively to maintain management's standards for overall performance.

The control system uses standards to evaluate performance. The variance from the standard is assessed and quantified in dollars, percentages, ratios, or numbers on a scale. Performance in any unit is measured in a manner appropriate to the standard being used: dollars, hours, square meters per hour, percentage increase, sacks of potatoes, rate of return on investment, times per week, and so on. Performance can also be measured on a scale. Employee attitudes can be measured by standardized tests that produce scores particular to the test; the results of a morale-building effort could thus be measured.

The seriousness of the variance from the standard is important; a one percent or one dollar variation is of less concern than a deviation of 10 percent or $1,000. The need for corrective action depends on the seriousness of the deviation.

5. *To correct deviations*   The control system should correct a deviation from the standard of performance appropriately and to the extent of the variance, just as a thermostat regulates a heating system to keep a room at a particular temperature. Most control systems achieve correction by stimulating managerial action: the control system identifies and quantifies the problem that is blocking goal attainment. Management initiates and implements an appropriate corrective action. For example, comparison of present inventory with perpetual inventory records—a control procedure—reveals shortages that management then seeks to prevent in the future through better security.

Current Practices in Control Systems   A control system that meets the specific objectives listed in the previous section would contribute substantially to the success of a foodservice operation. It is apparent in the most cursory examination of the industry that many foodservice operations do not have control systems with these capabilities. A few large companies, a few companies owned by conglomerates, a few institutions with control systems imposed on them by their sponsors, and a few small, individually run companies use control procedures effectively. Others—the vast majority—do not, for a variety of reasons.

LACK OF NEED   Many foodservice operations are small enterprises, owned, managed, and sometimes staffed by one or two individuals. It is possible to substitute personal management for control procedures. Through daily contact, the owner/operator gathers the information needed to manage his or her business and then acts on that information personally. Likewise, standards in a small operation may be known although not formally stated. The owner/operator of a roadside frankfurter stand realizes immediately that business one day is worse than another and reacts quickly by purchasing fewer frankfurters to replace stock, by hanging out a sign offering a special of the day, and so on. The owner/operator assesses the status of the enterprise directly on a continuing basis.

More formal control systems would not necessarily enable the owner/operator to deal more effectively with the conditions in which the enterprise functions. A detailed evaluation procedure could not tell the owner/operator any more about how to make the enterprise prosper in adverse business conditions than data recorded on a brown paper bag.

Many foodservice operations that began as small personal enterprises prosper, but their control procedures fail to grow with them. This failure to institute a satisfactory control system generally goes unrecognized, and operators attempt to control operations with a $500,000 volume and 15 workers as though they were operations with a $50,000 volume run by family members. Not only more, but more complex, control procedures are needed. While a cigar box may have sufficed for cash control in the past, current operating conditions require more sophisticated procedures and equipment—not several more cigar boxes.

LACK OF
KNOWLEDGE   Some operators or managers are unfamiliar with the concept of control. A lack of experience with control systems prompts them to seek elaborate solutions to problems that could be solved simply by effective control. For example, a decline in profitability may prompt increased promotion activities when, in fact, more careful control of production would eliminate the waste and spoilage that are eroding profits. Or, the menu program may be changed unnecessarily when a market audit would reveal that the operation remains unknown to a market segment that would find the original menu attractive.

Sometimes operators or managers are uncomfortable with the formalities and paperwork that control usually entails. They choose to emphasize employee relations instead of work-system productivity or patron accommodation instead of production forecasting. However, management may err as well in pretending that work-system productivity or production forecasting provides an exclusive means to meet the challenges confronting a complex enterprise.

MISCONCEPTION OF CONTROL

Many operations, although managed by people aware of the need for effective control, do not set up appropriate control systems. They fail to make the system as relevant to the operation as its production, service, or supply system. They fail to meet the needs of the operation. Activities, procedures, techniques, and equipment for control must be as appropriate to the particular operation as production or service activities, procedures, techniques, and equipment are to those systems.

This failure is exemplified by operations that have extensive control activities in some areas and virtually none in others. They may have elaborate personnel procedures that strictly govern the hiring and dismissal of employees but virtually no control of training programs for those same employees. An operation's accounting practices may be excellent, but cash receipts may be the only standard by which the operation can evaluate its menu program. Every penny the operation earns may be accounted for, but there may be no procedures for evaluating food waste, dish breakage, or energy use.

Other organizations fail to view their control activities as anything more than security functions. Often, operators and managers attempt to make the operation secure instead of making it work. They use control as policing activities: checking employee time cards against schedules signed by unit managers; checking bar records for the receipt of merchandise against storeroom records; checking cash register tapes against totals from guest checks that are then checked against kitchen duplicates that are then checked against kitchen production figures, and so on. Although the necessity of many of these procedures is evident, limitation of control tends to have four effects:

- Police efforts may replace the legitimate concerns of management: strategic management, personnel management, and adaptation to change as well as the organization's progress toward achievement of its objectives. Foodservice managers with this mentality can be found hiding in storerooms counting cans of sauerkraut while the operations they are supposed to be managing are producing substandard food, alienating consumers, and losing good employees.
- The operation's performance suffers because control activities do not ease the functioning of the operation. Control activities are not di-

rected toward product utilization, marketing effectiveness, productivity, inventory costs, menu-program performance, and other operating areas. Consequently, a lack of information about these areas makes effective managerial decision making impossible.

• Control activities may cost more to staff, equip and support than the profits they save or the losses they prevent. The result is overcontrol —a waste of time and money. Although the possibility of overcontrol exists in every area of the operation, it is more likely when control consists of internal checking procedures for security purposes. The frequency of control procedures for security purposes should decrease when few or no problems are detected; for instance, physical inventories may be conducted once a month instead of once a week and intensified only when problems occur.

• Overcontrol can also limit managerial flexibility. Maintaining consistency within the control system is a legitimate goal. However, exceptions to normal procedures must also be legitimized by making managers who authorize a deviation accountable for their actions. Control procedures are developed in conditions of uncertainty. Implementation of control procedures should depend on operational circumstances. Managers should be sufficiently skilled to recognize the difference between overriding procedures legitimately and compromising them unnecessarily.

Limitations on Control

Managers who seek to create an effective control system for a particular foodservice operation may find themselves limited by a lack of three basics: satisfactory models, basic research, and appropriate control techniques.

LACK OF MODELS FOR CONTROL

Foodservice operations differ greatly. The control system that worked in hospital Y may not work in a commercial foodservice operation or even in hospital X. If each operating system has been individually structured, then the system that guides them must reflect that structure.

The literature of the foodservice industry provides perhaps a dozen descriptions of control systems—in contrast to the thousands of descriptions of production systems and service systems. Most foodservice managers cannot identify their own operations closely enough with those few control systems described to use them as models. The only exception to this scarcity of models is the abundant literature concerning control procedures as internal checks.

LACK OF RESEARCH ON CONTROL

Foodservice is a large industry of many small enterprises. Very little research has been conducted on which a manager could objectively base standards for control: how much should it cost to process a purchase order or peel an onion?

LACK OF TECHNIQUES
FOR CONTROL

There are few techniques and little equipment specifically designed for control of foodservice operations. Unlike the manager of a large manufacturing enterprise for which both control techniques and equipment have been developed, the foodservice manager attempting to structure an operation's control system is limited both by a lack of resources and information. Creating an effective control system in these circumstances requires time and commitment. Managers who structure an effective control system, however, generally are rewarded by the longevity of their enterprises and by the extent of their resources.

Interaction of the
Control System
with Other
Systems

Control system activities interact with all other systems individually and as a group. Through control activities, the systems of a foodservice operation are monitored, and their performance is measured to ensure that each system meets standards individually. In addition, interactions between various systems are controlled. For example, the movement of goods from supply to production is monitored to avoid waste. If control procedures were rigorously applied to all systems (management, marketing, menu-planning, work, purchasing, supply, service, and business) as prior chapters have suggested, then the foodservice operation would:

- substantially comply with government regulations for equal opportunity, health, safety, sanitation, and so on.
- have a marketing mix that most efficiently allowed it to reach its market segment.
- have a menu program that reflects market-segment preferences.
- attempt continuously to improve labor productivity.
- make food purchases in light of price trends and product alternatives.
- maximize storage space and minimize inventory cost.
- forecast production needs accurately.
- manipulate the menu mix to correspond to current prices by merchandising selectively.
- forecast the impact of price changes on profitability.

DEVELOPING A CONTROL SYSTEM

Foodservice operations differ in the organization of their control systems. The assignment of particular control responsibilities to certain individuals in a specific operation is based on an assessment of how this best serves the operation's overall interests. An effective control system should be appropriate and specific to an operation and suited to its environment and employees.

Control responsibilities may be assigned to specialists who have few, if any, other responsibilities. These individuals may belong to the comptroller's department, the food and beverage control department, the accounting department, administrative services department, research and standards department, or even the operations department. Other enterprises assign the control of specific areas to separate specialized groups such as a personnel administration department or a quality control department.

Either of these organizational schemes presumes a large enough organization to justify substantial commitment of resources to control activities. They are characteristic of those few foodservice operations that are large enough to organize themselves on the model of industrial corporations.

However, most foodservice enterprises make control activities the responsibility of general management and operational, or unit, managers. Each foodservice system, department, or operational unit engages in control activities. Every manager, and to some extent every worker, has control responsibilities.

An operation's control system may be designed so that operational managers are primarily concerned with short-term activities, measurement, and record keeping or so that they are involved in long-term control procedures (those that have long-term implications on the success of the operation), allowed to evaluate the information they collect, and initiate appropriate corrective action. Likewise, nonmanagerial workers can be delegated control responsibilities that involve either record keeping or action. Does an inventory clerk simply count and record inventories, or does the clerk initiate a purchase order to replace stock? Does the cook simply report the portions produced by a recipe or does the cook reformulate the recipe or change its procedures to produce the standard number of portions?

Control activities concerned with evaluation, long-term planning, and action tend to increase in proportion to the individual's responsibilities in the organization. The chief executive of an organization measures less and evaluates more, is less involved in day-to-day control and more involved in long-term activities, has fewer record-keeping responsibilities and more responsibility for initiation of action. The unit manager of a foodservice chain may have only short-term measurement and record-keeping responsibilities, while workers are responsible only for the maintenance of their own performance standards.

However, shifting more evaluation and initiation to lower levels of the organization could result in better control by speeding corrective action. Likewise, information—the result of evaluation and not of record keeping—would more quickly be placed in the hands of the people who could use it best.

Shifting more evaluation and correction to lower levels may also increase employee motivation: the operation's standards would become a personal goal of each employee. As lower-level managers and workers initiate corrective actions, they determine more fully the structure of their jobs. Increased participation may lead to increased job satisfaction and productivity.

To achieve control system objectives, the management of an operation should seek to design a system that is consistent in organization, priorities, measurements, and devices with the operation's other systems. In broadest outline, this control system would consist of four major activities: establishing standards, measuring, evaluating, and correcting. Through these activities, the management of an operation expects to control key resources like capital and inventory; key operational areas such as food preparation; and key areas of its internal environment like consumer satisfaction. The design of the control system and the manner in which these activities are carried out must not unduly disrupt other systems or violate the objectives of control if smooth operation of all systems is to be achieved.

There are a number of distinct processes for establishing standards, measuring, evaluating, and correcting. For example, an operation should use surveys instead of accounting to measure consumer satisfaction because surveys are more appropriate to the measurement of opinion than accounting is. Budgeting and accounting are more useful when the standards established and performance measured can be expressed in dollars and cents. Thus, they would be more appropriate to the control of capital. A number of control processes used by the foodservice industry can be identified. Establishment of standards includes planning, budgeting, policy making, operational analysis, and research. Measurement includes accounting, internal checking, surveying, and observation. Evaluation includes auditing and information gathering, while correction includes the implementation and direction of remedies. Proper design of a control system should also include timing of control activities and useful control devices.

Although each of the above-mentioned activities may seem important in itself, the control system must be designed to foster a dynamic interaction of all activities of control with every system in a foodservice operation. For example, as important as the techniques, procedures, and process of food and beverage cost control may be to a particular operation, it should be recognized that a control system based on this alone is defective. Its design is defective because food and beverage cost control—let alone any single procedure or technique—does not provide for evaluation or correction. More important, it is defective unless it can be proven that consumer satisfaction, productivity, capital, food quality, and the score of other areas that cannot be controlled through food and beverage cost control alone, are unimportant to a particular operation. In other words, a comprehensive control system is needed: there may be no waste, theft, or other loss of food and alcoholic beverages—with or without food-cost control—but the operation may be overstaffed, revenues may barely meet expenses, the food may be virtually unacceptable to the operation's market, and so on.

However, in the development of a control system it should be noted that control is basically a routine. The employees concerned with control evaluate performance in terms of quantity. The number of meals served, the number of employees, the number of pounds of flour in the storeroom, and the minutes needed to cook a steak are all the province of the control system. Through the standards that it implements, the properly designed control system will gather data about the foodservice operation's performance and forward that information—in numbers and percentages—to management. It is the duty of management to decide whether or not the unit is overstaffed, what the proper ratio of revenues to expenses is, how to attract a certain market segment, and so on. Management retains the decision-making powers in a foodservice unit; management must not depend on the control system to uphold antiquated or useless standards. Instead, changes should be ordered.

Establishment of Standards

Control procedures must be applied to every area of operational performance. Standards should be established for every part of the operation so that the performance of each part can be measured.

Management must determine standards and establish some order of priorities for control procedures. This ordering should parallel the importance the management of an operation attaches to the areas that are to be controlled. Key areas are controlled intensively, less important areas are given less management time, or very little. In effect, management—through the control system—determines standards for the operation as well as standards for the functioning of the control system itself.

Standards must be particular to an operation. However, priorities need not be assigned by department. Various resources like capital and results like consumer satisfaction can be controlled using different standards. For example, within the operation's service system, management could choose to establish stringent standards to ensure consumer satisfaction while giving employee satisfaction only sporadic attention.

There are foodservice operations that legitimately ignore an area which other operations control intensively. Few noncommercial operations are concerned with monitoring market share—they serve most of the people they could possibly serve—while large commercial operations produce reams of control documents related to their current competitive positions.

There are five control processes related to establishment of standards: planning, budgeting, policy making, operational analysis, and research.

Planning   In general, a plan is a detailed statement of a course of action that is expected to achieve a definite result. Planning is the process of developing the overall plan as well as secondary plans for particular elements of the foodservice operation. Plans developed by management with the assistance of the control system become standards for performance. For example, planning for a marketing program is directed to achieving some market objective, such as influencing demand in order to increase sales volume. Scheduling—planning employee work hours—should result in satisfactory performance at minimum cost.

Budgeting   Planning can be effective only if it considers budget limits as well as long-term objectives. Budgets are a statement of quantified standards for a plan, that is, they are expressed in numbers. Courses of action should result in the attainment of objectives without exceeding stated expenses for labor, capital investment, materials, or even managerial time.

Policy making   Policies, procedures, regulations, and rules are statements of the organization's standards that either define quality of performance or prescribe the acceptable ways to achieve it. The owners or managers of a foodservice enterprise usually want the operation to be characterized by performance of a certain quality. Results can be compared to the stated quality of performance; ongoing activities can be compared to accepted ways of proceeding.

Policies, procedures, regulations, and rules are usually the result of a careful decision process and are in fact part of a plan to achieve broad objectives. Or, they may simply formalize plans that have worked repeatedly and seem valid for future achievement of objectives. For example, it may be the policy of the operation not to charge patrons for food products about which they complain. This policy can be seen as part of a plan to achieve marketing objectives and ultimately investment objectives, and as an element in a plan that has been demonstrated to be successful in achieving marketing objectives and investment objectives over a period of time.

Certain standards may be established by persons or agencies outside the operation. For example, after analyzing risks and benefits that alternative courses of action will create for the public, government agencies establish standards for the service of alcoholic beverages to persons under a certain age, the handling of food, the construction of buildings, the work environment, the installation of fire protection equipment, and so on. Policies established by outside agencies are much less flexible than the policies of management and the persons charged with control responsibilities. Nevertheless, performance of the operation must be measured against these externally determined standards as well.

Operational analysis   Planning and establishing standards involve operational analysis: a detailed study of the operation. If the operation has been effective in achieving its past goals, past performance can become the standard. If no other factors have intervened, then repeating all the activities of the past period and achieving all the intermediate results that were achieved should result in similarly successful performance. However, if other factors have intervened, if there have been fundamental changes in the operation or in its environment, then the effect of these changes will also be apparent through measurement and evaluation.

Establishing standards on this basis is common for a foodservice operation because of the repetitive nature of most foodservice activities. Most foodservice operations have a functional cycle of one day as compared to some manufacturing companies that may not sell their products until several months after they were manufactured, several years after the materials for them were ordered, and several decades after they had been developed. In a foodservice operation, it is fairly safe to assume that few factors change from day to day, and that by managing situations, the operation can deal with minor fluctuations. The danger inherent in accepting past performance as a standard is in assuming that a standard is still valid when it in fact has become inappropriate, hence, the necessity of closely watched control activities in the form of frequent measurement and evaluation. Variance from a standard can reveal that the standard is inappropriate. Managers must reassess standards to determine whether acceptable performance is possible without the standard and whether the old standard needs to be rethought because it has become a hindrance to performance. If the performance of the operation is adapted to the changed circumstance, substantial damage to the organization can be avoided.

Simulation is a form of operational analysis. Standards are established by projecting future performance and then measuring and evaluating the projection. A projected performance or achievement that is deemed acceptable becomes the standard. Large organizations may formally simulate future performance by the use of mathematical models manipulated by electronic data processing equipment. In smaller organizations—most foodservice enterprises—the process is virtually indistinguishable from decision making; by forecasting and examining future trends and demand, an operation projects simulated conditions fairly accurately and decides how to adapt to them. Forecasts of any kind, however, are the weakest type of standard since they are often little more than educated guesses.

Research   Establishing standards for some operational areas is occasionally done simply by determining the standards by which other operations have chosen to operate. The management of an operation must research health code standards, construction standards, and certainly market standards. If wooden cutting boards cannot be used, or if the people in an area will not eat pie crust made with lard, then operational standards are already defined.

In many industries, there are published standards in a great many areas that are fairly valid for most of the companies engaged in similar activities. For example, in the lodging business, each roomkeeper in a typical operation cleans about 14 rooms a day. For a new hotel this might be an acceptable provisional standard. In the foodservice industry, standards that can be applied to a wide number of operations are much less common. Few are published or available since it is difficult to establish parallels between operations. A published standard for labor cost (expressed as a percentage of sales) for a table-service restaurant is too general to be valid for operations with table service in common but vastly different investment costs, marketing objectives, production systems, materials costs, and so on. In general, standards that can be established by research are successful only when there are exact parallels between operations.

Use of Measurements

After deciding on standards, management must decide what measurements will produce the best data for assessing performance. Control procedures cannot be addressed to the total functioning or performance of an operation. The control system is concerned exclusively with the internal operations of a foodservice unit. Specific aspects of the production, service, or other systems can be monitored, and then the system as a whole may be evaluated by management on that basis. Just as a physician makes judgments about the overall health of a person by measuring body temperature or blood pressure, a manager evaluates performance by measuring certain indicators of performance and compares those measurements to a standard.

Measurements must be truly reflective of performance. Measured units of output are almost always satisfactory indicators. The amount of onions peeled, drinks sold, patrons served, or dollars returned on investment can indicate the performance of a food preparation worker, bar merchandising program, dining room staff, or business project.

Ratios and percentages can also be useful—although they tend to be abused—in evaluating performance if they are truly indicative. It is widely accepted that the ratio of food cost to sales of a commercial restaurant should be 30 percent. Unfortunately, having a 30 percent food cost may not be the least bit indicative of the operation's performance. It is possible to sell only one hamburger a day for a dollar. If the hamburger costs thirty cents, the food cost is 30 percent, although the volume of sales in this case is almost too tiny to matter. It is also possible to sell 5,000 hamburgers a day and have a food cost of 30 percent. It is also possible to have a 50 percent food cost and make a profit of a million dollars if enough products are sold so that revenues exceed all costs by a million dollars.

Ratios and percentages are legitimate indicators when they correspond to operational performance. The percentage of purchase orders under five dollars can be indicative of the performance of the purchasing system.

A manager using an indicator on any basis must validate it in the particular operation. A high rate of employee turnover may be very significant in one operation and not very significant in another that is not disrupted by employee comings and goings. A traditional gourmet restaurant that requires workers to be trained for its particular service and preparation style would be more affected than a limited-menu, take-in/take-out restaurant where each worker does only one narrowly defined and easily learned task. A great many broken dishes may mean that business is brisk or that warehandling is inefficient. Reliability of indicators, therefore, is very important.

Using several different indicators to assess the same performance increases the reliability of the indicators. Employee productivity and consumer satisfaction could both be measured to evaluate the performance of the service system.

With this perspective, it is not surprising that the indicators management uses for effective control may be unique to each operation, just as standards should be. A manager transferring from one operation to another may confront a substantially different control system. An entrepreneur or foodservice organization developing a new operation may have to abandon past practices and develop control procedures and indicators appropriate to the new operation.

The four basic ways of measuring are accounting, internal checking, surveying, and observation.

Accounting   Accounting procedures measure operational performance in financial units. Profits, expenses, and return on investment are usually measured by accounting.

It is important to recognize that accounting, even if it is extended to measure more strategic indicators such as cost per unit, cannot measure every aspect of operational performance because not every standard can be expressed in financial units. For instance, food quality or employee attitudes for which standards can be established cannot be measured in dollars. Indicators may be established showing the effect of poor food quality or disloyal employees on the operation's profits, and perhaps the effect can be stated in dollars. This process involves evaluation based on measurement determined by methods other than accounting, although the results are often translated into financial units if business decisions must be made.

Internal checking   When accounting is inappropriate, management often uses internal checking to measure whether standards are being met. Internal checking is often simply *counting* with the purpose of future comparison. Cans on a shelf, drinks sold, employees at a work station, and worker hours in an operation are routinely counted. Internal checking is by far the most common way of measuring in foodservice operations for the purpose of control. The list of things to be counted may be extended to include patrons, patron complaints and compliments, paper cups, broken dishes, violations of policies or procedural rules, and a vast number of other material and nonmaterial indicators that reveal operational performance in some—not all—systems.

Since the involvement of many employees and managers in control is restricted to internal checking, workers tend to identify it as the entire system. Obviously, there are other aspects to control. Executives of a large company, although they are fully involved in control, may not even see the forms and devices on which the internal checking is recorded.

Surveying   Surveying is the third control method related to measuring. When indicators cannot be expressed in financial units or counted, they can still be measured formally. Human performance is conventionally quantified in hours, dollars, or units of output, but human attitudes, perceptions, and other qualities cannot be quantified. Surveying offers a comparative measurement of qualities of this type. For example, the acceptability of a menu item to a market segment might be measured by a survey. Likewise, the motivation, intelligence, or skill of employees could be measured by an appropriate instrument and expressed in appropriate terms. For example, management might decide that the operation will benefit if employees are substantially loyal to the operation. Substantial loyalty among employees becomes the standard. Constructing a valid survey instrument requires specialists—psychologists, sociologists, and other behavioral scientists. Employee loyalty would be surveyed, and the results reported to management.

Observation   The fourth and last control measurement method is observation. The manager of an operation in the midst of an operational activity, for example, food preparation, measures performance by observation. The manager simply notes the quality and quantity of goods, service, and performance of his or her operation: the color of the rolls being baked, the progress of people washing and trimming vegetables, the ease with which food is transferred from production to service. Observation may seem to be mere subjective judgment to an employee, who may wonder, "How clean is clean?" In fact, a well-trained manager embodies the standards of the operation and uses his or her senses— hearing, smell, taste, sight, and touch—to determine whether standards are being met. At a glance, a manager should know whether lettuce has become too wilted to use. One sip of coffee should be sufficient to determine whether the coffee is acceptable to the operation's patrons.

Evaluation Processes   After measurement is made either by accounting, internal checking, surveying, or observation, the manager compares performance with the standard and then evaluates the seriousness of the deviation. If the evaluation warrants it, the manager might initiate appropriate corrective action (the next part of the control process).

Evaluation includes a comparison of the indicated performance with the standard and a judgment of the seriousness of the variance from the standard and whether or not it is to be corrected. This second step—correction—should be automatic. Management should decide which matters should always require correction; procedures that do not follow policy set by management should be corrected.

Management must establish a standard to determine how much variance in each area will necessitate correction. It is uneconomical for the operation to react to a minor deviation. Not even the control system of a mechanical device reacts to every change from the exact standard. If the standard in an operation is ten units, then perhaps correction should be initiated only when the indicator measures less than nine units of output.

If the correction step is not automatic, management may choose to control the particular area more closely to determine whether the variance represents a trend or is merely chance. It will do this monitoring through auditing, and information gathering.

Auditing   An operation can audit performance by formal assessment or survey methods or by observation. An operation can audit the measurements produced by internal checking and evaluate the significance of a shortage of five cans of sauerkraut, or of having only 1,000 customers instead of 2,000 during the month of July.

Information gathering   There are a number of informal processes of evaluation. The gathering of information does not have to be a detailed and formal process with many forms. The manager supervising an operational activity observes and measures, then evaluates, and finally, decides whether deviations have enough significance to warrant corrective action. Managers gather information in a number of informal ways; they learn the standards of management, observe workers in action, look over the forms and control devices used in their operations, and familiarize themselves with any skills their employees may have learned. The manager concerned with control would have pie crust made by determining the operation's standards for pie crust, assigning the task to an employee who knew how to mix the crust, and then inspecting the crusts before and after baking. Through dozens of informal processes, quality control is assured.

In addition, the measurement of an indicator may be straightforward and may facilitate evaluation. Information gathering is similar to observation; the information the control system needs for evaluation is readily available: for example, employee attitudes toward the night shift.

Mechanisms for Correction   The basis of a well-designed control system is a useful and flexible routine for the detection, evaluation, and elimination of any serious deviations from the operation's standards. If corrective action should be routine and automatic, it is a control process. On the other hand, if decision making is necessary before corrective action can be undertaken, then corrective action in that case becomes a managerial activity. A shortage of five cans of sauerkraut can simply result in the routine ordering of sauerkraut either through control of inventory or control of purchasing. If, on the other hand, profits have declined significantly, it is unlikely that corrective action will be simply to order the local newspaper to print the operation's advertisement three times a week instead of once a week. Management is concerned with the total performance of the operation. A decline in profits is a symptom of a deficiency in management. The province of the control system is internal operations. Corrective action can be taken in a straightforward manner because the information gathered by the control system, if interpreted correctly, should point up any errors within any system.

In other words, corrective action is a control process if it primarily involves directing of people or resources in some readily apparent and straightforward manner. It is a management process if it involves decision making and planning based on new information (information the control system is able to provide).

The manager of the control system remedies problems by directing changes in procedures or operations to maintain the organization's standards. If bread is not brown enough, he or she directs the baker to leave the loaves in the oven longer. The manager of the control system makes sure that employee appearance and behavior conform to the operation's standards. Through constant measurement, evaluation, and correction, the control system ensures evenness of quality in a foodservice operation.

Timing of Control Activities	Control objectives can best be achieved by implementing control procedures in one of three ways: before operational activities (precontrol); during operational activities (concurrent control); or after operational activities (postcontrol). The amount of time elapsing between the operational activity and the control procedure is also significant.

Ideally, all operational activities would be precontrolled. The control system then could predict the effectiveness of future activities, and future performance could be corrected before the operation suffered the consequences of a deviation from standards. Unfortunately, only certain operational activities can be precontrolled. For example, a direct mail advertising campaign can be tested; recipes can be tried before large batches are made; work systems can be studied before they are made operational. In the absence of intervening factors, actual performance should be equal to standards determined in precontrol. In other cases, precontrol can measure capability. Is the operating system or unit capable of, or adequately prepared for, meeting the operation's standards? In this instance, the service manager may evaluate the capabilities of the service system (staff, cleanliness, serviceware), or the food production manager may evaluate the capabilities of the food production system (staff and equipment).

For the service system and the production system, control procedures are also carried out during operations. A manager frequently compares ongoing performance and makes adjustments so the functioning of people, machines, or materials meets standards. On the other hand, it may be impractical to correct deficiencies in the work system by rearrangement of equipment or impossible even to measure the performance of an advertising campaign during its presentation.

Postcontrol compares measurements of results with standards. It has two limitations that make it inferior to precontrol or concurrent control: first, the operation may have already been damaged by the deviation from the standard, and second, the time lag between postcontrol and the operational activity can make it very difficult to identify the cause of the deviation, although its consequences may be apparent.

If postcontrol cannot at least be accompanied by precontrol and concurrent control, managers seek to minimize its disadvantages by compressing control periods and by speeding information about the results of an operational activity to those persons who can take corrective action. For example, instead of evaluating the menu program once a month by use of a menu scatter sheet or similar device and delaying the preparation of the report another month, the menu program can be evaluated daily and the report prepared overnight for action the next morning.

Postcontrol can present a third disadvantage. Because performance tends to be averaged over a period of time, the results may be deceptive. For instance, an operation's standard may be a 22 percent bar cost (an entirely hypothetical number). Postcontrol figures from a monthly audit that met this standard might be the result of $5,000 of business in the first part of the month at 33 percent and $5,000 of business in the second part of the month at 11 percent. Control by the week would present more accurate data that would result in questioning why the 11 percent cost could not be maintained all month.

From the perspective of the people whose activities are being controlled, these three types of control have other implications. The attitudes of employees can influence the timing of control. Precontrols may be viewed as directives, and thus will be welcomed by employees who are aided by direction and resented by employees who are not. For example, in catering a large wedding, most employees—even seasoned professionals—gain confidence if the unit's preparedness is carefully assessed and strengthened. On the other hand, an employee whose job involves much repetition, warewashing for example, would probably resent daily precontrol.

Concurrent controls receive strong employee reactions as well. These controls are usually yes-or-no devices that do not motivate workers or invite employee participation. To accept them without resentment, employees must recognize their appropriateness to the situation. Under conditions of operational stress because of unusual business activity, material shortages, understaffing, intense competition, or other major problems that threaten the organization, close concurrent control is seen as legitimate by almost everyone. On the other hand, in the absence of operational stress, it can be seen as overly oppressive.

Postcontrol devices can be equated with scorecards. Some individuals enjoy beating the standard. Others are uneasy with the all-or-nothing aspects of postcontrol.

Use of Control Devices
Foodservice operations employ various means to communicate the information that control procedures produce. A very simple control system may involve only oral communication. An owner/operator exercising only concurrent control observes performance, compares it with standards, and prescribes corrective action directly to workers.

More often control procedures involve written communication. Reports and directives in narrative form may be used, or forms and devices with data bases relevant to particular control activities may be developed. Preceding chapters have offered examples of such forms and devices. Forms and devices produced by government agencies for the control of certain areas of foodservice operations are in widespread use. Operational activities are also controlled internally through standards imposed from outside the organization such as unemployment insurance, Social Security, the Occupational Safety and Health Act, sales tax, and other governmental controls.

Some operations have succeeded in using automatic electronic data processing equipment for control information. With properly designed equipment, information gathering, comparison with standards, and initiation of corrective action are facilitated.

Attainment of control objectives may be severely limited by an operation's control devices. An operation that cannot afford to allocate managerial or clerical time to the preparation of reports and forms may be limited to superficial and ineffective control of only one or two areas. The operation may attempt financial control by compiling a monthly profit-and-loss statement and may attempt labor cost control merely by using information compiled by government-mandated payroll forms, instead of developing control devices appropriate to the operation.

Even in fairly large enterprises, the foodservice operation's fast pace, many transactions, complex operating systems, changing operating conditions, large personnel structure, and limited management structure make it difficult to exert control with written forms and devices at a cost consistent with investment objectives. The commercial operation that can neither afford the data processing equipment used by the large chains nor the clerical costs that many noncommercial operations tolerate may be unable to gather the information necessary for a comprehensive control system.

CONTROL ROUTINE

Routine includes all the daily activities and processes that must be done in order for any foodservice operation to function. If a representative control routine exists in the foodservice industry, it is the day-to-day control responsibilities of the manager of a foodservice unit of a large company. The manager of a unit of a chain of restaurants—a limited-menu, take-in/take-out restaurant—or of an account in a hospital, university, or factory of a contract foodservice company is generally part of a well-organized control system. Although there are thousands of people in this position, the control routine of the unit manager may not be typical of the present-day foodservice industry; owner-operated small restaurants still predominate. The tendency of the industry to larger economic entities suggests, however, that professional managers shall soon outnumber owner/operators.

Control Routine of a Unit Manager

The day-to-day operations of the control system of a large company are entrusted to the unit manager—the person directly responsible for the operation and success of a single foodservice unit. The company managing the food service of a large hospital is entrusting a significant amount of capital, the company's reputation, substantial revenues, the jobs of perhaps 50 employees, and the health of hundreds of people to an individual who may be based 500 miles from company headquarters. The unit manager of each operation is also responsible for the successful marketing of the operation's product in the locality.

The unit manager's control routine covers seven areas: (1) policy administration; (2) office maintenance; (3) control of operating systems; (4) control of personnel; (5) control of cash; (6) communication and reporting to headquarters; and (7) corrective action.

POLICY ADMINISTRATION

Whatever policies, standards, and practices are articulated by headquarters must be followed by the unit. In effect, the unit manager is being asked to match the unit's capabilities, operating procedures, products, and performance with established standards. The unit manager is supplied with a manual, sometimes called a "Standards and Practices Manual," that is periodically supplemented by additions and policy communications. Standards and practices manuals typically cover:

- Responsibilities and duties of management.
- Pricing of menu items.
- Credit policies.
- Relations with vendors.
- Communication with headquarters.
- Payroll procedures.
- Food quality and portions.
- Labor organization as it affects the company as a whole.
- Insurance.
- Legal matters.
- Worker privileges (meals, purchase of products).
- Matters which affect the company's image, for example, the sale of certain items, dress codes, and advertising.
- Client relations (for those operations serving a contract client).
- Procedures for control of the operating systems.

Exhibit 13.1 shows what might be contained in representative sections of a policy manual.

OFFICE MAINTENANCE The maintenance of the control system as a work system made up of equipment, workers, and materials requires attention. In addition to personnel and large office equipment and furnishings, it is necessary to organize and maintain forms, devices, stationery, menus, printed merchandising materials, cash control devices such as coin rolls and seals for night deposit bags, reference materials such as manuals, recipe files, and record files of forms, reports, memos, applications for employment, and so on.

The typical unit is controlled with at least 50 different forms and devices, although each may not be used daily. The unit must maintain control records for several years, along with files on hundreds of products and scores of vendors. A certain amount of correspondence with individuals and companies outside the organization is also likely. Exhibit 13.2 shows part of a typical forms list that might be used by a unit foodservice manager.

CONTROL OF OPERATING SYSTEMS Forms and devices are concrete expressions of the manager's control of the various operating systems: menu planning, work, purchasing, supply, production, and service. The control routine is formalized by record-keeping devices that assist in communicating information to management. Although not every form and device described in preceding chapters is used by any single operation, the unit manager is likely to be charged with numerous control procedures important to his or her particular operation. The list that follows is fairly representative but not

EXHIBIT 13.1   Excerpts from a Typical Standards and Practices Manual

Section 100

114   Unit Schedule
Intent of using definite established and posted hours of full operation is to contribute to a reputation of professionalism and consistency. Once established, there can be no variation without expressed authorization.

114.1   Opening Time
a.   Opening time shall be 8:00 a.m. local time.
b.   No food or beverage will be served prior to this time.
c.   All employees assigned to opening shift will be in complete uniform and on station fifteen (15) minutes prior to opening time.

114.2   Closing Time
a.   Unit will close at 11:00 p.m. local time.
b.   Customers who enter the unit prior to that time will be served.
c.   Customers who seek to enter the unit after that time will be politely refused service.
d.   Customers in unit after that time will be allowed to finish their meals in a leisurely fashion.
e.   Employees will be scheduled to complete closing routine as soon as possible after official closing time.
f.   Only a la carte menu (not dinner menu) will be used after 10:00 p.m. local time.

Section 800

842   Salad and Sandwich Vegetable Preparation

842.5   Preparation of Tomatoes for Sandwiches
a.   Use only firm ripe 6 x 6 standard lugs. See specification #212.
b.   Slice tomatoes to yield 45 slices per kilo.
c.   Pre-portion 4 slices of tomato on patty paper for speed in handling, quality control, and proper portioning by pantry workers.
d.   Keep tomatoes refrigerated in a covered container (P-15) at all times.

875   Beverage Preparation

875.4   Coffee Preparation and Handling
a.   Use only coffee from authorized vendors.
b.   Coffee must conform to specification #339.
c.   Prepare coffee according to procedure outlined in Section 412 in Recipe and Preparation Manual.
d.   Make coffee no sooner than 5 minutes before opening of unit.
e.   Dispose of unsold coffee 20 minutes after brewing.
f.   Clean machine after each brewing cycle.
g.   Clean and sanitize machine each day.
h.   Rotate coffee stocks to ensure freshness.
i.   A management employee must sample coffee from each brewing.

EXHIBIT 13.2 Forms and Devices Used by a Unit Manager

Form Number	Form Name	Purpose
FS 1.00	Receiving Record	Recording merchandise received from outside purveyors
FS 1.01	Food Purchased for Cash	Recording cash purchases
FS 2.00	Inventory	Maintain inventory records
FS 3.00	Monthly Report	
FS 4.00	Operating Statistics	Worksheets for preparation of monthly reports
FS 5.00	Management Checklist	
FS 6.00	Weekly Performance Record	Report to headquarters
FS 7.00	Daily Order Sheet	Order from commissary
FS 8.00	Guest Check Daily Record	
FS 9.00	Uniform Issue Record	
FS 10.00	Service Worker Production Record	Productivity studies
FS 11.00	Menu Analysis	Menu item popularity survey
FS 12.00	Sales by Hour Record	Business performance record
FS 13.00	Counter Guest Checks	
FS 14.00	Dining Room Guest Checks	
FS 15.00	Fixture Order	Authorization to purchase equipment

inclusive of the procedures a unit manager must deal with through control system forms and devices:

- Menu precosting and abstracting.
- Menu analysis.
- Recipe costing.
- Beverage costing.
- Inventory of food, serviceware, linen, equipment, and so on.
- Forecasting of expenditures, covers, business, and labor.
- Record keeping for purchasing.
- Record keeping of food transfers within the unit and within the company (from the storage area to the production department; from a central commissary to the unit).
- Business volume analysis.
- Labor budgeting.
- Labor scheduling.
- Labor productivity analysis.
- Production scheduling.
- Preventive maintenance.
- Value analysis.
- Yield and cost analysis of purchased products.

Employees are obviously an important part of the foodservice operation; the control of personnel is an important part of a manager's routine. The induction of an individual into the operation involves the unit manager in a lengthy control procedure. An employee must fill out an application form. In addition, the manager usually has to prepare other forms and records:

- Employee personnel record (usually with copies to headquarters).
- Employee's withholding allowance certificate.
- Applications for hospitalization and other benefit plans.
- Surety bond applications, if necessary.
- Union documents, if necessary.
- Insurance forms.

It is also necessary for the manager on the basis of these records, and with reference to company policies, to control payroll records, if not the actual checks of employees. In a given period, in addition to the hours the employee worked and basic rate of pay, the manager must deduct Social Security tax and the appropriate city, state, and federal withholding taxes, and maintain records for payroll purposes on such matters as cash advances to the employee, vacations, vacation pay, sick benefits, overtime, holiday pay, and savings bond contributions.

Other control procedures may be necessary when a worker is laid off, fired, or disciplined; when the worker's pay rate or job status changes; when the worker is transferred to another location; or when the worker falls ill or is injured on the job.

None of these procedures requires judgment or decision making; they are performed according to rules set by the company, a government agency, or an outside company such as a bonding company. These procedures principally involve computation and clerical efforts.

CONTROL OF CASH   Procedures for handling cash are of considerable concern to the foodservice company. The unit manager uses control procedures to prevent losses and make it obvious to every employee that any losses that do occur will be promptly identified. Frequently, the control of cash involves the unit manager in

- Counting cash.
- Approving payments by credit card.
- Approving the cashing of checks.
- Balancing cash with cash accounts using such control devices as dining room recapitulation sheets and cash register data.
- Preparing bank deposits and, sometimes, making them.
- Supervising persons who handle cash.
- Authorizing cash disbursements.

- Managing petty cash accounts.
- Monitoring documents which represent cash such as void guest checks and officers' meal tickets.

Although none of these procedures is in itself time-consuming, the manager of a unit with a dining room, a customer service area with five registers, and some coffee wagons spends a considerable amount of time on cash control procedures.

COMMUNICATION AND REPORTING TO HEADQUARTERS   Most foodservice chain companies require weekly or monthly business reports from the unit manager. The performance of the operation is measured in financial units on the basis of indicators such as total sales volume, check average, cost of food products used, cost of labor, and so on. These measurements can be expressed in simple numerical units or as ratios or percentages. Other report forms are used to compare present figures with either forecasts, budgets, or past performance figures.

Some of the largest foodservice companies require daily reports. When the unit manager must keep daily records, developing weekly or monthly reports is facilitated. The use of electronic cash registers that store data and report it on the register tape greatly facilitates daily record keeping.

Other operations with electronic data processing equipment in the headquarters unit require the manager to report data directly to the computer. The unit manager either sends the data to headquarters over telephone lines from a small device that resembles a hand calculator or prepares magnetic cards on a specialized electronic typewriter. One or two companies, through the use of special telephone lines, have connected the electronic cash registers in the operation with the computer at headquarters. The data accumulated can be sent without an intermediate device. In some instances, the data sent to the company headquarters are interpreted and organized to produce reports, payrolls, and inventory records for the unit. If the operational unit is linked to a central commissary, the reported data might also be used to produce a food order for the operation's purchasing department.

Other communications with the headquarters from the unit tend to be in three categories:

Requests for authorization   It may be necessary for the unit manager to request authorization to purchase equipment or advertising; to change vendors from those the company has authorized; to make menu changes; to change specifications, standards, portions, or procedures.

Duplication of records   Copies of records concerning sales, personnel, equipment maintenance, waste, quality control, or other operational activities may be required by headquarters.

Written reports   The unit manager may be required to submit written reports on areas that are not described by standard forms and devices: reports on health inspections, employee relations, labor organization activity, consumer reactions, merchandising programs, and plans for all areas.

Headquarters communicates back to the unit manager. Requests for authorizations are either granted or denied; duplicates of the reports headquarters has prepared from operational records are supplied to the unit manager; and periodic memos or bulletins are sent to the unit.

CORRECTIVE ACTION   The effective unit manager routinely initiates corrective action. Any deviation from standards—articulated in policy manuals or known to the manager through managerial training or education—that has been disclosed by measurement procedures is corrected. In the simplest instance, the loss of materials, determined by internal checking or by observation, results in action appropriate to its cause: improving physical security, retraining personnel, modifying preparation, service, or handling procedures, and so on.

Some corrective action is initiated by headquarters: the manager is told to take action on a specific problem. Headquarters may have greater expertise, standards that the manager is unaware of, or more information. Corrective action initiated by headquarters can affect any operational area. Direction provided by headquarters depends on the organization of the company's control system. Highly centralized systems may direct details of day-to-day operations. Decentralized systems allow the unit manager to initiate most corrective actions within the limits of broad policy statements. Exhibit 13.3 offers some hypothetical examples of corrective action initiated by headquarters.

MAKING THE CONTROL ROUTINE MORE EFFECTIVE

Only a limited discussion of the control routine of a foodservice organization was presented in the preceding sections on the unit manager. At hierarchical levels above the unit manager in the headquarters office and perhaps in regional offices, executives have their own routines. At levels below the unit manager, supervisors such as the kitchen production manager and the purchasing agent may have overlapping or complementary routines. Foodservice control entails a considerable amount of human effort. It is possible in many instances to improve the efficiency of control without sacrificing the attainment of objectives and without violating the principles of control. Indeed, increased efficiency often results in a speedier flow of information and generally more effective functioning of the system.

Two approaches to the improvement of systems are used widely in the foodservice industry: (1) improved techniques of information flow,

EXHIBIT 13.3 **Examples of Corrective Actions Taken by a Company Headquarters**

To:	The unit manager
From:	Company Headquarters, Quality Control and Standards Division
By:	Quality Control Technician
Re:	Three-Day Quality Control Assessment

Item	Problem	Solution
1. Tomato juice	Stored in can	Must be stored in plastic juice container
2. Stale coffee	Served old because it is made too far in advance and not rotated	Train for proper handling and make only enough to be served in the next 20 minutes
3. Lettuce	Not soaked in cold water and cut with a knife causing rust	Tear with fingers, soak in ice water
4. Hard boiled eggs	Allowed to stand in hot water causing dark yolks	See standards book for proper handling
5. Cole slaw	Served warm, too dry or too wet	Store on ice or refrigerate. Follow standards book
6. Soup	Served cold or served without proper proportion of vegetables to broth	Keep hot—stir from bottom
7. Gravy	Served lumpy, cold or watery	Keep hot—whip with whisk
8. Bacon	Cooked ahead and served cold or cooked too well done and served crumbly	Follow standards book for preparation
9. Bread	Allowed to dry out	Store in closed bread drawer
10. Hamburger rolls	Not toasted properly, not buttered properly and allowed to dry out	Follow standards in standards book

and (2) use of data processing equipment to release managers and other workers from routine clerical tasks.

Improved
Information Flow

Information can be considered a raw material to be transferred from one location to another where it is modified by selection, consolidation, or interpretation, or simply stored. Like any raw material, information from control procedures can be transferred more efficiently using a number of techniques:

• The flow of information can be improved by eliminating backtracking and crisscrossing.
• Methods of handling information can be made more efficient by better design of forms.
• Procedures can be combined or eliminated.
• Storage of information can be eliminated if it is unnecessary.
• Flow can be directed to people who need the information; delays, readings, and reviews eliminated when unnecessary.
• Human engineering concepts can be introduced: forms and devices can be made more legible and permit easier entry of information.
• Reproduction by photocopying can be substituted for actual duplication of information.
• Preprinted multipurpose form sets can be developed and used so that consolidation of information from various individuals does not require progressively more duplication of information as it is transferred from one form to another.
• Transfer of information from one place to another can be improved.
• High-speed equipment can be introduced such as electric typewriters and programmable desk calculators.
• Control routines can be integrated effectively: reports, forms, devices, and other documents used in a control routine at one level can become part of another routine so that information does not have to be transferred; for example, combination purchase order/inventory/requisition devices can also allow for accounting information.

Use of Data
Processing

There are data processing devices in many commercial foodservice operations: the more sophisticated electronic cash registers collect, process, and present data. The preset register supplies data such as sales per hour by item, total sales by item, cash receipts, charge receipts, payouts, and so on.

Certain systems also allow the manager to produce control devices, in the form of printouts that can be used as service workers' duplicate checks or customer receipts. Some registers scan pencil-marked guest checks, display relevant information for different cooking stations, and submit totals for collection.

Some automated bar systems combine basic control capabilities with the ability to mix drinks and dispense them according to predetermined formulas. Other operations monitor food and beverage sales by converting guest checks to key punch cards so that sales can be tabulated and compared with projections and cost figures.

Of course, there is also widespread use of data processing for traditional business information purposes such as payroll and accounts receivable. Often, the foodservice operation uses an accounting service which in turn uses data processing for these purposes.

As electronic cash registers have become more sophisticated, for example, in the number of preset items possible, the potential for extending menu items sales to inventory has developed. The newest equipment allows the manager to preset an inventory figure for certain items at the beginning of service, and then, at the end of service after keying in the amount of the item left, compare actual usage with projected usage.

A total system on this basis would have additional capabilities: all inventory files would be updated constantly, purchase orders would be generated from par-levels programmed into the system, precosts would be compared with actual costs and management would be supplied with summary reports. At the moment, only the custom-made installations used by the very largest commercial companies and institutions have this capability.

While it is apparent that data processing is approaching some sophistication in the areas of control of cash and sales, the larger problems of foodservice management are in areas other than these. Control of cash and sales are important concerns, but control of a foodservice operation involves much more, and other items are much higher among the manager's priorities: menu planning, production forecasting, portion control, and recipe formulation are among the areas in which the modern manager is so overwhelmed by data and tedious computation that often a timely, meaningful decision is impossible, thereby providing classic problems for solution by data processing.

As an example, the foodservice management of any property with several restaurants or outlets, for instance, a large hotel or resort complex, may have difficulty forecasting sales by menu item in a particular unit. While 3,000 lunches may be served, where will they be eaten... in the main dining room, in the cafe, in the club, on the terrace... and what items in what quantities of these different menus will be chosen? There is a tendency to overproduce in each of these outlets. A computer could present data accumulated from sales records, guest history, and operating logs for use in forecasting sales by the menu item in each outlet.

The problems of recipe formulation may be similarly relieved by the ability of the computer to present appropriate and accurate data. For example, the cost of the popular salad bar varies greatly from week to week because of the changing cost of produce. Fresh greens can vary by several hundred percent in the course of a season. The operator aided by an appropriately programmed computer might be able to vary the formula for a specific day to meet cost parameters and maintain quality acceptable to patrons.

Labor scheduling offers another opportunity to apply information processing. Many service operations could benefit by stagger scheduling—assigning different starting times to each worker—yet only 20 percent of those operations surveyed use it. In effect, this means that many operations use labor unnecessarily. Based on a forecast of business supplied by the computer combined with an analysis of individual worker's productivity—also supplied by the computer—the manager could prepare a schedule that would closely correspond to real needs. The computer could also project labor cost on the basis of sales, make overtime projections, be programmed to schedule on the basis of seniority, and so on.

Even foodservice organizations with management that is fully aware of the potential of data processing for control may be frustrated by the cost of data processing for specific applications. The equipment itself does not present the greatest financial problem: the use of a computer can be rented (a practice called "time-sharing"). However, the financial obstacle to many foodservice organizations that have investigated data processing is the cost of programming. A computer is incapable of processing data without specific instructions on how it is to be done. It is necessary to program, or instruct, the computer for each step in data processing. If the manager wishes to produce recipes with the use of the computer, a computer procedure has to be developed so that, on receiving the various data, the computer will calculate an accurate result.

Either the computer must be programmed by an individual working with it, or a commercial program must be purchased from an outside source. The expense in the first instance is considerable. Only operations associated with large organizations such as universities or hospitals or very large commercial organizations can afford the services of a programmer for a full range of data processing applications. On the other hand, commercial programs are expensive, and none specifically for the foodservice industry yet exists. The foodservice organization can purchase programs and associated materials (collectively called software) related to general business applications, but no menu planning, recipe development, or forecasting programs exist. This situation may be remedied as foodservice operations adapt to the most modern methods of control.

Chapter 14
Foodservice: Principles, Prospects, and Projections

Paradoxically, generalizations about foodservice management, foodservice operations, and the foodservice industry are always right and always wrong. These generalizations can at once be proved with specific examples and disproved with other specific examples.

In spite of this paradox, it is possible to suggest that the success of foodservice managers lies in their appreciation and application of principles of foodservice management; that the prosperity of an operation is due to its ability to adapt to changed or changing conditions; and that the foodservice industry is not the sole creation of individuals and companies but rather an evolving part of the changing society it serves.

PRINCIPLES OF FOODSERVICE MANAGEMENT

Foodservice management constantly confronts uncertainty and change in areas critical to its functioning. The management, marketing, menu-planning, work, purchasing, supply, production, service, business, and control systems cannot be designed to forever withstand the battering of future events. Markets, costs, technologies, workers, competitors, economies, and societies change—and to prosper, the foodservice operation must adapt. It may be necessary to alter market strategies, restructure menus, redesign work systems, modify production strategies, change service procedures, refinance, and adjust control processes to ensure continuance of the operation. To fail to change is to fail. The history of the foodservice industry is littered with failures of once-successful companies that could not adapt to new conditions. There are, however, also examples of companies that have continued to prosper despite fundamental changes that have affected their every operational area.

EXHIBIT 14.1   Principles of Foodservice Management

Principle	Description
Objective Principle	Operational activities are directed to some objective or goal.
Environment Principle	The formulation of objectives and the attainment of objectives is influenced by factors outside the foodservice organization.
Limited-Resource Principle	The resources of the foodservice organization must be used efficiently.
Systems Principle	The functioning of any element of a foodservice operation is dependent on the functioning of other elements.
Adaptation Principle	The growth and continuance of a foodservice organization is related to its ability to adapt to change.
Market Principle	A particular foodservice organization prospers because it provides a significant market benefit.
Planning Principle	Foodservice organizations best achieve their objectives if their managers anticipate rather than react to situations.
People Principle	The contribution of people to the foodservice organization must be maximized with respect to the total functioning of the organization.

The enduring strength of a foodservice operation is the ability of management to foresee challenges and opportunities and to meet them effectively. Fundamental to this ability is the recognition of a number of principles (discussed earlier in their applications to individual foodservice systems) that can become the basis for the progressive management of a total foodservice organization. Exhibit 14.1 summarizes and describes these principles.

Objective Principle   The formulation of objectives and the maintenance of a goal orientation are fundamental to the management of foodservice organizations. An examination of the practices of many foodservice operations suggests that two factors—tradition and momentum—make this a difficult principle to apply consistently. Tradition legitimatizes courses of action that are ineffective and perhaps purposeless; momentum shortens perspectives so that means are sometimes confused with ends. Tradition may cause some managers to justify current actions with reference to the past without consideration of objectives or their effectiveness under changed circumstances. Likewise, momentum may gather around a particular managerial technique, such as food cost control, obscuring its purpose. For example, a manager proves the operation has a 32 percent food cost without acting further to improve the operation. Similarly, an advertising campaign may achieve sufficient momentum so that it becomes an end in itself instead of a means to an end, producing advertisements without producing results. Gallons of soup may be produced without producing satisfaction of consumer wants; splendid decors may be installed without producing the derivative product that satisfies the market; or tremendous growth can occur without producing profitability; and so on.

Consistent with this objective principle of foodservice management is the concept that managers should be judged by their results, not by their efforts. Voluminous studies, new procedure manuals, rampant generation of control forms are symptoms of managerial activity that has lost its objective orientation.

Managerial accountability must be accompanied by adequate control procedures that measure the progress of any activity toward achieving a definite goal and that provide feedback concerning excessive deviations or changes in circumstances. These situations—or changes in objectives—may prompt changes and adjustments in operational activities. Foodservice operations are not missiles launched on some predetermined course with the expectation of hitting a distant target; rather, they can be guided continuously to the better achievement of objectives or toward new objectives.

Environment Principle A foodservice operation is influenced directly and significantly by factors outside the foodservice organization that its management cannot control. It is necessary to recognize these factors in both the immediate circumstance in which the operation functions and in the larger economic and social environment. It is necessary to understand their implications for the foodservice operation—either as opportunities or as constraints—and to control their impact on the operation.

Foodservice managers cannot defy world economic conditions that affect basic commodities, market imperatives, the objectives of suppliers or workers, the goals of sponsors, laws of community and country, and so on, without compromising the foodservice organization.

The fast pace of foodservice operations and their extreme sensitivity to external factors makes it impossible to plan for every contingency. The quality of managerial reactions to immediate events affects the attainment of organizational objectives. For the operation to prosper, managers must have the ability to manage situations; they must have organizational resources with which to act; and they must perform within an organizational climate that encourages managers to confront challenging situations.

To deal with these contingencies, managers must develop operational standards suitable to their particular foodservice operation. Each operation must confront its own particular opportunities and limits within the framework of its own particular abilities and resources. Specified operational standards for construction, for labor use, for advertising copywriting, for menu planning, for the creation of a service concept, and so on, are the result of a reconciliation of the foodservice organization's objectives and resources with its environment.

Both the immediate environment of the foodservice operation and the larger economic and social environment must be dealt with. Local events as they affect the operation must be taken into account: changes in population, employment conditions that affect disposable income of the market segment, alternative opportunities of employment of foodservice workers, merger of a local supplier with a national company, and so on, can affect the foodservice operation. Equally, the rate of inflation, interest rates, political events that affect the price of basic commodities, national legislation, and other larger events must also be considered in planning and decision making.

Social values as well as economic ones influence the foodservice operation. Consumerism, tastes, community attitudes about foodservice occupations, esthetic sensibilities, and moral codes all have implications for the prosperity of the foodservice operation.

Limited-Resources Principle

The resources of a foodservice organization must be used efficiently to achieve the organization's objectives. Achieving objectives without regard for available resources or costs is seldom acceptable.

Limitations on resources prompt managers to establish strategic priorities in an attempt to achieve overall objectives. In a commercial operation, goals usually include some investment objective that must be reconciled with other objectives. In noncommercial operations, goals include some objective reflecting the financial resources of the operation by which other objectives are qualified. Necessarily, there must be some rationing of resources so that objectives of higher priority are achieved before objectives of lower priority.

The resources of a foodservice operation are best utilized by its performing those operational activities that it performs best. Any operational activity that can be better performed by an outside organization should be performed by an outside organization—partial or full production of food products, cleaning and maintenance, advertising and promotion, work-system design, operational management, and so on.

In allocating resources either inside or outside the organization, management must undertake to expend the minimum amount of resources to achieve a desired result. It must compare input to output to establish standards for efficient allocation of resources. To achieve this, management examines costs, conducts value analysis, and gauges the time value of money.

Cost effectiveness   Cost effectiveness is an almost universal criterion for the evaluation of alternative courses of action directed to some objective. Clearly, if two courses of action will readily achieve the objective, then the less costly would be chosen. Many choices, however, are not that simple. Relative effectiveness—the capacity to achieve the objective—has to be compared to the relative cost of achieving the objective. It is possible to choose a less effective method, system, or piece of equipment because it is less costly. In a simple case, a foodservice operator might elect to slice cold cuts by hand instead of purchasing an electric slicer because the cost of the slicer is not justified by the benefits it provides.

Even when cost effectiveness cannot be directly expressed in dollars and cents as it can be in making the decision about the slicer, it can be an important consideration. "Costs" can be expressed in terms of managerial effort, effect on the market image, worker stress, operation-patron interactions, and so on.

Value analysis   It is necessary to examine every product used, every work method, every procedure, every piece of equipment to eliminate any feature, quality, procedure, or component that expends resources but does not directly contribute to the attainment of objectives.

Directed to products or things, this effort is called value analysis. It results in specification of food products and equipment so that there are no superfluous costly qualities or features. Directed to work methods or procedures, this effort is called value engineering, and it results in very careful work planning so that there is no wasted activity or time and so that input in terms of human efforts in hours or in dollars is the minimum necessary to achieve the desired output.

Time value of money   The numerous possible uses of monetary resources and their capacity to be used again and again add other dimensions to a consideration of efficiency. Time and timing become important. For a long-term use of funds to be as efficient as a short-term use of the same funds, output must increase. Hence, values can be placed on postponability and on turnover of investment. Consideration of the time value of money is relevant to almost all managerial decision making from the study of the feasibility of a new enterprise to the management of inventory.

Systems Principle   The functioning of any element of a foodservice operation is dependent on the functioning of other elements. For its successful management, a larger view of a functioning foodservice organization as dependent on the effective interaction of all its elements must be taken. Management is obliged to address the total functioning of the organization in making specific decisions relative to any aspect of it. While there may be a single starting point in a specific decision process, the implications for the organization of any proposed course of action must be considered.

The planning and decision making related to one operational system must take into account the constraints and opportunities presented by other operational systems. Likewise, the planning and decision making related to an element of an operational system (such as a specific operational activity, human resources, or equipment resources) has to take into account the functioning of all the other elements.

In many instances the objectives of one system or element are in conflict with one another. For example, production efficiency might be gained at the expense of competitive advantage (a marketing objective) by reducing the number of menu items offered. An overall perspective that places the objectives of the organization before the particular objectives of a system or element of a system is needed to effect a compromise that will achieve the optimum result for the organization.

Adaptation Principle   The growth and continuance of a foodservice organization is related to its ability to adapt to change; future events will make the current elements and systems of a foodservice organization—regardless of its success—obsolete. Although the example of many foodservice companies would seem to suggest the contrary, a decline in prosperity need not inevitably follow a period of success. Continuous renewal and adaptation to changed circumstances are possible. The foodservice organization can prosper in new situations if it has the capacity to adapt. This capacity lies in management's problem-solving orientation, flexibility, and sense of purpose.

Managerial problem solving is the process by which changes in the organization are effected. Instead of conforming to some absolute standard or ideal, managers fashion a solution that is appropriate to the particular problems confronting the organization. This flexibility in meeting problems because of changed circumstances should be a criterion for the design and redesign of systems, for structuring the organization itself, its jobs, and its menus, and, in fact, for every element of the foodservice organization.

Individuals, organizations, and systems tend to become rigid and resist change. It is possible to strengthen the ability of the foodservice organization to meet new challenges by developing its sense of purpose. Constant orientation to objectives prevents stagnation and complacency.

Market Principle   A particular foodservice organization prospers because it provides a significant market benefit. The objectives of the foodservice operation must be reconciled with market objectives if it is to prosper. The investment objectives of a commercial operation or the nutritional objectives of a noncommercial operation cannot be achieved in defiance of the values, needs, and wants of the people it can serve.

The tastes, needs, and wants of the market segment are the ultimate referents in operational decisions concerning the foodservice product. Standards for the foodservice product with regard to price, presentation, flavor profile, decor, and service are also established by the foodservice operation's customers, guests, or clients.

Planning Principle   Foodservice organizations best achieve their objectives if their managements anticipate rather than react to situations. Anticipation of future events and their implications for the foodservice operations is essential to effective management. The future vulnerability of the operation can be reduced by information about the operation's environment and about the operation. Not everything can be known about the external factors that may influence the operation, but some future events can be anticipated and contingency plans developed. Information about the operation's current functioning leads to an understanding of its capacity to prosper in the conditions that can be anticipated. Deficiencies can be corrected and vulnerabilities minimized. The creative function of management—developing the organization's ability to meet the challenges that face it—depends on understanding the workings and capacities of an organization through an analysis of its performance.

The planning and decision making that follow this analysis of performance must be undertaken with intellectual rigor. The same intellectual rigor must also be applied to the daily management of a foodservice operation. Although a single decision involving minor elements of the foodservice operation does not significantly affect the organization's effectiveness, collectively a series of many small decisions may have great impact.

People Principle   The contribution of the people to the foodservice organization must be maximized with respect to the total functioning of the operation. The nature of the foodservice operation and its product makes people particularly important to its success. People have to be recognized as an economic resource. People also have to be recognized as having emotional, psychological, and social qualities that affect the performance of the foodservice operation. The contribution of people can be maximized through motivation, control of labor, and management of service.

Motivation   Individuals are motivated in diverse ways. Motivation must be appropriate to the individual and appropriate to the objectives of the organization. Ideally, motivation serves to fully integrate human elements with the technical elements of the foodservice organization.

Control of labor   The people of the foodservice organization have to be considered an economic resource. Problems with regard to the availability and quality of labor have to be recognized. Efficiency and productivity are also considerations, as labor units must be rationed, budgeted, and controlled.

Management of service   The interaction of the people of the food-service operation with its market is a partial product of the foodservice operation. To the extent that this partial product is important to the success of the operation, these interactions must be managed.

PROSPECTS FOR FOODSERVICE

Depending on their objectives, management, resources, and the particular situations that confront them, individual foodservice organizations are variously affected by the opportunities and challenges that the foodservice industry faces. Some of the components of change—the factors and events that will cause some operations to prosper and others to decline—are apparent, but only the management of the individual foodservice organization can judge their specific implications. No one has to manage the 85-billion-dollar foodservice industry; someone must manage each of the more than 500,000 foodservice operations.

Four factors should be considered as potential influences on the prosperity of the foodservice operation and the nature of the foodservice industry: (1) market factors; (2) economic factors; (3) social factors; and (4) technological factors.

Market Factors   Stimulated by a variety of factors ranging from population changes to health information, the foodservice market is changing. The wants and needs of certain market segments are changing. Some segments are growing larger and others smaller. New markets are emerging. Some operations will be unaffected by these changes while others will face new opportunities and challenges. The foodservice market does not break up like a logjam and reform differently somewhere downstream. Rather, it changes piecemeal. Some operations feel the effects of change immediately: changes in the market occur at their doorsteps, among their patrons and potential patrons. Others more remote must wait for changes, should they come at all, to be diffused throughout the market. For example, three generations of Americans have eaten a light breakfast, but there still are many persons who remain immune to the temptations of corn flakes. Perhaps the successful operations that serve traditional ham, egg, and grits, or steak, egg, and potato specials may have to change their menus.

Although the implications for specific operations cannot be predicted, a number of sources of major changes can be identified.

POPULATION CHANGES   Numerous population changes are apparent in the United States: an increasing number of older people, smaller families, slowed population growth, more divorced people, more working women, growth of certain cities, a movement of people to the "sun-belt" states, and so on. As the makeup of the population changes and as shifts of population occur, new markets will become accessible to foodservice operations.

ECONOMIC
CHANGES

There are two economic changes of significance: continuing growth of discretionary income for most Americans, and the increasing number of Americans willing or obliged to spend some of their income on food away from home. Both trends augur well for the continued prosperity of the foodservice industry.

CHANGES IN
MOTIVATION

Changes in motivation are necessarily much more fragmented (less likely to apply across the board for the entire foodservice industry) than either population or economic changes. But since few foodservice companies, perhaps only those seven with more than 1,000 units, have national markets, changes in motivation are much more important to the prosperity of individual foodservice organizations. The people in the foodservice operation, on the sidewalk or highway outside, may be changing significantly in their wants, needs, likes, and expectations for satisfaction. Several recent phenomena are likely to significantly affect the foodservice operation's basic systems.

Diet awareness   People are becoming increasingly concerned about their intake of dietary fat from animal sources, their weight, and the amount of chemical food additives they eat. Although the basis of these concerns can perhaps be disputed, changes in market perceptions cannot be denied. A "health food" industry has developed consisting of specialized food manufacturers and retail outlets as well as a few restaurants. There are scores of health-through-food magazines, hundreds of diet books, and thousands of articles on "proper diet" in consumer publications, as well as government concern as evidenced by presidential commissions and congressional hearings.

Leisure   People have more leisure time and spend it away from home more than ever before. Eating away from home is an increasingly frequent leisure activity. Today's average American dines out more often than the person of a generation ago.

Increasing sophistication   People are increasingly willing to experiment with new foods. Supermarkets now devote large amounts of space to ethnic food specialties, wine and liqueurs, and imported cheese. Regional cuisines have become less isolated, and certain specialties like Tex-Mex chili and Southern pecan pie are now widespread. At the same time, a strong European influence has made possible the introduction of such dishes as quiche lorraine, crepes, and chicken paprikash. A largely vegetarian school of cooking may also be emerging.

Rising service expectations   The derivative foodservice product— the concept, service style, decor, and so on—is gaining importance in consumer motivation. People are less tolerant of unsatisfactory interactions with personnel.

Rise of the snack   The increasing consumption of numerous small meals or snacks is changing the traditional pattern of three square meals. Some people believe that the traditional pattern is unhealthy; others leave no time in their daily schedules for a dinner hour.

Epicurism   People are enjoying the smell of food, the look of food, the texture of food as well as the taste of food. The American Puritan heritage is giving way to frank indulgence in the pleasure of eating. A fine meal is considered the work of a craftsperson; food is becoming a refuge from an increasingly mechanized world.

Consumerism   People are becoming careful shoppers, more aware of price and value. There is more resistance to price changes and more comparison shopping. Expectations are rising. Consumers in both commercial and noncommercial foodservice operations are becoming increasingly demanding.

Shortened product life   Consumer loyalty to specific food products or operations is short-lived. Habits, tastes, and eating routines are less rigid. People are more influenced by friends, newspaper and television critics, and advertising. Food cults develop and disappear.

Economic Factors   The economic environment of the foodservice operation is always changing. Existing operations and those created in the future will face economic conditions that vary substantially from those of the foodservice industry during the boom years of the 1960s. Individual operations will prosper magnificently, strong existing companies will continue to grow— although perhaps at reduced rates—but many companies will be severely tested by economic circumstances.

CHANGES IN FINANCIAL RESOURCES   Foodservice is emerging from its "entrepreneurial" phase. It will be increasingly difficult to finance foodservice ventures, both the expansion or renewal of existing companies and the financing of new companies. Basic investment requirements for construction, equipment, furnishings, and accessories are increasing. In some areas, foodservice operations that cost $50,000 to initiate a few years ago now cost two and three times that amount, without a commensurate increase in potential return.

Investment capital may be in short supply. The foodservice operation must compete with other industries for available monies. General economic conditions, government activities, world economic circumstances, and a variety of other factors may make capital extremely expensive to procure.

CHANGES IN THE COSTS OF OPERATION   Operating costs are increasing. In several areas cost increases will be especially dramatic: labor, energy, and food products.

Labor   Rising labor costs may pose additional problems for foodservice operations. Several factors cause increases in the cost of labor. The minimum wage is being raised by government action. It is likely that it will be "pegged" to a percentage of the average wage paid manufacturing workers. Foodservice operations, unlike most manufacturing enterprises, are labor intensive: they do not have the same opportunities to substitute automated equipment for human labor.

Labor costs may also rise if fewer workers seek employment at foodservice operations. Participation in welfare programs may seem acceptable to many individuals who might otherwise seek foodservice employment. A shortage of qualified workers would cause foodservice operations to compete by offering higher wages, more fringe benefits, and so on.

Unionization affects only a small part of the foodservice industry today, but is growing. The tip credit is vulnerable to both federal and state legislative action.

Obviously, there are managerial solutions to these problems that will increase or at least maintain the productivity of labor, but, in absolute terms, the cost of a person's time for an hour's work will increase.

Energy   Energy crises, government reactions to energy crises, and government programs to prevent energy crises tend to increase the cost of energy to the foodservice operation. Increased energy costs will be compounded by an increased use of equipment in an effort to reduce labor costs.

Food products   Farming is becoming a highly complex, mechanized business. Farmers are affected by the rising prices of equipment, fertilizer, pesticides, and labor as well as natural disasters such as drought, hail, flooding, and frosts. They have become increasingly militant in their demands for higher prices.

In addition, the agricultural production of the United States will increasingly be devoted to providing exports to balance imports of commodities such as oil, minerals, and manufactured products from countries that have "cheap" labor. A diversion of supply from domestic markets tends to result in an increase in domestic prices. In recent times the sale of wheat stimulated increases in the price of flour and baked foods and in the price of meat.

The success of the oil-producing countries in the manipulation of world prices for oil has provided the model for other producers of commodities. Imported products such as sugar, bananas, and coffee may be much more costly in the future.

CHANGES IN COMPETITION   Competition is intensifying for many foodservice operations. Certain market areas are saturated: the growth of one foodservice operation can only be at the expense of another.

Competition is "in place." The foodservice operation opening in a particular market must fight for a market share against operations that have resources to fight back and the advantages of an established market image, loyal patrons, and long experience in the market.

The "food retailing" industry—the supermarkets and grocery stores—has recognized that the foodservice industry is competing for the same consumer dollars. As eating out has become more common, food retailers have adopted a variety of strategies to combat the foodservice industry. Any success they enjoy will be at the expense of the foodservice operation. Retailers are making an "economic" argument through media advertising of the advantages of eating restaurant-type, completely prepared products at home. Retailers are also offering "take home" freshly prepared products and establishing foodservice operations such as restaurants, "deli" counters, juice bars, and bakeries in retail outlets.

Major food processors are developing or purchasing independent foodservice operations. To nearby competing operations, they are more than just another "rival." They bring huge capital resources and expertise in purchasing, product development, marketing, and food preparation.

In the largest sense, the expertise of food processors makes them competitors to the foodservice industry as a whole, even when they do not own foodservice operations. They can increase the competitive pressure on the foodservice industry by substantially improving the quality, variety, and distribution of the pre-prepared foods sold in supermarkets as eating-out substitutes.

Social Factors The foodservice operation is influenced by the values, priorities, and problems of the society in which it functions. Social values, priorities, and problems change. The market of the foodservice operation reflects some of these social changes, and frequently the foodservice operation is directly affected. For example, in a simple instance, a foodservice operation in a penal institution or residential facility for the elderly is more likely to be affected by the prevailing attitudes of society toward prisoners and the elderly than by the complaints of inmates or residents.

Social values, priorities, and problems have some impact on the foodservice industry through labor legislation, welfare programs, political alliances with economic implications, liquor legislation, and public education. Government agencies are often the instruments of social change. The policies of government agencies reflect society's concern with public health, worker safety, and pure food, although these policies may not become the standards for consumers' buying decisions.

Ultimately, the foodservice industry is affected by the changes in values, priorities, and problems that are caused by ferment in American society. Changes in the mission and nature of employee feeding reflect a fundamental change in social values: a business's "right to make a profit" has been limited by social values that reflect concern for workers.

A change in social priorities from consumption to conservation has resulted in a variety of imperatives for foodservice from moral condemnation of "waste" to ecological legislation. The social problems of drug abuse and alcoholism are significant problems for the foodservice industry.

With this perspective, some social trends that will have implications for foodservice operations can be identified.

CHANGES IN
WORKERS' VALUES

The changes in social values that will most affect foodservice operations are manifest in the changes in worker expectations and attitudes. Universal education, widespread exposure to other life-styles through television viewing, and a host of other factors have increased the expectations of the worker and altered fundamental attitudes toward work. Fewer and fewer individuals will be content with foodservice industry jobs that offer no career possibilities or individual satisfaction. The increasing difficulty of entering the foodservice industry as an owner/operator because of the investment costs compounds the problem. Becoming an entrepreneur may no longer serve as an exit from a dead-end job.

Changes in social values are apparent in other areas. Moral pressure, and the force of law, are making American industry accept some responsibility for the integration of the economically, socially, and physically disadvantaged into American society. Affirmative action is only one manifestation of this emerging concern.

Society's current sense of responsibility to the aged, the infirm, and the young is creating new opportunities for the foodservice industry. Medicare, Medicaid, broadened Social Security programs, and child nutrition programs challenge the resourcefulness of the managements of both commercial and noncommercial foodservice operations.

CHANGES IN
SOCIAL PRIORITIES

The recent appreciation that the world's limited and irreplaceable resources are rapidly being exhausted will have profound implications on the foodservice industry in coming years. Conservation of natural resources and the preservation of the quality of the environment have gained in importance over industrial development and consumption. Energy use, pollution, and the production of single-service articles from petrochemicals, and the commercialization of residential and historic areas and park lands are among the social issues that the foodservice industry will face.

The increasing pressure of the world's population on the world's food supply may create other challenges for the American foodservice industry. The portion of the land presently used as pasturage or for the production of grain for cattle and that can be used instead for the cultivation of food crops may be allocated to this use. More people could be fed worldwide, but radical changes in the American diet, and certainly radical changes in the foodservice industry, would be necessary.

CHANGES IN
SOCIAL PROBLEMS

The foodservice industry is directly affected by the significant problems of American society such as crime in the streets, the economic decline of the central cities, drug addiction, employee crime, and social unrest. Some mitigation of these problems will provide opportunities for the foodservice industry; an intensification of them will confront the foodservice industry with additional constraints on its operational activities.

The issue of "crime in the streets" amply illustrates the effect of social problems on foodservice operations. Establishments are limited to daylight hours of operation where people fear violence in the streets. In safer areas, such as downtown entertainment and shopping districts and suburban malls, operations can serve patrons in the evening as well as during the day. Six additional hours of business activity without a very large increase in expenses can mean the difference between success and failure, between an adequate return on investment and a marginally profitable operation, and between fair compensation for effort and scant living for the independent operator. In high crime areas, the problems of a foodservice operation—even if it is open only during the day—are compounded by frequent robberies, undesirables using the facility, and difficulty in recruiting workers for service in hazardous conditions.

Technological Factors

The continuing development of the technologies involved in the foodservice industry may provide ways to meet the challenges and opportunities posed by changes in other areas. For example, equipment sophistication or the improvement of food preservation techniques may assist foodservice operations in coping with market demands for diverse products on the one hand and mounting labor costs on the other.

Technology also entails challenges and opportunities. The sophistication of equipment generally implies increased costs and increased investment requirements. The development of food preservation techniques will also serve the food retailer and fuel competition with retail establishments.

Technological change of some order can be expected in food, equipment, facilities, marketing, and management.

CHANGES IN
FOOD-RELATED
TECHNOLOGIES

There is the possibility of significant technological progress in food product development, food preservation, food preparation, and food distribution.

Food product development   Many recently developed products show great promise if they can be successfully attuned to market standards and integrated into the foodservice system: spun or extruded soybean products, encapsulated essential oils or isolates of spices, fish meal flour, high protein grains, synthetic flavors, meat analogues, and so on. The transition from the laboratory, the test field, or the pilot plant to the marketplace is long and arduous. Spun soy technologies used in the production of meatlike or cheeselike high protein foods have been known for 30 years. Of the scores of product ventures attempted, none as yet has had a great impact on the market.

Food preservation development The general improvement of freezing and canning technologies has been evinced by the introduction of some products preserved by sophisticated methods. For example, the cost of freeze drying will likely be reduced because of several recent technological advances. It will be possible to offer freeze-dried low-cost products such as vegetables as well as the high-cost items such as shrimp or coffee that are widely available now.

Preservation of foods in pouches has been demonstrated to be economical and satisfactory. And progress is being made in the development of starch for thickening foods that can then withstand heat treatment or freezing without losing their quality.

Other preservation technologies may increase the foods available to the foodservice operation as they become more practical, such as dehydro-freezing (drying, then freezing), chemical conservation, and irradiation.

Food preparation More and more information is being developed about the effects of heat on food, the properties of food products, and the technical aspects of cooking. Food preparation is evolving from domestic cookery into a true technology—an applied science—based on chemistry, physics, microbiology, nutrition, biochemistry, and engineering. Food preparation is becoming "controllable." Technical problems are being solved so that objectives of any kind—"creative," commercial, nutritional, or hygienic—are becoming easier to achieve.

Food distribution The distribution of food from agricultural producers and from processors of raw food to the foodservice unit shows promise of great progress.

• American agriculture is becoming more sophisticated in the planting and harvesting of crops and the development of hybrids that expand the traditional seasons of food products.

• Transportation may be significantly improved by the increased cost effectiveness of air transport and the development of a rail system that is more responsive to the needs of growers and buyers.

• The food distribution industry that supplies the foodservice industry is becoming technologically sophisticated and more aware of the needs of the foodservice operation.

• Foodservice operations are streamlining their buying procedures through the use of buying systems, central commissaries, and cooperatives.

• Greater efficiency and effectiveness are being introduced into materials-handling procedures at all levels of food distribution.

• Information systems are improving on a worldwide basis through the use of modern communication equipment.

• Fluctuations of supply and price of major commodities are being smoothed by international agreements.

EXHIBIT 14.2   Technological Opportunities for Foodservice

Food Safety

Development of passive food safety equipment to automatically monitor bacterial levels of products and facilities.

Serviceware

Creation of cost effective nondisposable serviceware processing systems to replace disposable, single-use serviceware in many applications.

Environmental Control

Development of cost-effective cleansing systems for kitchen exhausts; development of biodegradable packaging materials for take-out products; preprocessing of solid waste products to permit passive removal from the operation.

Production

Development of reconstitution devices that allow reconstitution of meal items with different specific heats (rates of heating); preservation-reconstitution techniques that permit efficient central large-batch production of items now requiring labor intensive on-site production.

Packaging

Development of packaging materials and formats that combine preparation compatibility, insulation properties, effective merchandising and ultimate utility as serviceware.

Meat Preparation

Elimination or reduction of waste generated by conventional boning techniques by either mechanical separation or laser beam boning.

Cooking Equipment

Development of energy conserving ranges, steamers, and fryers; large capacity dielectric heating units (microwaves); completely mobile, modular major equipment.

Merchandising

Development of automated vending machines that prepare and dispense whole meals, hot sandwiches, cold plates; automatic restaurants.

CHANGES IN FOODSERVICE EQUIPMENT TECHNOLOGY   Foodservice equipment technology may develop in several directions: the increased cost effectiveness of existing sophisticated equipment; new inventions; an increased awareness by foodservice equipment manufacturers of the evolving needs of the foodservice industry. Exhibit 14.2 suggests some of the more imminent technological advances in this area.

Increased cost effectiveness   Equipment such as sophisticated freezers, vegetable processing equipment, tunnel broilers, and "computerized" and continuous fryers may become cost effective for a greater number of foodservice operations. The cost of the equipment itself may be reduced, but it is more likely that foodservice operations will be able to make better use of this equipment because of fundamental changes in labor costs, management sophistication, new products, and so on.

New inventions   The future may bring significant new developments in equipment technology on the order of commercial-size microwave ovens, convection steamers, automated vending machines, modern ventilation systems, quartz ovens, pressure fryers, and other recently developed devices that have had a great effect on food preparation techniques.

Increased awareness of foodservice industry needs   Many manufacturers of foodservice equipment have recognized the needs of specific foodservice operations and are adapting existing technologies to serve them. The development of chilled food systems for foodservice operations such as hospitals or universities which must feed a great number of people in a short time is such an example. Foods can be cooked efficiently, stored without reducing their quality, and brought to serving temperature as needed. Time and labor are saved and can be allocated effectively. Manufacturers aware of the problems of the modern foodservice operation can combine existing technologies in ways suited to specific applications.

CHANGES IN FACILITIES TECHNOLOGY   The continuing development of construction technologies has been signaled by such advances as modular construction, alternative energy systems, and the development of new construction materials. Presumably, this development will continue, prompted by general economic factors.

Knowledge about foodservice facilities construction, lighting, heating, cooling, ventilation, decoration, work-system design, and waste removal is also increasing. A greater understanding of foodservice industry facilities and the operation's problems is also apparent on the part of architects, facilities designers, and engineers. Future facilities are more likely to incorporate technical innovations that can maximize the resources of the operation, while still meeting market standards, government codes, and operational criteria.

CHANGES IN MARKETING TECHNOLOGY   Marketing techniques from primary research to the selection of media mix to the auditing of advertising are gaining in precision. Using modern marketing techniques, the initiation of a foodservice operation, demand, product development, concept development, and efforts to influence demand can be approached with increasing surety. In other words, as the stakes get higher and higher, and the competition gets tougher and tougher, some of the risk is being reduced. As American industry changes from a manufacturing to a service orientation, there is every likelihood that marketing technologies will become even more exact.

CHANGES IN
MANAGEMENT
TECHNOLOGY

Foodservice management is developing in the direction mandated by the challenges and opportunities of future events. Advances can be noted in management education, and information and systems technologies.

Management education   Foodservice education is responding to the demands placed on the foodservice manager. In many institutions, curricula have been broadened to include courses relevant to the changes in the environment of the foodservice industry: finance, food production management, cost control, personnel management, purchasing, kitchen sanitation, food hygiene, and so on. Courses that do little more than perpetuate the styles of other periods are being deemphasized: classic French cuisine, "continental" dining room service, ice carving, and cake decoration. The ultimate result will be a corps of professional foodservice managers capable of guiding any foodservice operation regardless of its objectives, systems, market segment, and operating circumstances.

Management information   Exhibit 14.3 presents a summary from a government report that assessed the information available to the foodservice manager in 1969 and pointed to significant research "gaps." Although efforts by individuals in the foodservice industry, government and academic researchers, and the staffs of industry associations and publications have narrowed some of these gaps, their elimination remains a future challenge to serious students of the foodservice industry. As the excerpt suggests, the availability of this information will be of critical importance to the foodservice operation's future effectiveness.

Management systems   Prompted by circumstances and aided by their educations, foodservice managers are making use of some of the technologies that have long helped the managers of other industries, specifically, quantitative management techniques (variously called "management science" and operations research) and electronic data processing. The future undoubtedly will see further development of these technologies for management in general and for the foodservice industry in particular.

PROJECTIONS FOR FOODSERVICE

As managers seek to apply the principles of foodservice management to the present-day challenges of the foodservice industry, certain directions for the future may be suggested by their efforts. Future developments may be seen, even now, in managers' tentative adaptations to market, economic, social, and technological changes. These adaptations may grow to characterize the foodservice industry of the future or they may give way to other—as yet unforeseen—adaptive measures.

Projecting the future of the foodservice industry on such limited observations is risky but useful. As the pace of change accelerates, managers must learn to look forward in order to anticipate future prospects and prepare for them.

Foodservice Industry Trends   The characteristics of the foodservice industry of the future, and the prosperity of individual operations will depend on the effectiveness of managers in dealing with complex situations that can only be generally hypothesized today. Certain emerging trends can be identified.

Hybridization   Rigid categorizations of foodservice operations are becoming less relevant as foodservice managers create and operate foodservice establishments strategically rather than according to rules and traditional models. For example, hospitals and so-called fast food restaurants serve wine, once the privilege of only the so-called gourmet restaurants. Military feeding installations introduce alternative service systems and individualized feeding programs, while posh restaurants, once the bastions of table service, introduce salad bars and soup lines. Employee foodservice operations are decorated by the same designers who decorate luxury hotels. University and school lunch programs replace the institutional food that typified them with venturesome foods such as ethnic cuisines and vegetarian menus. If elements previously thought to be characteristics of one segment of the industry are increasingly adopted by other segments, such categories as "fast food," gourmet, institutional, cafeteria, and coffee shop will be entirely devoid of meaning.

A corollary of hybridization is the multipurpose restaurant that at various times or in various areas is a banquet hall, restaurant, take-out stand, bar, cafeteria, and, perhaps, a commissary for catering to a not-for-profit organization such as a school system.

Consolidation   Small operations with fragile financial structures and little impact as purchasers or advertisers are more vulnerable to adversity. In response to increasing difficulties in maintaining profitability and market share, these smaller organizations will either cease or merge with larger enterprises. In common with the beer, auto, food retailing, and appliance industry, the foodservice industry is consolidating into fewer and larger operations, mirroring the trend in other segments of the American economy, though many years later.

Vertical integration   Food processing companies that already own agricultural and distribution companies are purchasing foodservice operations so that they can complete their control of the manufacture and retailing of the foodservice product. In like fashion, and for the same purposes, foodservice operations are buying wholesale distributors, warehouse companies, trucking firms, equipment manufacturers, meat packers, bakeries, maintenance companies, and food processors.

Diversification   Foodservice companies are acquiring or developing other service or retailing companies—clothing stores, record shops,

EXHIBIT 14.3 Prospective Future Developments in Management Information for Foodservice

In reality, the degree of success, or status, of a particular type of foodservice operation cannot be measured only in terms of sales volume, profit and loss figures, and the rate of return on capital investment. Such intangible factors as employee morale, menu acceptance, and the psychological impact of the dining atmosphere upon the consumer have a dynamic impact on such consumer decisions as "where to eat, or should I bother to eat out?" An increasing number of operators, mainly the larger ones, recognize these intangible factors and are attempting to evaluate their impact upon financial progress. There is also a growing realization that survival in an expanding competitive market is dependent upon the determination of profit margins and production costs for specific menu items. Management is being forced to discontinue the practice of increasing menu prices of popular items to offset suspected cost increases of less popular items because an ever increasing number of specialty houses offer low-priced, limited menus.

Management will be able to meet these challenges when it has available, through research and analysis, a system to evaluate the foregoing tangible and intangible factors. This can be speeded up for the benefit of the entire foodservice industry if Government, universities, associations, operators, and research and development specialists determine common objectives and agree (at least tacitly) on methods of accomplishing them. To expedite this effort, some of the more important areas in which research should be conducted are listed. The sequence of the following listing is in the same order as the chapters in which these recommendations are presented in greater detail and not necessarily in order of priority.

1. Conduct research to determine the relative importance of such factors as population growth and concentration, economic growth, disposable income, family origin, travel, and location and size on the success or failure of foodservice operations. Quantitative values should be determined for these variable factors. Develop mathematical models for electronic data processing, or simplified models for manual calculation, or both.

2. Design and conduct research to reevaluate and revise the statistical data available to the industry for adequacy and timeliness. Standardize the categories or types of operations that are causing increasing confusion in comparing statistics and calculations. A vast multiplicity of categories has resulted from the individualization of foodservice operations to achieve merchandising distinctiveness. Often, the statistical data presented in trade journals, university publications, and trade association magazines or papers cannot be correlated to data published by the Census Bureau. It is recommended that the data published every 5 years by the Census Bureau be used as a statistical base. The Census Bureau categories should be reclassified. Trade journals, university publications, and trade associations should update the base figures within the 5-year interim.

3. The relative importance of various factors that have a significant impact upon merchandising, such as menu pricing, menu variety, physical environment, gratification of psychological needs, and advertising should be quantitatively evaluated. Approximate evaluations of the relative importance of these factors could be determined in a preliminary or pilot research study by (1) determining what the consumer requirements are for specific types of food service operations and (2) evaluating the merchandising practices in successful foodservice operations by type to determine the degree of correlation to consumer requirements.

4.   A survey of food manufacturers and processors should be conducted to determine optimum order sizes for "convenience foods" produced exclusively for the foodservice industry. These products would be manufactured or processed by the food manufacturer to the foodservice operator's specifications.

5.   Design and conduct operations analysis research of successful foodservice operations by type to (1) quantitatively evaluate specific production elements and establish the criteria for basic production costs, (2) determine which production elements of various foodservice systems are similar and which are not, and (3) determine the overall efficiency of various foodservice production systems. Conduct research to improve deficient production operations which are common to most foodservice operations. Develop a mathematical model for computer application to evaluate foodservice systems. Upon refinement, this model could be utilized for various simulation applications such as the evaluation of proposed changes in work methods and the impact of automated equipment upon various foodservice systems.

6.   Conduct research to determine the minimum and maximum number of foodservice outlets by type of operation and the sales volume required to justify capital investment for a commissary operation versus purchasing "made-to-order" convenience foods from a food manufacturer.

7.   Conduct research to determine the specific cost controls required of an information system to evaluate various types of foodservice systems. The practicality of such factors as volume variance (the projected sales volume by menu item compared with actual sales volume), material variance (food required for production compared with actual usage), performance variance (cost of labor and equipment required for menu production compared with actual usage), advertising variance, and other significant cost factors should be determined.

8.   In-depth research studies of successful foodservice operations should be made with the collaboration of social scientists to determine what output is needed of a good manager, supervisor, waitress, or cook, and what input is required (I.Q. levels, personal characteristics, etc.). The input will serve as guidelines for recruiting personnel. Analyze the characteristics of people available in the labor market and design training programs which supply the required skills. Develop the feedback or monitoring subsystem necessary to evaluate the training program. Once such systems are developed, the National Restaurant Association, American Hotel and Motel Association, State and local associations, and colleges can provide invaluable services to foodservice operators, most of whom do not have the time or the resources or both to conduct and evaluate effective training programs.

From the "Summary" prepared by John F. Freshwater, Transportation and Facilities Research Division, Agricultural Research Service, USDA, in the report "Selected Research Abstracts of Published and Unpublished Reports Pertaining to the Food Service Industry" by Leo Nejelski for Market Research and Agricultural Research Service, United States Department of Agriculture, December 1969.

amusement parks, arcades, hotels, and so on. Diversification protects against economic reversals in a single area, but it also provides opportunities for increased cash flow, better use of management, better use of construction investment, and more effective marketing efforts per dollar spent.

Increased emphasis on marketing   Advertising and other efforts to influence demand have become, and will continue to be, pivotal elements in ensuring the success of many foodservice operations. Foodservice operations with largely similar products are fighting for the shares of the same market instead of introducing new products to capture additional or different market segments.

Automation   The foodservice industry has learned the lesson of American industrial companies and is trading capital investment for operating costs in an effort to increase overall productivity.

Product diversity   After recognizing that the foodservice unit is a retail outlet and not a food factory, the next logical step is expansion of the product line. Supermarkets may add take-out, ready-to-eat products, and on-premises areas where these products may be consumed, but foodservice operations are adding grocery lines, selling commodity products such as coffee, and offering their own specialties such as baked goods or salad dressings. Some foodservice operations are diversifying their product lines beyond foodservice's traditional products: serviceware, clothing, records, gift items, antiques, and many others.

Increased market definition   As the number of foodservice operations in a geographical market multiplies, competition increases. Easy generalizations about market wants such as "everyone likes hamburgers," or "everyone likes lunch in a clean restaurant," can no longer be the basis for a foodservice operation's market appeal. When hamburgers are readily available at lunchtime in clean restaurants, market segmentation on this broad basis is no longer useful. More market definition is necessary. Smaller market segments must be identified more precisely. Foodservice managers are becoming sensitive to the needs and wants of market minorities—groups of people who want vegetarian or health food lunches; people who wish hamburgers in a theme restaurant; people who want to be served their hamburgers or something else at a table with a tablecloth, and so on. This trend, as much as any other, has obscured the boundaries between such traditional foodservice forms as the coffee shop and the restaurant or the diner and the "fast food" restaurant.

Repersonalization   The quality of personal interactions between the people of the foodservice operation and the people of the market segment may be changed as the foodservice operation grows larger. Consumers recognize that they are dealing with a larger, perhaps mammoth corporation, not an individual operator who can be directly responsive to them. Many foodservice managers wish to reverse this trend by personalizing the foodservice operation regardless of its size. Management approaches vary but include such efforts as individual restaurant concepts for each of the units of a chain; the development of the human relations abilities of the staff; and advertising campaigns that emphasize that the foodservice operation offers a customized product.

Investment minimization   A number of factors prompt the managements of foodservice operations to reduce their investment. Shortened product life, high investment costs, and capital shortages are but a few examples. New forms of foodservice business organization have emerged as a result—second generation franchising, foodservice management contracting, and joint ventures.

Second generation franchising does not differ substantially from first generation franchising except in one vital respect. The new franchisee is likely to be a businessperson with funds to invest instead of a prospective entrepreneur wishing to create a livelihood.

Foodservice management contracting places the investment obligations with other organizations rather than with the foodservice company. Instead of building foodservice operations, the foodservice company sells management expertise. The customers for these services include school systems, hospitals, recreation facilities, hotels, clubs, transportation companies, government agencies, universities, and groups of private investors.

Foodservice companies may initiate joint ventures by sharing with another enterprise in the construction of facilities. The result is a somewhat lower initial investment for the foodservice operation. For example, the cost of a building, land, parking lots, heating, ventilation, and air conditioning equipment may be shared by a foodservice company and a foodstore, or a foodservice company and a private club.

Market expansion   Foodservice companies are expanding into market areas that do not have the large population concentrations of earlier markets—small cities, small towns, shopping malls in the suburbs, and, ironically, central cities. The trend is prompted by somewhat lower investment costs, the dispersion of some traditional market segments, and intense competition in primary markets.

Nontraditional risk taking   Commercial and noncommercial foodservice organizations are becoming more venturesome in response to market, economic, social, and technological pressures. Traditional safe approaches to marketing, menu planning, purchasing, business organization, financing, production, and service may not be sure routes to prosperity. Manifestations of this enterprising approach include expansion abroad by chain restaurants, new restaurant concepts and even new restaurant chains developed by companies with already proven success formulas, explorations of ethnic menus, a la carte food service in hospitals, and foodservice contracting or joint venturing by schools and universities, social catering and commissary operations.

Meal as sensual experience   The meal experience is becoming an important element in the marketing of the foodservice enterprise. The ready-to-eat food product and other derivative products such as speed of service or speed of production may be losing ground to the experiential aspects of the food product. Take-out, limited-menu restaurants are offering a meal experience enhanced by music, decor, movies, and table seating if not table service. Pricing may begin to reflect the length of time of the meal experience as well as the operation's fundamental costs. Already in many operations, a rough relationship exists between the time the consumer spends in the establishment and the price structure. A restaurant that provides only atmosphere would be the ultimate expression of this trend. Customers would "rent" space in a mood-altering setting to consume food products purchased elsewhere.

A countertrend can also be discerned. In some markets, foodservice operations are offering value and substance in the form of quality food products and reducing the synthetic ambiance of their establishments.

Participative management   Foodservice companies are seeking new forms of organization that are consistent with rising expectations of workers and with the market, economic, social, and technological changes confronting the foodservice enterprise. Many foodservice managers are recognizing that hierarchical authoritarian organizations with central decision making by a managerial elite—an elite which the average worker cannot ever expect to join—is losing its validity. Other participative management trends include the introduction of a middle-management level, career ladder development, involvement of workers in decision making, consultation with workers on matters that affect them, and management training in human relations skills.

Intense cost control   Competition, market pressures, rising costs, stagnant productivity, and a host of other factors have intensified efforts to increase or maintain profitability through cost control efforts. As operators find it difficult to significantly increase volume, efforts may be directed toward cost control in the areas of labor, food products, waste, energy, theft, and so on.

Off-premises labor   Performance of a particular operational activity within the walls of the foodservice operation is no longer considered an absolute virtue. Management's pride in preparing food on premises or in using in-house expertise to write advertising copy is not always worth upholding especially if the cost of the activity is excessive and the product inferior. The tendency is to concentrate the operation's resources and efforts on those activities that are best done by the operation and most central to its essential business—the marketing of ready-to-eat food products.

Fundamental research   Foodservice management decisions are being made increasingly on the basis of objective data collected and handled in ways already validated by other segments of the American economy. Managers rely more on fundamental research than on guesswork, instinct, or tradition. Increased market research, formal product development programs, the use of statistical techniques for investment decisions, and work study preceding facilities design and layout are among the many instances of this new approach.

Foodservice
Management
Trends

Foodservice industry trends, prospects for change, and the principles on which the modern foodservice industry is based have a number of implications for present and prospective managers of foodservice organizations:

• Foodservice managers at all levels will be challenged by future events.
• Foodservice managers will need more education, more formal training, and more professionalism than was necessary for foodservice management in the past.
• The work of foodservice managers will involve increasing amounts of problem solving and systematic thinking.
• Foodservice managers, as individuals, will be presented with unprecedented opportunities for material success and personal achievement.

Challenges to foodservice managers   The increasing complexity of the foodservice operation and the conditions in which it must function provide the fundamental challenge to foodservice management. Some foodservice companies are billion-dollar enterprises; some foodservice departments in large enterprises employ hundreds of people and use millions of dollars worth of products; some foodservice units of large companies and thousands of independent restaurants produce more than a million dollars a year in revenues; some foodservice operations have the responsibility for the health and well-being of thousands of people. Management must rise to these challenges: small errors of judgment have far-reaching significance for profits, for jobs, for investments, for lives.

Education of foodservice managers   The increase in size and complexity of the foodservice operation and the changes that are affecting the foodservice industry require the foodservice manager of today to be more knowledgeable than foodservice managers of the past. Effective foodservice managers of today must have competencies and information in areas that managers of the past could ignore. Even at the operational level, foodservice management today is much more than simply seeing if the chef is in the kitchen, making sure that hot food is hot and cold food is cold, taking the money to the bank, and checking the doors on the way out. Day-to-day decisions affect the overall effectiveness of the organization and the efficiency of its operating systems. Consider only that today the operational manager is faced with responsibilities that were hardly among the priorities of the manager of a few years ago: energy conservation, protection of the public health, security, productivity, technical training of personnel, personnel relations, aggressive purchasing, market-oriented menu planning, financial planning, organization, work design, motivation, and recruitment—all of which require specialized knowledge.

Managerial problem solving   At all levels and in all areas of foodservice management, changing conditions require solutions to specific problems, not routine "cookbook" responses. In other times characterized by stable, well-defined markets, the absence of consumerism, inexpensive labor and materials, minimal government intervention in operations, limited operational options, minimal competition, and the general absence of convulsive change, universal rules and standards worked most of the time. When they did not work, ample profit margins and the slow pace of business reduced the impact of error. A foodservice manager could buy the highest grades of food products without attention to value analysis, schedule one service worker for eight hours for every five tables without attention to the cost of labor, plan the day's menus from leftovers without attention to market satisfaction, accommodate the convenience of the chef without attention to food hygiene, organize foodservice operations without attention to worker needs, and so on. At higher levels of management it was possible to write policies that had the force and rigidity of law, to establish restaurants on the basis of a few simplistic criteria such as traffic count, to tell the customers, guests, or clients what they should eat, and to otherwise act without risking the contravention of circumstances.

These approaches are no longer appropriate: rules of thumb, past practices, neat guidelines, and formulas do not work well at all when their fundamental premises have been eroded by change. Decision processes that acknowledge changed situations must take their place.

Opportunities for foodservice managers   The challenges to the foodservice industry create opportunities for management that are unprecedented. There will always be small jobs for small people, but the growth and complexity of the foodservice industry creates thousands of meaningful career opportunities.

Perhaps 25,000 new managers are inducted into the foodservice industry each year. Thousands of individuals are promoted to higher levels of responsibility and reward. In no other industry does a person advance as rapidly on the basis of performance and merit, and regardless of age, sex, or background. There are 30-year-old presidents of companies who started as management trainees; there are owner/operators who just a few years ago were warewashers in someone else's restaurant; there are foodservice administrators a few years out of school who have responsibilities and compensation comparable to the responsibilities and compensation of veteran executives in other areas.

Moreover, few industries can match the excitement and personal achievement that comes with being part of the foodservice industry as it meets the challenges of American society and an ever-changing world.

The Foodservice
Manager's Library

Ammer, Dean S. *Materials Management.* 3rd ed. Homewood, Ill.: Richard D. Irwin, 1974.

Anderson, David R. *Practical Controllership.* 3rd ed. Homewood, Ill.: Richard D. Irwin, 1973.

Anthony, Robert N., and Welsch, Glenn A. *Fundamentals of Management Accounting.* Homewood, Ill.: Richard D. Irwin, 1974.

Ayers Press. *Public Relations and Publicity Style Book.* Philadelphia: Ayers Press, 1978.

Backus, Harry. *Designing Restaurant Interiors: A Guide for Foodservice Operators.* New York: Lebhar-Friedman, 1977.

Beal, Edwin F. *Practice of Collective Bargaining.* 5th ed. Homewood, Ill.: Richard D. Irwin, 1976.

Beaton, William R., and Robertson, Terry. *Real Estate Investment.* 2nd ed. Englewood Cliffs, N.J.: Prentice-Hall, 1977.

Borsenik, Frank D. *The Management of Maintenance and Engineering Systems in Hospitality Industries.* New York: John Wiley & Sons, 1979.

Bowers, David. *Systems of Organization: Management of the Human Resource.* Ann Arbor: University of Michigan Press, 1977.

Boyd, Harper W., and Westfall, Ralph. *Marketing Research.* 3rd ed. Homewood, Ill.: Richard D. Irwin, 1972.

Buzby, Walter J. *Restaurant and Bar Security.* Los Angeles: Security World Publishing, 1974.

Carson, Charles R. *Managing Employee Honesty.* Los Angeles: Security World Publishing, 1977.

Claus, R. James, and Claus, Karen. *Visual Communication Through Signage.* Cincinnati: Signs of the Times Publishing Company, 1975.

Coltman, Michael M. *Financial Management for the Hospital Industry.* Boston: CBI Publishing Company, 1979.

Corder, Antony S. *Maintenance Management Techniques.* New York:

McGraw-Hill Book Company, 1976.

Coyle, R. G. *Management System Dynamics.* New York: John Wiley & Sons, 1977.

Craig, Robert L. *Training and Development Handbook: A Guide to Human Resource Development.* 2nd ed. New York: McGraw-Hill Book Company, 1976.

Credit Research Foundation. *Credit Management Handbook.* 2nd ed. Homewood, Ill.: Richard D. Irwin, 1965.

Dahl, Crete. *Food and Menu Dictionary.* Boston: CBI Publishing Company, 1972.

Demachy, Alain. *Interior Architecture and Decoration.* New York: William Morrow and Company, 1974.

Department of Energy. "Guide to Energy Conservation for Food Service." In cooperation with the Federal Energy Administration Food Industry Advisory Committee. Washington, D.C.: U.S. Government Printing Office, 1977. Publication No. FEA/D-75/411R. Stock No. 041-018-00127-1.

Drucker, Peter F. *The Effective Executive.* New York: Harper & Row, 1967.

_____. *Management.* New York: Harper & Row, 1974.

Dubin, Fred S.; Mindell, Harold L.; and Bloome, Selwyn. *How to Save Energy and Cut Costs in Existing Industrial and Commercial Buildings.* Park Ridge, N.J.: Noyes Data Corporation, 1976.

Escoffier, Auguste. *The Escoffier Cook Book: A Guide to the Fine Art of Cookery.* Translation of *Guide Culinaire.* New York: Crown, 1969.

Firth, Michael. *Forecasting Methods in Business and Management.* Philadelphia: International Ideas, 1977.

Folsom, LeRoi, ed. *The Professional Chef.* 4th ed. Boston: CBI Publishing Company, 1974.

Grossman, Harold J. *Grossman's Guide to Wines, Spirits, and Beers.* 6th ed. New York: Scribner, 1977.

Guthrie, Helen Andrews. *Introductory Nutrition.* 3rd ed. St. Louis: C. V. Mosby Company, 1975.

Hayes, Rich Stephan. *Business Loans: A Guide to Money Sources and How to Approach Them Successfully.* Boston: CBI Publishing Company, 1977.

Heaton, Herbert. *Productivity in Service Organizations: Organizing for People.* New York: McGraw-Hill Book Company, 1978.

Howell, William S., and Bormann, Ernest G. *Presentational Speaking for Business and the Professions.* New York: Harper & Row, 1971.

Ireland, Richard C. *Selling in the Restaurant.* Wheaton, Ill.: Hospitality Institute, 1974.

Jackson, Michael. *The World Guide to Beer.* Englewood Cliffs, N.J.: Prentice-Hall, 1977.

Johnson, Ross H., and Winn, Paul R. *Quantitative Methods for Management*. Boston: Houghton Mifflin, 1976.

Kazarian, Edward A. *Work Analysis and Design for Hotels, Restaurants, and Institutions*. Westport, Conn.: AVI Publishing Company, 1969.

Keiser, Ralph J., and Kallio, Elmer. *Controlling and Analyzing Costs in Food Service Operations*. New York: John Wiley & Sons, 1974.

Kepner, Charles H., and Tregoe, B. B. *Rational Manager: A Systematic Approach to Problem Solving and Decision Making*. New York: McGraw-Hill Book Company, 1965.

Knight, John, and Kotschevar, Lendal H. *Quantity Food Production, Planning and Management*. Boston: CBI Publishing Company, 1979.

Koontz, Harold D., and O'Donnell, Cyril. *Essentials of Management*. 2nd ed. New York: McGraw-Hill Book Company, 1978.

Kotler, Philip. *Marketing Management: Analysis, Planning, and Control*. 3rd ed. Englewood Cliffs, N.J.: Prentice-Hall, 1976.

Kotschevar, Lendal H., and Terrell, Margaret E. *Foodservice Planning: Layout and Equipment*. 2nd ed. New York: John Wiley & Sons, 1977.

Kotschevar, Lendal H. *Quantity Food Purchasing*. 2nd ed. New York: John Wiley & Sons, 1975.

Labuza, Theodore P. *Food and Your Well-Being*. St. Paul, Minn.: West Publishing Company, 1977.

Larsen, Jack Lenor, and Weeks, Jeanne. *Fabrics for Interiors: A Guide for Architects, Designers, and Consumers*. New York: Van Nostrand Reinhold Company, 1975.

Laventhal, Krekstein, Horwath & Horwath. *Uniform System of Accounts for Restaurants*. 4th rev. ed. Chicago: National Restaurant Association, 1968.

Levie, Albert. *The Meat Handbook*. 3rd ed. Westport, Conn.: AVI Publishing Company, 1970.

Lundberg, Donald E. *The Hotel and Restaurant Business*. 3rd ed. Boston: CBI Publishing Company, 1979.

McCarthy, E. Jerome. *Basic Marketing: A Managerial Approach*. 4th ed. Homewood, Ill.: Richard D. Irwin, 1971.

McGuinness, William J., and Steen, Benjamin. *Building Technology: Mechanical and Electrical Systems*. New York: John Wiley & Sons, 1977.

Matthews, Lawrence M. *Practical Operating Budgeting*. New York: McGraw-Hill Book Company, 1977.

Mizer, David A., and Porter, Mary. *Food Preparation for the Professional*. San Francisco: Canfield Press, 1978.

Montagné, Prosper. *Larousse Gastronomique: The Encyclopedia of Food, Wine, and Cookery*. New York: Crown, 1961.

Moyer, William C. *The Buying Guide for Fresh Fruits, Vegetables, Herbs, and Nuts*. 5th rev. ed. Fullerton, Cal.: Blue Goose, 1974.

National Institute for the Foodservice Industry. *Applied Foodservice Sanitation.* 2nd ed. Lexington, Mass.: D. C. Heath and Company, 1978.

Neswonger, C. Rollin, and Fess, Philip E. *Accounting Principles.* 11th ed. Cincinnati: South-Western Publishing Company, 1973.

Odiorne, George S. *Management Decisions by Objectives.* Englewood Cliffs, N.J.: Prentice-Hall, 1968.

Parsons, Robert. *Statistics for Decision Makers.* New York: Harper & Row, 1974.

Peddersen, Raymond B. *Specs: The Comprehensive Foodservice Purchasing and Specification Manual.* Boston: CBI Publishing Company, 1977.

Pépin, Jacques. *La Technique, The Fundamental Techniques of Cooking: An Illustrated Guide.* New York: Quadrangle/New York Times, 1976.

Pigors, Paul, and Myers, Charles A. *Personnel Administration: A Point of View and a Method.* 8th ed. New York: McGraw-Hill Book Company, 1977.

Potter, Norman N. *Food Science.* 2nd ed. Westport, Conn.: AVI Publishing Company, 1973.

Roberts, Louise. *How to Write for Business.* New York: Harper & Row, 1976.

Root, Waverly, and Rochemont, Richard. *Eating in America, A History.* New York: William Morrow and Company, 1976.

Sanders, Donald. *Computers in Business.* 3rd ed. New York: McGraw-Hill Book Company, 1975.

Seaburg, Albin G. *Menu Design, Merchandising, and Marketing.* 2nd ed. Boston: CBI Publishing Company, 1973.

Shenkel, William M. *Real Estate Investment Decisions.* Chicago: Institute of Real Estate Management, n. d.

Sherry, John H. *The Laws of Innkeepers for Hotels, Motels, Restaurants, and Clubs.* Ithaca, N.Y.: Cornell University Press, 1972.

Siegal, Harry. *The Business of Interior Design, A Practical Checklist for Analyzing the Various Conditions of a Design Project and the Related Clauses for a Letter of Agreement.* New York: Whitney Library of Design, 1976.

Smith, Theodore. *Dynamic Business Strategy: The Art of Planning for Success.* New York: McGraw-Hill Book Company, 1977.

Stanton, Erwin S. *Successful Personnel Recruiting and Selection.* New York: American Management Association, 1977.

Steinmetz, Lawrence L. *Interviewing Skills for Supervisory Personnel.* Reading, Mass.: Addison-Wesley Publishing Company, 1971.

Stokes, Arch. *The Equal Opportunity Handbook for Hotels, Restaurants, and Institutions.* Boston: CBI Publishing Company, 1979.

———. *The Wage and Hour Handbook for Hotels, Restaurants, and Institutions.* Boston: CBI Publishing Company, 1978.

Tannahill, Reay. *Food in History.* New York: Stein & Day, 1973.

Thorner, Marvin E., and Manning, Peter B. *Quality Control in Food Service.* Westport, Conn.: AVI Publishing Company, 1976.

Todes, Jay L.; McKinney, John; and Ferguson, Wendell. *Management and Motivation: An Introduction to Supervision.* New York: Harper & Row, 1977.

Tourism Education Corporation. *A Hospitality Industry Guide for Writing and Using Task Unit Job Descriptions.* Boston: CBI Publishing Company, 1976.

Tuck, Charles A., Jr. ed. *NFPA Inspection Manual.* 4th ed. Boston: National Fire Protection Association, 1976.

U.S. Department of Agriculture. Food and Nutrition Service. Child Nutrition Division. *Food Storage Guide for Schools and Nutrition.* Washington, D.C.: Government Printing Office.

Vancil, Richard F. *Financial Executive's Handbook.* Homewood, Ill.: Richard D. Irwin, 1970.

Van Horne, James C. *Fundamentals of Financial Management.* 3rd ed. Englewood Cliffs, N.J.: Prentice-Hall, 1977.

Wendell, Paul J., and Wakely, Maxwell A. H. *Modern Accounting and Auditing Checklists.* Boston: Warren, Gorham & Lamont, 1975.

Weston, John Frederick, and Brigham, Eugene F. *Managerial Finance.* 5th ed. Hinsdale, Ill.: Dryden Press, 1975.

Wheelwright, Steven C., and Makridakis, Spyros. *Forecasting Methods for Management.* 2nd ed. New York: John Wiley & Sons, 1977.

Wiest, Jerome D., and Levy, Ferdinand K. *A Management Guide to PERT-CPM.* Englewood Cliffs, N.J.: Prentice-Hall, 1977.

Wilkinson, Jule. *The Complete Book of Cooking Equipment.* Boston: CBI Publishing Company, 1975.

Witzky, Herbert. *The Labor Management Relations Handbook for Hotels, Motels, Restaurants, and Institutions.* Boston: CBI Publishing Company, 1976.

Index